PENGUIN CLASSICS

# AMERICAN SCRIPTURES

LAURIE F. MAFFLY-KIPP is Professor and Chair of the Department of Religious Studies at the University of North Carolina at Chapel Hill.

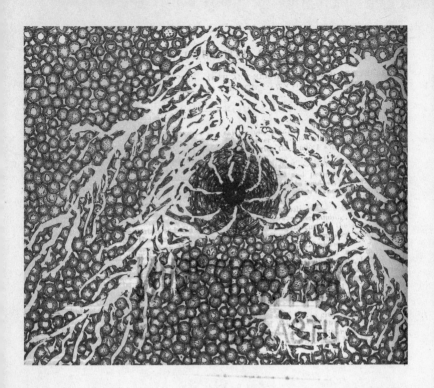

Showing the earth in the thirty-second year of the kosmon era. Jehovih said: When the world approacheth dan'ha in Sabea, the nations shall be quickened with new light; for kosmon cometh out of the midst. And My etherean hosts shall press upon the understanding of men, and they shall fill all the nations and kingdoms with new discoveries and inventions and books of learning. And men shall be conceited of themselves above all the ages past, and they shall deny Me and quarrel with My name, and cast Me out. But I will come upon them as a Father, in love and mercy: and My hosts of heaven shall cause babes and fools to confound the wise, by signs and miracles. My hosts from heaven shall cause chairs to speak; and inanimate things to walk, and dance. The dead shall reappear to the living, and talk with them face to face, and eat and drink, and prove themselves to the children of earth, and make My kingdoms known. Yea, they shall encompass the whole earth around about with signs and wonders, and set at naught the philosophy of men and the idolatries of the ancients. For both, the living and dead, shall know that I, Jehovih, live and reign over heaven and earth. This shall be a new era, and it shall be called, kosmon, because it embraceth the present and all the past. Then will I reveal Myself; and they that deny Me shall accept Me: of their own accord will they put away their Lords and their Gods and their Saviors; nor shall they more have idols of Me, either on earth or in heaven, for I am sufficient unto all.

—Arc of Kosmon, *OAHSPE*, p. 728

# American Scriptures

## AN ANTHOLOGY OF
## SACRED WRITINGS

*Edited with an Introduction by*
LAURIE F. MAFFLY-KIPP

PENGUIN BOOKS

PENGUIN BOOKS
Published by the Penguin Group
Penguin Group (USA) Inc., 375 Hudson Street, New York, New York 10014, U.S.A.
Penguin Group (Canada), 90 Eglinton Avenue East, Suite 700, Toronto, Ontario, Canada M4P 2Y3
(a division of Pearson Penguin Canada Inc.)
Penguin Books Ltd, 80 Strand, London WC2R 0RL, England
Penguin Ireland, 25 St Stephen's Green, Dublin 2, Ireland (a division of Penguin Books Ltd)
Penguin Group (Australia), 250 Camberwell Road, Camberwell, Victoria 3124, Australia
(a division of Pearson Australia Group Pty Ltd)
Penguin Books India Pvt Ltd, 11 Community Centre, Panchsheel Park, New Delhi - 110 017, India
Penguin Group (NZ), 67 Apollo Drive, Rosedale, North Shore 0632, New Zealand
(a division of Pearson New Zealand Ltd)
Penguin Books (South Africa) (Pty) Ltd, 24 Sturdee Avenue, Rosebank, Johannesburg 2196, South Africa

Penguin Books Ltd, Registered Offices:
80 Strand, London WC2R 0RL, England

First published in Penguin Books 2010

1   3   5   7   9   10   8   6   4   2

Selection and introduction copyright © Laurie F. Maffly-Kipp, 2010
All rights reserved

ISBN 978-0-14-310619-7
CIP data available

Printed in the United States of America
Set in Adobe Sabon

# Contents

# Introduction

Many Americans are, and always have been, fascinated with the Bible. But the interest extends far beyond simply reading the texts. The popularity in recent decades of Elaine Pagel's *Gnostic Gospels* (1979), the growth industry surrounding work on lost and forgotten Christian manuscripts, and the fascination evidenced about the possibility of lost traditions broached in the novel *The Da Vinci Code* (2003) suggest an enduring preoccupation with filling out, correcting, or extending the stories and teachings of the Bible. Thomas Carlyle once suggested that "Every man that writes is writing a new Bible, or a new Apocrypha," and there is an important truth contained in his words: Many Christians, especially those in the United States, view their sacred texts not simply as vessels of divine revelation but as occasions for devotional creativity. They improvise and engage with religious texts in many ways, transforming the very objects of their devotion in the process.

This tendency to engage scripture through emendation and addition was especially apparent in the United States after the American Revolution, when the promise of a new nation smiled upon by divine providence gripped Euro-American Protestants and unleashed religious energies in unprecedented ways. In the heady and tumultuous decades of the early nineteenth century, many Americans sought religious truths that would help them make sense of this new republic and allow them to communicate their understandings to others. Sacred texts that would both connect them to their (predominantly Christian) past and take them into an uncertain future proved a remarkably potent way of expressing and transforming faith and of wedding the twin imperatives of stability and flexibility. Writings as diverse as the *Book of*

*Mormon* (1830), the Shakers' *Holy, Sacred and Divine Roll and Book* (1843), James Colin Brewster's "A Warning to the Latter Day Saints" (1845), Andrew Jackson Davis's *Principles of Nature* (1847), Ellen White's *The Great Controversy* (1888), Lorenzo Dow Blackson's *The Rise and Progress of the Kingdoms of Light and Darkness* (1867), Mary Baker Eddy's *Science and Health with Key to the Scriptures* (1875), and John Ballou Newbrough's *OAHSPE: A New Bible in the Words of Jehovih and his Angel Embassadors* (1882) all claimed to extend or complete the promises of the Bible; many of these new scriptures caught the attention of growing numbers of believers willing to commit themselves to the truth of their teachings. Authors including Thomas Jefferson and Elizabeth Cady Stanton rewrote the scriptures they already had to conform to changing religious views.

By the mid-nineteenth century, readers of the Bible also began to question the veracity and completeness of the life of Jesus as it was presented in the four canonized Christian Gospels. In response, ministers, visionaries, anonymous authors, and even dentists began to produce new gospels, claiming a variety of sacred origins for their works. The results of their labors included Alexander Smyth, *Occult Life of Jesus of Nazareth* (1864); Olive G. Pettis, the *Autobiography by Jesus of Nazareth* (1870); Rev. W. D. Mahan, *The Archko Volume* (1887); Nicolas Notovitch, *The Unknown Life of Jesus Christ* (1890); and Levi Dowling, *The Aquarian Gospel of Jesus the Christ* (1907). Indeed, this list does not exhaust the list of "American Scriptures" that one might consult from this intensely creative era.

This volume introduces fifteen of these texts written between 1794 and 1907. These works are compelling and historically valuable because they represent the wide range of popular writings catalyzed by the democratization of religious life in the decades after the American Revolution, an era when men and women, African Americans and whites, and elites and nonelites felt empowered to enact and even design their own scriptural traditions. The texts they produced demonstrate that the hunger for theological improvisation ran deep; rather than listening solely to the words of ministers and scholars, or simply absorbing the teachings of charismatic revivalist preachers, these Americans and their followers were ready, quite literally, to take the Bible into their own hands. As the bestselling book in the nation by the 1820s, the Bible thereby stimulated the composition of other kinds of scriptures.

Though clearly of interest to scholars of the Christian tradition, the importance of these works extends beyond and allows us to question doctrinal boundaries. These texts suggest new ways of thinking about the varieties of Christianity in the United States and its connections to other religious movements. Many of these sources, such as the *Book of Mormon* and *Science and Health*, formed the basis for the collective worship of new faith communities on the American scene. Other texts moved away from Christianity in ways that are perhaps not so readily apparent (sometimes because their lineage has been effaced by orthodox Christians): Lorenzo Dow Blackson's *The Rise and Progress of the Kingdoms of Light and Darkness* (1867), a book written right after the Civil War by an unschooled member of the African Union Church, may be considered an odd or even idiosyncratic apocalyptic text. But it dramatizes racial themes and perspectives that infused the writings of other African American Protestants at the time. Similarly, *The Aquarian Gospel of Jesus the Christ* (1907) by Levi Dowling, while very much in keeping with a "life of Christ" text, would become the basis for New Age thought in the 1960s and 1970s, famously providing the designation the "age of Aquarius."

This creative output leads to a host of intriguing questions. Should we understand these texts as Christian commentary and exegesis in the tradition of Augustine and Aquinas, or are they additions to the Bible? At what point do they become something else, such as fiction or heresy, and how have Americans negotiated the shifting intellectual terrain that their publication represents? One might rightly argue that they represent "Lost Christianities," traditions as important as those indicated by the rogue gospels of Gnosticism or other ancient Christian groups. At the very least, reading these texts together provides a startlingly different view of the narrative of Christianity in the United States from what many of us have learned. Glimpsed through these examples, American Christianity becomes a sprawling, chaotic, intensely generative intellectual force that can fruitfully be compared to movements during the early church or Reformation era.

The selections in this volume also compel reconsideration of religious communities that are rarely studied for their intellectual production. Anthologies that address Shakers, Mormons, Christian Scientists, Seventh-Day Adventists, and others more often focus on their exotic social practices and precepts (e.g., celibacy, polygamy, spiritual healing, unusual dietary practices) rather than examining their sacred texts. This tendency can leave readers with the mistaken impression that groups outside of orthodox Christianity do not have legitimate intellectual traditions on which to draw; even worse, it obscures the fact that these traditions derive their power precisely from their close relationship to orthodox Christianity, and that their adoption of novel religious practices are often justified in characteristically "Christian" ways (through visions, revelation, and various interpretive strategies). Thus, comparing them with each other and with more conventional works demonstrates how the Christian system of revealed text, communal authority, and ritual work together, as well as how mainstream Christians enforced the boundaries of orthodoxy by excluding particular ideas and claims.

The term *scriptures* becomes a case in point: the texts in this volume prompt us to interrogate and define this crucial term. What is a scripture, and who gets to write one? Derived from a Judeo-Christian context, the term is now used freely and comparatively to encompass almost any text considered religiously significant by someone. The scholar Wilfred Cantwell Smith helpfully explains that there is nothing in the nature of a text itself that makes it scriptural; rather it is the relationship between a text and a community that imbues a text with scriptural qualities. The texts collected in this volume stimulate us to think about the historically situated, collective process of "scripturalizing," of investing a text with sacred meaning. These documents raise a host of provocative questions: How does something become a scripture? How do various people and communities use scriptures? How do scriptures bind communities together? What makes some claims of scriptural status more persuasive than others? What do people do with scriptures?

The official status of scriptures within historical religious communities are a subject of intense interest among scholars of religion. While many people have produced religious texts, relatively few of those writings have become part of an authorized set of documents recognized as definitive, or "canonized." The process by which this happens is fascinating and often quite complex. The earliest Christians, for example, adopted the Jewish Scriptures as their own, and only gradually came to incorporate books of what would become the New Testament into their communal life. Marcion of Sinope was perhaps the first follower to designate a given body of texts as Christian canon circa 160 C.E.: He proposed the compilation of ten epistles of the Apostle Paul that had been circulating among Christian communities, along with parts of the Gospel of Luke, into an official Christian Gospel. Not long after, Irenaeus proposed a four-gospel canon. By the fourth century the western Church had settled on a limited group of books for the New Testament that articulated an orthodox set of beliefs. But even then, the Bible was hardly set in stone. Many apocryphal texts—those religious writings considered valuable but not universally accepted as part of the canon—circulated among various Christian groups. The major divisions of the Church that existed by the sixteenth century (Catholic, Orthodox, and Protestant) disagreed on the inclusion of a number of documents, and each moved to declare their canons complete and closed.

Textual heterogeneity was not, in other words, a problem confined to the nineteenth century or to the United States. Even when early churches were able to agree on which texts to include, new questions arose about design and language translation. Bibles in the medieval period contained a chaotic sprawl of words and images presented in a variety of formats. And church leaders, although they had prescribed the texts contained within the canon, had never dictated their order or prescribed any standardized formatting or punctuation. Scribes, therefore, had little guidance as they created new copies, a situation that led to creativity and variety, from psalm books to personalized illuminated Scriptures. Within the growing Protestant communities in Europe and the Americas by the 1600s, the impulse to translate the Bible into local languages—to bring the Bible to the people—further multiplied the choices made by individual artists, scholars, rulers, and publishers as they created Bibles. By 1611, when the King James "authorized version" appeared in England, it was only the latest of many texts containing different formats, words, and images that were all considered canonized scripture.

One might well assume that this multiplication of Bible versions was only a cosmetic concern, a matter of placing the same content between different covers for all to see. But textual formatting and especially translation were seen as intimately related to scriptural interpretation. In the fifteenth century the Archbishop of Canterbury banned John Wycliffe's translation of the Bible for precisely that reason: it was feared that Wycliffe's heretical views would be transmitted in his interpretive choices. By 1408 England had enacted the strictest religious censorship laws in Europe, outlawing all unauthorized translations. Even the composition of the King James version of 1611, for all of its aesthetic appeal and endurance, was motivated far more by the desire for a uniform interpretive framework controlled by the crown's appointed leaders than by any desire to put the Bible into the hands of individual believers.

Yet the Bible, even in the European context, was also a book of the streets and popular life as much as it was an object for private devotional, political, and liturgical use. Although ordinary folk in the Middle Ages were not likely to have owned a personal copy, given the costs of creating individual texts by hand, they were intimately familiar with Scripture and knew the stories well. Laypeople had heard the Bible recited weekly throughout their lives, even if they had not read it for themselves. By the fifteenth century, well before Bibles were produced in mass quantities, plays based on scriptural accounts were staged in urban settings; plots and endings were transformed or reframed to fit the occasion. In an important sense, European Christians understood the Bible as a malleable set of narratives, a "voice of the street" that articulated their experiences and expressed their views of life's mysteries. The innovations of the nineteenth-century American texts included in this volume, in other words, should not be seen as sui generis, but an extension of practices familiar from the earliest years of European print culture.

All of this is to say that the notion of the Bible as a stable, unchanging text is a very recent idea, a product of the modern era, and one that hardly reflects the realities of the multiple ways that believers have historically made use of scriptures. As much as the development of Christianity relied on the introduction and acceptance of a whole new set of sacred texts, the process was never smooth or complete; there never has been a "final version" of the Bible on which all believers claiming the name Christian could agree. And believers have done all sorts of things *with* their scriptures: the Bible has been as much a book of stories to be enacted as a tome to be read aloud in church or a text to serve as an object of private devotion. That said, religious leaders in nearly all eras have nonetheless tried to control its meaning, to regularize its content, and to repress uses that the Church has found illicit and subversive. It is also true that, despite the fluid nature of Christian scripture, certain periods have witnessed unusual eruptions of creative activity. The early years of church formation and the era of the Reformation were such moments, marked by outbursts of interest in finding new meanings or adding to the content of Holy Writ. So, too, was the revival-infused period of the United States in the nineteenth century, a time when Christians claimed to discover, channel, translate, and otherwise recover sacred writings that challenged views of orthodox belief and behavior.

This lack of standardization, one might well assume, would be tempered if not resolved by the development of the printing press and the industrial revolution, events that began to put the Bible into mass production and made copies of Christian scripture available to ever larger communities. By 1850 the United States was certainly the most Bible-saturated nation on earth. This was due to a combination of new technologies beginning in the 1810s, including the advent of the power printing press, machine-made paper, new binding techniques, and enhanced distribution strategies. Energetic organizations like the American Bible Society (founded in 1816) dedicated themselves to placing a copy of the Bible in the hands of every American, while changes in social values, such as a rising literacy rate and access to educational opportunities among middle-class citizens, expanded the reading population across the country. All of these factors led to enormous growth in the number and variety of Bibles available to average Americans. Publishers, catalyzed by the growth of markets, began in the 1820s to produce illustrated Bibles, versions with maps and articles on the Holy Land, and other specialized details to distinguish their products. In trying to unite Americans around the "good book," Bible peddlers and producers led to the further proliferation of scriptural variations and a waning common sense of what constituted the Bible itself. Despite the growing numbers of Bible editions, and without a state church to regulate and control an authorized edition of Holy Writ, Americans seemed less and less sure of what the book, in its essence, *was*, even as they clamored for more of it.

Adding to the multiplication of scriptures was the lack of state-sponsored orthodoxy. Governments in Europe generally had an easier time regulating the distribution of authorized Bible editions: England, where the magisterial King James Version had remained the standard of the church since its introduction in the early seventeenth century, could well have been described as a country that knew what the Bible was because the crown countenanced only one official version. In the United States, however, the unyoking of church from state after the American Revolution threw wide the doors to all manner of scriptural transformation and dissemination. If no Bible version was orthodox anymore, none could be categorically censored as heretical, either.

At about the same time, European and American scholars raised new questions about the plausibility of the Bible as history, including its origins, manuscript variants, and relation to the natural and social sciences. In keeping with new scientific currents that listed and typed biological variety, eighteenth-century biblical scholars had begun to catalog and date the thousands of New Testament manuscripts that continued to be discovered throughout the Mediterranean world. Listing their variations, however, only brought into sharper relief the problems of deciding which should be taken as closest to the truth when discrepancies were found. By the mid-nineteenth century, German scholars seized on a more eclectic approach to ascertaining knowledge about Jesus and the early church by weighing evidence presented by a variety of witnesses. A few decades later Darwin's evolutionary theories, premised on eons of steady but chaotic and nondirected biological change, raised equally troubling questions about the historical chronology of creation as described in the Hebrew Scriptures: where were Adam and Eve to be found in the book of nature? How could one reconcile the origins of the earth as described in Genesis with the millennia of change implied in evolutionary theories? Suddenly, the problems of reading the Bible as a straightforward account of human origins and purpose came to the fore, and without a state church to mandate an answer, American Christians were left to adjudicate for themselves what would constitute persuasive proof of biblical truth.

The Bible, in short, for all its enormous popularity, had also become a huge problem for American Christians by the mid-nineteenth century. While the cadences of the King James Version echoed throughout the land, and the book as a religious object was revered and protected in public schools and courthouses, it would have been difficult to find any agreement about what the Bible looked like (since so many versions were available) or exactly what it said (since its conformity to history and science had become so confusing). The Bible had enormous importance and influence, to be sure. But what, exactly, was it? And what verifiable evidence did believers have for its authority as a sacred text?

It is no accident, then, that in a society in which the Bible was invested with tremendous cultural power but simultaneously was increasingly contested, religious innovators stepped in with new interpretations, commentaries, and even additions to Christian Scripture. The earliest scriptural innovator in the new nation was the founding father Thomas Jefferson himself, who was known to have kept next to him on his nightstand a copy of the Bible that he had "personalized" by cutting and pasting the passages of the New Testament that he found both believable (as in non-miraculous) and ethically inspiring. But many others would soon follow. They included Joseph Smith, Jr., founder of the Church of Jesus Christ of Latter-day Saints (Mormons), who claimed to have discovered ancient golden plates in a hillside in the 1820s that he then translated with the aid of divine revelation; a host of spiritualists, who "channeled" the communications of deceased spirits through their writings; Mary Baker Eddy, who founded the Church of Christ, Scientist, on the basis of her inspired discovery of scientific religious principles outlined in her companion to the Bible, *Science and Health with Key to the Scriptures*; and a dozen or more extra-biblical gospels or "lives of Jesus" that sought to explain or amplify aspects of the earthly history of the Nazarene prophet.

These diverse texts, many of which became scripture to a variety of American religious communities, asserted authority in divergent ways. Some were presented as ancient texts newly discovered or revealed (and, as we have seen previously, many verifiably ancient manuscripts relating to biblical events were still being recovered in the nineteenth century). Others came through inspiration, revelation, or channeled communication, declaring they recovered old truths or revealed new meanings to ancient tales. But what connected all of these texts is the linkage they claimed, either explicitly or implicitly, to some aspect of the Bible itself. They borrowed cultural authority from the Bible to stake their own claim to religious value, and to convince a biblically literate reading public of their importance.

The works selected here thus share several important features that bear upon their status as scripture. First, their authors, translators, editors, or discoverers all affirm to have received this wisdom from a source outside themselves, be it revelation, an enlightened philosophy, or an ancient archive. In doing so, they claim an external, usually transcendent, authority for their ideas and proposals. Second, the authors situate their texts in some kind of relationship to the Christian Bible—making them all, arguably, Christian texts that draw power from that connection even as they challenge traditional religious understandings. Third, all of these texts point, either explicitly or implicitly, to a community of the faithful for whom the text should be authoritative. In a few cases, that community is largely an "imagined" or prospective one, a cohort that the author hopes to unify by providing them with a text around which to unite. Finally, many of these texts, like the Bible itself, have an "afterlife" in which their meaning continues to change: some are canonized (as in the case of the *Book of Mormon* or *Science and Health with Key to the Scriptures*), others eventually are dropped from use (the Shaker *Divine Roll*), and still others are picked up by new groups and rediscovered as authoritative writings in entirely different settings (the *Aquarian Gospel*).

We have seen, then, how these "American Scriptures" fit into Christian history, broadly conceived. Those interested in the history of the United States will also encounter here an illuminating window into American life in the first century of the new republic, since nearly all of these texts also connect the nation's past to the religious present. Many of the issues that these works address relate to perennial philosophical and theological questions, but others speak to the historical context of the post-Enlightenment United States, placing readers squarely in an American framework. The themes of national destiny; millennialism (speculations about the end of this era of world history); issues of racial and gender difference in religious life; the relationship of science to religious experience; reconsiderations of the significance of beliefs in Jesus' life, death, and resurrection; and the relationship of other world religions to the Christian faith all weave their way in and out of these accounts, reflecting pressing social, intellectual, and political concerns of the day. Authors used scriptural accounts not just to describe eternal truth but also to make sense of current events and to understand their place in the world; in turn, they invoked the religious authority of Christian tradition, scientific thought, departed spirits, or revelation to convince others of the truths they told and to invite them to follow.

Worldly concerns frequently meet sacred history in these works. A number of these scriptures make important assertions about the millennial role of the United States, taking the founding of the nation as an auspicious sign of divine favor. Thomas Jefferson, for example, linked his efforts in *The Life and Morals of Jesus of Nazareth* to cull the grain of Christian ethics from the chaff of the superstitious events and miracles in the Bible because he felt that social harmony in the young nation could not be assured without a common morality based on the best of human reason. In this sense, America would model true Christianity for the rest of the world. *The Book of Mormon*, on the other hand, places iconic sites in sacred history (the Garden of Eden, the future home of a restored Zion) in U.S. territory, asserting that the nation was to be, geographically speaking, the alpha and omega of historical progression. *OAHSPE*, a lengthy text that outlines all of world history beginning with creation, details the founding of the American Republic as a signal event in the development of international social harmony and the beginning of a more peaceful sacred dispensation.

Several of these scriptures also reflected the millennial expectations of many Protestants in this era, hopes that were tied to a heightened optimism about national destiny and equation of America with the kingdom of God. Independence from England was followed within decades by a remarkable wave of religious revivals, events that convinced many people in the 1830s and 1840s that God was preparing for the "end times" as described in the Bible and that God's people must repent and prepare for the return of Jesus to the earth. For some Christians, millennial expectations intensified the urgency to spread the news and were accompanied by gifts of revelation so that this could be accomplished. The clearest example of a community formed in millennial expectation was the following of William Miller, described by Ellen Gould White in her 1888 text *The Great Controversy Between Christ and Satan*. In her telling, Miller was the latest in a long series of messengers sent to announce the imminent return of Christ. Many other religious groups shared that hope, including the Mormons, who looked forward to the rebuilding of God's Kingdom as a key element in the latter days of the earth. One ten-year-old follower of Joseph Smith, Jr.'s, young church, James Colin Brewster, began having visions that predicted cataclysmic events for Mormons who strayed from the true path: in his "Warning to the Latter Day Saints," Brewster called on believers to leave the larger group of Mormon followers and flee to California, where God would surely restore his Zion in the end times. The Shakers, a celibate and separatist religious order with communities scattered from Maine to Indiana, believed that the millennium had already arrived and they were in its midst. Their 1843 text, *A Holy, Sacred and Divine Roll and Book*, called on its readers to accept their teachings and recognize that the kingdom was available to them now.

While many apocryphal accounts depict the United States as a holy republic, they did not shy away from describing social problems that required divine resolution, frequently presenting ideas that ran counter to mainstream Christian church organization of the day. The Shaker scriptures announced the arrival of an egali-

tarian social order of men and women with the second coming of
Christ in female form (Mother Ann Lee), a development that was
counterposed to the wicked ways of most of Protestant America.
In similar fashion Mary Baker Eddy announced the arrival of
Christ's principles in the form of a woman through her own
teachings in *Science and Health with Key to the Scriptures*. Elizabeth Cady Stanton and her cadre of female writers composed
the *Woman's Bible* as a commentary on male patriarchy in the
Christian tradition and in modern life; they hoped, much like
Thomas Jefferson, to distill Christian teachings to their essential meanings and cast off centuries of male-dominated social
customs in the process. In another register, Lorenzo Dow Blackson figured Christian history as an extended battle over racial
oppression, a war in which God's warriors from Genesis to
the present contested with evil purveyors of injustice. In many
ways, the social battles of the nineteenth century can be tracked
through these documents, even as their authors announced the
ultimate resolution of discord.

Achievements in the scientific world came fast in this era, and
many of these texts struggle to understand the relationship between novel technologies and timeless truths. Authors were quick
to use newly developed techniques, to be sure. John Ballou Newbrough's 1882 *OAHSPE* was typed on the earliest edition of the
manual typewriter, although he claimed to be writing "automatically" and channeling the words of a spirit. Andrew Jackson Davis's lectures relied on the electromagnetic aura that spiritualists
believed surrounded human beings in order to access predeceased
spirits. But many writers also wanted to link their ideas to science as a foundational and unchanging principle, one that provided new explanations for Christian faith that moved away from
older notions of the interventionist God of history. Thomas Jefferson and Mary Baker Eddy both saw their improvements on
the Bible as an underscoring of natural law, believing their texts
to set forth truths that were there all along but simply needed to
be cultivated in religious communities. So, too, did Andrew Jackson Davis, a follower of the nascent theories of Spiritualism, who
believed that access to the spiritual realm required only a sustained focus on the innate powers of human perception. Olive
Pettis's *Autobiography by Jesus of Nazareth* explained Jesus'

"miraculous" powers as the workings of electrical currents rather than divine intervention, an explanation that ushered Christian teachings into the modern era. Even the resurrection of Jesus, the paradigmatic account of supernatural intervention in human affairs, was tamed by the steady principles of science and updated for a generation that reverenced rationality.

The study of history was also becoming a science by the late nineteenth century, and so it is not surprising that this era witnessed the publication of dozens of new gospel accounts that claimed to correct or amplify earlier texts and thereby to render a more accurate and complete biblical history. Some of these accounts are fairly conventional in their interpretations, such as the documents contained in the *Archko Volume* of 1884. The novelty of that text resides in its assertion of the existence of court documents dating back to the time of the life of Jesus, but when all was said and done, those found scriptures reassert a relatively orthodox theology. Other gospel accounts, however, especially those that professed to fill in the missing years of Jesus' life (since the Bible does not mention Jesus' whereabouts between the ages of thirteen and thirty), presented radically new interpretations of the man of Nazareth. Consider, for example, Alexander Smyth's Jesus in *The Occult Life of Jesus of Nazareth*, a volume that not only uncovers a secret love affair between Jesus and Mary Magdalene, but also reveals the existence of a vast conspiracy spearheaded by Saul of Tarsus and Judas Iscariot to misrepresent Jesus' true message to the world. The text implicitly indicts church leaders from the first century to the present for their misapprehensions and explains that only today, because of the revelations of this new gospel, can readers grasp real Christianity in its original intent.

Many of these texts challenge orthodox interpretations of the Christian tradition, either by recourse to science as explanation or through the implementation of a new science of history. By the early twentieth century Americans also were introduced to a host of other world religions by virtue of increasing globalization and immigration, which provided occasions for incorporating alternative religious understandings into older stories. Two of the gospel accounts included here, Nicholas Notovitch's *Unknown Life of Jesus Christ* and Levi Dowling's *The Aquarian Gospel*, blend

Christian traditions with currents from eastern philosophy by taking Jesus eastward prior to his ministry in Palestine. There, the text sets forth, he was schooled by adepts in Buddhism, Hinduism, Zoroastrianism, and other faiths, and incorporated his experiences into his ministry on his return.

These American scriptures would never be mistaken for mainstream Protestantism. Most American Christians, to be sure, dismissed them all as false and even heretical teachings, the work of madmen and cranks. Whatever one thinks of their ultimate value as religious truth, their study invites reflection on the varieties of Christianity in the American past and present, the formative role of texts in shaping religious experience, and the enduring power of the Bible in American life. One need only glance today at the proliferation of Bibles on the market, including the Green Bible, the Patriot's Bible, the Coach's Bible, the Athlete's Bible, the Glo Bible, and the Personal Promise Bible, to understand that there is an enormous desire for biblical texts and a host of purveyors eager to meet that demand. While this market can be traced in part to our contemporary desires as consumers, it must also be seen as a religiously creative practice elaborated and continued for centuries within communities of the book.

# Suggested Reading

Albanese, Catherine L. *A Republic of Mind and Spirit: A Cultural History of American Metaphysical Religion*. New Haven: Yale University Press, 2007.

Beskow, Per. *Strange Tales about Jesus: A Survey of Unfamiliar Gospels*. Philadelphia: Fortress Press, 1983.

Bushman, Richard L. *Joseph Smith: Rough Stone Rolling, A Cultural History of Mormonism's Founder*. New York: Knopf, 2005.

Ehrman, Bart D. *Lost Christianities: The Battles for Scripture and the Faiths We Never Knew*. New York: Oxford University Press, 2003.

Ferrell, Lori Anne. *The Bible and the People*. New Haven: Yale University Press, 2008.

Gaustad, Edwin. *Sworn on the Altar of God: A Religious Biography of Thomas Jefferson*. Grand Rapids: William B. Eerdmans, 1996.

Givens, Terryl L. *By the Hand of Mormon: The American Scripture that Launched a New World Religion*. New York: Oxford University Press, 2002.

Goodspeed, Edgar J. *Modern Apocrypha*. Boston: Beacon Press, 1956.

Gottschalk, Stephen. *Rolling Away the Stone: Mary Baker Eddy's Challenge to Materialism*. Bloomington: Indiana University Press, 2006.

Graham, William. *Beyond the Written Word: Oral Aspects of Scripture in the History of Religion*. New York: Cambridge University Press, 1987.

Gutjahr, Paul C. *An American Bible: A History of the Good Book in the United States, 1777–1880*. Stanford, CA: Stanford University Press, 1999.

Hatch, Nathan O. *The Democratization of American Christianity*. New Haven: Yale University Press, 1989.

Kern, Kathi. *Mrs. Stanton's Bible*. Ithaca: Cornell University Press, 2001.

King, Richard. *Orientalism and Religion: Postcolonial Theory, India, and "The Mystic East."* New York: Routledge, 1999.

McGarry, Molly. *Ghosts of Futures Past: Spiritualism and the Cultural Politics of Nineteenth-Century America.* Berkeley: University of California Press, 2008.

Maffly-Kipp, Laurie F. *Setting Down the Sacred Past: African American Race Histories.* Cambridge, MA: Belknap Press, 2010.

Numbers, Ronald L. *Prophetess of Health: A Study of Ellen G. White.* Grand Rapids: William B. Eerdmans, 2008.

Pelikan, Jaroslav. *Whose Bible Is It? A Short History of the Scriptures.* New York: Penguin Books, 2005.

Pike, Sarah M. *New Age and Neopagan Religions in America.* New York: Columbia University Press, 2004.

Stein, Stephen J. "America's Bibles: Canon, Commentary, and Community." *Church History,* v. 64, no. 2 (June 1995), 169–184.

Stein, Stephen J. *Communities of Dissent: A History of Alternative Religions in America.* New York: Oxford University Press, 2003.

Stoes, K. D. "The Land of Shalam: A Strange Experience in Child Life." *New Mexico Historical Review,* v. 33, no. 1 (January 1958).

Thuesen, Peter J. *In Discordance with the Scriptures: American Protestant Battles over Translating the Bible.* New York: Oxford University Press, 1999.

# American Scriptures

# The Life and Morals of
# Jesus of Nazareth

People often have accused Thomas Jefferson of being hostile to Christianity, but his relationship to churches, beliefs, and practices was far more variegated. The philosopher and politician harbored an intense desire to separate the purity of Jesus's original teachings from the corruptions of organized church life and the claims of his divinity. This was Jefferson's goal in composing what has come to be known as *The Jefferson Bible*, which he constructed sometime around 1819–20. His motives compelled him to literally cut and paste those elements of the Gospels that he felt were truest to the "genuine precepts" of Jesus as the exemplar of human excellence. In doing so, Jefferson produced what he termed a "wee-little book" that traced the life of Jesus. Yet it was a text shorn of the miraculous healings, resurrections, and claims of divine intervention that Jefferson felt clouded the true accomplishments of the Nazarene as an ethical instructor for humanity. Jefferson's Jesus was a man who died on a cross in Jerusalem, never to rise again; instead, Jesus's lasting legacy was a set of eternal moral principles that would inspire the American president throughout his life.

Jefferson never intended his words to be shown to the public, however, believing, as he did, that religion was essentially a private affair. He was leery of the tendency of the public to construct an "inquisition over the rights of conscience," rights that he held to be sacred. Nonetheless, he held to the principles of a growing number of liberal Christians in the late eighteenth and early nineteenth centuries, specifically the Unitarians that he numbered among his friends, that human reason, rather than supernatural revelation, was the ultimate arbiter of religious truth. He also believed that social harmony in the young republic could only be ensured through the cultivation of a common morality based on universal principles with which all could agree, and he felt that the teachings of Jesus contained that "natural religion" required in a pluralistic society. Jefferson was certainly reviled by his political critics for his unorthodox views, and he declared that he was "of a sect by myself, as far as I know." Nonetheless, his humanistic liberal views of Christian teachings as a commonsense way to unify civil society would inspire generations of admirers.

The following selections include the major events of Jesus' life story drawn from all four Gospels as well as examples of his teachings. To those familiar with the biblical accounts, these excerpts are most significant for the miraculous events and claims of divinity that are omitted—most notably, the resurrection of Jesus himself.

The verse numbers represent Jefferson's cutting of the text. In this respect, they demonstrate his willingness to disrupt the standard versification imposed by compilers of the King James version.

# The Life and Morals of
# Jesus of Nazareth

And it came to pass in those days, that there went out a decree from Caesar Augustus, that all the world should be taxed.

2   (And this taxing was first made when Cyrenius was governor of Syria.)

3   And all went to be taxed, every one into his own city.

4   And Joseph also went up from Galilee, out of the city of Nazareth, into Judaea, unto the city of David, which is called Bethlehem, (because he was of the house and lineage of David,)

5   To be taxed with Mary his espoused wife, being great with child.

6   And so it was, that, while they were there, the days were accomplished that she should be delivered.

7   And she brought forth her firstborn son, and wrapped him in swaddling clothes, and laid him in a manger; because there was no room for them in the inn.

And when eight days were accomplished for the circumcising of the child, his name was called JESUS.

2   And when they had performed all things according to the law of the Lord, they returned into Galilee, to their own city Nazareth.

And the child grew, and waxed strong in spirit, filled with wisdom:

2   And when he was twelve years old, they went up to Jerusalem after the custom of the feast.

3   And when they had fulfilled the days, as they returned, the

child Jesus tarried behind in Jerusalem; and Joseph and his mother knew not *of it*.

4 But they, supposing him to have been in the company, went a day's journey; and they sought him among *their* kinsfolk and acquaintance.

5 And when they found him not, they turned back again to Jerusalem, seeking him.

6 And it came to pass, that after three days they found him in the temple, sitting in the midst of the doctors, both hearing them, and asking them questions.

7 And all that heard him were astonished at his understanding and answers.

8 And when they saw him, they were amazed: and his mother said unto him, Son, why hast thou thus dealt with us? behold, thy father and I have sought thee sorrowing.

9 And he went down with them, and came to Nazareth, and was subject unto them:

10 And Jesus increased in wisdom and stature,

[. . .]

After this he went down to Capernaum, he, and his mother, and his brethren, and his disciples: and they continued there not many days,

2 ¶ And the Jews' passover was at hand, and Jesus went up to Jerusalem;

3 And found in the temple those that sold oxen and sheep and doves, and the changers of money sitting:

4 And when he had made a scourge of small cords, he drove them all out of the temple, and the sheep, and the oxen; and poured out the changers' money, and overthrew the tables;

5 And said unto them that sold doves, Take these things hence; make not my Father's house an house of merchandise.

[. . .]

And they went into Capernaum; and straightway on the sabbath day he entered into the synagogue, and taught.

2 And they were astonished at his doctrine: for he taught them as one that had authority, and not as the scribes.

At that time Jesus went on the sabbath day through the corn; and his disciples were an hungred, and began to pluck the ears of corn, and to eat.

2 But when the Pharisees saw it, they said unto him, Behold, thy disciples do that which is not lawful to do upon the sabbath day.

3 But he said unto them, Have ye not read what David did, when he was an hungred, and they that were with him;

4 How he entered into the house of God, and did eat the shew-bread, which was not lawful for him to eat, neither for them which; were with him, but only for the priests?

5 Or have ye not read in the law, how that on the sabbath days the priests in the temple profane the sabbath, and are blameless?

6 ¶ And when he was departed thence, he went into their synagogue:

7 And, behold, there was a man which had his hand withered. And they asked him, saying, Is it lawful to heal on the sabbath days? that they might accuse him.

8 And he said unto them, What man shall there be among you, that shall have one sheep, and if it fall into a pit on the sabbath day, will he not lay hold on it, and lift it out?

9 How much then is a man better than a sheep? Wherefore it is lawful to do well on the sabbath days.

10 And he said unto them, The sabbath was made for man, and not man for the sabbath.

11 ¶ Then the Pharisees went out, and held a council against him, how they might destroy him.

12 But when Jesus knew it, he withdrew himself from thence: and great multitudes followed him, and he healed them all.

[. . .]

And seeing the multitudes, he went up into a mountain: and when he was set, his disciples came unto him:

2 And he opened his mouth, and taught them, saying,

3     Blessed *are* the poor in spirit: for theirs is the kingdom of heaven.

4     Blessed *are* they that mourn: for they shall be comforted.

5     Blessed *are* the meek: for they shall inherit the earth.

6     Blessed *are* they which do hunger and thirst after righteousness: for they shall be filled.

7     Blessed *are* the merciful: for they shall obtain mercy.

8     Blessed *are* the pure in heart: for they shall see God.

9     Blessed *are* the peacemakers; for they shall be called the children of God.

10    Blessed *are* they which are persecuted for righteousness' sake: for theirs is the kingdom of heaven.

11    Blessed are ye, when *men* shall revile you, and persecute *you*, and shall say all manner of evil against you falsely, for my sake.

12    Rejoice, and be exceeding glad: for great *is* your reward in heaven: for so persecuted they the prophets which were before you.

13    But woe unto you that are rich! for ye have received your consolation.

14    Woe unto you that are full! for ye shall hunger. Woe unto you that laugh now! for ye shall mourn and weep.

15    Woe unto you, when all men shall speak well of you! for so did their fathers to the false prophets.

16    ¶ Ye are the salt of the earth: but if the salt have lost his savour, wherewith shall it be salted? it is thenceforth good for nothing, but to be cast out, and to be trodden under foot of men.

17    Ye are the light of the world. A city that is set on an hill cannot be hid.

18    Neither do men light a candle, and put it under a bushel, but on a candlestick; and it giveth light unto all that are in the house.

19    Let your light so shine before men, that they may see your good works, and glorify your Father which is in heaven.

20    ¶ Think not that I am come to destroy the law, or the prophets: I am not come to destroy, but to fulfil.

21    For verily I say unto you, Till heaven and earth pass, one jot or one tittle shall in no wise pass from the law, till all be fulfilled.

22    Whosoever therefore shall break one of these least commandments, and shall teach men so, he shall be called the least in the kingdom of heaven: but whosoever shall do and teach *them*, the same shall be called great in the kingdom of heaven.

23   For I say unto you, That except your righteousness shall exceed *the righteousness* of the scribes and Pharisees, ye shall in no case enter into the kingdom of heaven.

[. . .]

41   ¶ Ye have heard that it hath been said, An eye for an eye, and a tooth for a tooth:

42   But I say unto you, That ye resist not evil: but whosoever shall smite thee on thy right cheek, turn to him the other also.

43   And if any man will sue thee at the law, and take away thy coat, let him have *thy* cloak also.

44   And whosoever shall compel thee to go a mile, go with him twain.

45   Give to him that asketh thee, and from him that would borrow of thee turn not thou away.

46   ¶ Ye have heard that it hath been said, Thou shalt love thy neighbour, and hate thine enemy.

47   But I say unto you, Love your enemies, bless them that curse you, do good to them that hate you, and pray for them which despitefully use you, and persecute you;

48   That ye may be the children of your Father which is in heaven: for he maketh his sun to rise on the evil and on the good, and sendeth rain on the just and on the unjust.

49   For if ye love them which love you, what reward have ye? do not even the publicans the same?

50   And if ye salute your brethren only, what do ye more *than others?* do not even the publicans so?

51   And if ye lend to *them* of whom ye hope to receive, what thank have ye? for sinners also lend to sinners, to receive as much again.

52   But love ye your enemies, and do good, and lend, hoping for nothing again; and your reward shall be great, and ye shall be the children of the Highest: for he is kind unto the unthankful and *to* the evil.

53   Be ye therefore merciful, as your Father also is merciful.

54   Take heed that ye do not your alms before men, to be seen of them: otherwise ye have no reward of your Father which is in heaven.

55   Therefore when thou doest *thine* alms, do not sound a trumpet before thee, as the hypocrites do in the synagogues and in the streets, that they may have glory of men. Verily I say unto you, They have their reward.

56   But when thou doest alms, let not thy left hand know what thy right hand doeth:

57   That thine alms may be in secret: and thy Father which seeth in secret himself shall reward thee openly.

58   ¶ And when thou prayest, thou shalt not be as the hypocrites *are:* for they love to pray standing in the synagogues and in the corners of the streets, that they may be seen of men. Verily I say unto you, They have their reward.

59   But thou, when thou prayest, enter into thy closet, and when thou hast shut thy door, pray to thy Father which is in secret; and thy Father which seeth in secret shall reward thee openly.

60   But when ye pray, use not vain repetitions, as the heathen *do:* for they think that they shall be heard for their much speaking.

61   Be not ye therefore like unto them: for your Father knoweth what things ye have need of, before ye ask him.

62   After this manner therefore pray ye: Our Father which art in heaven, Hallowed be thy name.

63   Thy kingdom come. Thy will be done in earth, as *it is* in heaven.

64   Give us this day our daily bread.

65   And forgive us our debts, as we forgive our debtors.

66   And lead us not into temptation, but deliver us from evil: For thine is the kingdom, and the power, and the glory, for ever. Amen.

67   For if ye forgive men their trespasses, your heavenly Father will also forgive you:

68   But if ye forgive not men their trespasses, neither will your Father forgive your trespasses.

[. . .]

72   ¶ Lay not up for yourselves treasures upon earth, where moth and rust doth corrupt, and where thieves break through and steal:

73   But lay up for yourselves treasures in heaven, where nei-

ther moth nor rust doth corrupt, and where thieves do not break through nor steal.

74 For where your treasure is, there will your heart be also.

75 The light of the body is the eye: if therefore thine eye be single, thy whole body shall be full of light.

76 But if thine eye be evil, thy whole body shall be full of darkness. If therefore the light that is in thee be darkness, how great *is* that darkness!

77 No man can serve two masters: for either he will hate the one, and love the other; or else he will hold to the one, and despise the other. Ye cannot serve God and mammon.

78 Therefore I say unto you, Take no thought for your life, what ye shall eat, or what ye shall drink; nor yet for your body, what ye shall put on. Is not the life more than meat, and the body than raiment?

79 Behold the fowls of the air: for they sow not, neither do they reap, nor gather into barns; yet your heavenly Father feedeth them. Are ye not much better than they?

80 Which of you by taking thought can add one cubit unto his stature?

81 And why take ye thought for raiment? Consider the lilies of the field, how they grow; they toil not, neither do they spin:

82 And yet I say unto you, That even Solomon in all his glory was not arrayed like one of these.

83 Wherefore, if God so clothe the grass of the field, which today is, and tomorrow is cast into the oven, *shall he* not much more *clothe* you, O ye of little faith?

84 Therefore take no thought, saying, What shall we eat? or, What shall we drink? or, Wherewithal shall we be clothed?

85 (For after all these things do the Gentiles seek:) for your heavenly Father knoweth that ye have need of all these things.

86 But seek ye first the kingdom of God, and his righteousness; and all these things shall be added unto you.

87 Take therefore no thought for the morrow: for the morrow shall take thought for the things of itself. Sufficient unto the day *is* the evil thereof.

88 Judge not, that ye be not judged.

89 For with what judgment ye judge, ye shall be judged: and with what measure ye mete, it shall be measured to you again.

90    Give, and it shall be given unto you; good measure, pressed down, and shaken together, and running over, shall men give into your bosom. For with the same measure that ye mete withal it shall be measured to you again.

91    And why beholdest thou the mote that is in thy brother's eye, but considerest not the beam that is in thine own eye?

92    Or how wilt thou say to thy brother, Let me pull out the mote out of thine eye; and, behold, a beam *is* in thine own eye?

93    Thou hypocrite, first cast out the beam out of thine own eye; and then shalt thou see clearly to cast out the mote out of thy brother's eye.

94    ¶ Give not that which is holy unto the dogs, neither cast ye your pearls before swine, lest they trample them under their feet, and turn again and rend you.

95    ¶ Ask, and it shall be given you; seek, and ye shall find; knock, and it shall be opened unto you:

96    For every one that asketh receiveth; and he that seeketh findeth; and to him that knocketh it shall be opened.

97    Or what man is there of you, whom if his son ask bread, will he give him a stone?

98    Or if he ask a fish, will he give him a serpent?

99    If ye then, being evil, know how to give good gifts unto your children, how much more shall your Father which is in heaven give good things to them that ask him?

100    Therefore all things whatsoever ye would that men should do to you, do ye even so to them: for this is the law and the prophets.

101    ¶ Enter ye in at the strait gate; for wide *is* the gate, and broad *is* the way, that leadeth to destruction, and many there be which go in thereat:

102    Because strait *is* the gate, and narrow *is* the way, which leadeth unto life, and few there be that find it.

103    ¶ Beware of false prophets, which come to you in sheep's clothing, but inwardly they are ravening wolves.

104    Ye shall know them by their fruits. Do men gather grapes of thorns, or figs of thistles?

105    Even so every good tree bringeth forth good fruit; but a corrupt tree bringeth forth evil fruit.

106   A good tree cannot bring forth evil fruit, neither *can* a corrupt tree bring forth good fruit.

107   Every tree that bringeth not forth good fruit is hewn down, and cast into the fire.

108   Wherefore by their fruits ye shall know them.

109   A good man out of the good treasure of the heart bringeth forth good things: and an evil man out of the evil treasure bringeth forth evil things.

110   But I say unto you, That every idle word that men shall speak, they shall give account thereof in the day of judgment.

111   For by thy words thou shalt be justified, and by thy words thou shalt be condemned.

112   ¶ Therefore whosoever heareth these sayings of mine, and doeth them, I will liken him unto a wise man, which built his house upon a rock:

113   And the rain descended, and the floods came, and the winds blew, and beat upon that house; and it fell not: for it was founded upon a rock.

114   And every one that heareth these sayings of mine, and doeth them not, shall be likened unto a foolish man, which built his house upon the sand:

115   And the rain descended, and the floods came, and the winds blew and beat upon that house; and it fell: and great was the fall of it.

116   ¶ And it came to pass, when Jesus had ended these sayings, the people were astonished at his doctrine:

117   For he taught them as *one* having authority, and not as the scribes.

[. . .]

There came then his brethren and his mother, and, standing without, sent unto him, calling him.

2   And the multitude sat about him, and they said unto him, Behold, thy mother and thy brethren without seek for thee.

3   And he answered them, saying, Who is my mother, or my brethren?

4   And he looked round about on them which sat about him, and said, Behold my mother and my brethren!

5   For whosoever shall do the will of God, the same is my brother, and my sister, and mother.

6   In the mean time, when there were gathered together an innumerable multitude of people, insomuch that they trode one upon another, he began to say unto his disciples first of all, Beware ye of the leaven of the Pharisees, which is hypocrisy.

7   For there is nothing covered, that shall not be revealed; neither hid, that shall not be known.

8   Therefore whatsoever ye have spoken in darkness shall be heard in the light; and that which ye have spoken in the ear in closets shall be proclaimed upon the housetops.

9   And I say unto you my friends, Be not afraid of them that kill the body, and after that have no more that they can do.

10   But I will forewarn you whom ye shall fear: Fear him, which after he hath killed hath power to cast into hell; yea, I say unto you, Fear him.

11   Are not five sparrows sold for two farthings, and not one of them is forgotten before God?

12   But even the very hairs of your head are all numbered. Fear not therefore; ye are of more value than many sparrows.

13   ¶ And one of the company said unto him, Master, speak to my brother, that he divide the inheritance with me.

14   And he said unto him, Man, who made me a judge or a divider over you?

15   And he said unto them, Take heed, and beware of covetousness: for a man's life consisteth not in the abundance of the things which he possesseth.

[. . .]

The same day went Jesus out of the house, and sat by the sea side.

2   And great multitudes were gathered together unto him, so that he went into a ship, and sat; and the whole multitude stood on the shore.

3   And he spoke many things unto them in parables, saying, Behold, a sower went forth to sow;

4   And when he sowed, some *seeds* fell by the way side, and the fowls came and devoured them up:

5   Some fell upon stony places, where they had not much earth: and forthwith they sprung up, because they had no deepness of earth:

6   And when the sun was up, they were scorched; and because they had no root, they withered away.

7   And some fell among thorns; and the thorns sprung up, and choked them:

8   But other fell into good ground, and brought forth fruit, some an hundredfold, some sixtyfold, some thirtyfold.

9   Who hath ears to hear, let him hear.

10   ¶ And when he was alone, they that were about him with the twelve asked of him the parable.

11   ¶ Hear ye therefore the parable of the sower.

12   When any one heareth the word of the kingdom, and understandeth *it* not, then cometh the wicked *one*, and catcheth away that which was sown in his heart. This is he which received seed by the way side.

13   But he that received the seed into stony places, the same is he that heareth the word, and anon with joy receiveth it;

14   Yet hath he not root in himself, but dureth for a while; for when tribulation or persecution ariseth because of the word, by and by he is offended.

15   He also that received seed among the thorns is he that heareth the word; and the care of this world, and the deceitfulness of riches choke the word, and he becometh unfruitful.

16   But he that received seed into the good ground is he that heareth the word, and understandeth *it;* which also beareth fruit, and bringeth forth, some an hundredfold, some sixty, some thirty.

[. . .]

But when he saw the multitudes, he was moved with compassion on them, because they fainted and were scattered abroad, as sheep having no shepherd.

2   ¶ And he called *unto him* the twelve, and began to send them forth by two and two; and gave them power over unclean spirits;

3   These twelve Jesus sent forth, and commanded them, say-

ing, Go not into the way of the Gentiles, and into *any* city of the Samaritans enter ye not:

4   But go rather to the lost sheep of the house of Israel.

5   Provide neither gold, nor silver, nor brass in your purses,

6   Nor scrip for *your* journey, neither two coats, neither shoes, nor yet staves: for the workman is worthy of his meat.

7   And into whatsoever city or town ye shall enter, enquire who in it is worthy; and there abide till ye go thence.

8   And when you come into an house, salute it.

9   And if the house be worthy, let your peace come upon it: but if it be not worthy, let your peace return to you.

10   And whosoever shall not receive you, nor hear your words, when ye depart out of that house or city, shake off the dust of your feet.

11   Verily I say unto you, It shall be more tolerable for the land of Sodom and Gomorrah in the day of judgment, than for that city.

12   ¶ Behold, I send you forth as sheep in the midst of wolves: be ye therefore wise as serpents, and harmless as doves.

13   But beware of men: for they will deliver you up to the councils, and they will scourge you in their synagogues;

14   And ye shall be brought before governors and kings for my sake, for a testimony against them and the Gentiles.

15   But when they persecute you in this city, flee ye into another: for verily I say unto you, Ye shall not have gone over the cities of Israel, till the Son of man be come.

16   Fear them not therefore: for there is nothing covered, that shall not be revealed; and hid, that shall not be known.

17   What I tell you in darkness, *that* speak ye in light: and what ye hear in the ear, that preach ye upon the housetops.

18   And fear not them which kill the body, but are not able to kill the soul: but rather fear him which is able to destroy both soul and body in hell.

19   Are not two sparrows sold for a farthing? and one of them shall not fall on the ground without your Father.

20   But the very hairs of your head are all numbered.

21   Fear ye not therefore, ye are of more value than many sparrows.

22   And they went out, and preached that men should repent.

23   ¶ And the apostles gathered themselves together unto Jesus,

and told him all things, both what they had done, and what they
had taught.

[. . .]

Therefore is the kingdom of heaven likened unto a certain king,
which would take account of his servants.

2   And when he had begun to reckon, one was brought unto
him, which owed him ten thousand talents.

3   But forasmuch as he had not to pay, his lord commanded
him to be sold, and his wife, and children, and all that he had,
and payment to be made.

4   The servant therefore fell down, and worshipped him, saying, Lord, have patience with me, and I will pay thee all.

5   Then the lord of that servant was moved with compassion,
and loosed him, and forgave him the debt.

6   But the same servant went out, and found one of his fellow-
servants, which owed him an hundred pence: and he laid hands on
him, and took *him* by the throat, saying, Pay me that thou owest.

7   And his fellow-servant fell down at his feet, and besought
him, saying, Have patience with me, and I will pay thee all.

8   And he would not: but went and cast him into prison, till
he should pay the debt.

9   So when his fellow-servants saw what was done, they were
very sorry, and came and told unto their lord all that was done.

10   Then his lord, after that he had called him, said unto him,
O thou wicked servant, I forgave thee all that debt, because thou
desiredst me;

11   Shouldest not thou also have had compassion on thy fellow-
servant, even as I had pity on thee?

12   And his lord was wroth, and delivered him to the tormen-
tors, till he should pay all that was due unto him.

13   So likewise shall my heavenly Father do also unto you, if ye
from your hearts forgive not every one his brother their trespasses.

[. . .]

And, behold, a certain lawyer stood up, and tempted him, saying, Master, what shall I do to inherit eternal life?

2   He said unto him, What is written in the law? how readest thou?

3   And he answering said, Thou shalt love the Lord thy God with all thy heart, and with all thy soul, and with all thy strength, and with all thy mind; and thy neighbour as thyself.

4   And he said unto him, Thou hast answered right: this do, and thou shalt live.

5   But he, willing to justify himself, said unto Jesus, And who is my neighbour?

6   And Jesus answering said, A certain *man* went down from Jerusalem to Jericho, and fell among thieves, which stripped him of his raiment, and wounded *him*, and departed, leaving *him* half dead.

7   And by chance there came down a certain priest that way: and when he saw him he passed by on the other side.

8   And likewise a Levite, when he was at the place, came and looked *on him*, and passed by on the other side.

9   But a certain Samaritan, as he journeyed, came where he was: and when he saw him, he had compassion *on him*,

10   And went to *him*, and bound up his wounds, pouring in oil and wine, and set him on his own beast, and brought him to an inn, and took care of him.

11   And on the morrow when he departed, he took out two pence, and gave *them* to the host, and said unto him, Take care of him; and whatsoever thou spendest more, when I come again, I will repay thee.

12   Which now of these three, thinkest thou, was neighbour unto him that fell among the thieves?

13   And he said, He that shewed mercy on him. Then said Jesus unto him, Go, and do thou likewise.

And it came to pass, that, as he was praying in a certain place, when he ceased, one of his disciples said unto him, Lord, teach us to pray, as John also taught his disciples.

2   And he said unto them, When ye pray, say, Our Father which art in heaven, Hallowed be thy name. Thy kingdom come. Thy will be done, as in heaven, so in earth.

3   Give us day by day our daily bread.

4   And forgive us our sins; for we also forgive every one that

is indebted to us. And lead us not into temptation; but deliver us from evil.

5 And he said unto them, Which of you shall have a friend, and shall go unto him at midnight, and say unto him, Friend, lend me three loaves;

6 For a friend of mine in his journey is come to me, and I have nothing to set before him?

7 And he from within shall answer and say, Trouble me not: the door is now shut; and my children are with me in bed; I cannot rise and give thee.

8 I say unto you, Though he will not rise and give him because he is his friend, yet because of his importunity he will rise and give him as many as he needeth.

9 And I say unto you, Ask, and it shall be given you; seek, and ye shall find; knock, and it shall be opened unto you.

10 For every one that asketh receiveth; and he that seeketh findeth; and to him that knocketh it shall be opened.

11 If a son shall ask bread of any of you that is a father, will he give him a stone? or if *he ask* a fish, will he for a fish give him a serpent?

12 Or if he shall ask an egg, will he offer him a scorpion?

13 If ye then, being evil, know how to give good gifts unto your children: how much more shall *your* heavenly Father give the Holy Spirit to them that ask him?

[. . .]

And *Jesus* entered and passed through Jericho.

2 And, behold, *there was* a man named Zacchaeus, which was the chief among the publicans, and he was rich.

3 And he sought to see Jesus who he was; and could not for the press, because he was little of stature.

4 And he ran before, and climbed up into a sycamore tree to see him: for he was to pass that *way*.

5 And when Jesus came to the place, he looked up, and saw him, and said unto him, Zacchaeus, make haste, and come down; for today I must abide at thy house.

6 And he made haste, and came down, and received him joyfully.

7   And when they saw *it*, they all murmured, saying, That he was gone to be guest with a man that is a sinner.

8   And Zacchaeus stood, and said unto the Lord; Behold, Lord, the half of my goods I give to the poor; and if I have taken anything from any man by false accusation, I restore *him* fourfold.

9   And Jesus said unto him, This day is salvation come to this house, forsomuch as he also is a son of Abraham.

10   For the Son of man is come to seek and to save that which was lost.

11   ¶ And as they heard these things, he added and spake a parable, because he was nigh to Jerusalem, and because they thought that the kingdom of God should immediately appear.

12   He said therefore, A certain nobleman went into a far country to receive for himself a kingdom, and to return.

13   And he called his ten servants, and delivered them ten pounds, and said unto them, Occupy till I come.

14   But his citizens hated him, and sent a message after him, saying, We will not have this *man* to reign over us.

15   And it came to pass, that when he was returned, having received the kingdom, then he commanded these servants to be called unto him, to whom he had given the money, that he might know how much every man had gained by trading.

16   Then came the first, saying, Lord, thy pound hath gained ten pounds.

17   And he said unto him, Well, thou good servant: because thou hast been faithful in a very little, have thou authority over ten cities.

18   And the second came, saying, Lord, thy pound hath gained five pounds.

19   And he said likewise to him, Be thou also over five cities.

20   And another came, saying, Lord, behold, *here is* thy pound, which I have kept laid up in a napkin:

21   For I feared thee, because thou art an austere man: thou takest up that thou layedst not down, and reapest that thou didst not sow.

22   And he saith unto him, Out of thine own mouth will I judge thee, *thou* wicked servant. Thou knewest that I was an austere man, taking up that I laid not down, and reaping that I did not sow:

23 Wherefore then gavest not thou my money into the bank, that at my coming I might have required mine own with usury?

24 And he said unto them that stood by, Take from him the pound, and give *it* to him that hath ten pounds.

25 (And they said unto him, Lord, he hath ten pounds.)

26 For I say unto you, That unto every one which hath shall be given; and from him that hath not, even that he hath shall be taken away from him.

27 But those mine enemies which would not that I should reign over them, bring hither, and slay *them* before me.

28 And when he had thus spoken, he went before, ascending up to Jerusalem.

[. . .]

And Jesus answered and spake unto them again by parables, and said,

2 The kingdom of heaven is like unto a certain king, which made a marriage for his son;

3 And sent forth his servants to call them that were bidden to the wedding; and they would not come.

4 Again, he sent forth other servants, saying, Tell them which are bidden, Behold, I have prepared my dinner; my oxen and *my* fatlings *are* killed, and all things *are* ready: come unto the marriage.

5 But they made light of *it*, and went their ways, one to his farm, another to his merchandise:

6 And the remnant took his servants, and entreated *them* spitefully, and slew *them*.

7 But when the king heard *thereof*, he was wroth: and he sent forth his armies, and destroyed those murderers, and burned up their city.

8 Then saith he to his servants, The wedding is ready, but they which were bidden were not worthy.

9 Go ye therefore into the highways, and as many as ye shall find, bid to the marriage.

10 So those servants went out into the highways, and gathered together all as many as they found, both bad and good; and the wedding was furnished with guests.

11  And when the king came in to see the guests, he saw there a man which had not on a wedding garment:

12  And he saith unto him, Friend, how camest thou in hither not having a wedding garment? And he was speechless.

13  Then the king said to the servants, Bind him hand and foot, and take him away and cast *him* into outer darkness: there shall be weeping and gnashing of teeth.

14  For many are called, but few *are* chosen.

Then went the Pharisees, and took counsel how they might entangle him in *his* talk.

2  And they sent out unto him their disciples with the Herodians, saying, Master, we know that thou art true, and teachest the way of God in truth, neither carest thou for any *man:* for thou regardest not the person of men.

3  Tell us therefore, What thinkest thou? Is it lawful to give tribute unto Caesar, or not?

4  But Jesus perceived their wickedness, and said, Why tempt ye me, *ye* hypocrites?

5  Shew me the tribute money. And they brought unto him a penny.

6  And he saith unto them, Whose *is* this image and superscription?

7  They say unto him, Caesar's. Then saith he unto them, Render therefore unto Caesar the things which are Caesar's; and unto God the things that are God's.

8  When they had heard *these words*, they marvelled, and left him and went their way.

9  The same day came to him the Sadducees, which say that there is no resurrection, and asked him,

10  Saying, Master, Moses said, If a man die, having no children, his brother shall marry his wife, and raise up seed unto his brother.

11  Now there were with us seven brethren: and the first, when he had married a wife, deceased, and, having no issue, left his wife unto his brother:

12  Likewise the second also, and the third, unto the seventh.

13  And last of all the woman died also.

14  Therefore in the resurrection whose wife shall she be of the seven? for they all had her.

15  Jesus answered and said unto them, Ye do err, not knowing the scriptures, nor the power of God.

16  For in the resurrection they neither marry, nor are given in marriage, but are as the angels of God in heaven.

17  But as touching the resurrection of the dead, have ye not read that which was spoken unto you by God, saying,

18  I am the God of Abraham, and the God of Isaac and the God of Jacob? God is not the God of the dead, but of the living.

19  And when the multitude heard *this*, they were astonished at his doctrine.

And one of the scribes came, and having heard them reasoning together, and perceiving that he had answered them well, asked him, Which is the first commandment of all?

2  And Jesus answered him, The first of all the commandments *is*, Hear, O Israel; The Lord our God is one Lord:

3  And thou shalt love the Lord thy God with all thy heart, and with all thy soul, and with all thy mind, and with all thy strength: this *is* the first commandment.

4  And the second *is* like, *namely* this, Thou shalt love thy neighbour as thyself. There is none other commandment greater than these.

5  On these two commandments hang all the law and the prophets.

6  And the scribe said unto him, Well, Master, thou hast said the truth: for there is one God; and there is none other but he:

7  And to love him with all the heart, and with all the understanding, and with all the soul, and with all the strength, and to love *his* neighbour as himself, is more than all whole burnt offerings and sacrifices.

[. . .]

And take heed to yourselves, lest at any time your hearts be overcharged with surfeiting, and drunkenness, and cares of this life, and *so* that day come upon you unawares.

2    For as a snare shall it come on all them that dwell on the face of the whole earth.

3    Watch ye therefore, and pray always, that ye may be accounted worthy to escape all these things that shall come to pass, and to stand before the Son of man.

4    When the Son of man shall come in his glory, and all the holy angels with him, then shall he sit upon the throne of his glory:

5    And before him shall be gathered all nations: and he shall separate them one from another, as a shepherd divideth *his* sheep from the goats:

6    And he shall set the sheep on his right hand, but the goats on the left.

7    Then shall the King say unto them on his right hand, Come, ye blessed of my Father, inherit the kingdom prepared for you from the foundation of the world:

8    For I was an hungred, and ye gave me meat: I was thirsty, and ye gave me drink: I was a stranger, and ye took me in:

9    Naked, and ye clothed me: I was sick, and ye visited me: I was, in prison, and ye came unto me,

10    Then shall the righteous answer him, saying, Lord, when saw we thee an hungred, and fed *thee?* or thirsty, and gave *thee* drink?

11    When saw we thee a stranger, and took *thee* in? or naked, and clothed *thee?*

12    Or when saw we thee sick, or in prison, and came unto thee?

13    And the King shall answer and say unto them, Verily I say unto you, Inasmuch as ye have done *it* unto one of the least of these my brethren, ye have done *it* unto me.

14    Then shall he say also unto them on the left hand, Depart from me, ye cursed, into everlasting fire, prepared for the devil and his angels:

15    For I was an hungred, and ye gave me no meat: I was thirsty, and ye gave me no drink:

16    I was a stranger, and ye took me not in: naked, and ye clothed me not: sick, and in prison, and ye visited me not.

17    Then shall they also answer him, saying, Lord, when saw we thee an hungred, or athirst, or a stranger, or naked, or sick, or in prison, and did not minister unto thee?

18 Then shall he answer them, saying, Verily, I say unto you, Inasmuch as ye did *it* not to one of the least of these, ye did *it* not to me.

19 And these shall go away into everlasting punishment: but the righteous into life eternal.

After two days was *the feast of* the passover, and of unleavened bread: and the chief priests and the scribes sought how they might take him by craft, and put *him* to death.

2 But they said, Not on the feast *day*, lest there be an uproar of the people.

3 ¶ And being in Bethany in the house of Simon the leper, as he sat at meat, there came a woman having an alabaster box of ointment of spikenard very precious; and she brake the box, and poured *it* on his head.

4 And there were some that had indignation within themselves, and said, Why was this waste of the ointment made?

5 For it might have been sold for more than three hundred pence, and have been given to the poor. And they murmured against her.

6 And Jesus said, Let her alone; why trouble ye her? she hath wrought a good work on me.

7 For ye have the poor with you always, and whensoever ye will ye may do them good: but me ye have not always.

8 She hath done what she could: she is come aforehand to anoint my body to the burying.

[. . .]

When Jesus had spoken these words, he went forth with his disciples over the brook Cedron, where was a garden, into the which he entered, and his disciples.

2 And Judas also, which betrayed him, knew the place: for Jesus ofttimes resorted thither with his disciples.

3 Judas then, having received a band of *men* and officers from the chief priests and Pharisees, cometh thither with lanterns and torches and weapons.

4 Now he that betrayed him gave them a sign, saying, Whomsoever I shall kiss, that same is he: hold him fast.

5   And forthwith he came to Jesus, and said, Hail, master; and kissed him.

6   And Jesus said unto him, Friend, wherefore art thou come? Then came they, and laid hands on Jesus, and took him.

Jesus therefore, knowing all things that should come upon him, went forth, and said unto them, Whom seek ye?

2   They answered him, Jesus of Nazareth. Jesus saith unto them, I am *he*. And Judas also, which betrayed him, stood with them.

3   As soon then as he had said unto them, I am *he*, they went backward, and fell to the ground.

4   Then asked he them again, Whom seek ye? And they said, Jesus of Nazareth.

5   Jesus answered, I have told you that I am *he*; if therefore ye seek me, let these go their way:

6   And Jesus said unto him, Friend, wherefore art thou come? Then came they, and laid hands on Jesus, and took him.

7   And, behold, one of them which were with Jesus stretched out *his* hand, and drew his sword, and struck a servant of the high priest's, and smote off his ear.

8   Then said Jesus unto him, Put up again thy sword into his place: for all they that take the sword shall perish with the sword.

9   In that same hour said Jesus to the multitudes, Are ye come out as against a thief with swords and staves for to take me? I sat daily with you teaching in the temple, and ye laid no hold on me.

10   But all this was done, that the scriptures of the prophets might be fulfilled. Then all the disciples forsook him, and fled.

11   And there followed him a certain young man, having a linen cloth cast about *his* naked *body;* and the young men laid hold on him:

12   And he left the linen cloth, and fled from them naked.

13   ¶ And they that had laid hold on Jesus led *him* away to Caiaphas the high priest, where the scribes and the elders were assembled.

14   And Simon Peter followed Jesus, and *so did* another disciple: that disciple was known unto the high priest, and went in with Jesus into the palace of the high priest.

15   But Peter stood at the door without. Then went out that

other disciple, which was known unto the high priest, and spake unto her that kept the door, and brought in Peter.

16 Then saith the damsel that kept the door, unto Peter, Art not thou also *one* of this man's disciples? He saith, I am not.

17 And the servants and officers stood there, who had made a fire of coals; for it was cold: and they warmed themselves: and Peter stood with them, and warmed himself.

18 ¶ And Simon Peter stood and warmed himself. They said therefore unto him, Art not thou also *one* of his disciples? He denied *it*, and said, I am not.

19 One of the servants of the high priest, being *his* kinsman whose ear Peter cut off, saith, Did not I see thee in the garden with him?

20 Peter then denied again: and immediately the cock crew.

21 And Peter remembered the word of Jesus, which said unto him, Before the cock crow, thou shalt deny me thrice. And he went out, and wept bitterly.

22 ¶ The high priest then asked Jesus of his disciples, and of his doctrine.

23 Jesus answered him, I spake openly to the world; I ever taught in the synagogue, and in the temple, whither the Jews always resort; and in secret have I said nothing.

24 Why askest thou me? ask them which heard me, what I have said unto them: behold, they know what I said.

25 And when he had thus spoken, one of the officers which stood by struck Jesus with the palm of his hand, saying, Answerest thou the high priest so?

26 Jesus answered him, If I have spoken evil, bear witness of the evil; but if well, why smitest thou me?

27 And the chief priests and all the council sought for witness against Jesus to put him to death; and found none.

28 For many bare false witness against him, but their witness agreed not together.

29 And there arose certain, and bare false witness against him, saying,

30 We heard him say, I will destroy this temple that is made with hands, and within three days I will build another made without hands.

31 But neither so did their witness agree together,

32   And the high priest stood up in the midst, and asked Jesus, saying, Answerest thou nothing? what *is it which* these witness against thee?

33   But he held his peace, and answered nothing. Again the high priest asked him, and said unto him, Art thou the Christ, the Son of the Blessed?

34   Art thou the Christ? tell us. And he said unto them, If I tell you, ye will not believe:

35   And if I also ask *you*, ye will not answer me, nor let *me* go.

36   Then said they all, Art thou then the Son of God? And he said unto them, Ye say that I am.

37   Then the high priest rent his clothes, and saith, What need we any further witnesses?

38   Ye have heard the blasphemy: what think ye? And they all condemned him to be guilty of death.

39   And some began to spit on him, and to cover his face, and to buffet him, and to say unto him, Prophesy: and the servants did strike him with the palms of their hands.

Then led they Jesus from Caiaphas unto the hall of judgment: and it was early; and they themselves went not into the judgment hall, lest they should be defiled; but that they might eat the passover.

2   Pilate then went out unto them, and said, What accusation bring ye against this man?

3   They answered and said unto him, If he were not a malefactor, we would not have delivered him up unto thee.

4   Then said Pilate unto them, Take ye him, and judge him according to your law. The Jews therefore said unto him, It is not lawful for us to put any man to death.

5   Then Pilate entered into the judgment hall again, and called Jesus, and said unto him, Art thou the King of the Jews?

6   Jesus answered him, Sayest thou this thing of thyself, or did others tell it thee of me?

7   Pilate answered, Am I a Jew? Thine own nation and the chief priests have delivered thee unto me: what hast thou done?

8   Jesus answered, My kingdom is not of this world; if my kingdom were of this world, then would my servants fight, that I

should not be delivered to the Jews: but now is my kingdom not from hence.

9    Pilate therefore said unto him, Art thou a king then? Jesus answered, Thou sayest that I am a king. To this end was I born, and for this cause came I into the world, that I should bear witness unto the truth. Every one that is of the truth heareth my voice.

10    Pilate saith unto him, What is truth? And when he had said this, he went out again unto the Jews, and saith unto them, I find in him no fault *at all*.

11    And they were the more fierce, saying, He stirreth up the people, teaching throughout all Jewry, beginning from Galilee to this place.

12    Then said Pilate unto him, Hearest thou not how many things they witness against thee?

When Pilate heard of Galilee, he asked whether the man were a Galilean.

2    And as soon as he knew that he belonged unto Herod's jurisdiction, he sent him to Herod, who himself also was at Jerusalem at that time.

3    ¶ And when Herod saw Jesus, he was exceeding glad: for he was desirous to see him of a long *season*, because he had heard many things of him; and he hoped to have seen some miracle done by him.

4    Then he questioned with him in many words; but he answered him nothing.

5    And the chief priests and scribes stood and vehemently accused him.

6    And Herod with his men of war set him at naught, and mocked *him*, and arrayed him in a gorgeous robe, and sent him again to Pilate.

7    And the same day Pilate and Herod were made friends together: for before they were at enmity between themselves.

And Pilate, when he had called together the chief priests and the rulers and the people,

2    Said unto them, Ye have brought this man unto me, as one that perverteth the people: and, behold, I, having examined *him*

before you, have found no fault in this man touching those things whereof ye accuse him:

3  No, nor yet Herod: for I sent you to him; and, lo, nothing worthy of death is done unto him.

4  I will therefore chastise him, and release *him*.

5  ¶ Now at *that* feast the governor was wont to release unto the people a prisoner, whom they would.

6  And they had then a notable prisoner, called Barabbas.

7  Therefore when they were gathered together, Pilate said unto them, Whom will ye that I release unto you? Barabbas, or Jesus which is called Christ?

8  For he knew that for envy they had delivered him.

9  ¶ When he was set down on the judgment seat, his wife sent unto him, saying, Have thou nothing to do with that just man: for I have suffered many things this day in a dream because of him.

10  But the chief priests and elders persuaded the multitude that they should ask Barabbas, and destroy Jesus.

11  The governor answered and said unto them, Whether of the twain will ye that I release unto you? They said, Barabbas.

12  Pilate saith unto them, What shall I do then with Jesus which is called Christ? *They* all say unto him, Let him be crucified.

13  And the governor said, Why, what evil hath he done? But they cried out the more, saying, Let him be crucified.

14  Then released he Barabbas unto them: and when he had scourged Jesus, he delivered *him* to be crucified.

Then the soldiers of the governor took Jesus into the common hall, and gathered unto him the whole band of *soldiers*.

2  And when they had platted a crown of thorns, they put *it* upon his head, and a reed in his right hand: and they bowed the knee before him, and mocked him, saying, Hail, King of the Jews!

3  And they spit upon him, and took the reed and smote him on the head.

4  And after that they had mocked him, they took the robe off from him, and put his own raiment on him, and led him away to crucify *him*.

5  ¶ Then Judas, which had betrayed him, when he saw that he was condemned, repented himself, and brought again the thirty pieces of silver to the chief priests and elders,

6    Saying, I have sinned in that I have betrayed the innocent blood. And they said, What *is that* to us? see thou *to that*.

7    And he cast down the pieces of silver in the temple, and departed, and went and hanged himself.

8    And the chief priests took the silver pieces, and said, It is not lawful for to put them into the treasury, because it is the price of blood.

9    And they took counsel, and bought with them the potter's field, to bury strangers in.

10    Wherefore that field was called, The field of blood, unto this day.

11    ¶ And as they led him away, they laid hold upon one Simon, a Cyrenian, coming out of the country, and on him they laid the cross, that he might bear *it* after Jesus.

12    And there followed him a great company of people, and of women, which also bewailed and lamented him.

13    But Jesus turning unto them said, Daughters of Jerusalem, weep not for me, but weep for yourselves, and for your children.

14    For, behold, the days are coming, in the which they shall say, Blessed *are* the barren, and the wombs that never bare, and the paps which never gave suck.

15    Then shall they begin to say to the mountains, Fall on us; and to the hills, Cover us.

16    For if they do these things in a green tree, what shall be done in the dry?

17    ¶ And there were also two other, malefactors, led with him to be put to death.

18    And he bearing his cross went forth into a place called *the place* of a skull, which is called in the Hebrew, Golgotha:

19    Where they crucified him, and two other with him, on either side one, and Jesus in the midst.

20    ¶ And Pilate wrote a title, and put *it* on the cross. And the writing was, JESUS OF NAZARETH THE KING OF THE JEWS.

21    This title then read many of the Jews: for the place where Jesus was crucified was nigh to the city: and it was written in Hebrew, *and* Greek, *and* Latin.

22    Then said the chief priests of the Jews to Pilate, Write not, The King of the Jews; but that he said, I am King of the Jews.

23   Pilate answered, What I have written I have written.

24   ¶ Then the soldiers, when they had crucified Jesus, took his garments, and made four parts, to every soldier a part; and also *his* coat: now the coat was without seam, woven from the top throughout.

25   They said therefore among themselves, Let us not rend it, but cast lots for it, whose it shall be: that the scripture might be fulfilled, which saith, They parted my raiment among them, and for my vesture they did cast lots. These things therefore the soldiers did.

26   ¶ And they that passed by reviled him, wagging their heads,

27   And saying, Thou that destroyest the temple, and buildest *it* in three days, save thyself. If thou be the Son of God, come down from the cross.

28   Likewise also the chief priests mocking *him*, with the scribes and elders, said,

29   He saved others; himself he cannot save. If he be the King of Israel, let him now come down from the cross, and we will believe him.

30   He trusted in God; let him deliver him now, if he will have him: for he said, I am the Son of God.

31   ¶ And one of the malefactors which were hanged railed on him, saying, If thou be Christ, save thyself and us.

32   But the other answering rebuked him, saying, Dost not thou fear God, seeing thou art in the same condemnation?

33   And we indeed justly; for we receive the due reward of our deeds: but this man hath done nothing amiss.

34   Then said Jesus, Father, forgive them; for they know not what they do. And they parted his raiment, and cast lots.

35   ¶ Now there stood by the cross of Jesus his mother, and his mother's sister, Mary the *wife* of Cleophas, and Mary Magdalene.

36   When Jesus therefore saw his mother, and the disciple standing by, whom he loved, he saith unto his mother, Woman, behold thy son!

37   Then, saith he to the disciple, Behold thy mother! And from that hour that disciple took her unto his own *home*.

38   And about the ninth hour Jesus cried with a loud voice, saying, Eli, Eli, lama sabachthani? that is to say, My God, my God, why hast thou forsaken me?

39 Some of them that stood there, when they heard *that*, said, This *man* calleth for Elias.

40 And straightway one of them ran, and took a spunge, and filled *it* with vinegar, and put *it* on a reed, and gave him to drink.

41 The rest said, Let be, let us see whether Elias will come to save him.

42 ¶ Jesus, when he had cried again with a loud voice, yielded up the ghost.

43 And many women were there beholding afar off, which followed Jesus from Galilee, ministering unto him:

44 Among which was Mary Magdalene, and Mary the mother of James and Joses, and the mother of Zebedee's children.

The Jews therefore, because it was the preparation, that the bodies should not remain upon the cross on the sabbath day, (for that sabbath day was an high day,) besought Pilate that their legs might be broken, and *that* they might be taken away.

2 Then came the soldiers, and brake the legs of the first, and of the other which was crucified with him.

3 But when they came to Jesus, and saw that he was dead already, they brake not his legs:

4 But one of the soldiers with a spear pierced his side, and forthwith came there out blood and water.

5 ¶ And after this Joseph of Arimathaea, being a disciple of Jesus, but secretly for fear of the Jews, besought Pilate that he might take away the body of Jesus: and Pilate gave *him* leave. He came therefore, and took the body of Jesus.

6 And there came also Nicodemus, which at the first came to Jesus by night, and brought a mixture of myrrh and aloes, about an hundred pound *weight*.

7 Then took they the body of Jesus, and wound it in linen clothes with the spices, as the manner of the Jews is to bury.

8 Now in the place where he was crucified there was a garden; and in the garden a new sepulchre, wherein never man yet laid.

9 There laid they Jesus: and rolled a great stone to the door of the sepulchre, and departed.

(THOMAS JEFFERSON, 1794; REPRINT ED., ST. LOUIS, MO: 1902)

# The Book of Mormon

In the spring of 1830 Joseph Smith, Jr., a young farmhand, published a work that he claimed had miraculous origins. According to his later written account, an angel had led him to the hiding place of a set of golden plates some years earlier, buried in a hillside near his home in Palmyra, New York. With the aid of several divining implements, including seer stones and an ancient Israelite priestly apparatus known as the Urim and Thummim, the self-taught Smith had translated the hieroglyphics on the plates and dictated them into their final form. Shortly after this translation was published as the Book of Mormon, Joseph Smith, Jr., founded a small church consisting of those who believed in his revelatory experiences and the divine origins of the text.

The story that unfolded in those pages initiated both the beginnings of a major religious movement and violent opposition from many Americans who scorned Smith's "gold bible" and rejected his claim of its divine origins. For his followers, the Book of Mormon was more than a gripping story that explained the place of their homeland in a Christian universe; it was also a sign that God was once again communicating with those who believed his word. Through the prophet Joseph Smith, the record of ancient peoples detailed in the text authorized Mormons to recapture divine authority, to heal illness, to speak in tongues, and to gather once again to rebuild Zion, God's kingdom on earth. While a variety of religious groups since Joseph Smith's day take the Book of Mormon as "another testament" alongside the Bible itself, the largest of these, the Church of Jesus Christ of Latter-day Saints, now claims over thirteen million members worldwide. In meeting houses around the globe, Mormons use this scripture as a guide to daily living and a devotional touchstone.

The selections below tell the beginning, middle, and end of a cosmology that links the Book of Mormon to biblical prophecy. It relates the saga of ancient peoples who traveled from Jerusalem to the New World by boat many centuries before the birth of Jesus. Led by religious prophets with names such as Lehi, Nephi, Mormon, and Moroni, those New World peoples (known as the Nephites and the Lamanites, after some members of their founding family) built societies, populated the area, warred against one another, and worshipped the god of their ancestors. After the resurrection of Jesus Christ and his appearance to his disciples in Palestine, the Savior visited his followers in the Americas, delivering many of the same messages that he reportedly conveyed in the Old World. As the text relates, several centuries of peace followed his appearance, but eventually the Nephites and Lamanites began to war again. Overcome by the Lamanites by the fifth century C.E., the last of the Nephites, Moroni, buried the records of his peoples and their origins in the hillside where the final battle took place.

# THE

# BOOK OF MORMON

## AN ACCOUNT WRITTEN BY THE HAND OF MORMON UPON PLATES TAKEN FROM THE PLATES OF NEPHI.

Wherefore, it is an abridgment of the record of the people of Nephi, and also of the Lamanites; written to the Lamanites, who are a remnant of the house of Israel; and also to Jew and Gentile; written by way of commandment, and also by the spirit of prophecy and of revelation. Written, and sealed up, and hid up unto the LORD, that they might not be destroyed; to come forth by the gift and power of God unto the interpretation thereof; sealed by the hand of Moroni, and hid up unto the LORD, to come forth in due time by the way of Gentile; the interpretation thereof by the gift of God:

An abridgment taken from the book of Ether: also, which is a record of the people of Jared; who were scattered at the time the LORD confounded the language of the people, when they were building a tower to get to heaven: which is to shew unto the remnant of the house of Israel what great things the LORD hath done for their fathers; and that they may know the covenants of the LORD, that they are not cast off forever; and also to the convincing of the Jew and Gentile that JESUS is the CHRIST, the ETERNAL GOD, manifesting himself unto all nations. And now if there are faults, they are the mistakes of men; wherefore, condemn not the things of GOD, that ye may be found spotless at the judgment seat of CHRIST.

MORONI.

# The First Book of Nephi

## His Reign and Ministry

### CHAPTER I

*An account of Lehi and his wife, Sariah, and his four sons, being called, (beginning at the eldest,) Laman, Lemuel, Sam, and Nephi. The Lord warns Lehi to depart out of the Land of Jerusalem, because he prophesieth unto the people concerning their iniquity: and they seek to destroy his life. He taketh three day's journey into the wilderness with his family. Nephi taketh his brethren and returns to the land of Jerusalem after the record of the Jews. The account of their sufferings. They take the daughters Ithmael to wife. They take their families and depart into the wilderness. Their sufferings and afflictions in the wilderness. The course of their travels. They come to the large waters. Nephi's brethren rebelleth against him. He confoundeth them, and buildeth a ship. They call the name of the place Bountiful. They cross the large waters into the promised land, &c. This is according to the account of Nephi; or, in other words, I, Nephi, wrote this record.*

I, Nephi, having been born of goodly parents, therefore I was taught somewhat in all the learning of my father: and having seen many afflictions in the course of my days—nevertheless, having been highly favored of the Lord in all my days; yea, having had a great knowledge of the goodness and the mysteries of God, therefore I make a record of my proceedings in my days; yea, I make a record in the language of my father, which consists of the learning of the Jews and the language of the Egyptians. And I know that the record which I make is true; and I make it with mine own hand; and I make it according to my knowledge.

For it came to pass, in the commencement of the first year of the reign of Zedekiah, king of Judah, (my father Lehi having dwelt at Jerusalem in all his days;) and in that same year there came many prophets, prophesying unto the people, that they must repent, or the great city Jerusalem must be destroyed. Wherefore, it came to pass, that my father Lehi, as he went forth, prayed unto the Lord, yea, even with all his heart, in behalf of his people.

And it came to pass, as he prayed unto the Lord, there came a pillar of fire and dwelt upon a rock before him; and he saw and heard much; and because of the things which he saw and heard, he did quake and tremble exceedingly.

And it came to pass that he returned to his own house at Jerusalem; and he cast himself upon his bed, being overcome with the spirit and the things which he had seen; and being thus overcome with the spirit, he was carried away in a vision, even that he saw the heavens open, and he thought he saw God sitting upon his throne, surrounded with numberless concourses of angels in the attitude of singing and praising their God.

And it came to pass that he saw one descending out of the midst of heaven, and he beheld that his lustre was above that of the sun at noon-day; and he also saw twelve others following him, and their brightness did exceed that of the stars in the firmament; and they came down and went forth upon the face of the earth; and the first came and stood before my father, and gave unto him a book, and bade him that he should read.

And it came to pass that as he read, he was filled with the spirit of the Lord, and he read saying, Wo, wo unto Jerusalem! for I have seen thine abominations; yea, and many things did my father read concerning Jerusalem—that it should be destroyed, and the inhabitants thereof, many should perish by the sword, and many should be carried away captive into Babylon.

And it came to pass that when my father had read and saw many great and marvellous things, he did exclaim many things unto the Lord: such as, great and marvellous are thy works, O Lord God Almighty! Thy throne is high in the heavens, and thy power, and goodness, and mercy are over all the inhabitants of the earth; and because thou art merciful, thou wilt not suffer those who come unto thee that they shall perish! And after this manner was the language of my father in the praising of his God; for his soul did rejoice, and his whole heart was filled because of the things which he had seen; yea, which the Lord had shewn unto him. And now I, Nephi, do not make a full account of the things which my father had written, for he hath written many things which he saw in visions and in dreams, and he also hath written many things which he prophesied and spake unto his children, of which I shall not make a full account; but I shall make an account of my proceedings in my days. Behold I make an abridgement of the record of my father, upon plates which I have made with mine own hands; wherefore, after I have abridged the record of my father, then will I make an account of mine own life.

Therefore, I would that ye should know, that after the Lord had shewn so many marvellous things unto my father Lehi, yea, concerning the destruction of Jerusalem, behold he went forth among the people, and began to prophesy and to declare unto them concerning the things which he had both seen and heard.

And it came to pass that the Jews did mock him because of the things which he testified of them: for he truly testified of their wickedness and their abominations; and he testified that the things which he saw and heard, and also the things which he read in the book, manifested plainly of the coming of a Messiah, and also the redemption of the world.

And when the Jews heard these things, they were angry with him; yea, even as with the prophets of old, whom they had cast out and stoned and slain; and they also sought his life, that they might take it away. But behold, I, Nephi, will shew unto you that the tender mercies of the Lord are over all those whom he hath chosen, because of their faith, to make them mighty even unto the power of deliverance.

For behold it came to pass that the Lord spake unto my father, yea, even in a dream, and said unto him, blessed art thou Lehi, because of the things which thou hast done; and because thou hast been faithful and declared unto this people the things which I commanded thee, behold they seek to take away thy life.

And it came to pass that the Lord commanded my father, even in a dream, that he should take his family and depart into the wilderness. And it came to pass that he was obedient unto the word of the Lord, wherefore he did as the Lord commanded him.

And it came to pass that he departed into the wilderness. And he left his house, and the land of his inheritance, and his gold, and his silver, and his precious things, and took nothing with him save it were his family, and provisions, and tents, and departed into the wilderness; and he came down by the borders near the shore of the Red Sea; and he travelled in the wilderness in the borders which are nearer the Red Sea; and he did travel in the wilderness with his family, which consisted of my mother, Sariah, and my elder brothers, who were Laman, Lemuel and Sam.

And it came to pass that when he had travelled three days in the wilderness, he pitched his tent in a valley by the side of a river of water. And it came to pass that he built an altar of stones, and made an offering unto the Lord, and gave thanks unto the Lord our God. And it came to pass that he called the name of the river, Laman, and it emptied into the Red Sea; and the valley was in the borders near the mouth thereof.

And when my father saw that the waters of the river emptied into the fountain of the Red Sea, he spake unto Laman, saying, O that thou mightest be like unto this river, continually running into the fountain of all righteousness. And he also spake unto Lemuel: O that thou mightest be like unto this valley, firm, and steadfast, and immovable in keeping the commandments of the Lord. Now this he spake because of the stiffneckedness of Laman and Lemuel, for behold they did murmur in many things against their father, because he was a visionary man, and had led them out of the land of Jerusalem, to leave the land of their inheritance, and their gold, and their silver, and their precious things, to perish in the wilderness. And this, they said, he had done, because of the foolish imaginations of his heart. And thus Laman and Lemuel, being the eldest, did murmur against their father. And they did murmur because they knew not the dealings of that God who had created them. Neither did they believe that Jerusalem, that great city, could be destroyed according to the words of the prophets. And they were like unto the Jews, who were at Jerusalem, who sought to take away the life of my father.

And it came to pass that my father did speak unto them in the valley of Lemuel, with power, being filled with the spirit, until their frames did shake before him. And he did confound them, that they durst not utter against him; wherefore, they did as he commanded them. And my father dwelt in a tent.

And it came to pass that I, Nephi, being exceeding young, nevertheless being large in stature, and also having great desires to know of the mysteries of God, wherefore I did cry unto the Lord; and behold he did visit me, and did soften my heart that I did believe all the words which had been spoken by my father; wherefore I did not rebel against him like unto my brothers. And I spake unto Sam, making known unto him the things which the Lord had manifested unto me by his Holy Spirit.

And it came to pass that he believed in my words; but behold Laman and Lemuel would not hearken unto my words. And being grieved because of the hardness of their hearts, I cried unto the Lord for them.

And it came to pass that the Lord spake unto me, saying: blessed art thou, Nephi, because of thy faith, for thou hast sought me diligently, with lowliness of heart. And inasmuch as ye shall keep my commandments, ye shall prosper, and shall be led to a land of promise; yea, even a land which I have prepared for you; yea, a land which is choice above all other lands. And inasmuch as thy brethren shall rebel against thee, they shall be cut off from the presence of the Lord. And inasmuch as thou shalt keep my commandments, thou shalt be made a ruler and a teacher over thy brethren. For behold, in that day that they shall rebel against me. I will curse them even with a sore curse, and they shall have no power over thy seed, except they shall rebel against me also. And if it so be that they rebel against me, they shall be a scourge unto thy seed, to stir them up in the ways of remembrance.

[. . .]

And it came to pass that they did worship the Lord, and did go forth with me; and we did work timbers of curious workmanship. And the Lord did shew me from time to time, after what manner I should work the timbers of the ship. Now I, Nephi, did not work the timbers after the manner which was learned by men, neither did I build the ship after the manner of men: but I did build it after the manner which the Lord had shewn unto me; wherefore, it was not after the manner of men.

And I, Nephi, did go into the mount oft, and I did pray oft unto the Lord; wherefore, the Lord shewed unto me great things.

And it came to pass that after I had finished the ship according to the word of the Lord, my brethren beheld that it was good, and that the workmanship thereof was exceeding fine; wherefore, they did humble themselves again before the Lord.

And it came to pass that the voice of the Lord came unto my father, that we should arise and go down into the ship. And it came to pass that on the morrow, after we had prepared all things, much fruits and meat from the wilderness, and honey in abundance, and provisions, according to that which the Lord had commanded us, we did go down into the ship with all our loading and our seeds, and whatsoever thing we had brought with us, every one according to his age; wherefore, we did all go down into the ship, with our wives and our children.

And now, my father had begat two sons, in the wilderness; The eldest was called Jacob, and the younger, Joseph. And it came to pass after we had all gone down into the ship, and had taken with us our provisions and things which had been commanded us, we did put forth into the sea, and were driven forth before the wind, towards the promised land; and after we had been driven forth before the wind, for the space of many days, behold my brethren, and the sons of Ishmael, and also their wives, began to make themselves merry, insomuch that they began to dance, and to sing, and to speak with much rudeness; yea, even that they did forget by what power they had been brought thither; yea, they were lifted up unto exceeding rudeness. And I, Nephi, began to fear exceedingly, lest the Lord should be angry with us, and smite us, because of our iniquity, that we should be swallowed up in the depths of the sea; wherefore, I, Nephi, began to speak to them with much soberness; but behold, they were angry with me, saying, we will not that our younger brother shall be a ruler over us.

And it came to pass that Laman and Lemuel did take me and bind me with cords, and they did treat me with much harshness; nevertheless, the Lord did suffer it, that he might shew forth his power, unto the fulfilling of his word which he had spoken, concerning the wicked.

And it came to pass that after they had bound me, insomuch that I could not move, the compass, which had been prepared of the Lord, did cease to work; wherefore, they knew not whither they should steer the ship, insomuch, that there arose a great storm, yea, a great and terrible tempest; and we were driven back upon the waters for the space of three days; and they began to be frightened exceedingly, lest they should be drowned in the sea: nevertheless, they did not loose me. And on the fourth day which we had been driven back, the tempest began to be exceeding sore.

And it came to pass that we were about to be swallowed up in the depths of the sea. And after we had been driven back upon the waters for the space of four days, my brethren began to see that the judgments of God were upon them, and that they must perish, save that they should repent of their iniquities; wherefore, they came unto me and loosed the bands which were upon my wrists, and behold, they had swollen exceedingly; and also mine ankles were much swollen, and great was the soreness thereof, Nevertheless, I did look unto my God, and I did praise him all the day long; and I did not murmur against the Lord, because of mine afflictions.

Now, my father Lehi, had said many things unto them, and also unto the sons of Ishmael; but behold, they did breathe out much threatnings against any one that should speak for me; and my parents being stricken in years, and having suffered much grief because of their children, they were brought down, yea, even upon their sick beds. Because of their grief, and much sorrow, and the iniquity of my brethren, they were brought near even to be carried out of this time, to meet their God; yea, their grey hairs were about to be brought down to lie low in the dust; yea, even they were near to be cast, with sorrow, into a watery grave. And Jacob and Joseph also, being young, having need of much nourishment, were grieved because of the afflictions of their mother; and also my wife, with her tears and prayers, and also my children, did not soften the hearts of my brethren, that they would loose me; and there was nothing, save it were the power of God, which threatened them with destruction, could soften their hearts: wherefore, when they saw that they were about to be swallowed up in the depths of the sea, they repented of the thing which they had done, insomuch that they loosed me.

And it came to pass after they had loosed me, behold, I took the compass, and it did work whither I desired it. And it came to pass that I prayed unto the Lord; and after I had prayed, the winds did cease, and the storm did cease, and there was a great calm.

And it came to pass that I, Nephi, did guide the ship, that we sailed again towards the promised land. And it came to pass that after we had sailed for the space of many days, we did arrive to the promised land; and we went forth upon the land, and did pitch our tents; and we did call it the promised land.

And it came to pass that we did begin to till the earth, and we began to plant seeds; yea, we did put all our seeds into the earth, which we had brought from the land of Jerusalem. And it came to pass that they did grow exceedingly; wherefore; we were blessed in abundance.

And it came to pass that we did find upon the land of promise, as we journeyed in the wilderness, that there were beasts in the forests of every kind, both the cow, and the ox, and the ass, and the horse, and the goat, and the wild goat, and all manner of wild animals, which were for the use of men. And we did find all manner of ore, both of gold, and of silver, and of copper.

[. . .]

Wo be unto the Gentiles, saith the Lord God of hosts; for notwithstanding I shall lengthen out mine arm unto them from day to day, they will deny me; nevertheless, I will be merciful unto them, saith the Lord God, if they will repent and come unto me: for mine arm is lengthened out all the day long saith the Lord God of hosts.

But behold, there shall be many at that day, when I shall proceed to do a marvellous work among them, that I may remember my covenants which I have made unto the children of men, that I may set my hand again the second time to recover my people, which are of the house of Israel; and also, that I may remember the promises which I have made unto thee, Nephi, and also unto thy father, that I would remember your seed; and that the words of your seed should proceed forth out of my mouth unto your seed. And my words shall hiss forth unto the ends of the earth, for a standard unto my people, which are of the house of Israel. And because my words shall hiss forth, many of the Gentiles shall say, a bible, a bible, we have got a bible, and there cannot be any more bible. But thus saith the Lord God: O fools, they shall have a bible; and it shall proceed forth from the Jews, mine ancient covenant people. And what thank they the Jews for the bible which they receive from them? Yea, what do the Gentiles mean? Do they remember the travels, and the labors, and the pains of the Jews, and their diligence unto me, in bringing forth salvation unto the Gentiles?

O ye Gentiles, have ye remembered the Jews, mine ancient covenant people? nay; but ye have cursed them, and have hated them, and have not sought to recover them. But behold, I will return all these things upon your own heads: for I the Lord, hath not forgotten my people. Thou fool, that shall say, a bible, we have got a bible, and we need no more bible. Have ye obtained a bible, save it were by the Jews? Know ye not that there are more nations than one? Know ye not that I, the Lord your God have created all men, and that I remember those who are upon the isles of the sea; and that I rule in the heavens above, and in the earth beneath; and I bring forth my word unto the children of men, yea, even upon all the nations of the earth? Wherefore murmur ye, because that ye shall receive more of my word? Know ye not that the testimony of two nations is a witness unto you that I am God, that I remember one nation like unto another? Wherefore, I speak the same words unto one nation like unto another. And when the two nations shall run together, the testimony of the two nations shall run together also. And I do this that I may prove unto many, that I am the same yesterday, to-day, and forever; and that I speak forth my words according to mine own pleasure. And because that I have spoken one word, ye need not suppose that I cannot speak another; for my work is not yet finished; neither shall it be, until the end of man; neither from that time henceforth and forever.

Wherefore, because that ye have a bible, ye need not suppose that it contains all my words; neither need ye suppose that I have not caused more to be written: for I command all men, both in the east, and in the west, and in the north, and in the south, and in the islands of the sea, that they shall write the words which I speak unto them: for out of the books which shall be written, I will judge the world, every man according to their works, according to that which is written. For behold, I shall speak unto the Jews, and they shall write it: and I shall also speak unto the Nephites, and they shall write it; And I shall also speak unto the other tribes of the house of Israel, which I have led away, and they shall write it; and I shall also speak unto all nations of the earth, and they shall write it.

And it shall come to pass that the Jews shall have the words of the Nephites, and the Nephites shall have the words of the Jews: and the Nephites and the Jews shall have the words of the lost tribes of Israel: and the lost tribes of Israel shall have the words of the Nephites and the Jews.

And it shall come to pass that my people which are of the House of Israel, shall be gathered home unto the lands of their possessions; and my word also shall be gathered in one. And I will shew unto them that fight against my word and against my people, who are of the house of Israel, that I am God, and that I covenanted with Abraham, that I would remember his seed forever.

# The Book of Nephi, The Son of Nephi, who was the Son of Helaman

## CHAPTER I

*And Helaman was the son of Helaman, who was the son of Alma, who was the son of Alma, being a descendant of Nephi who was the son of Lehi, who came out of Jerusalem in the first year of the reign of Zedekiah, the king of Judah.*

Now it came to pass that the ninety and first year had passed away; and it was six hundred years from the time that Lehi left Jerusalem; and it was in the year that Lachoneus was the chief judge and the governor over the land. And Nephi, the son of Helaman, had departed out of the land of Zarahemla, giving charge unto his son Nephi, who was his eldest son, concerning the plates of brass, and all the records which had been kept, and all those things which had been kept sacred, from the departure of Lehi out of Jerusalem; then he departed out of the land, and whither he went, no man knoweth; and his son Nephi did keep the records in his stead, yea, the record of this people.

And it came to pass that in the commencement of the ninety and second year, behold, the prophecies of the prophets began to be fulfilled more fully; for there began to be greater signs and greater miracles wrought among the people. But there were some who began to say, that the time was past for the words to be fulfilled, which were spoken by Samuel, the Lamanite. And they began to rejoice over their brethren, saying, behold, the time is past, and the words of Samuel are not fulfilled; therefore, your joy and your faith concerning this thing, hath been vain. And it came to pass that they did make a great uproar throughout the land; and the people who believed, began to be very sorrowful, lest by any means those things which had been spoken, might not come to pass. But behold, they did watch steadfastly for that day, and that night, and that day, which shall be as one day, as if there were no night, that they might know that their faith had not been vain.

Now it came to pass that there was a day set apart by the unbelievers, that all those who believed in those traditions should be put to death, except the sign should come to pass which had been given by Samuel the prophet. Now it came to pass that when Nephi, the son of Nephi, saw this wickedness of his people, his heart was exceeding sorrowful. And it came to pass that he went out and bowed himself down upon the earth, and cried mightily to his God, in behalf of his people; yea, those who were about to be destroyed because of their faith in the tradition of their fathers. And it came to pass that he cried mightily unto the Lord, all the day; and behold, the voice of the Lord came unto him, saying, lift up your head and be of good cheer, for behold, the time is at hand, and on this night shall the sign be given, and on the morrow come I into the world, to shew unto the world that I will fulfil all that which I have caused to be spoken by the mouth of my holy prophets. Behold, I come unto my own, to fulfil all things which I have made known unto the children of men, from the foundation of the world, and do the will, both of the Father, and of the Son of the Father, because of me, and of the Son, because of my flesh. And behold, the time is at hand, and this night shall the sign be given.

And it came to pass that the words which came unto Nephi were fulfilled, according as they had been spoken: for behold at the going down of the sun, there was no darkness; and the people began to be astonished, because there was no darkness when the night came. And there were many who had not believed the words of the prophets, fell to the earth, and became as if they were dead, for they knew that the great plan of destruction which they had laid for those who believed in the word of the prophets, had been frustrated, for the signal which had been given was already at hand; and they began to know that the Son of God must shortly appear; yea, in fine, all the people upon the face of the whole earth, from the west to the east, both in the land north and in the land south, were so exceedingly astonished, that they fell to the earth; for they knew that the prophets had testified of these things for many years, and that the sign which had been given, was already at hand; and they began to fear because of their iniquity and their unbelief.

And it came to pass that there was no darkness in all that night, but it was as light as though it was mid-day. And it came to pass that the sun did rise in the morning again, according to its proper order; and they knew that it was the day that the Lord should be born, because of the sign which had been given. And it had come to pass, yea, all things, every whit, according to the words of the prophets. And it came to pass also, that a new star did appear, according to the word. And it came to pass that from this time forth, there began to be lyings sent forth among the people, by satan, to harden their hearts, to the intent that they might not believe in those signs and wonders which they had seen; but notwithstanding these lyings and deceivings, the more part of the people did believe, and were converted unto the Lord. And it came to pass that Nephi went forth among the people, and also many others, baptizing unto repentance, in the which, there were a great remission of sins. And thus the people began again to have peace in the land; and there were no contentions, save it were a few that began to preach, endeavoring to prove by the scriptures, that it was no more expedient to observe the law of Moses. Now in this thing they did err, having not understood the scriptures. But it came to pass that they soon became converted, and were convinced of the error which they were in, for it was made known unto them that the law was not yet fulfilled, and that it must be fulfilled in every whit; yea, the word came unto them that it must be fulfilled; yea, that one jot nor tittle should not pass away, till it should all be fulfilled; therefore in this same year, were they brought to a knowledge of their error, and did confess their faults. And thus the ninety and second year did pass away, bringing glad tidings unto the people because of the signs which did come to pass, according to the words of the prophecy of all the holy prophets.

And it came to pass that the ninety and third year did also pass away in peace, save it were for the Gadianton robbers, who dwelt upon the mountains, who did infest the land; for so strong were their holds and their secret places, that the people could not overpower them; therefore they did commit many murders, and did do much slaughter among the people. And it came to pass that in the ninety and fourth year, they began to increase in a great degree, because there were many dissenters of the Nephites who did flee unto them, which did cause much sorrow unto those Nephites who did remain in the land; and there was also a cause of much sorrow among the Lamanites, for behold, they had many children who did grow up and began to wax strong in years, that they became for themselves, and were led away by some who were Zoramites, by their lyings and their flattering words, to join those Gadianton robbers; and thus were the Lamanites afflicted also, and began to decrease as to their faith and righteousness, because of the wickedness of the rising generation.

[. . .]

And now it came to pass that there were a great multitude gathered together, of the people of Nephi, round about the temple which was in the land Bountiful; and they were marveling and wondering one with another, and were shewing one to another the great and marvelous change which had taken place; and they were also conversing about this Jesus Christ, of whom the sign had been given, concerning his death.

And it came to pass that while they were thus conversing one with another, they heard a voice, as if it came out of heaven; and they cast their eyes round about, for they understood not the voice which they heard; and it was not a harsh voice, neither was it a loud voice; nevertheless, and notwithstanding it being a small voice, it did pierce them that did hear, to the centre, insomuch that there were no part of their frame that it did not cause to quake; yea, it did pierce them to the very soul, and did cause their hearts to burn. And it came to pass that again they heard the voice, and they understood it not; and again the third time they did hear the voice, and did open their ears to hear it; and their eyes were towards the sound thereof; and they did look steadfastly towards heaven, from whence the sound came; and behold, the third time they did understand the voice which they heard; and it said unto them, behold, my beloved Son, in whom I am well pleased, in whom I have glorified my name, hear ye him.

And it came to pass as they understood, they cast their eyes up again towards heaven; and behold, they saw a man descending out of heaven; and he was clothed in a white robe, and he came down and stood in the midst of them, and the eyes of the whole multitude were turned upon him, and they durst not open their mouths, even one to another, and wist not what it meant, for they thought it was an angel that had appeared unto them.

And it came to pass that he stretched forth his hand, and spake unto the people, saying, behold I am Jesus Christ, of whom the prophets testified shall come into the world: and behold I am the light and the life of the world, and I have drunk out of that bitter cup which the Father hath given me, and have glorified the Father in taking upon me the sins of the world, in the which I have suffered the will of the Father in all things, from the beginning.

And it came to pass that when Jesus had spoken these words, the whole multitude fell to the earth, for they remembered that it had been prophesied among them that Christ should shew himself unto them after his ascension into heaven.

And it came to pass that the Lord spake unto them saying, arise and come forth unto me, that ye may thrust your hands into my side, and also that ye may feel the prints of the nails in my hands, and in my feet, that ye may know that I am the God of Israel, and the God of the whole earth, and have been slain for the sins of the world.

And it came to pass that the multitude went forth, and thrust their hands into his side, and did feel the prints of the nails in his hands and in his feet; and this they did do, going forth one by one, until they had all gone forth, and did see with their eyes, and did feel with their hands, and did know of a surety, and did bear record, that it was he, of whom it was written by the prophets, should come.

And when they had all gone forth, and had witnessed for themselves, they did cry out with one accord, saying, hosanna! blessed be the name of the Most High God! And they did fall down at the feet of Jesus, and did worship him.

And it came to pass that he spake unto Nephi, (for Nephi was among the multitude,) and he commanded him that he should come forth. And Nephi arose and went forth, and bowed himself before the Lord, and he did kiss his feet. And the Lord commanded him that he should arise. And he arose and stood before him. And the Lord said unto him, I give unto you power that ye shall baptize this people, when I am again ascended into heaven. And again the Lord called others, and said unto them likewise; and he gave unto them power to baptize. And he said unto them, on this wise shall ye baptize; and there shall be no disputations among you. Verily I say unto you, that whoso repenteth of his sins through your words, and desireth to be baptized in my name, on this wise shall ye baptize them: behold, ye shall go down and stand in the water, and in my name shall ye baptize them. And now behold, these are the words which ye shall say, calling them by name, saying: Having authority given me of Jesus Christ, I baptize you in the name of the Father, and of the Son, and of the Holy Ghost. Amen. And then shall ye immerse them in the water, and come forth again out of the water. And after this manner shall ye baptize in my name, for behold, verily I say unto you, that the Father, and the Son, and the Holy Ghost are one; and I am in the Father, and the Father in me, and the Father and I are one. And according as I have commanded you, thus shall ye baptize. And there shall be no disputations among you, as there hath hitherto been; neither shall there be disputations among you concerning the points of my doctrine, as there hath hitherto been; for verily, verily I say unto you, he that hath the spirit of contention, is not of me, but is of the devil, who is the father of contention, and he stirreth up the hearts of men to contend with anger, one with another. Behold, this is not my doctrine, to stir up the hearts of men with anger, one against another; but this is my doctrine, that such things should be done away. Behold, verily, verily I say unto you, I will declare unto you my doctrine. And this is my doctrine, and it is the doctrine which the Father hath given unto me; and I bear record of the Father, and the Father beareth record of me, and the Holy Ghost beareth record of the Father and me, and I bear record that the Father commandeth all men, every where, to repent and believe in me; and whoso believeth in me, and is baptized, the same shall be saved; and they are they who shall inherit the kingdom of God. And whoso believeth not in me, and is not baptized, shall be damned. Verily, verily I say unto you, that this is my doctrine; and I bear record of it from the Father; and whoso believeth in me, believeth in the Father also; and unto him will the Father bear record of me; for he will visit him with fire, and with the Holy Ghost; and thus will the Father bear record of me; and the Holy Ghost will bear record unto him of the Father and me; for the Father, and I, and the Holy Ghost, are one. . . . Yea, blessed are the poor in spirit who come unto me, for theirs is the kingdom of heaven. And again, blessed are all they that mourn, for they shall be comforted; and blessed are the meek, for they shall inherit the earth. And blessed are all they who do hunger and thirst after righteousness, for they shall be filled with the Holy Ghost. And blessed are the merciful, for they shall obtain mercy. And blessed are all the pure in heart, for they shall see God. And blessed are all the peace-makers, for they shall be called the children of God. And blessed are all they who are persecuted, for my name's sake, for theirs is the kingdom of Heaven. And blessed are ye when men shall revile you, and persecute, and shall say all manner of evil against you falsely, for my sake, for ye shall have great joy and be exceeding glad, for great shall be your reward in heaven; for so persecuted they the prophets who were before you. Verily, verily I say unto you, I give unto you to be the salt of the earth; but if the salt shall lose its savor, wherewith shall the earth be salted? The salt shall be thenceforth good for nothing, but to be cast out, and to be trodden under foot of men. Verily, verily I say unto you, I give unto you to be the light of this people. A city that is set on a hill cannot be hid. Behold, do men light a candle and put it under a bushel? Nay, but on a candle-stick, and it giveth light to all that are in the house; therefore let your light so shine before this people, that they may see your good works and glorify your Father who is in heaven. Think not that I am come to destroy the law or the prophets. I am not come to destroy but to fulfil; for verily I say unto you, one jot nor one tittle hath not passed away from the law, but in me it hath all been fulfilled.

[. . .]

And now it came to pass that when Jesus had spoken these words, he said unto those twelve whom he had chosen, ye are my disciples; and ye are a light unto this people, who are a remnant of the house of Joseph. And behold, this is the land of your inheritance; and the Father hath given it unto you. And not at any time hath the Father given me commandment that I should tell it unto your brethren at Jerusalem; neither at any time hath the Father given me commandment, that I should tell unto them concerning the other tribes of the house of Israel, whom the Father hath led away out of the land. This much did the Father command me, that I should tell unto them, that other sheep I have, which are not of this fold; them also I must bring, and they shall hear my voice; and there shall be one fold, and one shepherd. And now because of stiffneckedness and unbelief, they understood not my word; therefore I was commanded to say no more of the Father concerning this thing unto them. But, verily, I say unto you, that the Father hath commanded me, and I tell it unto you, that ye were separated from among them because of their iniquity; therefore it is because of their iniquity, that they know not of you. And verily, I say unto you again, that the other tribes hath the Father separated from them; and it is because of their iniquity, that they know not of them. And verily, I say unto you, that ye are they of whom I said, other sheep I have which are not of this fold; them also I must bring, and they shall hear my voice; and there shall be one fold, and one shepherd. And they understood me not, for they supposed it had been the Gentiles; for they understood not that the Gentiles should be converted through their preaching; and they understood me not that I said they shall hear my voice; and they understood me not that the Gentiles should not at any time hear my voice; that I should not manifest myself unto them, save it were by the Holy Ghost. But behold, ye have both heard my voice, and seen me; and ye are my sheep, and ye are numbered among those whom the Father hath given me.

# The Book of Nephi, Who is the Son of Nephi, One of the Disciples of Jesus Christ

## CHAPTER I

*An account of the people of Nephi, according to his record.*

And it came to pass that the thirty and fourth year passed away, and also the thirty and fifth, and behold the disciples of Jesus had formed a church of Christ in all the lands round about. And as many as did come unto them, and did truly repent of their sins, were baptized in the name of Jesus; and they did also receive the Holy Ghost.

And it came to pass in the thirty and sixth year, the people were all converted unto the Lord, upon all the face of the land, both Nephites and Lamanites, and there were no contentions and disputations among them, and every man did deal justly one with another; and they had all things common among them, therefore there were not rich and poor, bond and free, but they were all made free, and partakers of the heavenly gift.

And it came to pass that the thirty and seventh year passed away also, and there still continued to be peace in the land. And there were great and marvellous works wrought by the disciples of Jesus, insomuch that they did heal the sick, and raise the dead, and cause the lame to walk, and the blind to receive their sight, and the deaf to hear; and all manner of miracles did they work among the children of men; and in nothing did they work miracles save it were in the name of Jesus. And thus did the thirty and eighth year pass away, and also the thirty and ninth, and the forty and first, and the forty and second; yea, even until forty and nine years had passed away, and also the fifty and first, and the fifty and second; yea, and even until fifty and nine years had passed away; and the Lord did prosper them exceedingly, in the land: yea, insomuch that they did fill cities again where there had been cities burned; yea, even that great city Zarahemla did they cause to be built again. But there were many cities which had been sunk, and waters came up in the stead thereof; therefore these cities could not be renewed.

And now behold it came to pass that the people of Nephi did wax strong, and did multiply exceeding fast, and became an exceeding fair and delightsome people. And they were married, and given in marriage, and were blessed according to the multitude of the promises which the Lord had made unto them. And they did not walk any more after the performances and ordinances of the law of Moses, but they did walk after the commandments which they had received from their Lord and their God, continuing in fasting and prayer, and in meeting together oft, both to pray and to hear the word of the Lord. And it came to pass that there was no contention among all the people, in all the land, but there were mighty miracles wrought among the disciples of Jesus.

And it came to pass that the seventy and first year passed away, and also the seventy and second year; yea, and in fine, till the seventy and ninth year had passed away; yea, even an hundred years had passed away, and the disciples of Jesus, whom he had chosen, had all gone to the paradise of God, save it were the three who should tarry; and there were other disciples ordained in their stead; and also many of that generation which had passed away. And it came to pass that there was no contention in the land, because of the love of God which did dwell in the hearts of the people. And there were no envyings, nor strifes, nor tumults, nor whoredoms, nor lyings, nor murders, nor any manner of lasciviousness; and surely there could not be a happier people among all the people who had been created by the hand of God; there were no robbers, nor murderers, neither were there Lamanites, or any manner of ites; but they were in one, the children of Christ, and heirs to the kingdom of God; and how blessed were they, for the Lord did bless them in all their doings; yea, even they were blessed and prospered, until an hundred and ten years had passed away; and the first generation from Christ had passed away, and there was no contention in all the land.

And it came to pass that Nephi, he that kept this last record, (and he kept it upon the plates of Nephi) died, and his son Amos kept it in his stead; and he kept it upon the plates of Nephi also; and he kept it eighty and four years, and there was still peace in the land, save it were a small part of the people who had revolted from the church, and took upon them the name of Lamanites; therefore there began to be Lamanites again in the land.

And it came to pass that Amos died also, (and it was an hundred and ninety and four years from the coming of Christ,) and his son Amos kept the record in his stead; and he also kept it upon the plates of Nephi; and it was also written in the book of Nephi, which is this book. And it came to pass that two hundred years had passed away, and the second generation had all passed away save it were a few. And now I, Mormon, would that ye should know that the people had multiplied, insomuch that they were spread upon all the face of the land, and that they had become exceeding rich, because of their prosperity in Christ. And now in this two hundred and first year, there began to be among them those who were lifted up in pride, such as the wearing of costly apparel, and all manner of fine pearls, and of the fine things of the world. And from that time forth they did have their goods and their substance no more common among them, and they began to be divided into classes, and they began to build up churches unto themselves, to get gain, and began to deny the true church of Christ.

And it came to pass that when two hundred and ten years had passed away, there were many churches in the land; yea, there were many churches which professed to know the Christ, and yet they did deny the more parts of his gospel, insomuch that they did receive all manner of wickedness, and did administer that which was sacred unto him to whom it had been forbidden, because of unworthiness. And this church did multiply exceedingly, because of iniquity, and because of the power of satan who did get hold upon their hearts. And again, there was another church which denied the Christ; and they did persecute the true church of Christ, because of their humility, and their belief in Christ;

and they did despise them, because of the many miracles which were wrought among them; therefore they did exercise power and authority over the disciples of Jesus who did tarry with them, and they did cast them into prison; but by the power of the word of God, which was in them, the prisons were rent in twain, and they went forth doing mighty miracles among them. Nevertheless, and notwithstanding all these miracles, the people did harden their hearts, and did seek to kill them, even as the Jews at Jerusalem sought to kill Jesus, according to his word, and they did cast them into furnaces of fire, and they came forth receiving no harm; and they also cast them into dens of wild beasts, and they did play with the wild beasts even as a child with a lamb; and they did come forth from among them, receiving no harm. Nevertheless, the people did harden their hearts, for they were led by many priests and false prophets to build up many churches, and to do all manner of iniquity. And they did smite upon the people of Jesus; but the people of Jesus did not smite again. And thus they did dwindle in unbelief and wickedness, from year to year, even until two hundred and thirty years had passed away. And now it came to pass in this year, yea, in the two hundred and thirty and first year, there was a great division among the people. And it came to pass that in this year there arose a people who were called the Nephites, and they were true believers in Christ; and among them there were those who were called by the Lamanites, Jacobites, and Josephites, and Zoramites; therefore the true believers in Christ, and the true worshipers of Christ, (among whom were the three disciples of Jesus who should tarry,) were called Nephites, and Jacobites, and Josephites, and Zoramites. And it came to pass that they who rejected the gospel, were called Lamanites, and Lemuelites, and Ishmaelites; and they did not dwindle in unbelief, but they did wilfully rebel against the gospel of Christ; and they did teach their children that they should not believe, even as their fathers, from the beginning, did dwindle. And it was because of the wickedness and abominations of their fathers, even as it was in the beginning. And they were taught to hate the children of God, even as the Lamanites were taught to hate the children of Nephi, from the beginning.

And it came to pass that two hundred and forty and four years had passed away, and thus were the affairs of the people. And the more wicked part of the people did wax strong, and became exceeding more numerous than were the people of God. And they did still continue to build up churches unto themselves, and adorn them with all manner of precious things. And thus did two hundred and fifty years pass away, and also two hundred and sixty years. And it came to pass that the wicked part of the people began again to build up the secret oaths and combinations of Gadianton. And also the people who were called the people of Nephi, began to be proud in their hearts, because of their exceeding riches, and become vain, like unto their brethren, the Lamanites. And from this time, the disciples began to sorrow for the sins of the world.

And it came to pass that when three hundred years had passed away, both the people of Nephi and the Lamanites had become exceeding wicked one like unto another. And it came to pass that the robbers of Gadianton did spread over all the face of the land; and there were none that were righteous, save it were the disciples of Jesus. And gold and silver did they lay up in store in abundance, and did traffic in all manner of traffic.

And it came to pass that after three hundred and five years had passed away, (and the people did still remain in wickedness.) Amos died, and his brother Ammaron did keep the record in his stead. And it came to pass that when three hundred and twenty years had passed away, Ammaron, being constrained by the Holy Ghost, did hide up the records which were sacred; yea, even all the sacred records which had been handed down from generation to generation, which were sacred, even until the three hundred and twentieth year from the coming of Christ. And he did hide them up unto the Lord, that they might come again unto the remnant of the house of Jacob, according to the prophecies and the promises of the Lord. And thus is the end of the record of Ammaron.

# The Book of Moroni

## CHAPTER IX

*The second epistle of Mormon to his son Moroni.*

My beloved son, I write unto you again, that ye may know that I am yet alive; but I write somewhat that which is grievous. For behold, I have had a sore battle with the Lamanites, in which we did not conquer; and Archeantus has fallen by the sword, and also Luram and Emron; yea, and we have lost a great number of our choice men. And now behold, my son, I fear lest the Lamanites shall destroy this people, for they do not repent, and satan stirreth them up continually to anger, one with another. Behold, I am laboring with them continually; and when I speak the word of God with sharpness, they tremble and anger against me; and when I use no sharpness, they harden their hearts against it; wherefore I fear lest the spirit of the Lord hath ceased striving with them. For so exceedingly do they anger, that it seemeth me that they have no fear of death; and they have lost their love, one towards another; and they thirst after blood and revenge continually. And now my beloved son, notwithstanding their hardness, let us labor diligently; for if we should cease to labor, we should be brought under condemnation; for we have a labor to perform whilst in this tabernacle of clay, that we may conquer the enemy of all righteousness, and rest our souls in the kingdom of God.

And now I write somewhat concerning the sufferings of this people. For according to the knowledge which I have received from Amoron, behold, the Lamanites have many prisoners, which they took from the tower of Sherrizah; and there were men, women and children. And the husbands and fathers of those women and children they have slain; and they feed the women upon the flesh of their husbands, and the children upon the flesh of their fathers; and no water, save a little, do they give unto them.

And notwithstanding this great abomination of the Lamanites, it doth not exceed that of our people in Moriantum. For behold many of the daughters of the Lamanites have they taken prisoners: and after depriving them of that which was most dear and precious above all things, which is chastity and virtue; and after they had done this thing, they did murder them in a most cruel manner, torturing their bodies even unto death; and after they have done this, they devour their flesh like unto wild beasts, because of the hardness of their hearts; and they do it for a token of bravery. O my beloved son, how can a people like this, that are without civilization; (and only a few years have passed away, and they were a civil and a delightsome people;) but O my son, how can a people like this, whose delight is in so much abomination, how can we expect that God will stay his hand in judgment against us? Behold, my heart cries wo unto this people. Come out in judgment, O God, and hide their sins, and wickedness, and abominations from before thy face. And again, my son, there are many widows and their daughters, who remain in Sherrizah; and that part of the provisions which the Lamanites did not carry away, behold, the army of Zenephi has carried away, and left them to wander whithersoever they can for food; and many old women do faint by the way and die. And the army which is with me, is weak; and the armies of the Lamanites are betwixt Sherrizah and me; and as many as have fled to the army of Aaron, have fallen victims to their awful brutality. O the depravity of my people! they are without order and without mercy. Behold, I am but a man, and I have but the strength of a man, and I cannot any longer enforce my commands; and they have become strong in their perversion; and they are alike brutal, sparing none, neither old nor young; and they delight in every thing save that which is good; and the sufferings of our women and our children upon all the face of this land, doth exceed every thing; yea, tongue cannot tell, neither can it be written. And now my son, I dwell no longer upon this horrible scene. Behold, thou knowest the wickedness of this people; thou knowest that they are without principle, and past feeling; and their wickedness doth exceed that of the Lamanites. Behold, my son, I cannot recommend them unto God lest he should smite me. But behold, my son, I recommend thee unto God, and I trust in Christ that thou wilt be saved; and I pray unto

God that he would spare thy life, to witness the return of his people unto him, or their utter destruction; for I know that they must perish, except they repent and return unto him; and if they perish it will be like unto the Jaredites, because of the wilfulness of their hearts, seeking for blood and revenge. And if it so be that they perish, we know that many of our brethren have dissented over unto the Lamanites, and many more will also dissent over unto them; wherefore, write somewhat a few things, if thou art spared; and I shall perish and not see thee; but I trust that I may see thee soon; for I have sacred records that I would deliver up unto thee. My son, be faithful in Christ; and may not the things which I have written, grieve thee, to weigh thee down unto death, but may Christ lift thee up, and may his sufferings and death, and the shewing his body unto our fathers, and his mercy and long suffering, and the hope of his glory and of eternal life, rest in your mind forever. And may the grace of God the Father, whose throne is high in the heavens, and our Lord Jesus Christ, who sitteth on the right hand of his power, until all things shall become subject unto him, be, and abide with you forever. Amen.

## CHAPTER X

Now I, Moroni, write somewhat as seemeth me good; and I write unto my brethren the Lamanites; and I would that they should know that more than four hundred and twenty years have passed away, since the sign was given of the coming of Christ. And I seal up these records, after I have spoken a few words by way of exhortation unto you. Behold, I would exhort you that when ye shall read these things if it be wisdom in God that ye should read them, that ye would remember how merciful the Lord hath been unto the children of men, from the creation of Adam, even down until the time that ye shall receive these things, and ponder it in your hearts. And when ye shall receive these things, I would exhort you that ye would ask God, the eternal Father, in the name of Christ, if these things are not true; and if ye shall ask with a sincere heart, with real intent, having faith in Christ, he will manifest the truth of it unto you, by the power of the Holy Ghost; and by the power of the Holy Ghost, ye may know the truth of all things. And whatsoever thing is good, is just and true; wherefore, nothing that is good denieth the Christ, but acknowledgeth that he is. And ye may know that he is, by the power of the Holy Ghost; wherefore I would exhort you, that ye deny not the power of God; for he worketh by power, according to the faith of the children of men, the same today and to-morrow, and forever. And again I exhort you, my brethren, that ye deny not the gifts of God, for they are many; and they come from the same God. And there are different ways that these gifts are administered; but it is the same God who worketh all in all; and they are given by the manifestations of the spirit of God unto men, to profit them. For behold, to one is given by the spirit of God, that he may teach the word of wisdom; and to another, that he may teach the word of knowledge by the same spirit; and to another exceeding great faith; and to another, the gifts of healing by the same spirit. And again, to another, that he may work mighty miracles; and again, to another that he may prophesy concerning all things; and again, to another, the beholding of angels and ministering spirits; and again, to another, all kinds of tongues; and again, to another, the interpretation of languages and of divers kinds of tongues. And all these gifts come by the spirit of Christ; and they come unto every man severally, according as he will. And I would exhort you, my beloved brethren, that ye remember that every good gift cometh of Christ. And I would exhort you, my beloved brethren, that ye remember that he is the same yesterday, to-day, and forever, and that all these gifts of which I have spoken, which are spiritual, never will be done away, even as long as the world shall stand, only according to the unbelief of the children of men. Wherefore, there must be faith; and if there must be faith, there must also be hope; and if there must be hope, there must also be charity; and except ye have charity, ye can in no wise be saved in the kingdom of God; neither can ye be saved in the kingdom of God, if ye have not faith; neither can ye if ye have no hope; and if ye have no hope, ye must needs be in despair; and despair cometh because of iniquity. And Christ truly said unto our fathers, if ye have faith, ye can do all things which is expedient unto me. And now I speak unto all the ends of the earth, that if the day cometh that the power and gifts of God shall be done away among you, it shall be because of unbelief. And wo be unto the children of men, if this be the case; for there shall be none that doeth good among you, no not one. For if there be one among you that doeth good, he shall work by the power and gifts of God. And wo unto them who shall do these things away and die, for they die in their sins, and they cannot be saved in the kingdom of God; and I speak it according to the words of Christ, and I lie not. And I exhort you to remember these things; for the time speedily cometh that ye shall know that I lie not, for ye shall see me at the bar of God, and the Lord God will say unto you, did I not declare my words unto you, which were written by this man, like as one crying from the dead? yea, even as one speaking out of the dust? I declare these things unto the fulfilling of the prophecies. And behold, they shall proceed forth out of the mouth of the everlasting God; and his word shall hiss forth from generation to generation. And God shall shew unto you, that that which I have written is true. And again I would exhort you, that ye would come unto Christ, and lay hold upon every good gift, and touch not the evil gift, nor the unclean thing. And awake, and arise from the dust, O Jerusalem; yea, and put on thy beautiful garments, O daughter of Zion, and strengthen thy stakes, and enlarge thy borders forever, that thou mayest no more be confounded, that the covenants of the eternal Father which he hath made unto thee, O house of Israel, may be fulfilled. Yea, come unto Christ, and be perfected in him, and deny yourselves of all ungodliness, and if ye shall deny yourselves of all ungodliness, and love God with all your might, mind and strength, then is his grace sufficient for you, that by his grace ye may be perfect in Christ; and if by the grace of God ye are perfect in Christ, ye can in no wise deny the power of God. And again, if ye, by the grace of God are perfect in Christ, and deny not his power, then are ye sanctified in Christ by the grace of God, through the shedding of the blood of Christ, which is in the covenant of the Father, unto the remission of your sins, that ye become holy without spot. And now I bid unto all, farewell. I soon go to rest in the paradise of God, until my spirit and body shall again reunite, and I am brought forth triumphant through the air, to meet you before the pleasing bar of the great Jehovah, the eternal Judge of both quick and dead. Amen.

(JOSEPH SMITH, JR., 1830; 3RD ED., NAUVOO, IL: 1840)

# A Holy, Sacred and Divine Roll and Book; from the Lord God of Heaven, to the Inhabitants of Earth

In February 1842 an angel named Al'sign te're Jah' directed Philemon Stewart, a member of the Shaker community in New Lebanon, New York, to a nearby hillside. Over fourteen days Stewart received revelations that confirmed the chosenness of the Shakers as the conveyors of divine truth to other earthly inhabitants, and detailed the role of Shaker founder Ann Lee as the second, female, manifestation of Jesus Christ, the "Anointed One." In language rich with biblical allusions, the revelation also warned the "inhabitants of a perishing earth, and languishing world" to repent of their sins, separate from the evils of the world, and heed the teachings revealed previously to Moses on Mount Sinai, to the prophets of Israel, and by Jesus Christ and his followers. Stewart was then instructed to publish these revelations and to distribute them widely as a sacred text to be used alongside the Bible. In 1843 they appeared as *A Holy, Sacred and Divine Roll and Book*.

For the several thousand members of the United Society of Believers in Christ's Second Appearing (more commonly known as Shakers), the text was immediately accepted as a distinctive but not unique demonstration of spiritual gifts and communications with angels, dead society members, and former leaders. Beginning in 1837, a new "era of manifestations" visited many followers within Shaker communities scattered across New York and New England; members received visions of direction, consolation, and warning that helped them better understand the divine role of Mother Ann

Lee, who had founded the American movement in the 1780s. Stewart's book was understood as scripture alongside the Bible and other "spirit messages" delivered to members. For the next decade it was read aloud by leaders and used liturgically by community members in the spiritual "family" groupings that made up their celibate order.

The selections presented here focus on the themes that make the Shaker interpretation of Christian history and the Bible distinctive. Amply demonstrated in these pages is their understanding of the dual nature of God as both male and female, instantiated in the appearances of Jesus Christ and Mother Ann Lee on Earth; their understanding that the millennium had arrived and God was calling believers to separate from the sinfulness of the world into celibate ("sinless") religious orders; and their belief that divine and earthly leaders past and present continued to communicate with their followers.

# A Holy, Sacred and Divine Roll and Book; from the Lord God of Heaven, to the Inhabitants of Earth

THE WORD OF GOD,

TO HIS HOLY SON JESUS CHRIST, THE SAVIOR OF MEN.

*Take this short Roll of my word, go forth to earth, and read aloud, upon the top of my holy Mountain, that one of my servants may understand and correctly write the same.*

*To this place, I will cause one of my holy Angels, who shall bear thee company, to lead the one whom I have chosen, even in the first watch of the rising sun, to the sacred spot of ground, whereon I will cause my word to be revealed in flames of burning fire.*

## PROCLAMATION.

Bow down your hearts, all ye who dwell in Zion, and humble yourselves to the dust before Me, O ye worms of mortal clay! All flesh shall wither at my presence, and the deceitful worker in Zion shall be consumed by the fire of my burning. For much have I given unto Zion, and much will I require at her hand, saith the Lord God of Heaven.

For I will have a pure people on the earth, whose hands are not stained with human blood, nor their souls defiled with sin and disobedience to the commands of my blessed Son, whom I, ALPHA and OMEGA, the beginning and the end, have twice sent forth to the inhabitants of earth, whom I created in my own image, that they might bring forth offerings pure and holy, before my sacred throne.

In tender mercy, and loving kindness, did I send forth my Son, both in his first and second appearance, that they might learn the way of peace and salvation, and gain an inheritance in my pure and holy gospel, while on earth, that would insure them a peaceful mansion of rest in my holy kingdom, when they had done with the things of time.

But, *Oh! Hálen si vaś ta vać la!* Mortal man hath never been ready, from the earliest ages of the world to the present day, to learn my will and obey my sacred word, through such means as I was pleased to send it forth to them.

But my sacred words have been trampled under their feet; my law of nature disregarded and set at nought; and in the sacred path of my gospel, which is the law of grace to the soul, their feet have not walked. But in other paths their feet have trodden, and [they have] shed much innocent blood. And other gods than Me, have their souls bowed down to worship.

Thus saith the Lord God of Heaven and earth; My All-seeing Eye hath beheld the doings of the children of men, for ages and ages long past, even to the present day. And a cruel, persecuting spirit, in all ages of the world, to the present time, hath invariably risen up against my most merciful offers, to persecute, even unto death, those who put their trust in Me, and would sooner suffer death, in any form, than disobey my righteous commands.

But give ear, O earth, and understand, O ye people that dwell in her! The day of my visitation hath begun, saith the Lord; and I will never cease, nor cause my hand of judgment to be stayed, until I have met all nations in their own paths. Mercy and judgment are in my grasp; and my hand of wrath and indignation is hovering over the earth, and my Angels are passing to and fro, through every quarter.

And where ever I find a people on the earth, saith the Lord, who are ready and prepared to keep the commands of my blessed Son, either in his first, or second appearance, and heed this, my present warning voice unto them, by humbling themselves, and bringing forth fruits meet for repentance, which are, humility of soul, peace, love and good will to all men, and a conscience void of offence, before Me, their God, and each other; my hand of judgment shall lightly pass them over; and in merciful rays of loving kindness, will I cause my blessings to distill upon them.

But unto such as make light, in this their day, of my warning voice, and will not even return to the law of nature, as I commanded the children of Israel, by my faithful servant Moses, in ancient days; but pass on, saying within their own hearts; *"These are the words of mortals and not of God";* I will surely visit them, in my own time and season, with sore destruction and desolating judgments, till mountains sink and valleys rise, and kingdoms into pieces rend.

For I will cause peace to depart from the earth, and an awful gloom of terror and dismay to spread itself over her face. For I am the God of yesterday, to-day, and forever; and my spirit shall not always strive with mortal man to no purpose.

But they shall hear my word in different parts of the earth, sent forth through the mouths of babes and sucklings. And the tongues of the dumb shall be loosed, to warn the people to turn from the error of their doings, and repent before the Lord their God, that his rolling judgments sweep them not from the earth.

And awful signs shall appear in the firmament of heaven, that shall cause the heart of man to faint; and his strength shall fail because of the judgments which my Almighty hand hath sent forth upon the earth. For she groaneth beneath her present weight of sin and wickedness; and crieth unto Me for vengeance to recompense unto the inhabitants thereof, who, by their own disobedience, have brought this curse upon her.

Therefore, have I, the God of Heaven, in mercy and loving kindness, seen fit to reveal, in these last days, my word and will unto my chosen witnesses. And this short roll of my word, saith the Lord of hosts, I command my witnesses to put up in the yard of my Holy Sanctuary; that all such of the children of men, as may pass this street, upon the side of my Holy Mountain, may read and understand the same.

But touch it not, saith the Lord of hosts; for I have placed four of my holy Angels, to guard my sacred word. And let him that readeth understand; and judge not my word, judge not my work; for my doings are marvelous in the sight of men; and who can comprehend my ways, saith the GREAT I AM.

I have commanded my chosen people, who dwell upon this

Mount, to bow down in low humility before Me, and separate themselves more from the children of this world; and worship Me, the coming season, in a retired situation, humbly supplicating the mercy of the Lord their God, both for themselves, and the rest of the inhabitants of the earth.

Therefore, trouble ye not my chosen ones; for I have called them, saith the Lord, and they shall not appear in pomp and splendor; but they shall be clothed in meekness, and humility of soul; clad in the spirit of the LAMB, and the garment of the SAVIOR. For my people are inoffensive, and will sooner suffer, even unto death, than resist unto blood. Therefore, in blessing I will bless; and in troubling I shall trouble, saith the Lord of hosts.

[. . .]

Then, O thou mighty and proclaiming Angel, take to thyself other Angels, and go to the Zion on earth, where, by my Almighty Power, the windows and doors of Heaven have been opened for several years past, that the indwellers thereof might converse with mortals on earth, or with such a portion of them as had forsaken all for the gospel's sake, in a more remarkable degree of nearness and freedom, than was ever before suffered, since the earth, by my hand was created.

There, take to thyself a servant of my name, an instrument whom I have chosen for this purpose, and prepare him, through deep tribulation, and anguish of soul, to write correctly, the words of this Roll, as thou shalt read them unto him.

But before this shall take place, thou shalt show forth strange and striking signs unto the people, which shall appear both awful and sublime. For in this Roll to the children of men, have I declared the Daughter of Zion, in her proper lot and place, as well as the Son.

THE
# SACRED, SOLEMN AND SEALED ROLL

OPENED AND READ, BY THE

## MIGHTY ANGEL

## CHAPTER I.
## THE LORD FIRST ANNOUNCES HIMSELF IN HIS TRUE CHARACTER, TO THE NATIONS OF THE EARTH.

1. I AM THAT I AM, A GOD OF JUSTICE, OF WISDOM, AND OF TRUTH. A GOD OF LONG FORBEARANCE, OF TENDER KINDNESS, AND LOVING MERCY. A GOD OF WHOM YE READ, WHO CREATED THE HEAVENS, AND THE EARTH, AND ALL THAT IS THEREIN.

A GOD who sent forth the overwhelming deluge, to sweep from the earth's face, even that which I had created in my own image, bearing immortality, because of their gross wickedness, in perverting the order of nature which I had given them.

2. A GOD that appeared on Sinai's top, and gave my law, engraven upon two tables of stone, into the hands of my true and faithful servant Moses, for the Children of Israel.

3. A GOD who fought their battles when they were obedient, and suffered their enemies to prevail when they were disobedient;

4. A GOD that led them to the promised land, and sent, in my own wisdom unto them, the promised Messiah.

5. A GOD who hath narrowly watched the doings of the nations and kingdoms of the earth, from the day they crucified my Son, up to the present time.

6. I AM, is GOD; whose power is Almighty, and whose glory and beauty filleth all immensity and space; yet the least creature of my creation, is an object of my particular notice; either in mercy or in judgment. And with Me, time does not exist, for before time was, I AM, existed; and the after Me can never come.

7. JEHOVAH JAH, is my name; through endless worlds I'm

known; fulfilling, to the least jot and tittle, that which I have promised through the mouths of my true and faithful servants.

8. All creation, that mortals can comprehend, should pass into oblivion, rather than one word from my mouth should fail of being accomplished, let it be spoken through whatever medium it may; if I have prepared that medium, I have also recorded it on the records of eternity; and all the power that earth and hell possess, can never falsify one word.

9. But times and seasons, I seldom give to any agent, to declare: they are reserved in true wisdom, by the ETERNAL TWAIN, united in one. I am that GOD that did promise, in ancient days, through the mouths of my faithful servants, that in the latter day, I would set up a kingdom that should never have an end. This I have done; I have begun a kingdom that shall never have an end.

10. I did also promise, that I would fill the whole earth with a stone, from the Mountain, cut out without hands: This I am also doing, in my own time and season. Remember that with Me, one day is as a thousand years, and a thousand years as one day: yet, the very hairs of your head are all numbered, and the moments of your lives all counted.

11. I did also promise to create a new heaven and a new earth, wherein should dwell righteousness. And I did furthermore declare, that my kingdom was a kingdom of peace; and for this purpose did I send my only begotten Son into the world. I did also promise, that I would cause the loftiness of man to be brought low; and bring into contempt the honorable and great ones of the earth, (or those who felt themselves as such,) that the pride of all flesh might be stained, and my name alone, exalted in that day. This work I am now doing, even in the present time in which you live.

12. I am that God who did promise, through the Lord Jesus Christ, that I would come as a thief in the night; and warned all to be prepared, with lamps well trimmed and burning, having oil in their vessels, ready to meet the Bridegroom and Bride, and not to be found sleeping, when their Master should return.

13. And lo, I have come, and cried aloud the watch, but few answered; therefore I called the lame, the halt and the blind to my feast, and they that were the children of the kingdom I did

cast out, and compelled those from the highways and hedges, to come in and sit at my table, that it might be filled.

14. I am that God who promised, through my blessed Son, that if any would forsake all, for the gospel's sake, take up their cross, and follow Me, they should be blessed while in time, an hundred fold; and in the world to come, with eternal life. And that all such as would lose their life for my sake, should find it; and all such as would save their life should lose it. For the Father and the Son are one, and from the Eternal Essence of my goodness, did I send him forth. [See St. John, Chap. xvii. 11, 21, 22.]

15. I AM, is God of yesterday, to day, and forever; my purposes alter not, neither do they change, with the passing events of time.

16. My attributes of goodness, justice and equity, with an offer of repentance, have always, in the wise dispensations of my providence, preceded, (in kind and merciful offers to the children of men,) the heavy hand of my judgment, that they who would, might turn and be saved.

17. And now, even in this your day, I am that God who does, through means of my own choosing, and vessels of my own preparing, send forth my word of truth, accompanied by a kind and friendly warning, to all nations, kindreds, tongues and people, who dwell upon the face of the whole earth.

18. Not through vessels polished by the arts and sciences, cultivated by man, but through such as are humble and dependent children, who seek to know, and do my will, as the first, and greatest object of their pursuit; who dwell in a humble and secluded position in life; choosing, rather to suffer persecution, tribulation and affliction with my people, than to enjoy the pleasures of sin for a season.

19. Such are the instruments and vessels, through whom the word of my law shall go forth, from the Zion of my likeness, to the ends of the earth. Through such as do, in truth, yield themselves as clay in the hands of the potter; giving all the honor and glory to my name, knowing and feeling themselves nought, but poor frail worms of the dust, whose life and breath is but as a vapor, that vanisheth quickly away.

# CHAPTER II.
## BRIEFLY SHOWING THE ORDER OF MY WORK WITH THE CHILDREN OF MEN IN EARLY AGES;

WHOM I HAD CREATED IN MY OWN IMAGE, SAITH THE LORD, TO FILL A MUCH MORE HONORABLE AND EXALTED STATION, IN MY VIEW, THAN THAT TO WHICH THEY HAVE APPLIED THEMSELVES

1. When I created the earth, and all that is therein, I created man in a state of free agency, possessing an immortal soul, endowed with reasonable faculties, and also with irrational, or opposite propensities.

2. These irrational, or opposite propensities, could never have gained such an influence over his rational mind, as to have perverted the order of his creation, had he kept my commandments, when first by my hand he was created, and placed in the garden, with full liberty to partake of every flower, and eat of the fruit of every tree, save the one that stood in the midst. This he was not to meddle with on pain of death.

3. But the irrational and inferior propensities working upon his animal part, seduced him to yield to the pleadings of the weaker vessel, and disobey the righteous command of his Creator God.

4. By giving way to indulge their natures, the seat of which gratification was placed in the midst of their bodies; and this is the tree, standing in the midst, bearing the forbidden fruit, from which they plucked, not for the sake of procreation, but wholly for the sake of gratification.

5. Therefore, the death, of which I had before told them, did now ensue; they could no longer stand before Me in a state of true innocence; for they had basely corrupted that order of nature which I had strictly commanded them to keep, and violate it not.

6. The times and seasons for them to come together merely for the sake of propagating their own species, could have been fulfilled, sufficient to accomplish that end, and [that work] been as justifiable in my sight, as that of eating or drinking; and they could have known no more shame in the transaction.

7. But by yielding to inordinate propensities, the seed of man was

basely corrupted; and by that means, the order of nature, which I had established for his protection while in a natural state, was wholly thrown aside, saith the Lord, by the great mass of mankind, until debauchery, bloodshed and violence, did fill the whole earth, save a small remnant, who had descended from him who was begotten strictly after the order of nature, in true obedience to my command.

8. I never intended, saith the Lord, that after having created man in our own image, to be an honor and glory unto us, by showing forth the image of his Creator, that he should have filled the earth with every species of abomination and violence, and caused it to be covered with bloodshed and carnage: by no means.

9. But I intended it should have been a terrestrial paradise, standing in its natural order uncorrupted, until in my wisdom, I should have seen fit to introduce an order of grace, or a spiritual dispensation, for such portions of its inhabitants as were adequately ripened for the calling.

10. I should have noticed, with my blessing and protection, in the order of my providence, those who had strictly kept the order and law of nature, uncorrupted, as really as those who were called into the order of my grace; or to a work so pure and holy, that it could allow of nothing pertaining to the works of generation;

11. But mankind, from the earliest ages of the world, have never ceased to pervert the order of nature, and turn it to subserve their own ungoverned and licentious passions, until their loss and darkness have become so great, that the whole earth is corrupted, and fast sinking under a curse, from my all righteous hand.

12. And all the judgments and calamities which I have suffered to come upon the earth in past dispensations and ages, to the present day, as a just recompense for their own doings, have been for the purpose that mankind might learn obedience to my law, by the things which they suffered.

13. Yet, notwithstanding all these solemn warnings, accompanied by awful judgments, if their lives were spared, they have never ceased to harden their hearts, and again provoke my Holy Spirit to anger by their gross wickedness, committed [by many,] with their eyes wide open, knowing that they were disobeying the commands of the Lord their God.

14. The whole world, and all the inhabitants that have heretofore lived on the earth's face, bear Me witness, that it hath now become ripe, for sore and heavy judgments.

15. Therefore, do I firstly send forth my warning voice in charity, and extend the offer of repentance to all who will accept it; for I delight not in the death of the wicked, saith the Lord.

16. But I would, that ye turn from the evil of your doings, and learn true righteousness; or come so far towards it, as to keep that law of nature which I first established for the protection of man, while yet in a natural state.

17. Hearken, O ye people, and hear my word, saith the Lord your God. Had man kept his rectitude in the order of nature, as I commanded him, no innocent blood would ever have been shed by his hand; no wars and fightings would ever have existed among the nations of the earth.

18. But because of their awful wickedness, and of their beastly abominations, I, the Lord God of Heaven and earth, have suffered the sword, with bloodshed and carnage, famine, destruction and pestilence, with sweeping blasts of my fury, in earthquakes and tornadoes, to devastate many parts of the earth, and swallow up in destruction, the living thereon; that others might take warning and behold the doings of an Almighty hand, that no mortal power could sway.

19. [These events were suffered,] that those who beheld the awful calamities, with which their fellow creatures had been visited in a stroke of my judgment, might take warning, and turn from the evil of their doings, before it be too late.

20. But how, saith the Lord, have they hardened their hearts? Truly, by saying to their fellows when the calamity was passed, "Why this is truly remarkable, the Lord must have done this; but perhaps the like never will take place again, and so we will go on as usual, [and do as we have done.]"

21. Others would say, "These things are unavoidable in the natural course and order of the elements; I do not consider that God has any thing to do with it."

22. And by this means, they would strengthen their fellow mortals in the belief, that my Almighty hand and power, hath nothing to do in bringing such sweeping calamities upon the earth, and by so doing, [they would] strengthen and encourage

their companions to go on, still adding to, and increasing the black catalogue of crimes that was attached to those whom I had swept from the face of the earth.

23. Yea, saith the Lord, instead of my judgments serving to work repentance and humiliation, in those who were unvisited by my judgments, it only served, (with many,) to harden them in their awful crimes of wickedness.

24. I deal, saith the Lord Almighty, with the creatures of my creation, according to my own wisdom. I deal with the different nations, kindreds, tongues and people, dwelling upon the face of the whole earth, both in mercy and in judgment; and in my own wisdom I deal with them as nations, and I deal with them as individuals.

25. Give ear, O Earth, and understand my words, all ye people who dwell in her, saith the Lord of hosts. Will you receive the word of the Lord your God in mercy, now while it is extended to you, in this, the latter day of his glory? Or will you forbear to hear, and refrain from repentance, as your fathers before you have done?

26. Eternity, and the souls dwelling therein, cry unto Me, as a witness, that from the earliest ages of the world to the present day, mankind, as a body, have stood against the most merciful offers of my hand, by refusing to hearken to my word, which I sent forth for their best good, their peace and their comfort.

27. But, as a few glimmering stars in the midst of midnight darkness, so have I preserved a few chosen witnesses, who were prepared, through deep tribulation, and much suffering, to testify of my word, and of my work in truth, through all the dispensations of my goodness to man, from the earliest ages of the world to the present day.

28. I have never promised salvation nor protection, to any souls, only in the path of true obedience to that revealed will and order, made known to them, through such instruments, as I had prepared and raised up to testify of Me, both by precept and example, in the age and day wherein they lived.

29. And, as a criterion by which to tell those who were the true witnesses of my word, I did proclaim, through my blessed Son, that *fruits* alone, should declare, for or against each soul; that I would know no man by his words; but by the *fruits* which he

brought forth, should he be judged. And this declaration from my eternal throne, must, and forever will remain unalterable, through time and in eternity.

30. For I AM, is a just God, dispensing unto every one according as their works shall merit; and weigh every nation, according to my wisdom, in the just balance of my power; and according to that measure which they have meted unto others, so shall it be meted to them again.

31. And according to that cup which they have filled with the waters of affliction for others to drink; so shall it again be filled to overflowing, and returned to their own mouths; and according to the effusion of blood which they have caused in other nations to flow; so shall it flow from their own veins, with an increased measure, saith the Lord their God.

## CHAPTER IV.
## OF THE LAW OF NATURE, AND ORDER OF GRACE. THE DAUGHTER OF ZION DECLARED &C.

THE CHILDREN OF MEN, IN THEIR OWN NATURAL WISDOM, CAN NEVER DISCERN THE TRUE SIGNS OF THE WORKING OF MY HOLY SPIRIT, SAITH THE LORD.

1. Thus saith the Lord to the inhabitants of the earth. Go search ye the records of my holy word, which many of you so highly venerate; for ye say that they testify of Me, and of my blessed Son.

2. But after all the warnings which I had sent for hundreds and hundreds of years, through the mouths of my faithful servants, to my chosen people, respecting the coming of the Messiah, what did it avail them, when the time for his appearance had arriven? The sacred volume by which ye pretend to be led and guided, does testify the truth so far as it goes, upon that ground.

3. Though much of the record of my sacred word, delivered in past ages, hath been destroyed, and much that is now handed down to the present generation, hath been greatly perverted by such as were enemies to the yoke and cross, which the Lord Jesus

required them daily to bear and wear; yet by the interposition of my Almighty hand, a sufficient portion of that record, containing the words sent forth from my eternal throne, hath been preserved unto the present day, and doth now stand before Me as a witness, testifying against the body of darkness which covereth the earth, and the gross darkness that covereth the people thereon.

4. For their sins and abominations are many, and their transgressions not a few, saith the Great I AM; whose eye beholdeth the thoughts and intents of every heart, and the leading motive of every action among the children of men.

5. But as I have said in ancient days, I would condescend to reason with my creature man; so do I now, in this the last age of the world, again say, I will this once, condescend to reason with the objects of my creation; for truly the earth is covered with many souls, and there be millions and millions who know not their right hand from their left; upon whom the rays of my true light hath never beamed.

6. Therefore, I will this once and again extend the arm of my mercy, holding forth the sceptre of true righteousness, to all such of the inhabitants of earth as hunger and thirst for salvation, and are ready to sacrifice all to obtain it. And to such as desire still longer to remain in the wilderness state of nature, the sceptre containeth my law and commandments for the same.

7. I do require, saith the Lord, (who is descending to earth in mercy, and in heavy judgment,) that all such as desire to live in nature, propagating their own species, keep the law of nature unviolated, as I have commanded from the beginning.

8. And all such as desire to come into the gospel of grace, must keep the law of grace, as I did command in the first appearing of my blessed Son, your Lord and Savior Jesus Christ, who stands as the first true Anointed One;

9. And, as I have commanded in the second manifestation of the same spirit, now in this your day, though you believe it not, which is through the Daughter of Zion, constituting a spiritual Mother, the second Anointed One, who now stands in her proper lot and place, with her blessed Lord and Savior; at the head of my new and spiritual Creation, now established on the earth; and her name is, and forever shall be, [called] MOTHER ANN LEE.

10. And now, the fulfillment of those predictions, from the

mouths of my servants, concerning the establishing and setting up of my kingdom in the latter day of glory, as recorded in the sacred volume of my word, which all those of you who profess to be Christians so highly esteem and venerate as sacred truths, are now by my own mouth, saith the Lord, declared unto you to be fulfilled.

11. But I will show unto you, O ye children of men, the most plain and prominent passages recorded in holy writ, which have come down to the age in which you live, referring to the coming of the Messiah upon earth, to teach the people of his way, that they might walk in his path, when the time should come, for him to descend to earth.

12. And observe ye, how little these things were understood or regarded by those who then dwelt upon the earth; and in a special manner the Jews, who, for hundreds of years, had been called the chosen people of my name, and to whom I had shown great notice, in leading them out from the bondage of Egypt, into a land flowing with milk and honey, which I had promised their forefathers, I would give unto their seed after them.

## CHAPTER XV.
### PASSAGES OF SCRIPTURE, REFERRING TO THE SECOND COMING OF CHRIST IN THE FEMALE.

Sec. 8. Remember, all ye inhabitants of the earth, saith the Lord, that a work without sin unto salvation, is a perfect work; and this is the work of Christ's kingdom, which is now set up on earth.

9. And this is the little stone, cut out from the mountain without hands, which hath smote the great image, or idol lust, [by destroying the filthy propensities in man,] and shall fill the whole earth in my own due time and season, saith the Lord.

10. Though it be small, among the countless millions of earth; yet, by my own hand has it been planted, and by my own hand shall it be watered with the dews of Heaven, until all the predictions which I have sent forth, concerning it, are fulfilled in its growth, in its power, and in its dominion. I require not the aid of mortals to defend the work of my hands.

11. Though mankind, in their own natural wisdom and understanding, darkened by the black veil of antichrist, apply and interpret those sacred passages referring to MOTHER, the BRIDE, and she shall be called, THE LORD OUR RIGHTEOUSNESS, as alluding to the Church; yet, this altereth not the true import of the sacred meaning; although the female had never been revealed in her sacred order, before this dispensation.

12. The vision seen by John, in the fourteenth chapter of Revelations, of the Lamb on mount Zion, and with him an hundred and forty and four thousand, was in a future day; which is, the day of his second coming, in the completed order of that new and spiritual kingdom, at the head of which he stands, with the Bride, whom I have prepared for him, saith the Lord.

13. Though mankind, from the earliest ages of the world to the present day, have ever applied their strength and faculties to carve out other ways, than that which I laid out for them, that they might indulge and gratify their own evil propensities, in contra-distinction to the laws and commandments that their Creator sent forth for their protection;

14. Yet, every step of disobedience, they must retrace in sorrow and humiliation, and enter in at the straight gate, and walk in the narrow way, or remain in endless shades of darkness and misery.

15. For my kingdom is a kingdom of peace and purity, and nothing that worketh abomination, or maketh a lie, shall in any wise enter therein. And such as come when called, enter my holy vineyard in due season: such are owned and accepted of Me, for their obedience and sincerity of heart, whether they be rich, or whether they be poor; whether they be bond, or whether they be free.

16. But remember, they that strip for the race and run for the prize, in the gospel dispensation of this day, must strip off all their old filthy garments, and be clad with the new, by honestly confessing every known sin, in the presence of one or more of my true and faithful witnesses, who have been tried in the furnace of affliction, and purified by the gospel fire.

17. And let all such as still desire to remain in the works of nature, return to the law and order of nature, as I have commanded from the beginning, saith the Lord.

18. Defile not your own bodies, nor those of each other, only

for the purpose of begetting your own offspring. And all such as name the name of Christ, as being ministers of his gospel, set ye this example to your people; or a curse, a heavy curse, from my Almighty hand, shall follow you and your seed.

19. All ye rulers, and great ones of the earth, set forth this example before those over whom you do preside; and bear against and suppress the haunts of debauchery, by your civil laws, as fast as is possibly in your power. You have no time to lose in doing this work; for delays will cast you from beneath the arm of my mercy; and when it is too late, you will cry unto Me saying, Lord, spare us, and we will mend our lives, by hearkening to thy word.

20. My times and seasons for utter destruction upon kingdoms, realms and cities, by reason of their wicked inhabitants, whose hearts are hardened in unbelief, and disregard of my solemn warnings, are reserved in my own power; even the Angels whom I have sent forth, as yet, know them not: therefore, they cannot be revealed as yet, unto mortals.

21. But timely warning I do give, to every nation, kindred, tongue and people, dwelling on the earth, saith the God of Heaven.

22. And all ye, of whatever grade or class ye may be, confine the gratifications of your own corrupt propensities, within the bounds of the law of nature. Cease, O inhabitants of earth, cease to promote and encourage works of licentiousness and debauchery; or I shall suffer you to sink into the earth's bowels, saith the Lord.

23. Beware, beware, and hearken to the voice of the Lord your God, who delighteth not in the destruction of human life; nor in the misery of those whom he hath created for a much higher calling, than to be slaves to their own wicked passions.

24. Turn, O inhabitants of mortality! turn, turn ye to the Lord your God, in deep repentance of heart, that the holy and swift winged Angels, that I have sent to pass and re-pass through the earth, to pass and re-pass again, until the time of my own appointing is fulfilled, may behold you clothed in sackcloth and mourning, turning from the evil of your doings, and learning to do well; and record your names upon the list of mercy for the same.

25. For I AM, is a God, whose mercy is reached by the penitent

heart, and whose judgment, in justice, will speedily follow the high, the lofty, and unabased. For the haughtiness of Monarchs, Kings, and the great ones of the earth, shall be bowed down, and the loftiness of man brought low, even with the dust; and my name alone, saith the Lord, shall be exalted.

26. Every dispensation of my goodness to man, from the creation of the world, to the present time, hath always been attended with an increasing degree of order, beauty and holiness, beyond that which preceded it.

27. The time had not come, when Christ first appeared on earth, for him to establish his kingdom, in that perfect order, glory and beauty, that he has now, in his second coming. For its order was not then completed, and never could be, until the female had found her proper lot and place, as the Mother of all who should ever after, enter the new and spiritual creation, which my Almighty hand hath established on the earth, inseparably connected with my holy kingdom in eternity.

28. I have caused a sufficient number of the sacred passages to be inserted, as do clearly show unto every reasonable mind, that Christ must necessarily make his appearance in the female, or the order of my kingdom would not have been made complete, nor the declarations given in past dispensations, from my holy spirit fulfilled.

29. And as I had before declared unto you, that I destroyed not that which hath proceeded from my own mouth, or disannulled the work of my own hands; but that heaven and earth should pass away, rather than that one jot or tittle should fail; so will all ye inhabitants of the earth find, that in my own time and season, all things which I declare unto you, will be fulfilled in their true spirit and sense.

30. But remember that a natural man, while under the influence of nature's darkness, understandeth not the givings of the spirit of God, for they appear like foolishness unto him: for the sinful indulgence and gratification of one's carnal and filthy propensities, out of the proper time and season for the purpose of begetting their own offspring, is one of the most soul-darkening, and sunken practices that man is capable of committing.

31. Even under the law, saith the Lord, if they went forth and

defiled themselves contrary to the law, they were required to take
an offering, and go to the priests, and there make an atonement
for their transgression.

32. And shall my requirement respecting self-denial, and the
laws of restriction, in this day, after having sent forth the gospel
dispensation, be less effective than under the darkened ages of
the Mosaic Law?

33. Shall my Almighty power suffer the children of men to go
on from age to age, regardless of every law and restriction which
hath been sent forth to the inhabitants of earth, even in the dark
and wilderness ages of the world, when light, knowledge and understanding had been, but in a very limited degree, suffered to
shine upon them? The voice of my eternal justice declareth, Not
so; for I have created man to be an honor and a glory unto Me,
his God and Creator; and my purpose, in the ultimate event of
my work with man, shall not be disannulled or destroyed. But as
yet, few, very few, in any previous age of the world, have answered the purpose of their creation.

34. And moreover, did not my servant Moses, when I sent him
to sanctify and prepare the people to meet Me before the mount,
require that none of them should come at their wives, for the
space of three days before they were called to appear before Me?
Surely he did; and does not this declare it to be the work of uncleanness? Surely it does; and every rational mind knoweth it to
be so. Works that are attended with a shame, and require the cur-
tains of darkness to be spread, wherein they are committed, every
rational mind knoweth must be impure.

## CHAPTER XVI.
### CHRIST'S SECOND APPEARING IN
### THE FEMALE; HER OFFICE AND CALLING
### AS THE BRIDE, OR SPIRITUAL MOTHER;
### AND THE CHARACTER OF HER
### TRUE FOLLOWERS.

1. Thus saith the Lord, the Holy and Eternal One, Give ear unto
my voice, all ye people, and hearken and understand my word,
all ye nations of the earth.

2. For whom are you looking, to usher in the rays of eternal life, and open the eyes of your souls, that ye may be saved from your sins?

3. Do you look for the Christ of God, the spirit of the Holy Savior, the Lamb who stood upon Mount Zion, with the hundred and forty and four thousand, having their Father's name written in their foreheads, who were virgins, not being defiled with sin?

4. Do you look and seek after a kingdom, of which the sacred volume does predict; which by the spirit of inspiration was told, That a pure and holy kingdom, by my Almighty hand, should, in the latter days, be set up, which should be called the house of the Lord, established in the top of the mountains, and exalted above the hills; of which nations should say, Come, and let us go up to the Mountain of the Lord, and to the house of the God of Jacob; for he will teach us of his ways, and we will walk in his paths?

5. Where the Law should go forth of Zion, and the word of the Lord from Jerusalem?

[. . .]

50. Whose subjects are *in* the world, yet are not *of* the world; for I their Lord and God, have chosen them out of the world?

51. Where holy Angels from the eternal world minister unto them, and ten thousand times ten thousand gather to behold their worship?

52. Where saints on earth, with saints in heaven do unite in one eternal song of praise, to Me their God and Maker?

53. Where, through great tribulation and sufferings of soul, by living the life of the Lamb, their garments are washed white?

54. Do you seek for that kingdom, against which, the hand of persecution hath ever been raised; and against which the envenomed tongue of slander and falsehood hath never ceased to pour forth its volumes of blackest epithets?

55. Where souls fulfill the law of Christ, as made known in his first appearing, and by that means, are able to fulfill the whole law in his second coming?

56. Where souls know, by actual experience of more than sixty years, that they have found the spirit of the Lord's Christ, revealed in a Mother, whose name was ANN LEE?

57. For it hath saved them from all sin, and clothed their souls in a garment of true righteousness, and created in their hearts, that love to Me, their God and Maker, which surpasseth, in a thousand fold ratio, all other loves;

58. Which has given them strength and power to resign their lives in martyrdom, if called so to do, rather than deny their faith, or the power by which they received this, [which was] from, and through the QUEEN of Zion, who stands as my first and chosen witness in this last dispensation of my goodness to man.

59. Do you seek for that kingdom, where the gospel of a CHRIST and of a MOTHER reigneth, united in one?

60. Were any of you born, and brought forth into a completed state of existence in the world, by a *father*,—or by a *mother*? Or were you only begotten by a *father*, and then, at the proper time and season, brought forth by the *mother*?

61. And by whom were you fed with milk, and dandled at the breast, while in your infancy; by the father,—or by the mother?

62. By whose caresses, and soothing hand of comfort, were your troubled spirits pacified to rest? Was it not the Mother's?

63. If We, the over-ruling and GREAT FIRST CAUSE of all created things, on earth and in the heavens, have, in our own wisdom, created the natural order of things, figurative of that which was spiritual, how can there be any spiritual order, or kingdom of glory completed, unless the woman is brought to stand in her place, according to the figure?

64. Have We not created an order and place for the woman, in the natural order of the creation? Was she not to travail in sorrow, and bring forth children? And in the absence of her husband, does she not stand at the head of her own family?

65. If these things in nature do exist, why stumble ye at the fulfillment of the true representation?

66. And if this is not the true representation, and this order does not exist in the spiritual heavens, why did not We create and send forth, all living upon earth, in the male order?

67. O ye blind and bigoted seers, who strain at your own pride, and must swallow your own folly! The woman you all want, and the man you all want; but the enjoyment of each other in fleshly gratifications, is your greatest desire. No longer wipe your lips,

and say you are guiltless; for the God of Heaven doth judge you, the Searcher of every heart, before whose eyes, your abominations are as plain as the whited walls of your houses are in your view.

68. But hearken; Do any of you seek for a kingdom, where the pride of vain mortals ruleth not, and the arrogance of frail, fallen nature, beareth not the sway? Where the high and the low, the rich and the poor, the lame, the halt and the blind, can all fare alike, upon terms of strict equality and justice?

69. Where all yield strict obedience to the revealed will of Heaven, through such agencies as are appointed, through the order of my holy anointing power, wherever I may have caused it to rest?

70. Where all the political strifes and contentions, and party feelings amongst the children of men, are disowned and rejected?

71. Where an avaricious spirit, to heap up treasures on earth where moth and rust doth corrupt, cannot dwell?

72. And again; Do ye sincerely seek for that city of refuge on earth, where you can know and do the will of your God, day by day? Where you can receive strength to crucify your own evil natures, and be born anew, as little innocent children, into the kingdom of your God?

73. Do you seek for that home and place, while in a terrestrial state, where you can live day by day, as ye would, if ye knew ye were to die on the morrow, and as ye would if ye were to live a thousand years?

74. Where the kingdom of Heaven, and the righteousness thereto belonging, is the soul's first pursuit; and where all that is needful for the body, through obedience and faithfulness, shall be given unto it? And where, to deal justly and walk humbly, to fear God and keep his commandments, comprise your whole duty?

75. If so, seek in earnest, and ye shall find; knock, and it shall be opened unto you; ask, and ye shall receive; follow that light which I shall cause to shine into your souls, and it shall lead you to the city of peace, saith the Lord your God; but not to ease and indulgence, thinking to procure your souls' salvation in that way; not where the manna of Heaven rains down, to feed and support you in idleness, without the soul's exertion;

76. Not where each one, or any part can do that which seemeth right in their own eyes, according to their own natural wisdom and understanding;

77. But where that wisdom, that knowledge and understanding, which is revealed in the order of my own appointment, beareth rule, and is the main spring of action throughout, in all things, spiritual and temporal;

78. According to the completed order of my new heavens and new earth, which I have, in this latter day, established on the earth for all nations, all kindreds, all tongues and all people, who will make the sacrifice which I require, saith the Lord, to obtain a home therein, beneath the wings of my protection.

79. I have now declared unto you; all ye nations and people, that the spirit of my blessed Son hath appeared the second time, without sin unto salvation, in the *female,* or *Spiritual Mother* in Israel.

80. And this, my kingdom, as represented by the stone from the mountain, has been established for more than sixty years upon the earth; and yet, ye believe it not; though various publications of its principles, have been circulated when called for, yet, ye know not the Christ or his true kingdom.

81. I have never required, saith the God of Heaven, that the subjects of Christ's second coming, or the children of the Bride, should compass sea and land to make proselytes;

82. This, my Church, the assembly of Saints, was never established upon the eternal foundation of righteousness and truth, for a popular show to the inhabitants of earth.

83. But I required her people to embody their strength in one united capacity, and conquer and subdue their own evil natures within, and travel in humility of soul, and tribulation of spirit, and gain a substance of the true oil of light, and life eternal; That when my time should come, in the order of my own wisdom, she might have wherewithal, to do her duty to other souls, as I have placed her, a city upon a hill, whose light and brightness can never more be hid.

84. And thus, the days of her seclusion are accomplished; and I, the God that formed her, do now declare her to the inhabitants of the earth; and I have also declared the true characters of all

who do, in truth, compose the subjects who dwell, and safely remain within her holy walls.

85. Though wolves in sheep's clothing, may creep within her gates, yet, their craving wants for flesh, or fleshly lust, will soon betray the borrowed coat they wear.

86. No ravenous beast can long remain within her holy borders; though many like the place, yet none but the true and honest hearted like the cross, nor will long endure the gospel fire of truth, which doth eternally burn to guard the tree of life.

87. And furthermore, saith the Almighty Power, I declare the *three first witnesses* unto you, who bore record on the earth, that I, the Almighty God of Heaven, had sent forth the likeness of my blessed Son, the second time, without sin unto salvation, to poor frail mortals on the earth.

88. And through a female was Christ made known, [*as a spiritual Mother,*] to complete the order of that kingdom which was begun in his first appearing. And I declare, to all nations, the spirit of this chosen female to be the Bride, the Lamb's wife, the Queen of Zion, and Mother of the new and spiritual creation which shall never be destroyed.

89. Though I, her Lord and God, should purge and refine her [inhabitants] to that degree of purity and holiness, that not more than ten souls were able to abide the fire within her holy courts; yet shall these stand, and be supported by the Almighty power of my hand, though armies against them should be arrayed for their destruction.

90. Remember, all ye people who dwell within the walls of my Zion, which is pure and holy, if ye walk not worthy of your holy calling, the great privilege, which in my mercy I have granted you, shall only prove as burning coals of fire upon your heads, to sink your souls from my presence; and a far heavier stroke of my judgments, shall come upon *you*, than upon those who have never been blessed with such a privilege of my notice, within the walls of my Zion.

91. It is not numbers that compose my Zion; but the purity of that life which souls live; and by the interestedness of their spirits, to build up the cause to which they are called; by spending and being spent, agreeable to that example which was invariably

set by the *three first witnesses*, who bore this gospel across the rolling deep, to fair Columbia's shore, and who, by my Almighty hand, were protected so to do.

92. And by my power, shall other faithful souls safely re-cross the foaming deep, to plant this gospel in distant lands, to feed the hungry souls who cry to Me for [the] bread [of life.]

## CHAPTER XXXI.
## OF HARMONY, PURITY AND INNOCENCE, AND THE TRUE ENJOYMENT OF THE TWO SEXES, IN THIS STATE. CLOSING OF THE ROLL.

1. And again, saith the Lord, I now call upon you, O ye inhabitants of the earth, to hearken to my words, and understand the truth concerning that of which ye are, as yet, strangers.

2. You do not see how it is possible, for male and female to dwell in societies together and enjoy each other's association, and good and kind feelings, and still have nothing to do with sexual indulgences. This, in truth, to natural man, who is absorbed in the things of nature, seems to be impossible; a mystery that he cannot comprehend, or understand.

3. And truly it is, saith the Lord, by natural man, while living after the ordinary course of nature, incomprehensible.

4. For this power of associating together, as little harmless children who know no evil, in harmony, purity and innocence, is given, and can be found, only in the completed order of my creation, wherein old things are done away, and all things become new.

5. All selfishness, quarrels, contention, strife, inveterate feelings of animosity, and attitudes of hostility, are effects proceeding from certain causes; and no body of people, [influenced by these causes,] can long dwell together in a united capacity, but that these effects, or consequences proceeding from these certain causes, will break them to pieces and scatter them asunder.

6. The cause of all those uncontrolled divisions of feeling emanates wholly from the region of darkness, where no true light, in its fullness, can ever shine; and that is the indulging and gratify-

ing of one's own carnal, fallen, and corrupt nature of fleshly lust, that is always at war against the soul's best good and comfort.

7. And while fed by indulgence and gratification, it will never suffer souls to enjoy true harmony, love, union and innocence, so that they can associate in societies together, further than the bounds of natural private families extend; and even they, come far short of existing together in a state of peace and harmony.

8. The gratification and indulgence in fleshly works, whether confined to one's self, or in connection with others, is continually strengthening the root of this evil tree, which bears the forbidden fruit, and hath many branches, that are continually strengthened and supported from this root.

9. Therefore did the followers of my blessed Son, even in his first appearance, teach souls to lay the axe at the root [of the tree,] and destroy the cause, and the effect will cease, and the branches and limbs of this evil tree will die.

10. When this is done, saith the Lord, then souls are again re-deemed unto Me, in a state of purity and innocence; and not until it is done, whether they be in time or in eternity, it maketh no difference further than this;

11. The more they indulge themselves while in time, in the gratification of these works, the greater are the guilt, condemna-tion and stains of sin and filthiness impressed upon their souls when entering eternity; and the greater must be their sufferings and tribulation to find their redemption.

12. For I created man, saith the Lord, in the beginning, pure and innocent; and when he is again redeemed unto Me, he will be pure and innocent; and the more sin he commits, after he is born into the world, the greater is the distance that he is carried from Me, his God and Creator; and consequently, the greater must be the length of his journey, in retracing his steps in sorrow and tribulation, again to find Me, his Creator God, in truth.

13. And this is rendering unto every one a just reward, accord-ing to their works; but mortals, when sinning against light and understanding, are rapidly hastening their souls at a great dis-tance from Me, and from the purity of my kingdom.

14. But in the completed order of my new creation, now estab-lished on earth, male and female dwell together as brethren and sisters, not as husband and wife; for in this completed order, they

can have nothing to do with those works belonging to the husband and wife dispensation; as that is wholly confined to the natural order, and not to the spiritual.

15. But that degree of comfort and true enjoyment which males and females take together, when living as brethren and sisters, in bonds of filial affection and gospel purity, is beyond any thing that can be enjoyed in a natural state. It is similar, saith the Lord, to that which two little children, brother and sister, who know no impurity or wickedness, take in their innocent plays together.

16. And for this very cause, did your Lord and Savior take little harmless and innocent children in his arms, and bless them; and told his disciples to suffer them to come unto him; for of such was the kingdom of Heaven.

17. This example of your Savior with little children, both in his first and second appearance, embraced the plainest and most striking figure that could be made use of, to show unto the people that state of true innocence, purity and harmlessness, that must be possessed by all such souls as would ever become true heirs of his kingdom.

18. But in order for souls to obtain a place in the completed order of my *new creation*, they must firstly confess their sins honestly, as before shown in this Roll; then give themselves up unto Me, as clay in the hands of the potter, to be led as little children, counseled and instructed through such visible agency as the influence of my Spirit, saith the Lord, hath appointed for that purpose; and to be admonished, in my holy fear, when found necessary.

19. All this is done by the influence and power of the spirit, without coercive measures; which measures I do not allow to be made use of, in my kingdom, save in the case of children, when all mild and persuasive means fail, I suffer them to be gently corrected with small rods; but never are they allowed to be abused, or cruelly treated, in any way, or meddled with by any one when under the least degree of excitement or passion.

20. This is briefly the law and order of my kingdom, now established on the earth, forever more to stand. It is, and forever will be, composed of subjects harmless and inoffensive, who bear no carnal weapons of warfare, but rely, in their true obedience

and devotedness of soul unto Me, upon my arm for protection from their enemies without and within;

21. Who will suffer at the hands of their fellow creatures, injustice, cruelty and abuse, without retaliation, saith the Lord; having this assurance from Me, That man can only destroy the body, but cannot injure the soul.

22. Therefore, O vain and mortal man, consider all your doings, and take heed unto your goings, lest ye are found fighting, even against the Almighty hand of your God.

23. For there is no person or spirit, that can rise and seek to stand against the eternal attributes of my goodness, purity, innocence and holiness, but what does fight against the Almighty hand of Him who created the Heavens and the earth, and whose power, in judgment, they must surely meet for so doing; for no weapon, formed against my Zion, shall prosper; and every tongue that shall rise against her in judgment, I will condemn, saith the Lord.

24. And now, my last and closing word in this sacred and solemn Roll of my mercy, I do send forth to all nations, kindreds, tongues and people, that dwell upon the face of the whole earth.

25. As you deal with one another, so will your God deal with you; as you treat this, his sacred and solemn word, so will He treat you, in the dispensation of his judgment, and of his mercy. As you regard the laws of nature herein required to be kept, so will He regard you.

26. As you regard the law of grace, or order of his new creation herein required to be kept, by all who feel their souls called upon to advance forward into this perfect order, so will his Almighty hand regard you, with his blessing and protection.

27. As you regard the requirement of Me, your God, respecting the reading of this solemn *Roll of my word,* and *Book of everlasting truth,* to the inhabitants of earth, in your solemn assemblies, so will the Lord your God, in the day of his heaviest visitation in judgment, regard, and cause his holy Angels to regard you.

28. As you regard, and treat the operations of my spirit, which shall go forth abroad in the world, of which I have before told you, so shall you be treated, by the over-ruling hand of your God.

29. According as you believe and obey, or disbelieve and disobey, the words contained in this Sacred Roll [and Book,] so shall the sincerity of your cries and lamentations, in the day that you are constrained to pour them forth for my mercy, be regarded or disregarded by your God.

30. And according to the zeal, enterprise and sincerity of such as are required to correctly translate and circulate this Book through different nations and languages, so shall their days of my notice, in peace and blessing, be prolonged.

31. It is my requirement, saith the Lord, that in two years from the commencement of the year *One thousand eight hundred and forty four*, copies of this, MY SOLEMN WARNING, be circulated throughout all professed Christendom on the face of the whole earth; and as far among the heathen nations, as missions for civilization and for instruction have been extended.

32. And so far as the inhabitants of the earth regard, in truth, the sacred requirements contained in the holy scriptures, and in this my Sacred Roll, now sent forth directly from my eternal throne, in the age and day in which they live, so far are they justified in my sight.

33. And by laboring, as fast as possible, to settle all feelings of collision, both in their own realms and kingdoms, [and with other nations,] without hostilities being commenced, or blood being shed, and to cease learning the arts of war, and cultivate the principles of peace, they will, so far, stay the heavy judgments which are already poured out without mixture, into the cup of the wrath of my indignation, to be sent forth upon the earth.

34. But this effort to do away the cause of war, and establish conciliatory measures, that justice, in all cases, may be done, and the effusion of blood, and the destruction of human life be prevented, I require, saith the Lord, should be made by nations, as well as by individuals.

35. And so far as mankind turn their attention to cultivate the soil and procure their subsistence by their own honest industry; so far will they evidently feel, as nations, the blessings of an overruling providence smiling upon them.

36. But let all nations and kingdoms remember, saith the God of Heaven, that they have advanced in wickedness, against the laws of their God and Creator, on to the very last stage in which

his Almighty hand, in offers of mercy, can be extended towards them.

37. And if they refuse, as nations, to hearken and take warning, sure destruction is their certain and final doom. Herein is contained my word, the only true GOD, the ALMIGHTY POWER of Heaven and earth, the *Over-ruling* and *Great first Cause* of all created things. The GOD who was, the GOD who is, through endless worlds made known.

38. Therefore, unto that God give thanks, whose omniscient eye is not confined to certain limits of time and space.

39. Trouble ye not the *little few* from whence this, my word, at my command, has now come forth: for I, the God of all, have commanded their seclusion, as a body, for a short season, from all public gaze and throng; that I may scourge them in my mercy, and teach them how, in tribulation's vale, to walk softly before Me their God.

40. Trouble ye not the mortal hand, or Instrument of flesh and blood, through whom I caused my holy and mighty Angel of eternal light, power and truth, to move and guide the pen in truth to write this, my Holy and Sacred Roll, for mortal eyes to view; for he is but mortal flesh and blood, like unto each one of you.

41. No honor there belongs, but that of obeying Me, the Lord his God, regardless of all other personal views or consequences. Holy and sacred things I do require, saith the Lord, to be kept holy and sacred, practiced in both heart and hand; and not to be made the daily subject of comment, yet still unheeded.

42. But when souls converse together on sacred subjects, let them be sincere in heart, possessing a degree of fear and reverence to that God by whom they were created, and before whose eternal throne of judgment and true justice, each soul must soon appear.

43. And thus endeth the Roll, sent forth from Me, the God of Heaven and earth, consigned to all possessing mortal clay, saith the AL FÍNO of all creation, the *Beginning* and the *Ending;* even so, eternally it shall stand, Amen.

(PHILEMON STEWART, CANTERBURY, NH: 1843)

# A Warning to the Latter Day Saints . . .
# An Abridgment of
# the Ninth Book of Esdras

The publication of the *Book of Mormon* in 1830 prompted a dramatic upsurge of interest in both the reality of modern-day revelation and the possibility that ancient scriptures might still be discovered and translated. These issues were most acute within the growing body of followers of Joseph Smith, Jr., and his claims emboldened other believers, a number of whom broke with Smith to found religious communities based on their own visionary outpourings. One such individual was James Colin Brewster (1826–?), whose family had moved to Kirtland, Ohio, to join with the Mormons when James was a young boy. In 1837 the ten-year-old claimed that he had been visited by an angel, who had shown him a better way to organize Smith's church. Initially encouraged in his spiritual precocity by church leaders, Brewster's continuing corrections to church teachings eventually caused a rift with Mormon leaders, and his family, while still connected to the faith, moved to Springfield, Illinois. From there Brewster began in 1842 to publish pamphlets that he asserted were abridgments of ancient documents furnished by the angel. Collectively called the Book of Esdras, Brewster claimed that they were the teachings of an ancient biblical prophet who lived in approximately 160 B.C.E. The publications contained many predictions related to the fate of the Mormons, criticized the emergence of Mormon temple ceremonies and Mormon economic practices, and prophesied the end of the world in 1878. Brewster and his family were excommunicated in 1842, but this hardly stopped his production of texts.

Several years later Brewster published "A Warning to the Latter Day Saints, Generally Called Mormons," which was alleged to be an abridgment of the Ninth Book of Esdras. In it he included poetry and fragments said to be from other ancient books, as well as a conclusion that details the prophecies already fulfilled from his 1842 pamphlet (including the murder of Joseph Smith, Jr., in 1844). The bulk of the text is an extended warning of impending doom to the sinful people who have fallen away from God's true teachings—namely, the Mormons in Nauvoo, Illinois. Like a Hebrew prophet the author details the many painful and destructive ways that they will perish for their trespasses, including floods, droughts, pestilence, and earthquakes. The document also predicts the fall of Nauvoo ("Idle city") and ultimately the destruction of the American government that will usher in God's kingdom. That realm, he prophesies, will be established in California ("Bashan"), which will be given to the faithful remnant of saints that keep God's commandments.

In June 1848, after Nauvoo had been destroyed and the majority of Mormons had migrated to Utah, Brewster reorganized his small band of perhaps one hundred believers, claiming that, while Joseph Smith had been called to establish the church, Brewster had been anointed to build the kingdom of God on Earth. The twenty-four-year-old prophet finally left for California in August 1850 with ninety members, two hundred head of cattle, and twenty-seven wagons, even as he continued to translate ancient documents (specifically, Mayan hieroglyphics and New Mexican Indian pictographs encountered in his travels). The group suffered schisms along the way, but Brewster settled briefly in Colonia, New Mexico; by 1853 he had returned to the United States with his family, where he lived a life of apparent obscurity, never to prophesy publicly again. Still, his documents vividly demonstrate the tenor of prophetic religion in antebellum America, the volatility of revelatory power in the early Mormon community, and the ways in which believers were eager to tie biblical history to their New World home.

# A Warning to the Latter Day Saints, Generally Called Mormons.

## AN ABRIDGMENT OF THE NINTH BOOK OF ESDRAS,

*by James Colin Brewster.*

Return unto the Lord your God, lest ye be cast off; for the wicked shall surely be destroyed, and the ungodly shall be consumed with unquenchable fire. They that know the way and walk not therein, shall find darkness, and not light; they that turn from the ways of God shall not be comforted; they shall go into darkness, and unless they repent, they shall be utterly destroyed; for speedy destruction cometh upon the ungodly, who have seen the way and walk not therein; who teach the word but turn aside from the commandments, walking in forbidden ways, and speaking vain and lying words; and turn aside after the temptations of satan. They lay a snare for their brother and dig a pit for their neighbor; they turn from light unto darkness, and because they cleave unto darkness, they shall have darkness, and shall stumble and fall, being taken in the snares which they set, and falling into the pits which they have dug. For the word of God is not in vain, neither shall it fail, but shall continue the same forever. Therefore the ungodly shall not stand, but shall perish in the midst of their days; for they that serve satan shall fall into darkness. Therefore be not led estray, for they that are led estray and do not return, shall be cut off. But they that serve God shall be made strong; they shall prosper and dwell in the land which the Lord their God shall give them. For his strength is above the strength of men, and his word cannot be broken. They that fight against their enemies shall be slain, and they that escape the sword shall pass through much tribulation and few of the ungodly,* even those that call themselves saints, shall escape; for they have been a wicked and rebellious people; they have been called but have turned aside from the right way. Therefore they shall be driven. They shall build houses but shall not inhabit them. They shall plant vineyards but shall not eat the fruit thereof. They shall be scourged for their iniquity and perish, because they will not repent. But they that will repent shall receive mercy; but they who are proud and rebelious shall receive affliction, they shall not be spared or pitied, for the hand of the destroyer is upon them. They shall be brought down and made desolate by fire and the sword. For this saith the Lord, I will bring upon them a strong people, whom they hate, and a terrible one whom they despise, and I will utterly bring them to nought. Though they be numerous as the sand of the sea shore, yet they shall be confounded and their multitude shall be afraid and tremble when the Lord God shall commence his great work, and begin to cut off the proud and destroy the ungodly, to whom judgement is as gall and righteousness as wormwood. Therefore, shall their destruction come quickly and their end shall come in an hour, for they are strong, yet they shall be brought down and they shall become weak. They shall all be smitten, but they shall not all perish. Therefore they that repent and turn unto the Lord their God, shall be preserved.

Let not the inhabitants of the Earth rejoice when God shall destroy the ungodly, for he will surely recompense upon the wicked their wickedness; for he will not suffer the wicked to escape, (i. e. the enemies of the Mormons,) and he will also punish the ungodly, for he is a God of justice and truth, and will not suffer any transgressor to escape. Turn unto the Lord your God, that ye be not utterly destroyed, for God will surely recompense the wickedness of the ungodly upon their own heads, for his judgement shall overtake them suddenly, neither shall the fire be quenched when it burneth in the stubble, neither shall the lion be turned aside from the prey. Therefore the judgments of God shall be as fire among the ungodly and as a lion among the wicked; for

* The ungodly is that part of the Mormons who profess righteousness but work iniquity.

on one hand shall be sword and fire, and on the other wild beasts and desolation. Therefore they shall be scourged, because their transgressions are as numerous as the sand of the sea shore. They shall not be spared, but they shall be driven out of the land of their inheritance. As Israel was driven forth by Nebuchanezzer, king of Babylon; even so shall the ungodly perish and be visited with utter destruction in the last days. Therefore let the ungodly fear and tremble, and the wicked be afraid, for God will not spare them any longer.

Serve God, therefore, that ye be not destroyed with the ungodly; for they shall be destroyed, and none can deliver them from the hand of the destroyer for destruction shall surely come upon this people, for the oppressor shall surely be oppressed, and they that break shall surely be broken, for the scorner shall be consumed and they that watch for iniquity shall be cut off. For the ways of the ungodly are in darkness, having turned aside from the right way, they shall surely stumble and fall. Therefore turn aside from the ways of the ungodly and walk not in their ways, for they go to destruction.

Let not them that do evil say that their works are good, they shall surely come to nought; they shall surely be destroyed by the sword of the Lord, for his hand is strong and he will destroy the enemies of his saints and will confound the Nations, and overcome their strength. He will send upon them pestilence, earthquakes and wild beasts to devour them. He will dry up their rivers that ships cannot sail therein, and make the glory of the earth vanity, and their strength as dust before the whirlwind.

He will make the fenced cities heaps, and the strong holds a desolation. He will smite the rich, that are in the plains and the strong that are upon the mountains, and make the vallies desolate. He will break the ships that are in the sea, and send upon the Islands a consuming fire. He will make the nations to mourn and the earth to weep. When men sow the seed he will withhold the rain, but in time of harvest he will send an abundance (of rain.) And on the Idle city he will bring fear, and the Prince of fear shall rule over them, though they say every man to his neighbor, let us be strong. Although they make to themselves swords and snares, and dig pits for their enemies, yet shall they turn back from the battle and they shall be snared, taken and broken, and the words of Alciba shall be fulfilled, which he wrote saying:—

"Strong is the God of the heavens, whose power is over the earth, and the sea and all things that is therein; at whose power the sun is darkened and the moon shall be turned to blood before whom Babylon is as stubble, and the Idle city as chaff, to be consumed or driven away by the whirlwind, yet will the transgressors transgress, will the wicked continue to do wickedly, will they seek after wickedness before him who created both the heavens and the earth. These shall be smitten with the sword of Jehovah who in his fierce anger, shall cast them away, who oppress the poor and lay up unto themselves riches—that feed themselves and regard not the needy, they clothe themselves with rich garments, but spare not those that are in want.

1   For these are judgments deep in store,
        Which on their guilty land shall pour,
    A torrent strong, not turned aside,
        To quench in blood their lofty pride.

2   What power shall quench the burning flame,
        That in the stubble still remaine,
    Or turn the whirlwind's wrath aside,
        That scatters chaff and lofty pride?

3   Or stop the arrow, strongly shot,
        Their name from off the earth to blot;
    Or drive the lion from his prey?
        For now is God's avenging day!

4   Or who shall stop the torrent's course,
        Or stop the sword with all its force,
    And drive again the hated power,
        Who came against them in an hour.

5   For these shall surely over-turn,
        That proud ungodly men may learn

> God is not in their secret ways,
>> But is the King and Prince of days.

> 6   Lord, save the righteous from all ill,
>>  And all thy promises fulfill;
>>  Smite the ungodly with thy rod.
>>  Till all repent and turn to God.

To whom shall strength be given or to whom shall righteousness be restored? Strength shall be given to them that keep the commandments and that obey the law.

They that keep the Sabbath holy and profane not the name of the Lord God.

That take not usury and abhor all works of darkness and secret combinations; for these are from Satan and multiply evil upon the sons of men. They that speak the truth and deceive not. Unto these shall strength be given and righteousness restored.

For beyond the everlasting hills is the land of Bashan.

For a terrible one shall stand up, before whom the ungodly shall tremble—for unto them the power of God is terrible, and they fear his glory more than the sword, for the servants of God shall be terrible, and they that go to Bashan (California) shall have strength given and righteousness restored unto them. Let not the ungodly prosper, saith the Lord, for upon the idle shepherds will I bring a strong people, and a terrible one will I raise up that they shall be broken and scattered, and upon every hill and in every valley shall they mourn; into whatever land they shall go, there shall they be afflicted. They shall in no wise escape for they are transgressors; they are rebellious, proud and haughty. Therefore they shall fall.

Against whom shall judgment be brought forth and against whom shall the battle be set in array! those who know the commandments and keep them not. These will the Lord cast down, and bring upon them sword, fire and desolation when their vallies over-flow with abundance and the plains are covered with grain and the sound of rejoicing, and mirth is heard in the city. Then shall be heard a voice on the waters of Cedron, crying, "We unto the land and the inhabitants thereof." For a fierce and a strong people, whose horses hoofs are as steel and the sound thereof as a whirlwind, these shall trample under foot the vineyards, and set on fire the fields of grain. And the Idle city* shall be confounded and the multitude thereof shall be of small power.

And the mighty man shall turn back from the battle and their swords shall be of no avail, and their enemies shall encompass them round about, and shall enter in and shall utterly make waste and destroy; they shall slay with the sword and burn with fire until they make the city a desolation, and a burying place for the people that are therein. But they who fear God shall escape through the wilderness, and go beyond the river Amli (Rio del Norte) unto the land of their inheritance, a land of hills, of vallies, of plains and pleasant places, which brings forth in abundance, that they who go there shall prosper.

The land of Bashan shall be given to the saints—those who shall escape from the midst of the ungodly. They who go there shall not be of the ungodly, they shall be those that speak the truth and lie not, that love peace and abhor war, that are not lovers of gain and seek not after riches.

These shall go there and inherit the land, for no one but the righteous shall dwell there. But they shall dwell there and no one shall make them afraid. They shall build cities; they shall plant vineyards, and they shall make the desolate lands a garden and the forsaken place a fruit field; they shall make the waste places a pleasant land.

Wo to the Idle city for their transgressions are many and the righteous among them are very few, and because of these they are spared, and when these turn to wickedness they shall be destroyed. Therefore repent and return unto the Lord, least ye be cut off, for God will sweep away the wicked and overthrow the ungodly, and they shall sink into darkness.

The strength of the saints shall not be shaken, neither shall they be overthrown, neither shall the ungodly have power to make them a prey, for the sword of the Lord is strong and it shall be terrible among the Nations, and the cities of the wicked shall fall before it. Their walls shall not stand, neither their towers de-

---

* The Idle city in Nauvoo, so called, because the inhabitants of that city profess to serve God but do not. Therefore they are called Idle, as they do not the works they profess to do. This does not apply to all, but a majority are of this description.

fend them; but they shall all fall and perish together, even in wickedness. Wo to the Idle city and to the inhabitants thereof, for they are a rebellious people—a people turned aside from the right way, in whom the Lord God hath no delight, because of their wickedness. They shall not rest, neither shall they have peace; because of their transgressions, they are driven and smitten their enemies; they shall not be spared nor saved from destruction; but shall perish from off the face of the earth. Such is the lot of those who have the light of the gospel and yet draw the sword against their enemies.

It shall come to pass that there shalt many great and marvellous things to be seen by all the inhabitants of the earth, even more than has been seen since the days of the flood; for the earth shall be shaken, and the moon shall be turned into blood; there shall be great tribulation upon the face of all the earth, and all the wicked shall fall, though they be many in number; who doeth good that they may be saved who serveth God, that they may not perish.

Who can find a righteous man or a friend that falleth not? Because there is none righteous, the earth mourneth. For no one serveth God continually; they have broken the commandments of God; they regard them not.

How are the mighty fallen and the righteous turned away? the pure in heart are not found and the righteous are few among men. The haughty left themselves up; the proud are not cast down; the ungodly are without number, and the wicked fill the whole earth. The Lord will destroy the wicked from off the face of the earth and the ungodly from among his saints.

Salvation cometh by good works; without obedience no man can be saved; for him who will not obey shall not receive the reward of righteousness, laid up for the saints of the most High, which are peace, glory and life everlasting; the inheritance of the saints of the Most High, a crown of eternal glory laid up for them who fear him and obey the Lord God who created them.

Who shall not see when the Lord setteth up his banner, when he calleth the wicked to repentance. Then shall his glory be shown unto the saints of the most high; therefore keep all the commandments which he has given you, lest Satan overcome you by his temptations, which are many. He seeketh to lead men astray into darkness, where the light cometh not, and the glory of God is not seen; for the power of satan is darkness, and his power is the shadow of death which leadeth unto death, even the first and second death, the destruction of the body and the spirits for the ungodly who have seen the way and walk not therein are reserved in chains of darkness unto the great and terrible day of the Lord, wherein all flesh shall be judged and rewarded according to the deeds done in the body. The power of God is light, and his strength is glorious; they that keep his commandments shall rejoice, and they that fear him shall learn wisdom; for wisdom cometh of God and glory is shown forth by his wisdom. The word of the Lord, like a two-edged sword, shall divide like a rock in the midst of the sea, so are the saints among the wicked. The anger of the Lord is terrible. As a fire among the stubble, so is his anger toward the ungodly. Hath not the Lord spoken by the mouth of his prophet Malachi, saying—

"The day cometh that shall burn as an oven, and all the proud and they that do wickedly shall burn as stubble; but unto such as fear my name shall the son of righteousness arise with healing in his wings, and they shall go forth and grow up as calves of the stalls, and the wicked shall be as ashes under the soles of their feet." Then shall the righteous have rest; for, as it is written, the wicked cease from troubling and the weary are at rest. The word of the Lord came unto Isaiah, saying: "I will smite the proud and the wicked shall be cut off; the scorner is consumed and they that watch for iniquity, are cut off." The wicked shall no longer triumph, and the righteous shall have rest. Vengeance is mine, and I will repay saith the Lord. A day of warning, and not of many words.

Behold and hearken, O ye people! behold the judgments of God about to be poured out upon the Nations. He will smite the wall, and it shall be destroyed. His lightnings have went forth and shall not return until they have gone to the ends of the earth, till they have smitten the proud and cast down the haughty; till they have humbled the pride of the rich or smitten them with destruction, for the Lord God hath spoken it, and it shall be accomplished, God will not spare the wicked unless they repent.

The saints who go to Bashan for safety, shall keep the commandments which the Lord their God shall give them. They shall not err, neither shall they stumble if they keep the commandments which the Lord God gave unto those who served him; for great is the power of the Lord, and his strength is above the strength of the Nations. Therefore fear not, but go forth to the land which the Lord God shall give you, for an inheritance; and the ungodly and wicked shall not have power to go there. And they who go there shall appoint one to be their leader, one whose trust is in God, vigilant, and not easily turned aside from the right way; and he shall lead them in the way which they should go to the land of their inheritance, and he shall be appointed by the voice of those who go there, and if he behave himself unworthily or break any of the commandments given them to observe, another shall be appointed in his place; but if he shall do that which is right, then he shall retain his office one year. And while he shall keep the commandments, they shall obey his word.

They shall not transgress the commandments, though he should command them so to do; but in all other things they shall obey him. [The foregoing was written in A. D. 1842.]

1   Let all earth rejoice and sing
   Their great Redeemer, Prince and King,
   Who comes to set them free from sin,
   And in the earth his work begin;
   Rejoice, rejoice, rejoice, again!
   The earth has long in darkness lain.

2   Let all the saints arise and sing,
   For all the earth when cleansed from sin,
   Shall, like a fruitful field appear,
   And bud and blossom all the year,
   Rejoice, rejoice, rejoice, again!
   The foe of righteousness is slain!

3   The saints shall prosper in the earth,
   The wicked fall by sword and dearth,
   The God of Righteousness declares
   He'll save you from the wicked snares,

Rejoice, rejoice, rejoice, again!
The righteous shall be freed from pain!

4 See all the righteous ones are saved,—
The wicked are destroyed, who gave
No glory to the glorious God,
Are smitten by his Iron rod.
Rejoice, rejoice, rejoice, again!
The saints are washed from every stain!

5 From every stain of sin made free,
That they may live to know and see,
The glory of their God sublime,
Whose wond'rous glory is divine,
Rejoice, rejoice, rejoice, again!
For satan and his power is slain!

## THE SONG OF ALCON,
*(Copied from The Tenth Book of Esdras.)*

1 In modern days when saints are few,
And wicked men their course pursue;
When unopposed they pass along,
A strong, a rich and powerful throng.

2 A people few, a people weak,
Upon this shore for peace shall seek;
And to the King and Prince of days,
A city on this land shall raise.

3 Whose glory all the world shall see,
Before which Kings shall bow the knee;
When every other land shall weep,
And war has spread both wide and deep;

4 When cities burn and Nations sink,
And the proud powers become extinct;

Then shall this land in glory rise,
Above all powers beneath the skies.

5   Regardless of the fire and flood,
They trust in God's prevailing word,
But not in numbers, forts or arms,
Or wars unrighteous vain alarms.

6   By these shall Joseph's son's find rest,
For Joseph's sons I see afar,
Dispersed o'er fair Bethsula's plains,
And Ophir's wide and rich domains.

7   Hated, and chased, and driven away,
And to their enemies a prey,
But times shall change, and nations fall,
When God shall spread his head o'er all.

8   When the strong Isle that rules the sea,
With all its glories cease to be;
When Divan sinks and Scythia falls,
With its strong armies towers and walls;

9   Then God shall save in the glorious land,
By the power of his own almighty hand.
The poor and the weak that by men are oppressed,
Where they can dwell safely, forever and rest.

10  Then truth shall flow down from the fountain of light,
And scatter the darkness and vapors of night,—
Until peace shall extend o'er the land and the sea,
And the nations rejoice that the righteous are free.

# EXPLANATION.

Bethsula is North America. Ophir is South America, "The strong Isle," is Great Britain. Divan is China. Scythia is Russia, and the sons of Joseph are a part of the Indian tribes.

## AN EXTRACT FROM THIS
## PROPHECY OF ENOCH.

"In the same year that this nation, (the United States) shall begin to fall, shall the Kingdom of righteousness arise. The power and authority of God shall then be given to those who strive to keep the commandments, and brake not his law. And they shall go forth and establish and build up the Kingdom. In the land that will be given unto them to possess, there shall be no earthquakes, tempests, wars or desolation. But they who have been oppressed and trodden under foot of men, shall gather together and shall inhabit the richest of all the countries of the world, even the land of peace, which none of the ungodly or unjust nation shall possess. For the space of ten years after this time, the saints shall not be considered by men, as one of the nations of the earth; but in this time they shall be preaching the gospel to those who have long dwelt in darkness, and shall change the wilderness to a garden, and the desert to a fruitful field. For thus saith the Lord God of both heavens and earth.

Then I, Enoch, looked and saw the judgments that shall be poured out upon the inhabitants of the world in the latter times. In those days the rulers of the lands shall be proud, and ungodly or wicked men who shall seek their own pleasure and not the good of the people, and the people shall increase in wickedness until the measure of their iniquity be full, and they shall commit all the crimes that ever have been committed by men, and then shall the judgments of God he poured out upon them, even storms and tempests, earthquakes, floods and pestilence. Thou shall the nations make war upon each other, and many shall be slain.

The people of Bethsula* shall be the first destroyed. For many years they shall be visited by signs in the heavens above, and judgments and destruction on the earth; but in the seventieth year of the nation, they shall begin to fall; they shall not rise again.

Therefore, repent all ye who do wickedly, and serve the Lord

---

* The United States are termed "the people of Bethsula," as they are the greatest nation on this continent.

you God: for his hand is upon the Nations, and his judgments on those who keep not his law: There shall be an end of the power of the ungodly and the wicked.

But those that will turn from the ways of satan shall be saved; they shall inhabit the earth and establish the Kingdom of righteousness which shall increase until all other nations have vanished away and are found no more for the Kingdom of God shall possess the whole world."

## A SONG OF ENOCH.
### The Kingdom of Righteousness.

1   I looked and beheld the regions of rest,
    The Kingdom of righteousness far in the west,
    Where health, peace and plenty and truth shall abound,
    And wars and oppression shall never be found.

2   Then the darkness of night shall spread over the earth,
    Fire, pestilence, tempests, blood-shed and dearth;
    Yea, darkness and gloom, and death and dismay,
    And all men shall perish that will not obey.

3   And then, O! Bethsula thy power and thy might
    Shall be gathered in vain for that terrible night;
    For the sun of thy glory in sorrow shall set,
    When by they of east thy armies are met.

4   Then swift from the battle thy warriors shall fly,
    And leave all the wounded to languish and die;
    And they who have conquered shall burn and destroy
    Until nothing is left to hurt or annoy.

5   With the sword they shall slay and with fire they shall burn,
    And the most fertile plains to a desert shall turn,
    Till the conquerors rule o'er the land and the sea;
    Until they are no more who so long have been free.

# THE FULFILMENT OF THE PROPHECIES.
## *Contained in the writings of Esdras.*

It is well known to many that a pamphlet was published in this city, about three years since, entitled "The words of righteousness to all men," being an abridgment of several books written by the Prophet Esdras, and containing many prophecies of important events that should take place in the last days; these have been in part literally fulfilled, as will be seen by the following:

The first prophecy is on the 6th page; it is there written:—"The trees of the forest shall be destroyed, (see also page 18th, "he will burn the forests with fire.") During the last few months the forests in this country have been on fire to a greater extent than ever before was known, in the States of North Carolina, Virginia, Maryland, Pennsylvania, Vermont and Massachusetts. Great destruction and loss of life, and property have been occasioned by the conflagrations of the forest.

*Destruction of the cattle and fish.*—On the same page it is said, "The fish shall be found on dry land," and "many beasts which are for the use of man, shall be destroyed." This has also been fulfilled. In the year 1843, a mortality broke out among the cattle in Egypt, which in a short time swept off two hundred thousand head of oxen; in 1844, a similar destruction commenced in Germany, and has since spread through all the countries of Northern Europe. A few months since a mortality was observed among the fish in the Atlantic. From the eastern extremity of Long Island to Chesapeake bay, the coast was strewed with thousands of dead fish, and millions more were floating dead in the ocean. In lake Ponchantrain the fish have been destroyed in the same manner, so that the waters were literally filled with the dead fish.

*Signs in the Heavens.*—On page 25th Esdras says, the signs in the heavens, "shall appear as fire." Within the last three years hundreds of instances have occurred in which singular and unaccountable appearances have been seen in the heavens, from various parts of the earth. The following is an account of one of the signs seen in the city of London, Sept. 5, 1842, from the London papers.

"The first indication of this singular phenomenon was about 10 minutes before 10 (on Tuesday night,) when a light crimson apparently vapor rose from the Northern portion of the hemisphere, and gradually extended to the centre of the heavens, and by 10 o'clock or a quarter past, the whole from east to west was one vast sheet of light. It had a most alarming appearance, and was exactly like that occasioned by a terrific fire. The light varied considerably. At one time it seemed to fall, and directly after rose, with intense brightness. There was to be seen mingled with it volumes of smoke, which rolled over and over, and every beholder seemed convinced that it was a terrible conflagration. The consternation in the metropolis was very great. Thousand of persons were running in the direction of the supposed awful catastrophe. The engines belonging to the fire brigade stations in Baker street, Farington street, Watling street, Waterloo road, and, in short, every fire engine in London were horsed and galloped after the supposed scene of destruction with more than ordinary energy, some of the engines, proceeded as far as High-gate and Holloway before the error was discovered.

These appearances lasted for upwards of two hours. * * * And towards morning the spectacle became one of more grandeur. At 2 o'clock in the morning the phenomenon presented a most gorgeous scene, and one very difficult to describe. The whole of London was illuminated as light as noonday."

*Earthquakes.*—"The signs on the earth shall be earthquakes and great storms." Since the prophecy of Esdras has been published, a greater number of earthquakes have been experienced in various parts of the world than ever before in so short a period. The earthquake in Hayti, 1842, destroyed a great number of towns, and about fifteen thousands of people. The great earthquake of 1843, at Gaudeloupe, and the neighboring Island, caused greater destruction than any before ever experienced in the West Indies. The number of people killed and wounded in Guadeloupe alone, was upwards of twenty thousands; besides those that perished in the other Islands. The earthquakes in Italy and Sicily destroyed many thousand of the inhabitants of those countries. The earthquakes in Armenia and Persia, have produced, immense destruction, overthrowing whole villages and burying all their inhabitants in the ruins.

Shocks of earthquakes have been experienced throughout the continent of Europe, Turkey in Asia and Northern Africa. Also in nearly all parts of the United States, Texas and Mexico; in the last named country doing great injury in the towns and cities; in some, great numbers of the inhabitants perished. Earthquakes have also occurred in Central America, and some parts of South America. And all this within the last four years, more than three fourths of the inhabitable globe has been shaken, hundreds of towns and villages have been destroyed, and the number of people that have perished is immense.

*Storms.*—The storms that have ravaged both land and sea for the last three years in all parts of the world, exceed in number, if not in extent and fury, those that have been known in former years. The storm of January 1843, extended from Great Britain to the coasts of Italy; destroyed nearly one hundred vessels of various nations, and several hundred persons perished. The storm destroyed all the fruit in the Island of Sicily and did great injury on the coasts of Italy.

The storm on the Gulf of Mexico, the same year, destroyed 20 ships, some of them men of war; another in 1843 was more destructive. The same year the gale that swept the south west coast of Florida, destroyed two or three towns, prostrated the forests for miles, and caused great destruction for more than 100 miles; thirty or forty people perished, at the mouth of the Rio Plain; 40 ships were destroyed by a hurricane, in one of them 50 men perished.

In October 1844 a gale at Buffalo, on Lake Erie, destroyed a number of vessels, and much property on land, and upwards of 50 persons were drowned.

A storm at Philadelphia and its vicinity in 1842, destroyed a great amount of property, and from 30 to 50 lives, were lost about the same time. A storm in North Carolina swept away $250,000 of various kinds of property, and another in Canada did great damage.

On the 5th of October, 1844, the Island of Cuba was visited by a terrible storm, which spread ruin and desolation for hundreds of miles; upwards of a hundred ships was wrecked, and the fruit and crops on that and the adjoining Islands destroyed or greatly injured. During the last four years some hundreds of tornados have occurred in the U. States and Europe, by which hundreds of lives have been lost and millions of dollars in property destroyed. Among other destructions might be mentioned, that fearful avalanche that rolled from the Cordilleras of South America upon the neighboring plains and buried 1200 inhabitants, together with their cattle, houses, &c.

*Overflowing of the Rivers.*—The song of Enoch, page 45, says, "And rising rivers next their banks o'erflow." This has been fulfilled in a terrible manner, for almost every river in the whole world has overflowed its banks within the last four years, inundating the countries through which they flow, causing the most dreadful destruction of life and property.

In 1843 the rivers in New York and the surrounding States rose to an alarming height, sweeping off the bridges and doing immense damage to the Canal, roads, and other improvements. In the same year, the rivers in Europe, the Rhine, the Rhone and the Tibor, overflowed their banks; one third of the city of Rome was under water, and some of the provinces of France were literally covered with water, so as to destroy almost the entire crops. In 1844, the rivers of the western States overflowed the country in a greater extent than ever before was known.

The Mississippi, Missouri, Arkansas, Red river, Osage, Illinois, and Sangamon, were all higher than ever before; and the destruction occasioned by these floods has been variously estimated at from 12 to 20 millions of dollars. The same year the rivers in New Grenada and Venezuela inundated those countries, and it is said, "It will require years of prosperity to repair the damages done by the floods of 1844." The great rivers of China rose to such a hight that they broke through the dykes and inundated two rich and populous provinces.

And this year, 1845, the destruction caused by floods has been greater than in any year before. Belgium, Holland, Germany, and Poland, have been literally covered with water for weeks. The Rhine, Elbe, Danube, Dwina, Vistula, Oder, Scheldt, and many other smaller rivers, have this year been higher than at any time, before in two hundred years, and some of them higher than ever before was known; many large towns have been covered with water. The great bridge at Dresden has been carried a way, the crops in those countries entirely ruined, and many hundred villages overwhelmed by the "rising rivers." The dykes being broken down, the roads destroyed, and many lives lost. The inundation on the Arno, in Italy, this year, caused such destruction that on the waters retiring the vallies were covered with the dead bodies of men and animals. Last year the river Maritz rose very suddenly and swept off three thousand houses in the city of Adrianople. The flood in the Adana destroyed 1,200 people about the same time.

Many other floods, storms and inundations have taken place, which I omit to mention for the want of space.

*Signs in the Moon.*—The song of Enoch also says, "signs in the sun and in the moon appear." The signs in the moon have appeared in the month of Feb. 1843, the moon was observed (from different parts of New York) having a cross on its surface. This appearance lasted some time and was seen by hundreds of persons. The same month, a still more remarkable appearance was seen from Fort Leavenworth, and some parts of Missouri. About four o'clock in the morning the moon was observed to be red as blood, with a black cross in the centre, it remained thus for an hour; when the moon changed to its natural color, but the black cross continued some time until the moon was hid from view by clouds. The signs in the sun have not yet been seen, but all the signs and judgments that are foretold in the books of Esdras will take place. The destructions that have been during the last four years are but the "beginning of sorrow." They will continue to increase with fearful rapidity until all are convinced that these prophecies are true. The people must not consider them as my prophecies. They are the writings of Esdras who was permitted by the Most High to re-write* the sacred books (that had been burned by the heathens) about one hundred and sixty years B.C.

Esdras also says, there shall be "blood fire and vapor of smoke." This, it is well known, has been fulfilled. As showers of flesh and blood have fallen in Tennessee and North Carolina, as well as in other parts of the world, within the last few years, and a greater number of fires have occurred in this country since the

---

* See second Esdras, 14 chapter, from the 19 to the 23d verse.

first of last Jan. than ever before took place in twice that length of time. To illustrate this I extract the following from the Chillicothe Gazette:—

> "It seems as if the frowns of an offended God rested upon this devoted land, and that the viole of His wrath were being poured without mixture upon the heads of this unhappy people. The whole country in filled with the "voice of lamentation and wo." Our villages, towns and cities throughout the length and breadth of the Union, have been visited by the devourling element, and several of them have become suddenly transformed into desolate piles of smoking ruins. Every paper that comes to hand teems with accounts of most heart rending calamities and appalling catastrophes, both by land and by water."

Some fifty or sixty steam boats and rail-road accidents to have happened in the short interval (of six weeks,) attendant with most lamentable sacrifice of life and loss of property. Probably not less than one thousand fires in different parts of the United States, (dating from the burning of the National Theatre at Washington on the night succeeding the inauguration,) have occurred, destroying in their frightful career not less than one hundred millions of property. Crime, too has reared its hideous form, and stalked abroad with unwanted boldness—even in the light of the sun at noonday. The hearts of men have always become estranged to one another; and the worst passions of the human breast seemed to have found full vent. Parents have destroyed their own offsprings, children have murdered their parents, brothers their sisters, and sisters their brothers; husbands their wives, and wives their husbands; while acquaintances and friends, alike with strangers, have selected the victims of the assassin's knife from their own midst.

These things have been matters of every day occurrence for the last six weeks. It may be safely estimated that the number of unnatural deaths, by accidents of various kinds, fire, water and the hand of violence, during the brief period above named, in different parts of the country, are not less than fifteen hundred, and yet those point only to the beginning of sorrow. Then to call to mind the unprecedented amount of all other kinds of crime which is committed around us, and of which every mail brings us the intelligence, we are truly astonished. Who ever heard of the perpetration of so many thefts, burglaries, arsons, riots and deeds of lawless outrage in so short a time? These facts are truly astonishing. They clearly indicate the chastening hand of the Almighty for our many and grevvious national sins, in characters too plain to be misunderstood. These are signs, in the language of scripture, "blood fire and vapor of smoke," warn us that the day of retributive justice is nigh; even at the door.

And I would add the terrible riots in Philadelphia; the Anti-rent disturbances in New York; and the disgraceful murder of Joseph and Hyrum Smith in Carthage prison; and the failure of all attempts to bring the murderers to merited punishment, are signs that the prophecy of Enoch concerning the fall of Bethsula (i.e. the United States) will be fulfilled.

SPRINGFIELD ILLINOIS, July 18, 1845.

(JAMES COLIN BREWSTER, SPRINGFIELD, IL: 1845)

# The Principles of Nature, Her Divine Revelations, and A Voice to Mankind

In the mid-1840s word began to spread around Poughkeepsie, New York, that a teenaged shoemaker's apprentice from a poor family could diagnose disease. Andrew Jackson Davis (1826–1910) had shown signs of clairvoyance at an early age, and he also seemed adept at entering altered states of consciousness. In such trances, he asserted that he encountered historic figures and could discern the underlying illness within people. Soon Davis, dubbed the "Poughkeepsie Seer," began to lecture publicly. His method was unusual. He was assisted by two aides: Dr. Lyons, the "magnetizer," would put Davis into a trance state; and the Universalist minister Reverend William Fishbough would write down his words as he spoke them. This technique, Davis insisted, closed off his external senses and opened the "perceptive powers of the internal" through which he could better access the spiritual realm. Between November 1845 and January 1847 Davis delivered 157 lectures in this manner, and then published them as *The Principles of Nature, Her Divine Revelations, and a Voice to Mankind*. Claiming that the truths he uttered were a new revelation to humanity, Davis's book opened with the creation of the world in "liquid fire" and continued up to the present.

While Davis's performance of new scripture might seem unusual today, his insights into the realm of spirits and writings on sundry subjects became foundational texts for growing numbers of Spiritualists in the nineteenth-century United States. Known as the "John the Baptist" of the movement, Davis proclaimed the reality of communication with beings beyond this life several years before the famous "spirit rappings" in the home of the Fox

Sisters sensationalized Hydesville, New York, and catalyzed the growth of interest in séances and spiritual mediums. Davis published more than forty books between 1845 and 1885 on cosmology, health, and the afterlife, and provided the intellectual structure of a belief system, along with key terms for spirit communicants. Like many Spiritualists he was also an activist for radical social reform, including women's rights, Spiritualist lycea for children, and communal experiments to further human development and align society with the laws of nature as he understood them. Davis's works are still regarded as revelatory wisdom by those who believe in the potential for communication beyond this life.

In this selection Davis voices his critique of the superstition and fanaticism of traditional religion that prevents humanity from attaining its full spiritual potential. Critical of biblical "superstition," he urges readers to turn to "the Universe" as the source of ultimate truth and throw off the shackles of organized religion that bind the human mind. Davis's remarks also illustrate an early recognition of non-Abrahamic religions, and he suggests that they have much wisdom to offer humanity. Prefiguring the "hidden gospels" published later in the century, and yet also echoing the naturalism of Thomas Jefferson, Davis provides a revised history of Jesus, portraying him as a compassionate, philanthropic, perfect man, but not as divine.

# The Principles of Nature, Her Divine Revelations, and A Voice to Mankind

## PART I.

### The Key,
### or
### The Principles of Nature.

§ 1. REASON is a principle belonging to man alone. The office of the mind is to investigate, search, and explore, the principles of Nature, and trace physical manifestations in their many and varied ramifications. Thought, in its proper nature, is uncontrolled—unlimited. It is free to investigate, and to rise into lofty aspirations. And the only hope for the amelioration of the world is free thought and unrestricted inquiry. Anything which opposes or tends to obstruct this sublime and lofty principle, is wrong.

The mind can not be chained! It will leave its resting-place, and explore the fields of science; and, not satisfied with the investigation of terrestrial things, it has soared to the heavens and counted the stars. It has familiarized itself with the motions of the planets, given names to laws that control the universe, and has proved the existence and qualities of these laws by mathematical analysis and demonstration. The mind is naturally unrestrained in its actions and thoughts—free from all shackles and bonds of the external world. Yet man has not been allowed to express sentiments irresistibly flowing into his mind. Ignorance, superstition, and bigotry, have wielded a tyrannical sceptre, and sectarianism has usurped the dominion over the human soul!

Man has rights founded in principles of Nature. These rights have been perverted, crushed, and prostrated. Folly has reigned in the place of reason; imbecility has reigned instead of thought; vice has reigned instead of virtue; ignorance has reigned instead of knowledge, and bigotry has reigned instead of benevolence! Thus the highest, holiest and sublimest powers of man have been repressed and distorted by the degrading shackles of superstition and false imagination.

The office of the mind is to hold dominion where the above evils have reigned. It is to become unchained and free from the prison of sectarian darkness, and ushered into the light of truth and the atmosphere of liberty. The tall monuments of ignorance which have existed, may be interrogated by generations yet unborn.

Man has not been permitted to enjoy the free and uncontrolled exercise of his powers and intellectual endowments. He has not had the liberty to express thoughts gushing from the depths of his mind, but has been compelled to restrain and repress them for want of an atmosphere of light and liberty. The few who have dared to express themselves freely, have done it at the immediate risk of their physical destruction. Truths that are eternal have been conceived of, yet smothered by the hand of a dominant and tyrannical Ignorance.

This ignorance still exists; this bigotry and superstition still exist; and where is the responsibility for the *cause* of their existence? Sectarian usurpation must bear the charge. It has, in its long career, crushed and prohibited the free exercise of moral and intellectual attainment. It has obstructed the progress of human knowledge. It has obscured the main features and manifestations of truth, and thrown a mantle of ignorance and fanaticism over the world. It has covered and concealed from the mind of man the real and only principle which constitutes his peculiar dignity. It has sapped the foundations of human happiness. It has produced a schism in the race, and a wasting prostitution of human powers yet uncorrected and uncontrolled. The true interests of mankind have thus been perverted to those of vice and misery. Wisdom has not existed, but folly has usurped her throne. Knowledge has been limited, while ignorance has been universal. Happiness has been crushed to the ground, while misery has everywhere raised her hideous head. Persecution, incited and sustained by ignorance and party prejudice, has destroyed thousands of human beings. The mind of man has thus become enslaved, and no principle or power of truth and virtue has been able to break its chains!

Deplorable have been the results of ignorance and vice. With a

ruthless hand they have grasped and held the interests, affections, and mental associations of men, until the voice of Nature
had no power to speak and tell of the victim's fate! Thus most
melancholy has been the condition of generations past. The cause
is vividly reflected on our minds; and the reflection induces the
conclusion that such conditions shall not again exist. Reflection
on things past and present show to the inquiring mind that the
*institutions* which have existed have been in direct opposition to
the interests, feelings, and affections, of human nature. Those institutions can not exist to the extent to which they have, because
the mind of man has become nearly unshackled, and free to act
and investigate, and boldly to express its earnest and serious convictions. And these investigations will remove the foundations of
illiberal institutions, which are based upon impure motive, and
not on true principle—which are sustained by motives of individual interest, and not by the interest and good of mankind.

The world is existing on wrong foundations. The interests of
one person are in direct opposition to the interests of another; and
what is one man's interest results in another's misfortune. The
interests of individuals are centred in their isolated and distinctive
principles and pursuits; and the corrupt condition of society and
the world is owing to the great amount of individual absorption
from the common rights of humanity. It is from this cause that
the world, instead of harmonizing in all its parts and ramifications, is in a disorganized state; and, from the fact that each part
is obstructed in so many ways from communicating and harmonizing with others, the whole has become disunited and confused.

As the world is situated, those elements that *are* united become
absorbents from those which *are not;* and hence, instead of an
harmoniously-organized condition of the world, one part is extraneous and excrescent to another. Hence, instead of being
united, the world is disunited; and instead of harmonizing, it is
confused. Instead of universal peace and good-will, war and dev-
astation have prevailed; and instead of the happiness and interests of one man consisting in the happiness and interests of the
whole, the interests of each one are in direct opposition to the
interests of others. This can not and shall not much longer exist.
Its causes are becoming revealed; and this revelation arouses the

feelings, interests, and crushed affections of man, to one vast rebellion against the dominions of vice and misery. Truth, in her
mighty power, shall prevail over ignorance; and all her enemies
shall be crushed, to rise no more! One principle, one foundation,
one faith, one interest, one universal and eternal asylum, shall
exist for the whole world of mankind! This result rises above the
utmost conceptions of the mind; and this will usher in that light
which has been hid so long from the world. This light is happiness and peace; and this, too, is the light which, when once it
expands, can not contract. And this is the resurrection from
moral and intellectual degradation!

———

§ 156. Thus, reader, you are believing a book voted as being the
word of God by three hundred and eighteen bishops, and sealed
as true by the emperor Constantine! You understand, now, the
origin and formation of what is called the "*Holy Bible*," which
means *excellent soft bark*. You understand, now, how that which
can boast of antiquity, can assume the ground of being sacred,
and how, being defended by a multitude of interested promulga-
tors, it can defy the yearnings of your thoughts to be free, and set
at naught all your attempts at investigation. You will now be able
to bear it in mind, that the *Hindoo* has a Bible which he venerates
as much as you do yours. So also has the *Mohammedan*, and the
*Persian*. Each equally impelled by prejudice and hereditary affection, will inquire, "If you deprive us of our Bible, what shall we
have in its stead?" Beloved reader, there is a Book in which beauties and divine truths are inexhaustible; a Book filled with texts
that no Egyptian, Jewish, Persian, or Hindoo priest or theologian
can counterfeit; a Book which can not be concealed—whose
teachings can not be misapprehended, and whose results will be
purity, virtue, morality, and celestial righteousness; a Book from
which the whole world may derive indestructible consolation,
and learn of that Divine Essence which is the Cause and Parent of
human existence. It will at the same time unfold the unspeakable
grandeur of your *celestial* habitations, each of which will be only
a sphere or step in the grand and magnificent gallery that leads to

the Flower of celestial Beauty, whose fragrance is the perfection of an unchangeable Universe. Will you ask, then, reader, what will be given you instead of a material book, composed of paper and impressed with type, when a UNIVERSE is open to the researches of your aspiring mind? Certainly nothing can be more unreasonable than the superstitious claims that are in the world for the teachings of a simple *book*, that can be altered in a thousand ways in going through the operations of a press! But there exists a BOOK that teaches purity, morality, and immortality, and demonstrates the loveliness of the GREAT CREATOR—a Book, too, that is as indestructible and unvarying as the constitution and divine qualities of NATURE.

I have but a few more remarks to offer concerning the Bible, and these are as follows: It does not teach that pure morality which belongs to the nature of man, and which will result from a superior condition of the race. From this remark must be excepted a few incidental expressions said to have been used by JESUS—such as "the Golden Rule,"—which was comprehensively taught six hundred years before, by CONFUCIUS, the Chinese philosopher. Again: it does not prove *immortality;* neither does it teach the mighty truths contained in the successive spheres or degrees of future existence. Nor does it even present any substantial proof of the transition from this rudimental condition, to a higher degree of material and physical organization; or in other words, it does not demonstrate a resurrection to a future life. Nor does it present one proper conception of the constitution, character, greatness, omnipotence, and majesty of the Divine Mind. Nor does it do justice to his works, except in those meditations upon which I have heretofore commented. Nor does it contain one substantial proof of an unvarying law upon which to found a hope of ever being regenerated, or of ascending to a sphere of more perfect and harmonious existence. Nor does it teach that holy virtue, morality, and refinement, which should receive the name of religion.

This term *religion*, however, is quite inexpressive, and needs, in order to be understood, a brief definition. The term *ligo* is a Latin word, signifying *to tie* or *bind*. *Re*-ligo is to *re*-tie or bind over again, and make still stronger. The *n* being attached, forms the word *religion*, which means to bind and rebind, and make secure. It is well to say that, understood in this sense, it has performed its office most effectually. For the term "religion," indeed, implies little more than being sacredly bound to *sectarianism*. The word as used by commentators is very potent, and very expressive; and it may be seen by these remarks that it is *very applicable*.

Thus the "Primitive History" is useful as a history of mythology, ancient theology, false and imaginary deities—as containing accounts of wars, pestilences, persecutions, desolations of cities, false prophesyings, long and tedious expeditions, most unjust assassinations, murders, adulteries, abominations, trials, afflictions, imagination, phantasm, rebellion; as presenting information concerning oriental customs, expressions, ordinances, prejudices, religious wars, martyrdoms, and all kinds of injustice, immorality, and unrighteousness. Viewed in the light of a *history*, I say, its writers should be respected, and its contents preserved. But as a *theological* book it should not be read; for it contains no absolute doctrine—and all those doctrines which are supposed to be taught therein, are merely the false interpretations given of it by various commentators in all ages since the book was compiled for the exclusive use of the adherents of Catholicism. From *falsifications* I would rescue its teachings. I therefore say, the book is good as a *history*, and would not have done the least harm in the world, had not forced interpretations been given of its contents, and had not claims been preferred in its behalf to a sacredness which it does not claim for itself, and, as I can positively say, which it does not inherently possess.

But the objection may arise, that some tribes and nations of the earth know nothing of this book, and yet they are miserable, ignorant, and wretched, in the extreme. The answer to this will be hereafter given and comprehended in the third part, or the Application, of this portion of the work.

§ 157. I NOW proceed to give a true history of JESUS, from his birth to his death, and to state the causes of so many unjust sayings contained in the New Testament concerning him and others.

In Nazareth in Galilee, there dwelt a family but little known to the world, or to the inhabitants of the town in which they resided. The father, whose name was JOSEPH, was a very active and industrious mechanic. He was a carver and sculptor, and was frequently engaged in various branches of carpentry. His associate, MARY, was a very gentle and kindly-disposed woman. They lived generally unknown, because of their domestic retirement, and love of the quietude pervading an undisturbed and happy home. They neither possessed an affection for literature, nor for the study of any science or philosophy that was then cultivated among the inhabitants, as derived from the Grecians and other enlightened nations. It was in this family that that little personage, about whose birth, life, and death, so many marvellous accounts have been written, was born.

Not long after his birth, Joseph and his wife were disinherited from the house they occupied, because of an unfavorable report that became extant, through the agency of some designing and evil-disposed persons. Before they left the house, however, Joseph dreamed that it was proper for him and his family to journey into Egypt.

Previous to this journey, a necessary circumstance compelled Mary to lay her child in a manger, in which place, as I am distinctly impressed, he lay not over forty minutes. Joseph, not knowing what else to do, obeyed the suggestion of his impressive dream, and departed into Egypt. They were not long there before a suitable relief was procured for them, which induced their return, and established them again comfortably in their previous habitation.

It is well that all should bear in mind that dreams were supposed in those days to be something more than the workings of the elements and imaginations of the mind, and the suggestions, especially, of those dreams which were highly impressive, were obeyed as a voice from an angel of the Divine Mind.

This much is related in the New Testament, in a truthful manner; and the account there given is correct, with the exception of the interpretation that was given to these simple occurrences, by people generally, and especially by the writers of this history.

But the New Testament leaves two chasms in the life of Christ, which are of great importance, inasmuch as they are periods in human life that as much as any other require attention. Matthew and others speak of his birth, and then are silent until they introduce him into the presence of learned doctors and philosophers, in the temple. And no account is given of him after this, again, until he became thirty years of age; and then he is said to have begun his preaching. It is plain, that from birth to the age of twelve years, and also from the age of twelve to thirty, many most important occurrences might have transpired, of which the world, through these sacred historians, have not the least intimation.

After Joseph returned with his family, all his secular and domestic affairs were rendered agreeable and easy; and he was likewise restored to the bosom of society, and was beloved as a worthy citizen. No particular impression existed among the inhabitants concerning their young and beautiful son, with the exception that he was generally admired for the perfect symmetry of his form and cerebral structure. I am presented with no such an occurrence as the command related by Matthew to have been issued by Herod. But as I proceed, the origin of this account will distinctly appear. The child was named JESUS—which was a name occasionally occurring, but seldom admired, because of its association in the mind with the supposed spirit of an Egyptian deity, much worshipped by the priests of the Sun, and spoken of in various portions of the second book of Kings. His physical constitution was beautifully proportioned, and he possessed a corresponding beauty of the mental faculties.

His general organization was indeed remarkable, inasmuch as he possessed combined the perfection of physical beauty, mental powers, and refined accomplishments. He was generally beloved during his youth, for his great powers of discernment, his thirst after knowledge, and his disposition to inquire into the causes of mental phenomena, of the conditions of society, and of the visible manifestations of Nature. He was also much beloved for his pure natural sympathy for all who were suffering afflictions either of a physical or mental character. His benevolence and love toward all without distinction; his constant yearning for the companionship of those who were considered good and righteous; his marked respect and affection for those who were much older than himself; his constant visits to those who required relief from their afflictions; and his kind words of consolation to those who were depressed either by disease or unhappy social circumstances—all contributed to render him an object of general love and attachment. These were the peculiarities which distinguished him from all other persons then living.

It is true that at the age of twelve years he was admitted to the presence of the learned doctors. There he manifested some of his powers of discernment, interior and natural philosophy, unsophisticated love, simplicity of expression, kindness of disposition, and universal sympathy and benevolence. These he displayed with all the naturalness and spontaneousness resulting from the promptings of an uncorrupted and purely-organized spiritual principle. He answered their pertinent interrogations with great benignity, promptitude, and freedom of conception and expression. What most astonished the doctors was the demonstration of his philosophical conceptions and mathematical powers—all of which were blended into a perfect system by the pervading element of his mind, which was LOVE.

§ 158. I would have the reader understand the reason why these things were to be expected from, and were manifested by, him. I have related that Jesus was perfectly constituted, both as to his physical and spiritual organization. This being the case, his mental faculties were early developed to a degree even transcending the capacities of those philosophers in whose presence he showed forth his wonderful mental qualifications. Even at the present time there is a youth whose mind is in a similar manner prematurely developed, especially his faculties of perception and causality, and his powers of mathematical calculation. He is in one of the eastern states—and is already surprising the learned doctors and philosophers by his astronomical and mathematical powers. Frequently there are persons who have one or more of the mental faculties fully developed while they are as yet in a youthful state. Many also have the power of perceiving material substances or colors, or reading, without employing the natural organs of vision. Others are capable of having the interior faculties of their minds opened by being thrown into an abnormal condition, which relieves the mind of much of its burdensome obstruction, and renders it suitable for the influx of superior knowledge. This fact is at the present day arresting the attention of many observing doctors and philosophers of the land.

JESUS while in youth, and especially at the age of twelve, possessed all those superior qualifications which many scarcely possess when their interiors are expanded by the modern discovery of manipulations. Hence I discover that he became noted, because of his superior and highly-refined powers of discernment, together with his gentleness, kindness, and sweetness of disposition.

After he had manifested his marvellous powers to the learned doctors in this instance, he courted no longer their presence, and lived principally among his brethren, spending a large portion of his time in the visitation of the diseased, depressed, disconsolate, and suffering inhabitants in various portions of the land. He seemed to possess an intuitive knowledge of the medicinal properties of plants, of mineral and animal substances—of their use, and of the proper time and manner of their application in the curing of various diseases. This qualification, however, he acquired during the period which elapsed from the age of fifteen to thirty-three. He also possessed a great *physical soothing power* over the disordered or disconcerted forces of the human system. This was because of his superior physical endowments. Hence it is related in various places in the New Testament, that he laid his hands upon persons, and they were cured. When relieving the palsy, he is reported as having said, "Thy faith hath cured thee: rise, take up thy bed, and walk." Also he is said to have laid wet sand or clay upon the eyes of the blind, and thus to have restored sight. And in various other instances he is represented as having made use of *physical means* to produce the cures which are by his biographers and others insignificantly termed "*miracles.*"

The reason is clear why those sacred historians employed expressions so mysterious and ambiguous—expressions which often did violence to the human judgment by conveying ideas which reason can never sanction. It was the general impression, after he became so noted for his many benevolent and charitable deeds, that he must either be actuated by the Spirit of the God of Abraham, Isaac, and Jacob, or by the Evil One whom their imaginations had promoted to an equal degree of almightiness. Finally, it became so general a belief that lie was actuated by the *first*, that they designated him by the title of "the Son of God." Then the ignorant and uninformed bowed with a trembling veneration at the mere mention of the name of "JESUS, the Son of God," although many of them had never beheld him.

The inhabitants in those days were greatly inclined to extremes of faith and incredulity. If any particular theory, principle, or philosophy, were presented for their consideration, they were accustomed to embrace or combat it violently. Thus it was that most of the Jews *despised* Jesus, while others *worshipped him*, and believed all the marvels that had been related of him. It is well to remark that Jesus never professed to be what they make him to say he was. He was a kind, amiable, and unassuming being, discarded by many because of his superior and benevolent traits, and as much beloved by those whom he immediately benefited by the smiles of his loving-kindness and by his soothing power.

He often during his youth, and also after ascending to manhood, preached for the purpose of consoling and instructing multitudes of those who were depressed in spirit, and unfortunately situated in the world. One of those beautiful lessons of consolation and exhortation is recorded in the fifth, sixth, and seventh chapters of Matthew—where, with all the simplicity of a confiding disposition, he consoles the multitude by saying, "Happy are they that mourn, for they shall be comforted; happy are the poor in spirit, for they shall see God; happy are the peace-makers, for theirs is the kingdom of heaven"; and in like manner he proceeds with his expressions of kindness and of all those sentiments that might be expected from the workings of such a well-constituted mind. In his preaching he employed the terms that were then in use, and he professed to be nothing more than a teacher of pure and unadultered love, and also a general sympathizer with all who needed relief, consolation, and sympathy.

I am exceedingly attracted by the purity of his life, disposition, teachings, and spirit of reform. He saw distinctly, and realized fully, the unhappy situation of his fellow-men; and he yearned for the time to come when there would be a new heaven and a new earth, wherein might dwell righteousness. He was anxious for the prevalence of a general harmony of interests and action, such as would join in one the whole race of mankind. He desired that prudence and industry should so reign throughout this material sphere, as that the desert might blossom as the rose, and the wilderness bloom with a smiling, inviting beauty. Thus he delighted to contemplate the establishment of the spiritual Zion—the great Temple of Knowledge and Righteousness so feelingly spoken of, and so earnestly desired by, that good and worthy writer, ISAIAH. Such are the yearnings of all naturally-philanthropic bosoms. Such are the aspirations of those exalted minds who behold the human race as a Whole, and in their superior benevolence cherish no self-ishness or pride.

§ 159. Thus Jesus lived, doing good to those who came and required assistance, exhorting those who were uneducated, and preaching to multitudes—*not* in the temple or the synagogue, because those places were *too pure* for his deeds and his philosophy—but on the mountain and by the wayside; thus lifting up his voice in what has before been termed "the sanctuary of the expanded earth and the unfolded heavens." He taught thus because he felt it an imperative duty devolving upon him to instruct the ignorant, and to deposite if possible that pure spirit of reform in the social world that might result in establishing the beauties of the spiritual Zion, and in perfecting the qualities of the Tree of Righteousness. He felt prompted to preach, what had been before conceived, that men should do unto others as they would have others do unto them; and he desired that the simple, good, and tranquillizing influence of this principle might be deposited and developed in the bosom of every human form. He desired that the day of righteousness should be ushered in, when there would be no more pain, sorrow, or crying, for the old things would all have been passed away, and all things would have become new. And in the accomplishment of his desires, sin would be destroyed, together with that which hath the power of sin, that is darkness, ignorance, folly, imagination, imbecility, and every species of sectarianism and unholy philosophy.

JESUS continued to obey those beneficent monitions of his mind (which were to cure the diseased, to visit the fatherless and widows in their afflictions, and to preach peace on earth and good-will to men) until prejudice became so strong against him, that he was unable to proceed any further in his career of purity and benevolence. He was censured by various learned, and, as they were thought to be, very *great*, theologians, and was persecuted to a great extent by the multitudes, who were exasperated from the workings of religious prejudice against him. So he was captured, brought before a council of judicature, who were all disposed to condemn him without a hearing, for disturbance of the peace, for interference with their long-cherished religious faiths, their social organization, their modes of worship, their rites and ceremonies, their long and loud prayers to Him whom they supposed to be the Lord of Abraham, Isaac, and Jacob, for blasphemy, and for doing deeds that were good on the sabbath-day. All these and many similar accusations were brought against him; and they exhibited a spirit of persecution that will be ere long fully exemplified in this nineteenth century. On these accusations they condemned him to die the death of a martyr! And as was the custom in cases of similar accusations in those days, they crucified him, two others sharing the same fate with him. During the infliction of this most unjust penalty, the Jews manifested the same spirit of sectarian vengeance, and the same desire for the destruction of all invasive philanthropy and purity of principle, that will ere long be exhibited again. Thus will be demonstrated the existence of precisely the same spirit as that which characterized the Jews of old, and the influence of this will clothe the rising and unborn generation in the armor of prejudice, hostility, and fanaticism!

Thus JESUS was a good man, a noble and unparalleled Moral Reformer, considering him as disconnected from all those unjust things that are in the New Testament recorded of him. He did not profess to be the Son of God in any other sense than that of a branch, as all are, of the great Tree of universal and eternal Causation. He did not profess to be directed and impelled by any other spirit than that of Divine love, the germ of which dwells in every other being undeveloped. And to this principle, as existing in others, he appealed so feelingly, in order that its qualities might be unfolded, and that they might advance to the degree of refinement in love and wisdom then occupied by himself. He was, then, A TYPE OF A PERFECT MAN, both in physical and spiritual qualifications. But those representations which make him more than this, I discover are all *untrue*, and express that only which was professed *for*, but never *by* him.

Thus, then, he died a martyr to the principles of truth, reason, and virtue. So likewise did Matthew, Paul, and others. And it is lamentable to reflect that the world has been guilty of such flagrant injustice that even many in subsequent generations have been subjected to the torturing rack, to the stake, and to the dissolving flames! Men have even rushed to the field of battle, and there, impelled by envy and sectarian prejudice, they have poured out each other's life's blood, thereby causing Nature to blush for shame for the degradation of her children! Brethren have joined in open hostility, actuated by no other cause than the terrible and fiery elements of sectarian envy, prejudice, and local affection! How fearful, indeed, is the gloom of the dark thought, that man has died a martyr to the natural promptings of the spirit within, and to the principles of virtue, morality, and love!

I behold Jesus, then, as a great and good Reformer; as connected with no marvellous or mysterious aristocracy, but as being born of lowly parents, and fostered in the bosom of their domestic habitation; as possessing intelligence to a surpassing degree; as manifesting unbounded love, benevolence, and sympathy; as healing the sick, restoring the blind, curing the lame, and visiting the disconsolate in their afflictions; as preaching love, morality, peace on earth and good will to men; as instructing the multitudes in the paths of pleasantness and peace; and as loving all and disliking none. I behold him as being condemned, nailed to the cross, and dying a martyr to the cause of love, wisdom, and virtue! Such is one of the parts in the great monument which an ignorant and misdirected world have erected to their own shame and folly!

[. . .]

§ 161. A long time elapsed after Jesus became noted for his moral teachings and benevolent acts, before any inquiries were instituted concerning the peculiarities of his birth and early life, or concerning the circumstances attending the same. It is well to say, that the chief inquiries, and the collection of facts, relative to the birth, life, and deeds of Jesus, were not made *until many years after his death*. Therefore the *general impressions* of his early followers were assumed *as a basis* whereon his subsequent historians and followers predicated their faith and doctrine. The unfavorable report concerning Joseph and Mary, heretofore mentioned, gave rise to the first impression as to the illegitimacy of Jesus. It was in consequence of this report that Joseph was disinherited for a season; but after the report subsided, he returned to his former home, and all the previous impressions, were obliterated entirely, and no more was thought upon the subject.

When the first inquiries were made concerning the birth of Jesus, the conclusion, as derived from superficial testimony, was as follows: That Jesus, doing good, performing many cures, and manifesting great powers of intellect, must necessarily be supposed to be the Son of the Good Spirit, or God. In confirmation of this, proof was supposed to exist in the report referred to; and Mary, the mother of Jesus, was supposed to have conceived, in her virginity, by the breathing influence of the Holy Ghost. And it was known that Joseph had a dream which caused his departure into Egypt; and this was believed to be angelic instruction. Jesus, it was thought, could not have been so perfect as he was, without having an origin unlike that of others. And as he had manifested brotherly-kindness, and accomplished benevolent acts, this was deemed conclusive evidence that his origin must have been *pure*. The conclusion, then, was irresistible, that Jesus was begotten of the Holy Spirit, and born of the Virgin Mary, and therefore was the Son of God. And they supposed that he was named Jesus because he was sent to save his people from their sins. All these things were retrospectively viewed by the generation succeeding the death of Jesus, and were considered undeniable evidences of his miraculous conception, of his immaculate purity, and that he must have been the Son of God. All this was in perfect harmony with their prepossessions of mind.

Here the New Testament leaves the history of Jesus until he arrives at the age of twelve years. But surely some things must have been said to have occurred as connected with his life during this period. But the accounts which were collected seemed too crude and imperfect to receive a canonical sanction; and they were hence rejected on account of their inconsistency and the unsound manner in which they were recorded. Some of the rejected books are still in existence, and are full of marvellous relations concerning the childhood of Jesus, and the peculiarities which distinguished his whole life. Some of these stories are not worthy a moment's consideration, inasmuch as they are derived from the marvellous and exaggerated impressions hereditarily received by the persons who wrote them. Among other things, it is related that while Jesus was a little boy, and associated with other children, the stars were seen to follow his course, while his companions were not in the least thus honored; and that the moon appeared to trace and retrace her steps, following the various movements of the boy Jesus: also that a peculiar illumination was visible on his countenance, which would blind the eyes of those near him: also that while a very little boy, he would with other boys approach the streams, and of the moistened clay make birds and other small forms; and it is related that those which were made by the other boys would remain inanimate, while those formed by Jesus would be immediately animated and transformed into beautiful birds! It is also related that seeds which were deposited in the earth by his hand would germinate and grow up in the space of thirty hours to full maturity. Much is also said concerning many visions and dreams that he had, all of which tended to confirm the opinion that he was the Son of God.

The account concerning Jesus being introduced among the learned doctors is strictly true, but it was not written until after his death. All the things accomplished by him which are called *miracles*, were related as such mainly by those who received the traditions from those who were the immediate followers and companions of Jesus. It was a general belief that he was the person whom many of the earlier historians and prophets foretold. Hence, in various instances, quotations are made from their writings which seemed to have an immediate bearing upon, or connexion with, the things they had heard concerning the birth, life, and deeds of Jesus.

The writers of the books in the New Testament could not resist the conviction that Christ was thus miraculously born; and that inasmuch as he accomplished so many miracles, discoursed so eloquently, harmed no one, but did good to all, and died ignominiously for his cause, he must have been the Son of God—the application of this title being in accordance with the general mode of expression and belief. They likewise cherished the conviction that he must have been foreseen by the prophets of previous generations. Hence by research among their writings, passages were found which seemingly had a connexion with the prominent circumstances in the life of Christ, which they were recording. Therefore they made those quotations with a serious conviction that they had immediate reference to the things which they were employed in relating.

§ 162. The history of the deeds accomplished by Jesus from the age of twelve to thirty, was registered promiscuously in various books, some of which are now called the Apocrypha of the New Testament. These relate more miraculous manifestations of the physical and mental powers of Jesus than are recorded in the New

Testament. Yet they were written more from hearsay than from actual knowledge. And I am impressed to say that the account of *the ascension* was also transmitted by others to those who wrote it, with the exception of one account preserved on bark, and said to have been written by Mark, who was present as an eye-witness of the occurrence. For be it remembered that the art of writing was then understood only by a very few, and that paper, ink, and the art of printing, were to them unknown. Hence the accounts impressed on bark and other substances would in some instances remain untranscribed for one, two, or three centuries. Some of these were preserved until a species of paper was invented upon which their contents were transcribed. Very few persons were able to write; while the vast multitude were only capable of conveying their thoughts verbally: and the constant verbal delivery of these accounts subjected them to constant modifications. Yet from impressions thus traditionally transmitted, the subsequent writers produced those records of which the world is in possession at the present day.

Still more emphatically am I impressed to say that the birth of Christ as related, the correspondingly-inconsistent stories of his youth, the accounts of the instantaneous cures effected by him, the pretensions that are made in his behalf in respect to his mediatorship, and of his being in a superior sense the Son of the Deity—and also the account of his literal ascension—are all strictly the traditional impressions imbibed and written of him, none of which are true as they are related. It is impossible to be in communion with, and possess a knowledge of, the unerring and unchangeable principles of the Divine Mind, and at the same time admit the truth of these traditional records. And it is given me to know that he who believes fully in their truth is not in communion with the laws, purposes, and Essence of the Great Positive Mind. But he who is interiorly enlightened concerning these, hesitates not to declare, from a serious conviction of the judgment, that such things *can not* be true; for their very nature precludes their possibility.

While I am thus compelled to speak, I am none the less conscious of having myself supposed these things to be true, and of having believed them with a vast degree of veneration, while my mind, like others, was trammelled by sensuous opinions and philosophy. Yet now, having the external senses closed, and the perceptive powers of the internal opened, I am acquainted with those things which in outward life appeared unaccountable mysteries. These historical accounts, concerning which I in common with others have had mysterious impressions, now appear entirely transparent, even to their origin, and their confirmation in the minds of mankind. And I now rejoice to know that this superficial theology has not the least connexion with the Divine Essence, or Great Creative Cause, with his laws, or with the great system of material and spiritual worlds. And the belief in these things forms no part of the theology which every department of Nature and the Universe unequivocally demonstrates and establishes.

*Now* my affections are directed entirely by that wisdom which discards a theology so impure and superficial. Yet when I return again to the exterior world, and know things only by sensuous impressions, then also will my affections return and control my superficial wisdom; and these affections will at once connect me again with all those superficial views, theories, and philosophies, that at this present moment occupy no tangible position in my conceptions of the structure of the Universe, or of the character of the Great Positive Mind. Hence, while I am in this condition, I am knowledging that which is opposed to the present affections of men, in the departments of theology and philosophy. But it is nevertheless proper—nay, it is an imperative duty—for me to develop that which I now perceive is seriously interfering with all social happiness and mental progression. Let it be, then, the serious effort of all vigorous minds, to learn soon to modify their affections for supposed truths, so that their *reason*, and not their *prejudices*, may in all cases be the governing principle of their minds. These developments will then lose their apparent irreverence, and become at once a vehicle to convey to the judgment truth and wisdom. I will have occasion to speak on this point again, when treating on the physical and spiritual constitution of man; but at the present time it is necessary still further to confine the attention to those things heretofore investigated.

[. . .]

§ 165. There exists no history or account of the birth and teachings of Jesus corresponding to that which is recorded in the New
Testament, with the exception of the account in Josephus; and that
occupies no conspicuous position, but is merely recorded as a passing remark of no very great importance. Some have supposed that
this passage is an interpolation. I do not discover that this supposition is true; for the record is genuine, although not contained in
some of the early versions of Josephus. Yet it is clear that this historian attached no such importance to the life and character of
Christ as was attached thereunto by those who wrote the gospels.
It is reasonable to suppose that if the birth and life of Christ had
been of such a supernatural character, more historians would have
received conviction accordingly, and would have devoted considerable portions of their writings to a relation of his miraculous manifestations, setting forth the importance of his birth, death, and
resurrection. But as no more historians devoted themselves to this
work, the conclusion inevitably follows that few, if any, firmly believed these things, except those who wrote the primitive manuscripts of the New Testament; and that the latter believed because
they received a mass of apparent evidence which no others were in
a situation to receive.

The object of speaking concerning these things is to free the
minds of men from all superstitious prejudice as connected with
a belief in the same, which prejudice has a tendency to retard the
physical and spiritual development of mankind. Society can not
be reorganized in harmony with the laws and requirements of
Nature, until all obstacles are removed which obstruct the un-
foldings of the general mind, and stand in the way of universal
action: and this superstitious belief in an unreal theology is one
of those obstacles that are to be of all others the most dreaded
and the most repulsed from the bosom of mankind. Such obstacles can be removed only by cautiously revealing the *causes* engaged in their creation; and a knowledge of these will cause the
mind to repulse and discard their effects as these are existing at
the present time in every portion of the world.

Therefore I have descended to the causes that were engaged in
creating the book that is now called *the Bible;* and a knowledge
of these removes at once all that superstition concerning it, and
all those ideas of its supernaturalness, that have preserved it in

the bosom of fanaticism from the period of its origin to the present day. The effects of these causes have been folly, ignorance, prejudice, bigotry, superstition, injustice, wretchedness, immorality, and aristocratic distinctions, among the various nations of the earth. Now he who can sympathize with these *effects*, may still continue to cherish their parent *causes;* but he who feels an inward repulsion at the very thought of their existence, will most certainly display his nobleness of mind in discarding for ever those unholy causes which produced them, as well as the effects themselves, and begin to live a new life in the physical and mental world, and thus be fitted to ascend to the highest point in the second sphere of knowledge and understanding.

Still nothing should be venerated more than the beautiful and truthful prophetic meditations of the early writers concerning a universal deliverance from tyranny, bondage, and wretchedness. And the many useful and beautiful moral precepts contained in the New Testament, as spoken by Jesus, demand equal reverence. All such moral teachings should be regarded with deep veneration, especially when that veneration is an offspring of the judgment, and not of the affections; for the affections are not the developed principles, but merely the elements of the judgment.

And it will be perceived that the nobleness of those early writers, and the superior physical and mental endowments of Jesus, are still preserved as a source of instruction, and that they even shine forth with a brilliancy they never have before displayed, because they have been so much obscured beneath a heterogeneous mass of unjust and useless materials. And what has been preserved of their characters and teachings is capable of being applied to the great subject of Moral Reform, which is only to be affected by first reforming the physical and social conditions of men. The beauty of their lives and characters, the perseverance which distinguished their efforts, and their adherence to the principles of virtue, goodness, and righteousness, even unto martyrdom—all stand forth as conspicuous examples by which all men may profit.

And let it be known that JESUS was the greatest of them all in this great field of labor—in this great vineyard of natural (not *un*natural) culture. He possessed pre-eminently those ennobling attributes which are worthy a living imitation in the lives and deeds of all men. I therefore place Jesus and these early writers or prophets in the same category with those worthy and noble philanthropists who have lived since their time, and those who still live to adorn the world. They were general sympathizers with the afflictions of men, general actors for the public good, general relievers of the widows and fatherless, general preachers of the great principles controlling the Universe and Man with an unerring government, and general relievers of despondency and mental wretchedness, by unfolding to the minds of men the great and glorious era when would exist universal peace, industry, and righteousness.

And it is an honor to the human race to become now acquainted with the pure characters of former days, as disconnected from all the extraneous obscurities that have shut out their real characters from the mental perceptions of the world. It is an honor now to know and appreciate the trueness, goodness, brotherly-kindness, and benevolence of JESUS, as disconnected from all the falsifications heretofore obscuring his intrinsic physical and spiritual qualifications.

Thus I close all reflections on the character and application of the principles of the early writers, and of JESUS, until the delivery of the third part of this work.

———

One facility, one most powerful engine of freedom and of the distribution of thought, must be attached to the superior association, and thus be a part of it, and that is THE PRESS. This wields an omnipotent sceptre over the public mind, and is a rightful vehicle for the dissemination of personal, local, scientific, and general information. A printing department, then, should be composed of a congregation of present proprietors, and conducted upon the most expeditious principles which the science of mechanism can without difficulty supply. A multitude of presses may be governed by one well-constructed engine, and labor may be so distributed as that as much labor as is at present accomplished may be performed in one third of the time.

This must form an important part of the superior association. The interest of printers must be concentrated on the great end of *social unity*, and on the *equal distribution of knowledge*. Until they agree to this, there will exist as much disunity in their pursuits as now exists. Those who are competent to preside at the editorial table should perceive at a glance the consistency of this proposed system. They, moreover, should exert their influence in promulgating the high principles of magnanimity and benevolence of soul.

One truth, however, is particularly impressive, and that is, that if he who wields the pen to inform the public mind through journals and books of the day, does not perceive the importance of these principles of social reform, he is most certainly not qualified for the office which he is compelled by circumstances to occupy. A movement can not be depended upon as commencing in this class, but only among the laboring classes—the *farmers* and the *mechanics*—who, when once organized, will draw the social world into their consociable embrace.

(ANDREW JACKSON DAVIS, 1847; 10TH ED., NEW YORK: 1852; PP. 5–8, 557–66, 569–73, 578–81, 774–75)

# The Occult Life of Jesus of Nazareth

In 1860 Alexander Smyth wrote to the Spiritualist Andrew Jackson Davis about a "series of extraordinary and mysterious internal experiences" that he had endured for several years. "Sometimes I saw or inwardly perceived the main branches of my nervous system burst forth suddenly into beautiful lights of blue and yellow; sometimes down my sides; sometimes along my arms; very often on one side of my face or across my brows." Smyth reported hearing music, sounds, and finally the voices of two men. The voices identified themselves as the spirits of Saul of Tarsus and Judas Iscariot from the spirit world. Their story is related in *The Occult Life of Jesus of Nazareth*, which explains that they had chosen Smyth to serve as their earthly agent as they confessed their evil deeds and revealed their conspiracy to cover up the true history of the life of Jesus. In so confessing, they sought to correct the lies perpetuated in their lifetimes and recorded in the books of the New Testament, a "compilation of misstatements, misconceptions, and perversions." Saul's conversion on the road to Damascus was, he explains, all an act to acquire power for himself; he convinced the Gospel writers of his fabricated account of Jesus' divine mission to further his own ends.

Smyth's life of Jesus was not a popular book, either in his lifetime or thereafter. It is more significant because of the tenacious hold of the ideas it communicates: Jesus was misunderstood in his lifetime and has a secret history that has only been revealed through contemporary communication with the spirit world, and even more intriguingly, his hidden story includes a romance with Mary Magdalene that has been lost to the ages. Both themes are threads that connect Smyth's work to twentieth-century New Age communities such as the Unarius Academy of Science, a system of ideas that combines belief in interplanetary space travel, advanced physics, reincarnation, and communication between this world and spirit worlds. Ruth Norman, or Uriel, one of the founders of the movement, has published several works claiming that Mary was engaged to Jesus and that Jesus' message has been corrupted by the Christian tradition. In like manner, the success of novels such as *The Da Vinci Code* are dependent on conspiracy theories about the efforts of the early church to obscure Mary's importance to Christian history. Although Smyth approaches these subjects in a decidedly Victorian style, the enduring questions about the mysteries of Jesus' life remain.

The selections here focus on the young Jesus (then known as Jose) and his friendship with John, his companion who mistakenly attributes Jose's ability to cure disease to supernatural causes. Meanwhile, Jose gains his knowledge through his travels around the world and work with spiritual adepts. A second episode relates a conversation with his beloved, Mary, in which he convinces her that the entire Jewish tradition is misguided, "nothing more than a figment of the human imagination." In declaring his love for her he also reveals his true mission: He has come to spread word of the True God of Nature and to rid the world of superstition and barbarism.

# The Occult Life of Jesus of Nazareth

## THE EARLY HISTORY OF JESUS.

Friend Alexander, I will not insult your intellect by supposing that you believe there is any truth in the vile and ridiculous account that Luke and I concocted when we wrote the history of Jesus, concerning Mary, the virgin mother—the Holy Ghost in the form of a dove, acting as a proxy for the God of Heaven, in begetting a son who was to be equal to himself, and had existed through all time before he was begotten. I will not insult your reason, by supposing you to believe any part of these silly lies; but I will give you the true account of his youthful days as far as I received it from Jesus himself.

A short time after I had passed into the spirit world, being exiled from all society, in dreary exclusion, I received a visit from the spirit of the much injured Jesus, whom I had caused to be sacrificed to the hatred of the Jewish priests. I quailed before his benign and noble presence, feeling myself unworthy to meet his gaze. He gently rebuked me for the many evils I had done him, saying that he was informed of all by Judas, whom I had sent to the spirit world the same night that Jesus died. He told me that he forgave me for all my wickedness in regard to him, and then he spoke in sympathizing tones of my suffering condition. He said he could not mitigate my agonies, or he would, advising me to repent, aspire after righteousness, and strive to renew my nature for the better; that my wretched exclusion would be terminated in course of time, and I then would be allowed to mingle with the blessed. He then spoke of many parts of his history, enlightening me on many points I knew not before.

As regards his early days, he said that Joseph the carpenter, and his wife, Mary, moved into Nazareth when he was not many days old. Nobody knew from whence they had come. They settled there, and gained the esteem of their neighbors as honest, prudent, working people. He never heard his parents speak of any mysterious or miraculous event in connection with his birth, yet as he grew up he perceived that there was some mystery or doubt concerning him, whispered among the neighbors. Some doubted his being the son of Joseph and Mary. Some went so far as to say that Mary never had a child; for little Jose, as Jesus was called in his youth, had been nourished on goat's milk, and the breast of Mary had never suckled a child, nor did she give any other indications of having become a mother. There were other instances the folks cited, as proof that Jose was not the son of Joseph and Mary. He bore no resemblance in person, disposition or character to them. Whose son was he, then? Nobody knew, if Joseph and Mary were not his parents. However, the child grew in health, strength and great beauty of person. He did not take pleasure in the ordinary mischievous freaks and follies of children, the characteristics of his disposition being mildness, general amiability, and susceptibility to all grave and pious impressions. He was sent to school at the ordinary age to the synagogue of the village, where, as soon as he had mastered the rudiments of the language, he studied with great avidity the subjects of morals, metaphysics and religion, as then taught in the schools. He seemed to possess great intellectual capacity and comprehension, for at the age of fifteen he was pronounced the most intelligent youth and greatest disputer in the synagogue of the village and neighborhood.

As he approached manhood he became acquainted with a youth about his own age, whose name was John, who was the son of a priest, being educated for one of the priesthood. This youth was of a restless, erratic and visionary disposition, not content with the ordinary routine and views of things, for his mind was directed to a series of changes, innovations and reforms, which he was continually suggesting and advocating with the greatest of energy and confidence in his illusions.

The two youths—though very different in dispositions—became inseparable companions, for they found great pleasure in each other's company—not so much because their views in general assimilated, but they found an intense interest in contrasting their dissimilar ideas. They took long rambles together, sometimes being so interested in their discourses that they did not know whither they were going or where they were. Mount Tabor and its environments were frequently the scenes of their disputes and rambles.

One day they were taking a ramble as usual, and they discoursed upon certain moral subjects which were extremely exciting. They had been walking for hours without heeding their course. At length having made a pause they discovered that they were completely lost. They looked around them to discover indications of their whereabouts, but nothing could they see that they knew. The scene presented a grassy vale, along which meandered a small stream. At a short distance, at the foot of a hill, they perceived a small hut constructed of logs, the roof of which being covered with branches, rushes and soil. In front of this building they perceived a human being sitting on a rock. To him they directed their steps, with the view of inquiring their way back to their village. When they arrived at the spot they found the person to be a hoary-headed old man, enveloped in a long black robe, bare-headed, and feet without sandals. They soon came to the conclusion that they had fallen in the way of a recluse.

Having greeted the old man and stated their case, he, with a pleasing smile upon his countenance, gave the desired information, telling them that their case was not an uncommon one, for he had once been a youth himself, and had frequently lost his way, and the sight of realities around him in the pleasing contemplation of airy visions. He then invited them into his habitation, and set before them some food, telling them to rest and refresh themselves. He also invited them to tarry with him the night, as the day was far spent. The young men expressed their sense of his kindness, and gratefully accepted the hospitable invitation. The recluse then replenished his fire with sticks, which was burning in the centre of the hut, and when the day was passed, they all three lounged around it, passing some hours in discourse. The old man seemed to be possessed of a great mind. Whether it came from experience, learning or supernal inspirations, they knew not; but most of his ideas were perfectly new to them, being of the most profound, philosophic nature, giving explanations and revelations of things, which to them had hitherto been as so many mysteries. He spoke of the great mysterious power pervading all nature under the name of God; of the multitude and magnitude of created things; of the different races of men; of their past and present errors; of the gradual progress and capacity of the human mind, and the probability that in course of time mankind will arrive at comparative perfection.

The two young men listened attentively to the old man's discourse, they never before having heard the like. Jose saw clearly that the recluse had got his ideas through experience and deep reflection, while John concluded that no man could speak as he had done unless he was supernaturally inspired. He said to himself, "Certainly this man is a prophet! I will question him, concerning myself."

"My worthy host," said John to the old man, "I must confess that I have never heard a man speak more startling truths than you have done. You certainly must possess the power of prevision and prophecy. I beg of you, if it be so, that you will try your powers upon me, and tell me what will be my career and end of life."

"Young man," answered the recluse, with a serious candor, "you are mistaken in your estimate of me. I candidly tell you that I do not possess the powers of which you speak; nor do I make any pretensions thereto, and all others who assume to be such I consider to be visionary enthusiasts or vile impostors. I consider it impossible with any person on earth, or spirit above, to see a thing that does not exist. Future events we all know do not exist, and as such, they consequently can not be seen or foreseen. But I will tell you what it is possible to do. A man is capable of speaking of probabilities according to the knowledge he may have of the thing in question. For instance, from the insight I have of you I can state some things that may probably occur to you during your lifetime."

"What may they be?" eagerly inquired John.

"They are to this effect," answered the recluse: "You will live a visionary life, meeting many disappointments and disgusts at what you will consider the perversity and wickedness of the world, because it does not prove to be such as you wish it or expect it to be. You will live an erratic and unsocial career, for your nature will find no pleasure in the general society of men. This disposition will lead you into many difficulties; your mind will become unhinged, and your end will be soon and unpleasant."

"Indeed!" exclaimed John, as he reclined himself back, with an air of one disappointed and mortified. "Your estimation of my career is not very promising or flattering. However, there is one comfort; you do not give them as facts, but only as probabilities. But what say you of my companion?" he added, as he pointed to Jose. "Can you not say something better of him?"

"With regard to your companion," said the recluse, as he gazed into the eyes of Jose, "there may be something said of him of a very extraordinary nature."

"If you can foresee anything that will add to my happiness or of that of my fellow men, I pray you let me hear it," observed Jose.

"I perceive, my dear youth," responded the old man as he continued his gaze upon Jose, at the same time feeling of his hand, fingers and wrist with some mysterious motive, "that within you lies latent a great power, which, when brought into action, will influence the minds and act upon the bodies of your fellow men, producing the most extraordinary and astounding results."

Jose started, and a tremulous emotion passed through him at this declaration of the recluse.

"I mean," continued the latter, "that there is within you a mine of nervous power, which, when exercised upon your fellow men, will be capable of ameliorating many of their miseries, by producing the cure of their bodily diseases, and mitigating the severities of others; at the same time it will enable you to command their minds, to lead them from their errors and vices, to better conditions and understandings."

"Oh! blessed will be the day, if that shall prove true," exclaimed Jose as he sprang forward and seized the hand of the old man, which he pressed fervently from the impulse of his joyful excitement. "Make me acquainted with its nature, and convince me of its truth; then I shall be one of the happiest of men."

"There is a principle or power that pervades all animated nature, by some termed life, by others, spirit," observed the old man. "This power is not the same in all beings, especially in man. In some, it is weak; in others it is very strong. Some men who possess this power in an extraordinary degree, are capable of acting upon their weaker fellows, producing good or evil effects, as their dispositions direct them to act. The nature of the effects produced are very various; but when this power is exercised with benevolent designs, much good can be produced to our fellow men, in curing certain diseases, and influencing the mind in the right direction of virtue."

"Oh, most worthy sir," exclaimed Jose, his eyes beaming with enthusiasm and rapture, "make me sensible how I possess this power, for my delight of life is to do good to my fellow men."

"The power, as I said, lies latent within you," replied the recluse. "It requires some other external power to arouse it; and when once brought into action, it will continue in force during your life. I have the happiness to possess that power to a certain extent; and I think, if you give your consent, I shall be enabled to call forth that which lies latent within you."

Jose gave his consent when he and the recluse rose from their seats, while John regarded them in speechless surprise as he remained in his place. The recluse desired Jose to stand erect against the wall of the hut. He then removed his garments, leaving his neck and breast bare; then placing his right hand upon the top of his head and taking his left hand in his other, they remained in this position for some minutes. Then he placed his right hand upon the back of his neck, and his left upon his breast, remaining thus for some minutes. Then he placed both hands upon the sides of his head, and moved them down to the soles of his feet; this he repeated several times. Then he placed both hands upon his shoulders, and slowly moved them down his arms to his fingers, which he repeated several times. At the commencement of this process, Jose felt a sudden icy chill pass through him, which was succeeded by a glow of heat and a tingling sensation all over him externally. All his vital organs seemed to expand and acquire force; his physical and moral energy seemed to become greater.

"Now," said the recluse, as he terminated the last mentioned actions, "let us see whether my anticipations are correct or not."

He then told Jose to stand in front of John, to fix upon his eyes his own steadfast gaze, and to will in his own mind that John should sleep, and then he gave directions to perform certain manipulations, all of which Jose performed accordingly. The result was as the recluse anticipated. John regarded his companion with an incredulous smile, as though he doubted the theory of the recluse; but soon his eyelids drooped, the smile vanished from his lips, his countenance became pale, and the relaxed state of his muscles gave evidence that he was no longer conscious of external things.

"He sleeps," remarked the recluse.

"Wonderful!" exclaimed Jose, as he regarded the result with astonishment, and felt for the old man a degree of profound reverence.

"This sleep," added the recluse, "is very different from the ordinary one of mortals. The mind and all the powers of life are totally abstracted from the corporeal senses, and his individual existence is quiescent to all influences, save that of your own. In fact, his body is totally insensible, and his spirit is subject to your will in all respects, as I will convince you."

The recluse then took a small stick, with which he beat the sleeper over the shoulders and legs, without eliciting any signs of sensibility or motions. Then he gave Jose some directions how to exercise his will-power over him. Jose then stood in front of the sleeper, and with the concentrated energies of his will, commanded the latter to arise and follow him. Immediately the sleeping John arose and stood erect; then, with a fearless step, he followed Jose around the hut, passed out of the door-way, and for a few minutes walked to and fro in front of it; then returning to the hut he was restored to his former position by the side of the fire.

Then Jose, having received instructions from the recluse, by certain counter manipulations restored John to his former state of wakefulness and sensibility. As soon as he had recovered his consciousness he looked around him with astonishment, and said: "Well, this is strange! I really believe that I have slept."

"You have," responded the recluse.

"But did I sleep from my own nature, or from any power exercised over me by my companion?" inquired John.

"You slept," answered the recluse, "through the influence of a power possessed by your companion, which was existing in a latent state within him, and which I aroused to action. This power he has exercised over you, causing your body to become insensible to touch, and your mind and life-powers to concentrate themselves, yet to become subservient to his will."

When the recluse had given this explanation, John raised his eyes to Jose, in which was an expression of reverence and awe; then raising his hands and clasping them together, he exclaimed exultingly, "Glory to the most High! His will is made manifest to me! My suspicions and anticipations are now become realities! The prophets have not spoken in vain assumptions; their words are true!" He then rushed from the hut.

When John had left, the recluse observed "the conduct of your companion is very strange."

"It is to those who know not his nature as well as I do," replied Jose. "He is naturally a great enthusiast, which has impelled him to gather up many chimerical and fanciful notions. From what he has just experienced, some new fanciful notion has just started in his mind concerning me; but I will reason with him to-morrow, and check its further growth."

The recluse and Jose passed some time discoursing upon the nature of the power newly developed in the latter. Full particulars were given by the recluse, according to his experience of its application to the benefit of men; the kind of diseases that would come under its influence; its mode of operation on the mind and body, and many other traits of its nature. To all of this Jose listened with intense interest and joy. Time became far advanced into the night, and as John did not return, they reclined themselves to repose.

About the break of day, John entered the hut, seeming to be much exhausted, as though he had passed the night in wrestling with intense emotions. The two companions then, after thanking their host, took leave of him, and departed for their homes.

As they went along, Jose imparted to John all that had taken place the previous evening concerning the induced sleep of the latter, and some important information he had acquired besides. He endeavored to impress his companion with the idea, that the power he possessed was a natural one, though not possessed by all men. John listened attentively without responding a word, but towards the conclusion of Jose's explanation, he shook his head, and looked up to his friend with an expression that seemed to doubt what he had heard.

"You seem to doubt what I have been saying," observed Jose as he caught the glance of his companion.

"I do, in one respect," replied John. "Your explanation of this mysterious power may be all true, excepting, as I think, your inference that it is natural to man. I doubt that."

"Then how do you view it?" inquired Jose with surprise.

"I have my ideas upon the subject," replied John, "but I do not wish to state them now. Let us cease to speak of it, and hasten home."

The two companions then continued their route in silence, each being absorbed in his own thoughts. As they came within a short distance of Nazareth, they entered an humble habitation by the roadside to see one of the neighboring families.

The people were poor, and the wife and mother was afflicted with severe neuralgic pains. As soon as Jose perceived the case of the poor woman, a thought struck him that this would be a good opportunity to test his mysterious power in the cure of diseases, and he therefore resolved to make the attempt. Calling the woman to him he addressed her in a soothing strain touching her malady; and when he perceived that he had wrought her mind to a befitting tone, he manipulated her from head to foot, exerting the full energy of his will to scatter the disease, and gently touched with his fingers the most afflicted parts. In a few seconds the woman declared herself relieved of her pains, and said she was cured. Unspeakable was the astonishment of the family, and great was their joy and gratitude. The eyes of Jose were lit up with great pleasure, while John stood with eyes fixed upon his companion.

"Come, John, let us depart," said Jose, as he took the latter by the wrist, and broke the spell that was upon him. They then passed into the road; but John, instead of walking by the side of Jose, followed a little in the rear.

"Why do you linger behind, John?" inquired Jose of his companion.

"It is not becoming in me to place myself on an equality with you any longer," replied John, in a troubled voice. "Hitherto we have been familiar companions, bound to each other by the bonds of friendship, but now a line of distinction must be drawn between us. Our companionship must give place to that of master and servant, and my friendship must be replaced by love, reverence and duty."

"By the Holy of Holies," exclaimed Jose, as he regarded his companion with the greatest astonishment. "Are you crazy, John? Whom do you take me to be?"

"The truth must no longer be withheld," replied John seriously. "The Lord has made his will and ways manifest to me this day, and the words of the prophet are come true, when he said,: 'Behold my servant whom I uphold; mine elect, in whom I am delighted. I have put my spirit upon him.' Yes, Jose, you are the blessed one of whom the prophet has been speaking. That mysterious power you have of doing good, is supernatural, which is confirmatory of the truth. I can no longer doubt of your being the—"

John paused, as though he were afraid to utter the next word that would have completed his declaration. Then Jose seized him by the upper part of his tunic, and gazed intently into his eyes for a few moments, and then said, "The what?"

"The Messiah!" responded John, humbly and reverently.

There was a pause in their discourse as the two youths regarded each other for some time with great intentness, the expression of John's countenance being that of humility and reverence, while that of Jose, in the commencement seemed to be astonishment and displeasure at what he considered John's infatuation. But as he continued his gaze the perception broke upon him that John was no longer of sane mind; then the sternness of his looks relaxed, assuming one of commiseration.

"John," exclaimed Jose at length, as he released hold of the former, "you certainly must be crazy to entertain so preposterous a thought. The foolish books you study have unhinged your mind. I beg of you, if you wish to be my friend and companion for the future, that you will never mention to me or anyone else the like again."

John made no response, but with a sullen air and dissatisfied feelings he followed his friend on their return to the village.

This event placed a restraint upon the friendly intercourse of the two young men, so that from that time their intercourse was much restricted. John confined himself to his studies, and Jose attended to his father's business. Nothing was known among the neighbors why the two young men were not so friendly as usual; but by some means it became known that Jose possessed a wonderful power of curing and mitigating certain diseases, which soon spread through the village and around the neighborhood. Jose was accordingly besought to exercise his power to the benefit of the afflicted. The result was, that many who were diseased were made sound, and many others were relieved, and by which he gained many friends bound to him in gratitude. Some persons there were who became jealous of his skill and popularity, and fearful of losing their own influence, thought proper to thwart and misrepresent him, so that while some were giving him all due praise, others were sarcastically hinting that he was a doubtful or bad character.

This state of circumstances surrounded Jose until he had arrived at the age of manhood, when an event happened which very much changed them. Joseph the carpenter, his reputed father, died. He had been prosperous at his business during his residence at Nazareth, one main cause of which was the industry and general good conduct of Jose, so that he had accumulated some wealth, which he had the good sense to divide between his wife and Jose.

Soon after the burial of his father, Jose converted all his means into money, and with the permission of his mother, he resolved to travel into distant countries to see the world and gain knowledge. His arrangements were soon made; but before taking his departure he had a friendly interview with his former companion, John. They discoursed long together. John was sorely distressed upon this occasion. He ventured to express once more to Jose that he believed him to be the true Messiah as spoken of by the prophets. He begged Jose to acknowledge himself to be such, and to let him declare it to the world; but Jose remained inflexible to all his beseechings in that respect. At length they parted, with the compromised understanding that after a number of years, when Jose should return from his travels, if they should accord in their general views, they would go forth together, and preach to the world reform and repentance.

Jose then set out upon his travels. He visited Egypt, Greece and Italy, and some other countries. After some years, when he was about thirty years of age, he returned to Judea. When at Jerusalem he met John. They soon after made their appearance in public, under conditions as will be explained hereafter.

"I have now, friend Alexander," resumed the spirit Saul, "given you the early history of Jesus of Nazareth, which was imparted to me by himself at the time he visited me in my exile from the happy Spiritual societies. I shall now with the assistance of Judas give you his after history—that tragic narrative in which Judas and I were the principal actors. I shall not pretend to give yon the incidents in detail and in such connection as to form a unity of the whole; but will deliver them as they occur to my memory: nor shall I take up your time in description more than is actually necessary. My intent will be to furnish you with all the material facts and scenes, but leave the rest to your own taste, skill, learning and prudence, to make any addition, illustration or embellishment you may think necessary, to produce a united and comprehensive true history, such as will be easy of comprehension and agreeable to the people you live among. When you shall have accomplished this task, you will then issue it to the world, calling upon all Christendom to read it, that they may no longer live in error and misconception of the truths therein stated. The Christian clergy, after reading my historical revelations, will no longer have a just excuse in maintaining a system of baneful doctrines, which I, Saul, expose and denounce.

The task I have assigned to you is a laborious one for a man in your circumstances; but be not discouraged. It is a debt of justice due to humanity that I owe, and shall be enabled to pay through your labors. You will confer great benefits upon your fellow men, and though you may not meet with a just reward in your mortal life, be assured that you will obtain it in the world of spirits."

"Before I proceed to my task, I wish to ask a question," I said to my communicating spirit.

"What is it?" demanded Saul.

"I wish to know," I said, "what has become of the spirit Jesus."

"After his kind visit to me," replied Saul, "in which he made me acquainted with many secret points of his history that was not known to any other spirit or mortal, he took leave of me, and soon after was translated to the highest sphere of beauty and bliss; since then, I have not seen or heard of him."

---

According to the desire and commands of the spirits, Saul and Judas, I had about forty communications with them, in which they presented me a series of facts and incidents concerning the history of Jesus during the latter part of his career on earth, and the parts they performed therein.

These communications were given to me by the spirits taking possession of my mind about one hour each day, when, usurping all my mental powers and functions, they produced a series of visions similar to beautiful and well connected dreams. Scenery, characters or personages, dialogues and actions transpired in regular succession and order, like a performance upon a theatrical stage. I was the only spectator, though I had no other conception of myself than that of a conscious perceptive essence, with the power of perceiving the hidden feelings and unspoken thoughts of the visionary personages before me, the medium.

---

## VISION FOURTH.

The dazzling orb of day had for hours disappeared below the horizon, and the less lustrous lamp of night was suspended high in the heavens above Mount Olivet, diffusing her silvery beams of tranquil light and soothing influence over and around the humble village of Bethany, which, like an eagle's eyry, was perched in the cleft of the mountain.

Within the vast expanse of the celestial vault myriads of stars with ceaseless light, unobstructed by cloud or mist, contributed their powers to illuminate and adorn the scene of night. The air was soft and agreeably tempered, redolent with numerous agreeable odors exhaled from trees, from blossoms, from healing shrubs and beauteous flowers. All lights were extinguished in the humble dwellings; all was peace and quietness, for all the worthy people, excepting two, had retired to rest from the toils of the day.

With noiseless steps and hand in hand that two emerged from the dwelling of Lazarus, crossed the enclosed yard, and entered the garden near by. One was a man of tall, commanding figure and majestic mein; the other a female much less in stature, of delicate, sylphlike form, whose sparkling eyes told a tale of love and present happiness. Both persons were enveloped in their mantles which covered their heads, shoulders and busts as a means of guarding against the night dew.

As soon as they had entered the garden the female leaned upon her companion's arm, and her eyes beaming with pure affection looked up to him, seeking an exchange of glances. The man with looks of tenderness and solicitude gently supported her delicate form, as in a voice sweet and musical he poured into her ears words of sacred intelligence, tales of interest, and declaration of secret thoughts and feelings congenial to her soul. As thus they discoursed they paced to and fro the smooth walks belonging to this beautiful parterre, or under the fruit trees on the borders thereof.

"Mary," said the female's companion, as he raised his hand and eyes towards the firmament with a serene expression of countenance, "does this scene not impress thee as being one of great beauty and magnificence?"

"Yes, Jose," replied the maiden in great sweetness of tone. "This scene of night is truly beautiful. This night seems to impress me with its beauty and magnificence more than any night I have noticed for many years. I know not how it is, for I am of simple mind, not knowing how to appreciate such scenes of grandeur; but I know that I have frequently paced this garden in the tranquil hours of night, and never have I felt as I do now. When I gazed upon the starry firmament with all its glittering lights, and endeavored to imagine what they were, I found my mind a blank. I seemed to be an insignificant speck not included in any of the great systems of greatness and grandeur. All things impressed me with a chill; the forest-covered hills and green sloping valleys seemed cheerless. I felt a sadness of heart. I found myself, as it were, alone in the world and unhappy. Ah! how great the change this day and night since thou hast returned to me, Jose! Now all things seem bright and smiling. My mountain home looks picturesque and beautiful. Mount Olivet never looked so gay, with her olive and fig trees, her orchards and vineyards with their luscious fruits. Even the red barren hills eastward down to Jordan, the dread Lake Asphaltis, and the mountains of Moab seem more cheerful to my view, while the humble dwelling of my father I would not exchange for a palace. Ah! Jose, my heart is now over-flowing with happiness so exquisite and ineffably sweet! Tell me, Jose, how all this change is produced within me."

As Mary uttered the latter part of her speech her companion seemed to undergo great emotion, as though some feeling or sentiment that his good nature prompted him to acknowledge he was about to reveal, yet prudence compelled him to suppress. His eyes became averted from the loving gaze of the fair maiden, and a slight tremor passed through him. After a few moments' silence in which he struggled to gain his composure, he replied with calmness:

"Mary, I am happy to perceive that the reminiscences of our youthful days are not obliterated from thy memory, and that the brotherly love and pure friendship we formerly entertained for each other burns as brightly and as holy as ever in thy pure heart. That it is so I am convinced from the pleasure and happiness thou dost manifest at my presence, giving to thee that happy tone of feeling which makes all things around thee appear so bright and beautiful; it is the re-awakening of thy sisterly love and pure friendship."

"Sisterly love and pure friendship!" exclaimed Mary, repeating the words of Jose in a tone of aversion. "I have a sincere love for my sister, a deep filial love for my father, and a great friendship for all mankind; yet none of these are like unto the affection which I entertain for thee, Jose."

"Mary, thou art all innocence and pure affection," replied Jose, as he placed his arm around the maiden and pressed her to his breast. "Thy love is beyond all price, and happy will be the lot of that man who shall possess and enjoy it. I am aware of the tender relations that exist between us, the claim and command I have over thy pure affections; yet, Mary, there is a Being greater than I who ought to command thy attention and share thy love before me; a Being who is the source or fountain of all love under whatever form it is manifested on earth. Every passional emotion of love that vibrates in the heart or thrills through the nerves, emanated from and once formed a part of that great mysterious power which we all feel, yet whose perfect nature we know not. Let us then for the present, Mary, cease to talk of our egotistical love, and talk of Him from whom all love cometh."

"Dost thou mean the God of our Fathers, Jose?" inquired Mary.

"I mean the God of the Universe, Mary," replied Jose sternly.

"I have been taught," said Mary, "to believe in one great God, Jehovah by name, who made this world and all mankind; who selected the Children of Israel as a choice and favored people; who sent his servant Moses to lead them from the bondage of Egypt, and then gave to him a table of laws, by which they should be governed. To this God I have been taught to render due homage, praise and glory. Such are the limits of my understanding thereon."

"Mary," replied Jose in a tone of gravity and with an expression of solemn earnestness, "I wish not to shock the self-reliance of thy young inexperienced mind; but the love of eternal justice and immutable truth as well as my duty to thee compel me to declare that all thy conceptions of the Deity, which thou callest the God of our Fathers, are but so many gross errors, that have no existence in the nature of the true God of the universe, who is the Master and Father of all things around us."

"Errors!" exclaimed Mary in surprise and trembling. "Errors sayest thou, Jose! Are not the words of our priesthood, and of our holy books all true? They declare that there is but one God, Jehovah, who descended upon Mount Sinai, and amidst lightnings and earthquakes made compacts for his favored people."

"No, Mary," answered Jose emphatically; and his eyes became expressive of an aroused energy and zeal. "It is all imposture, fiction and lies so gross and absurd in their nature that to connect them with the idea of the true God, is to utter blasphemy and wickedness.

"The God in whom thou hast been taught to believe under the name of Jehovah, is nothing more than a figment of the human imagination, bearing a correspondence in its nature and attributes to the traits of character and peculiarities of man. The Gods as worshiped by mankind in every country and in all ages, have been represented in their natures according to the gross conceptions of the people of the time and place. They are the ideal images designed by certain cunning men to represent and account for the various mysterious phenomena of nature of which man has hitherto been ignorant. Mankind in their primitive savage state worship the phenomena of nature under various hideous and fanciful forms; and as they progress in their social relations and expand in mind, so do their Gods make a corresponding change of form and attributes.

"When a nation of people are savage, cruel, fickle and unjust, the Gods of that people are the same, and as the nation advances in intelligence, virtue and reason, their conceptions of their Gods make a similar advance. This relation between mankind and their Gods has proven true in all times and countries, and is the case with the race of people of which we are. What were the Gods of our forefathers before the time of Moses? Were not our forefathers ignorant savages in bondage to the Egyptians, so void of intelligence that they knew not their origin? Did they not render homage to beasts, birds and reptiles as their Gods? Yes, such was their gross, groveling state, and such their gross conceptions of the superhuman powers!

"This state lasted for ages, and until one among them who had been reared under more favorable circumstances, possessing some intelligence, vast cunning and a bold spirit, called his brethren together, broke their bondage and led them forth in triumph from their masters, to seek a new country where he could establish them as a nation. This was Moses who, seeing the necessity of uniting his people by some powerful tie, seized the occasion to establish a new God. And what was this God, this Great Jehovah, but an ideal figment that originated in his mind, whose attributes correspond in nature to the character of Moses' self; a being of absolute rule—bold, terrible, cruel, vindictive and unrelenting; possessed of firmness and weakness; of power, and yet impotent; of justice, and yet unjust; of love and hatred; of steadfastness and fickleness; of intelligence, and yet ignorant; of truth and falsehood; and of all other qualities, some good and some evil. Such was the God established by Moses, and such was Moses in character. This God as established by Moses was good for the people under the time and circumstances in which they were placed, as it was somewhat superior to their previous state of gross ignorance. But now the times have changed; there is more knowledge existing in the minds of men than before; and the evils arising from this barbarous superstition are more apparent and more grievous to bear. Therefore it becomes our duty to discard the relics of previous barbarism, and to lift up our thoughts in search of the True God of Nature."

While Jose was delivering the preceding discourse, Mary continued to gaze upon him with the greatest astonishment, and with some degree of terror in her countenance, it being the first time she had ever heard sentiments expressed so opposed to the education she had received. In the simplicity of her mind she had never doubted or questioned the truth or origin of the Jewish theogony; and had they been uttered by any other lips she would have considered them as the greatest blasphemy; but coming from him whose word she had hitherto considered as truth and wisdom she felt confounded for a time, not knowing what to think or how to decide—whether to renounce the belief to which she had been educated, or admit the truths as delivered in Jose's words.

For a few moments there was silence in which Jose gazed penetratingly into the face of the maiden to discover what effect his words had produced, while she was struggling to collect her thoughts and regain sufficient composure to form them into words. At length, drawing closer to her companion and placing her right hand upon his shoulder, as she looked up to him with great seriousness of expression, she said in a grave tone of voice:

"O, Jose, what strange and fearful words are these thou hast uttered? Is it possible that thou art serious and true in all thou hast said, and that all my education on these matters is nothing but a system of error and imposture? Is it possible that the great system of Priesthood and all pertaining to it, as established by Moses and continued to the present day, is no more than a grand scheme of imposture and knavery? Is it possible that I, a true believer and humble devotee of the Great Jehovah, know nothing of the true God of the Universe?"

"It is even so," replied Jose in a tone of great sweetness. "Let not the truths I utter affright thy young mind. Look at them boldly, and thou wilt find that truth is more inviting and amiable when once seen, than error and falsehood, though the latter may be better known to thee. In that which I have said, I have spoken in seriousness, with a sense of its responsibility. Thou knowest I never speak otherwise. It is also true that the priesthood of Jerusalem's Temple and all pertaining to it are nothing but a grand scheme of imposture and knavery, and that its devotees know no more of the true God than the babe just born."

"O! Jose, Jose," cried Mary piteously. Reclining her head upon his breast, she clung to him as though for protection. "Have mercy upon my ignorance and weak nature. I have no reason to doubt thy words, for they have always had the power to sink deep into my mind, leaving there the impress of truth and wisdom. But now, dear Jose, this discourse of thine has wrought me great uneasiness. I feel a void in my mind since thou hast destroyed the main structure of my education. I feel as nothing compared to my former self. Do not, therefore, deprive me of those errors and false notions that I have been taught to believe sacred, unless thou canst fill up the void with something of greater substance and beauty. Give me at least one idea of that true God of whom thou hast hinted, but not yet fully spoken."

"I will, Mary," answered Jose quickly. "Let now all thy senses awaken to receive impressions from the beauteous and magnificent universe. Let thy soul open and expand its recipient powers so as to embrace the brilliant truths which the phenomena of nature shall present to thee. Let thy spirit awaken and expand its wings, soaring with me to various realms, where the beauty, power, wisdom and magnificence of the Universal God are displayed."

Jose then extended his right hand towards the starry heavens, and added in a tone of voice, calm and grave, as his countenance seemed to be illumined with a sacred fervor, while the glance of Mary following in the direction indicated, was of an absorbing, solemn interest.

"Behold, Mary, the vast expanse of firmament above and around us! Regard this beauteous moon whose silvery tranquil beams serve as a lamp of night to illumine this earth in the absence of the lustrous orb of day; and notice the twinkling stars whose numbers are innumerable, which not only contribute their share of nocturnal light but give to the celestial scene a solemn beauty and grandeur. What thinkest thou, Mary, constitute the substance and nature of these celestial lights? In other words, what are they?"

"What are they!" exclaimed Mary in surprise at the question. "Are they not what our reverend Rabbi have taught us that they are? Is not the moon a great light to rule the night as the sun does the day? Are not the stars so many smaller lights, like so many torches attached to the vault of the firmament, to light up and adorn the scene of night?"

"Such is the answer I expected from thy innocent but misinformed mind, Mary," replied Jose in a tone of gentleness, though a smile slightly curled his lip. "But mark me, such a view of things is erroneous. They are fabulous notions taken from the mystical lore of the Rabbi. I who have traveled and conversed with sages of many countries, have reason to know better. I, therefore, declare to thee, Mary, what thou considerest as so many lights to rule and adorn the scene of night, are so many suns and worlds, similar to the one we live in."

"Worlds!" ejaculated Mary in astonishment as she regarded Jose doubtingly for a moment, and then with steady gaze she peered into the starry firmament.

"Yes, Mary, worlds," resumed Jose. "Worlds and suns innumerable! Families of suns, worlds and moons similar to our own, so numerous that it would be as easy for a man to count the particles of sand in the desert as to number the worlds that exist through the vast extent of universal space. To thy naked eye these starry luminaries seem no larger than a common torch, and according to the deep and profound learning of the Rabbis they are represented as such, yet the smallest of them is nearly as large as the earth we inhabit, while the greater portion are hundreds and even thousands of times greater in bulk. Of such vast extent is the distance of the nearest star that a bird of the swiftest wing could not fly the same extent of space in many thousands of years. All these suns and worlds possess peculiar motions, giving the changes of night and day as well as seasons, which are continued incessantly to all eternity. Moons around worlds, worlds around suns, and suns with their families of worlds, making a gradual revolution around some central spot in the universe. Within this central spot we may suppose exists that Great Power, that Great Soul and Mind which is the source of all life that exists throughout the boundless expanse of matter and space; He, the great God of life, of light, of love and motion, whom all mankind feel and acknowledge, but whose nature and person no one has been enabled to define!"

"What wonderful and fearful ideas thou bringest to my view,

dear Jose," said Mary in a tremulous tone of voice. "How different are thy conceptions of these mysteries to that of our Rabbi!"

"Thou sayest truly, sweet maiden," replied Jose. "The God of our Fathers as represented by our Father Moses and his successors, was the creation of their ignorant minds, possessing all the weaknesses, limited powers and turbulent passions of the people of those days. But the great God of Nature, as I will represent him to thee according to my intuitive ideas, is a much different being to the Jehovah of Moses.

"Thus, Mary, thou must endeavor to imagine the mighty power, greatness and wisdom of this Great God who could and has done all these mighty works, for words will fail to describe them. Compare the mightiness of this great God with the absurd and ridiculous representation of the great Jehovah as given by our forefathers who waged a petty warfare with an Egyptian King to obtain the release of our forefathers from bondage. Consider how the great Jehovah entered into a contest with the Egyptian jugglers to see who could work the greatest feat; the palm of success being at length conceded to him by his producing some vermin of the meanest and most loathsome kind. After all the display of his mighty powers he could not bend the Egyptian King to his wishes, so he caused the Children of Israel to flee by night. Then he induced them to wander in the deserts for many years searching for a home where they suffered all kinds of deprivations and miseries. On the top of Mount Sinai he declares himself to his people, giving to them the Decalogue which he had inscribed on two tablets of stone; and though it is said he made the earth and whole universe in six days yet it took him forty to make the inscribed tablets. Under the guidance of this God and his servant Moses our poor ignorant forefathers wandered and suffered for forty years, when at last they were enabled to seize some land where to establish a home by murdering and robbing the Canaanites. This God of our forefathers is not only cruel and unjust to other nations, but he is full of wrath and vengeance to his favorite people, for at times he slaughtered them by thousands with sword, disease and famine.

"How great is the contrast, Mary, between the God of our forefathers and the great true God, whom I am endeavoring to bring to thy comprehension."

Jose paused for a few moments and regarded the countenance of Mary, to discover the effect of his words, while she, raising her beautiful hazel eyes, met his glance half-way. No terror or superstitious awe was expressed in her glance as before, when the name of Jehovah was mentioned, but the expression was indicative of rational thought and firmness, as she observed with a sober energy of voice:

"Jose, I now perceive that my education has been one of error and imposture. I now begin to comprehend some of the startling truths which thou hast endeavored to impress upon my young, misguided mind. Things which were taught me as sacred, I now begin to view in their true shapes and colors, as things of distorted imagination, ignorance and imposture. I henceforth discard all such absurdities, as lies and impositions, and I shall hold myself impressive to all the lights of truth, pertaining to the true and only God of the universe.

"O! Jose," added Mary after a slight pause, in which she drew herself closer to him, regarding him with a look of mingled love and reverence, "when I look upon thy noble person, hear the music of thy voice and consider the wisdom of thy words, it seems to me that I am in the presence of one far greater than human. I feel a spell come over me filling me with mingled love, admiration and reverence. I pray thee, then, to continue thy teaching, scattering a few more seeds of intelligence upon my simple mind, that they may take root and spring up like beauteous flowers, exhaling delicious odors, in honor of the great God of whom thou hast been speaking."

"O! Mary," replied Jose in a tone of great tenderness, "pure and innocent as thou art, thou art worthy of the love of thy Maker, and as such art capable of understanding his nature. Thou art now enabled to perceive that the God as worshiped by our forefathers and our present people, is a figment of barbarous imagination, worshiped only by such as are lost in ignorance and insensible to noble manhood; but the Great God of the universe is a Divine Father, by whose divine love all passive matter has been endowed with life. His wisdom and goodness conceived the plan which extends from the time of acting through all eternity. It was his divine essence of love that united atom to atom in bonds of sympathy and holy wedlock; from which sprang minerals, crystals, vegetables and animals of every kind, hue and figure. This ascending and progressive work of organization was prosecuted by a series of successive spheres of developments bound together by the bonds of mutual interest and dependence. The higher being developed from the combined energy of all the lower, until the powers of each sphere were developed to the ultimate design. When the organization of man became sufficiently developed and matured, it became qualified to receive the impress of the positive spirit of God upon the tablet of its interior life, and by which he became developed into a spiritual intelligence which constituted him an offspring of the divine essence of love and mind. It is thus by the development of this interior spiritual intelligence mankind became the children of God. When God's children can be no longer sustained upon earth, he receives them within his own mansion under his own especial care, where the elements of their spiritual being become developed into a still higher state of perfection, and they become more worthy of their Maker.

"Yes, Mary, the great God I am endeavoring to bring to thy notice is the father of us all as well as the life spring of the universe. His inherent and unchangeable attributes are power, wisdom and love. By his divine love, he felt the impulse to awaken and form all passive matter into the beauteous universe, as we behold it. By his infinite wisdom he was enabled to plan and design it to go into operation; and by his almighty power, he was enabled to put it into execution. By his fatherly solicitude for all that he had produced, he has controlled, and still continues to govern every thing in order, with the hope that his magnificent works will ultimately redound to his glory and satisfaction."

"Is the love that is felt in the human breast anything akin to the love of this divine Father?" inquired Mary timidly.

"It is, though not in the same degree," replied Jose. "It springs from the same source, modified to suit every sentient being of the earth. It comes from the divine essence of our heavenly Father's self. It penetrates through all material things, thrilling throughout the being, and swelling the bosom of our mother Nature. The most minute atoms are brought into holy alliance by its divine sympathy, and every germ of the vegetable world that bursts into life, expanding in beauty, kissed by the beams of light, and nursed by the honey dews of heaven, is conceived in love by this divine essence. Every creeping or aerial being, fly or insect, re-produces its kind from the same power. Every innocent bird with beautiful plumage that coos, bills and mates, is under the same divine influence; and all other animals are bound to transmit their kind to succeeding times by this process of love and parental solicitude. In mankind there is a modification of this passion of love which adds to his bliss and exaltation.

"The passion of love with all other animals is confined to the earth, dying out with the animal when it has run its course; but in man it is not so. The conjugal love of man and woman, coupled with pure and holy desires, develops all the divine affections which are necessary to man's happiness on earth; and when it is commingled with noble aspirations and exalted ideas, aspiring to all that is beautiful, lovely, good and magnanimous, then it will open to him an inheritance in the realms of bliss, after he shall have passed his terrestrial career. Then he enters the presence of his divine Father, to receive a welcome to his new home and state of everlasting bliss."

"Oh, Jose! dearest Jose!" exclaimed Mary in a tone expressive of great excitement, as she disengaged herself from his arms, and stood at a small distance before him, with one of her hands upon her breast and the other extended, her whole person seeming to be wrought up to an ungovernable pitch of intense feeling, her Cheeks glowing with the vermillion blood; her nostrils expanding and quivering, inhaling deep draughts from the external air; and her eyes gazing upon him with an intensity of love and suspense. After a few moments' pause, in which she endeavored to lessen the throbs of her heart, she added:

"Jose, pardon me if I do or say anything unseemly in thy sight, for the subtle powers of my nature are now beyond control. Eagerly have I listened to the wisdom of thy words, in bringing to my untutored mind a knowledge of the true God. Clearly and justly do I appreciate thy explanation of his divine nature; how his divine love is the active principle which has brought all things into existence, continuing them from age to age by the same power. With rapture have I understood that it is this same love that exists within the breasts of all mortal beings, the ties that bind us to each other, the parent to the child and the child to the parent;

man to woman, and woman to man. All this I can appreciate, therefore I know that thy words are true.

"Yes, Jose, for years has this subtle mysterious passion been nestling and growing within this breast of mine. From day to day and year to year has it been increasing in strength and purity, praying for the happy moment when it should burst from its concealment, and declare itself to the object of its adoration. That moment is now, Jose. I will not and cannot suppose that thou art ignorant as to whom my love is devoted; for thou with all thy wisdom can easily penetrate the innermost secrets of my heart, yet from some secret prudence thou hast delayed to call forth the confessions of my soul, therefore I am compelled to declare that it is thou, Jose, who art the object of my love. Think not amiss of me if I make this confession. If this love, as thou hast taught me, comes from the divine nature of the great God of the universe, is it not holy, just and pure? And if it be natural to all beings of our kind why should I conceal it? If thou seekest for a love of the highest type which shall open an inheritance for thee to that immortal blessed state of existence hereafter of which thou hast spoken, have I not a just plea in defence of my love? All my pure desires, noble aspirations and exalted ideas are concentrated in thee. Wilt thou accept my love, Jose?"

While Mary was making her passionate declaration Jose remained immovable, devouring with greedy ear the outpourings of her innocent and ardent love; but at the termination of her discourse he averted his eyes for a few moments, which he passed in reflection, and recovering the equilibrium of his emotions, he at length raised his eyes, which beamed with great tenderness, and replied in a tone of voice tremulous with emotion:

"Beloved maiden, the time, as thou sayest, has come when the ties that bind our hearts together should be defined and understood. When we were children strolling over the hills of Nazareth, we loved as children allied by the ties of brotherly affection; but as we grew older our attachment grew closer, more sacred and interesting; then we termed it friendship. Since our separation at our native village our attachment has become greater, deeper, more fervid and dependent upon each other for worldly bliss. Our hearts, though separated by distance, have communed with each other, and our two souls have mingled into one, like commingling dew drops on a flower. Our desires, our hopes and aspirations have reflected each other's image. Our hearts have beaten in unison, and our spirits spoken with the same tongue. In all this there has been a rapture too deep, heartfelt and abiding in this mysterious mutual feeling, to be expressed by the cold word of friendship. What then is it but love?"

"Then thou dost love me, Jose?" interposed Mary in a state of thrilling suspense.

"With a pure and holy love I love thee, Mary," answered Jose. Then a wild shrill shriek of joy was uttered by Mary as she sprang forward and threw herself upon the neck of Jose, who with loving fervor clasped her in his arms.

Some minutes elapsed in silence, during which the two lovers in close embrace intermingled that mysterious magnetic aura which under various external demonstrations produced the thrilling sensation of love.

At length when their ecstatic feelings of joy had somewhat subsided and consciousness returned to inferior objects of sense, Jose gently raised his head, after imprinting his lips for the last time upon those of the now happy maiden, and addressed her in tones of the greatest tenderness.

"Mary, beloved maiden, whose love is as pure and ardent as the rays of light emanating from the dazzling sun, long have I anticipated this happy moment, and long have I feasted in imaginary bliss that I should enjoy when our mutual love should be made known to each other. But perhaps thou hast thought me remiss or somewhat mysterious in my conduct if I loved thee, that I should be so long absent from thy side. Let me therefore explain."

"Jose," responded Mary in joyous emotion as she threw her arms around the neck of her lover, and gazed upon his manly countenance with a look of fond devotion; "Jose, I have no complaint to urge against thee. Since thou hast accepted my love and acknowledged a return, I feel myself extremely happy; all my past grievances, anxieties and suspense are banished forever, and I may say that I never felt a pang during thy absence that my present bliss does not more than repay."

"Sweet maiden," replied Jose, "thou art worthy of all the joy of which the human heart is susceptible. This I can declare in truth, that ever since we parted at Nazareth thy image has ever been present to me. Three objects have influenced and impelled me during my wanderings in foreign countries, which I have ever considered as so many sacred duties. One was to investigate and inquire as far as man possibly could into the nature of the Deity. Another was to render myself worthy of his love; and the other was to render myself worthy of my Mary's love. With a knowledge of God, possessing his love in heaven, with my Mary's love on earth, I thought I should be extremely blessed. This has been my aim and achievement. But now, Mary, I have something to say that will not be so pleasant for thee to hear."

Jose then proceeded to inform the maiden more in detail of the objects of his pursuits during his travels, which were to discover men's notions or positive knowledge of the Deity. That after ten years' travel and study he had been enabled to gain considerable knowledge thereon—at least enough to infer that the Jewish system of theology and theogony were base, vicious and absurd. He had, therefore, determined to return to his country, and would endeavor to enlighten his people as to the nature of the true God, and the vile system of things taught by the Priesthood and their books.

He told her also that since his return he had seen John the Baptist, who had invited and pressed him to receive baptism at his hand. He stated, that though he did not admire the character of John or his doctrines generally, yet as to baptism he saw nothing very objectionable. He thought it might possibly have a good effect on and among the people, therefore he consented that John should baptize him. After that he intended to commence his task of teaching the people.

Mary expressed her uneasiness at the prospect of being again separated from the object of her love; but Jose soothed her fears and reasoned away her objections by telling her that he would not be far away, nor long at a time; and after a while when he should have made some progress in establishing his views among the people, he would return to unite their loves in holy wedlock.

Mary at length gave her assent to all Jose proposed, agreeing to wait with cheerful resignation the deferred time of their happy union. Jose then stated that he must take his departure on the morrow for the neighborhood of the Jordan, to prepare for the forthcoming ceremony of John's baptism.

With a firm reliance on each other's love and faithfulness, with joyous hearts at the present, and blissful anticipations of the future, the two lovers returned to the house, and separated to their respective chambers.

(ALEXANDER SMYTH, 1864; REV. ED., CHICAGO, IL: 1899)

# The Rise and Progress of the Kingdoms of Light and Darkness

Lorenzo Dow Blackson was a self-educated Methodist preacher with grand ambitions—not for himself, but for the future of his fellow African Americans in the unfolding of sacred history. In keeping with his commitment to simplicity and humility, he referred to his 1867 work of more than three hundred pages as a "feeble essay," but in its pages he spun an elaborate tale of epic battles against the cosmic forces of evil. Modeling his work after John Bunyan's *Pilgrim's Progress,* Blackson's work is a Christian allegory; unlike Bunyan's classic tale of the individual traveler working toward eternal salvation, *Rise and Progress* tells a story of collective racial striving.

Blackson's text did not receive much attention in his lifetime, nor has it since. But it is a critically important window into the religious worlds of African American Protestants as they used literary means to combat white racism, boost the morale of their race, and secure their own places as Americans and as Christians. Both the form and content of Blackson's work counter the claims made by many whites of the day that Christian history was a story of a civilized Europe and America battling the evil heathens in other parts of the world. Instead, Blackson casts all of world history as a conflict between the kingdom of light and the kingdom of darkness, both of which exist in all nations; within this framework, he explains racialized oppression as one among many battles in an enduring contest. The analogy of Christian salvation and emancipation from slavery was essential to Blackson and other black ministers: Just as individuals needed redemption from the shackles of their personal sins, African Americans also sought collective liberation. In this sense, his work echoes the sentiments of many African American church leaders of his day.

The book opens with a recapitulation of the biblical account of creation described in the Book of Genesis, and then moves through key moments from the Old and New Testaments and into modern history, culminating in a "description of the last great battle between these two great powers . . . a war of extermination." In the course of his story, Blackson discusses the Reformation, the American Revolution, the rise of Protestant denominationalism, the major world religions, the independent black church movement, and the persistence of racism following the abolition of slavery in the United States. Blackson sets his account in a military framework, undoubtedly influenced by the recent Civil War. God became "King Alpha" or the "King of Light," and the heroes became the "Soldiers of Light" comprised of various "regiments" that the king led into battle. In these excerpts, Blackson discusses the significance of Christ's sacrifice and resurrection and outlines American history through the lens of racial and religious warfare. He combines racial, biblical, national, and ecclesiastical commentary as a way of situating African Americans and steering them toward a brighter future.

# The Rise and Progress of the Kingdoms of Light and Darkness

I left you where King Alpha, who is also called Shiloh, agreed at an appointed time and place to meet Justice, and then and there to pay him all of his demand. So now the day and time having come, he went forth unto a mountain called Calvary, where Justice met Him, having his whole bill and account fully made out, and he declared that silver and gold would avail nothing towards paying this demand, as they in this respect were corrupt. Neither would the blood of bullocks and heifers, nor turtle doves and pigeons, avail anything towards settling this claim legally held against man. But that the whole law must be kept, and that honor that is due to the great Majesty on high must be fully paid to Him. And to seal the whole and make man's pardon sure on condition of repentance and future obedience and believing in King Messiah, and that for this cause King Messiah should spill his own blood and giveup his own life for a time, and fall by the stroke of king Death, that thereby he might ransom his rebellious subjects from the power of sin and death, and blot out the handwriting that Justice had against them. Now Mercy, a very great princess, the darling of the bosom of the great Father, and the chosen and well-beloved of the almighty Son, was presented on this occasion, and also all the powers of darkness under Abadon, pleading the destruction of man, and desiring that he should be doomed to be forever under the power of Abadon, sin and death, as he had yielded obedience to the two former.

Death also claimed to have a right to have dominion over him, justice also agreeing to the legality of the claim, and therefore pronounced all mankind doomed to death and eternal imprisonment, unless an ample atonement were made for his transgression, and the debt he owed was fully paid, and therefore justice stood, and with a dreadful frown gave Death the keys of the prison, and summoned him to give man a thrust with his dreadful dart, and confine him in everlasting imprisonment and woe, the Great Majesty on high consenting to its justice. But mercy also stood, and smiling in the face of the Father and the Son, she plead in man's behalf, that if possible this awful sentence might be repealed, but as this could not be unless that Messiah in man's stead paid the debt; therefore she entreated the Father to give up the Son, and the Son to be willing to come and give his life a ransom for the transgressors. Now the time having fully come for these things to be done, King Death stood with the keys at his side, and his dart uplifted high, ready to give the fatal blow and make thereby a finishing stroke to man. But the most merciful King Messiah stood forth and in man's stead suffered Death's heavy stroke to fall on himself, and also suffered himself to be taken a prisoner by him for a time. Now this sentence having been pronounced by justice, was executed by death in the following manner: Abadon and Sin commanded their subjects to bring false accusations against Prince Messiah, and to pronounce him a deceiver, and as such to lay violent hands upon him, and after buffeting and spitting upon him, and putting a crown of thorns on his head, and then to nail his hands and feet to a tree, and leaving him hanging there in that suffering situation exposed to the inflicting of Death's dreadful dart, who eager to give the blow threw it with all his vengeful power, which Messiah to shelter man endured, but fell beneath the stroke and was taken prisoner by Death, and cast in his prison called the grave.

Now Messiah had previously told his trumpeters that these things were to be, and that he would lay under the power of death until the third day, and that he would then arise and overcome death, and take from him his keys, and take them in his own hands to possess them forever and come forth from his prison triumphantly over Abadon, Sin and Death, and all their dark and subtle powers, leading prisoners into captivity, and giving precious gifts to men, and then to re-ascend to his meritorial seat on his majestical throne, there to sit in glory, forever highly exalted over all. And according to his promise, on the third day early in the morning while it was yet dark, a flaming herald by the express order of the great King of Light, was despatched from on high, to the place where the reat [great] Messiah laid, where those who had been appointed to watch were stationed, to see whether his disciples came and stole him away, or whether he by his own power came forth. Now these men were undoubtedly picked and valient men, and had done what they could to secure the place, and were arrayed for battle, and had rolled a great stone to the prison door as a preventative, yet did this great messenger with ease remove every stumbling block out of the way, and so glorious was his appearance that for fear of him these guards trembled, and fell and became as dead men, then did the great and mighty King Messiah arise and lay violent hands upon Death and drew out his sting and took from him his keys and brought him under subjection, and then unlock his prison door and come forth triumphant and gloriously over sin and death, and all of Abadon's dark powers. Now, although death had stood from the beginning an unconquered foe to all the sons of men—yea had conquered all with whom he had come in contact, and was at this time armed with all his dreadful weapons of war, and stood ready to contend for every inch of the ground, and hoped never to be overcome, yet when the great King Messiah armed himself for battle, with all his weapons of war, and went forth conquering and to conquer, grim Death fell beneath the force of his Almighty power, and although Abadon also stood with all his combined powers of earth and Hades in battle array, when great Messiah mounted the chariot of his love which was stronger than death, then did he with ease ride through the thickest of the combined forces of Abadon, Sin and Death, spoiling their powers and leading them captives.—He dragged them bound in chains at his chariot wheels, and made them a show openly as vanquished and conquered foes. Thus did he triumph gloriously over all the powers beneath, giving very great and precious gifts to men. Now very soon after he had thus subdued these great foes to himself and his creature man, he showed himself to some of his chosen servants, who went early on the third day to the place where he had been laid, telling them that he had not yet ascended to his Father, to re-inherit the kingdom of his power and glory; therefore tell my brethren that I am going shortly to ascend to my Father, and your Father, my God, and your God. So these servants being thus informed by their heavenly and divine master, ran with great joy to tell their brethren these glad and glorious tidings; and that they had seen their king alive, and he had told them these things. So now the great King Alpha, having thus paid the debt his rebellious subjects owed, his almighty Father's wrath was appeased, and justice was satisfied. And therefore Mercy and Justice on this occasion, met on friendly terms, and kissed each other, for although they had previously been on very friendly terms together for an infinite period of time, even long before man had an existence; yet on the occasion of the debt that man owed through disobedience, and the penalty that was due to him, they had differed and disagreed. For justice demanded an infinite punishment, or an infinite atonement, as man had infinitely transgressed; but mercy demanded and asked that an infinite atonement should be made for him, and that he should be pardoned on conditions of true repentance for past offences, and future obedience.

So now therefore, each of their demands having been fully complied with, by the great sacrifice which Messiah had made, it was therefore, for this cause, that mercy and justice met on such friendly terms together, kissing and embracing each other, and mercy asked of justice and obtained a receipt in full for all that man owed to the majesty on high, and this receipt was deposited in the hands of King Alpha, to be given to man by him, through the interposition of the Comforter on conditions of repentance towards his Father, and faith in himself. Now king Messiah had told his body servants, while he was yet with them, that after he had taken his departure from them, and had fought and conquered the tyrannical powers of Abadon, Sin, and Death, to make up for the absence of his bodily presence amongst them, he would send the Comforter ever to remain with them to comfort, console, instruct, and teach them and bring all things in remembrance which he had previously told them. These and many other comfortable words, did our great and glorious king speak to them for their comfort, encouragement, and edification, and also for those who were to come after them, as his obedient servants; the records of which have been faithfully kept, and handed down to posterity unto the present day.

So now after King Alpha had alone, and single-handed, thus-fought this great battle against the combined powers of these three great kings, Abadon, Sin, and Death, and had as above described, gained a complete victory over them, and all their frightful powers, and having paid Justice all of his legal claims and demands against his rebellious subjects, previous to his re-ascending to his royal and majestic throne in the Celestial Land, he collected together his chosen body servants who had been with him while he sojourned in the terrestrial Land, and made known to them the conditions on which his Father and himself would acquit men from all the claims his steward Justice had previously held against them; also appointing and commissioning them, and their successors, to make known to all succeeding generations those conditions, and fully informing them of the manner of his kingdom on earth, and giving them power to establish it, and make his laws and decrees fully known to men. Having set apart twelve as his ministerial ambassadors, delivering to them the necessary documents and his message of reconciliation, and ordaining them to go unto all the terrestrial Land, and deliver it to every creature; and they that believed and complied therewith, should be acquited and live in his kingdom; whilst they that did not, should be condemned to death, and be cast forever out of it, and be consigned to Hades. Having finished all that was necessary for him to do, assuring them that he would be with them wherever his presence was needful, accompanied by his Father to help them, he led them to the number of five hundred, who had been his followers, to an appointed place, there to take his leave of them, the place being called the Mount of Olives. He then in the presence of them all, that there might be no lack of witnesses, got on a cloud, it serving as a chariot, and slowly in their sight made his ascension towards the Celestial Land, there to re-ascend his throne at his Father's right hand, to reign over all principalities and powers, both above and below through all immensity of space, and over all created beings.

[. . .]

And now, kind reader, having briefly sketched the outlines and history of the Rise and Progress of the Kingdoms of Light and

Darkness on the earth, in all its different divisions and districts, with the exception of the United States, and is supposed at this time to be one of the leading nations in literature, and the arts and science, and in the wealth of this world, but in her loyalty to King Alpha, she is a nation very far behind her privileges, coming far short of what she ought to be in consideration of the great favors and blessings she has received at his hands.

Now this division, like South America, was at first peopled by the Indians, a people as we have described, that were when first discovered, in gross darkness, being unenlightened by the glorious light of the gospel, as the watchmen of Zion had not sounded the gospel trumpet among them, and they had not yet heard its pleasing sound; but it was now to be blown among them by the gospel trumpeters, who were sent by the King of Light for that express purpose, being commissioned as ambassadors to negotiate with them, and propound conditions of reconciliation and peace to those, who through iguorance [ignorance], and the dark influence of Abadon, were in rebellion against him. Many of these rebellious ones, after receiving instructions from the ambassadors of Light, became reconciled to their rightful sovereign, and took the oath of allegiance to him, and became valiant soldiers in his cause, and faithfully served in his army until they were called home from the battle field, to receive with great joy his approval. Now it is supposed that the first officers and soldiers of the Army of Light, who came into the United States, was a detachment from the Puritan regiment, who being persecuted greatly in Europe, their native land, by the enemies of the King of Light, because of their adherence to him, and their opposition to Abadon and his vile cause, therefore being directed by the Comforter, they emigrated to this strange land, and began their base of operations in the Eastern or New England States, landing first at a place called Plymouth Rock.

They soon after organized a regiment, which grew fast and was very prosperous, for the recruiting officers being expeditious, soon enlisted many volunteers in the land of their adoption; and there were also many transferred to them from the army that occupied the eastern continent, for it was the king's will, that there should be a strong army of occupation concentrated in the western as well as in the eastern continent. And therefore after the Puritan regiment had first led the way, there were detachments from the various regiments composing the grand Army of Light, in the eastern continent, despatched unto the western, to fill up the ranks of the intended army of occupation therein; for here were there to be great battles fought, and victories gained in favor of the Kingdom of Light, for so had the king determined, and for this cause had sent his soldiers of the different regiments.

[. . .]

Now these Eastern districts were and are still in the advance of the Middle, Southern and Western ones in civilization and light, and were the first to do away with African slavery, which was long after supported and upheld by the most of the other districts, and what was worse, there the various regiments, professing to belong to the Army of Light, approved, or did not openly disapprove of this very great and crying evil, which, after having been introduced, went on increasing until it had in a large degree demoralized and corrupted the various regiments composing King Alpha's army of occupation in the western continent; for there were but very few regiments that wholly escaped the contaminating influence of slavery; and at length the very existence of the United States government was endangered thereby, for it occasioned the shedding of much blood to preserve it, all of which is due to the protection which slavery received from the United States government, this being at variance with the laws of King Alpha, all his attributes, which we term his cabinet, being opposed thereto. Now, as we have above said, the New England States, be it said to their praise, were the first to see and get rid of the sin of slavery, and early did they blot it out of the statute books of their moral law, even far in the advance of most of the regiments which professed to belong to the Army of Light, removing it out of their statute book, which is also termed the spiritual law, and is professed to be drawn from King Alpha's law book, which is known to be averse to all manner of sin and oppression. The Puritan regiment in the Eastern States knowing this, conformed thereto, and be it also said to the credit of the Quaker regiment, they at an early date ceased to maintain the

grand evil of slavery. Neither was it admitted in the first formation of the Methodist regiment, nor while those men lived who
were its founders, who received their orders immediately from
the Comforter, and were determined to die rather than to go contrary thereto. But after these valiant veteran soldiers were called
home from the field, their successors in arms, I am sorry to record, were not as attentive as they to observe all the orders of the
Commander-in-chief. This at last caused a division of the regiment into North and South portions, the North being determined
to carry out fully the orders of the commanding general, while
that of the South evaded it by attempting to misconstrue and to
interpret them differently. Thus did matters continue many days,
and the various other regiments were affected more or less by the
same cause. Now King Alpha and Omega had in the beginning
created all men free and equal, and endowed them with certain
rights and privileges, among which are life, liberty and the pursuit of happiness.

Now the well informed reader will know that what is now
called the United States, was formerly under, and subject to the
government of Great Britain, who founded the colonies, that afterwards became independent states, which thing was brought
on through, and by the oppression of the mother country's government, which enacted such laws, and made such restrictions as
was thought by the colonies to be unjust and oppressive; therefore did they rebel against the government of Great Britain and
took up arms in defence of what they thought were their just
rights, and they so far succeeded as to gain their independence,
for which they fought; and greatly did they rejoice when having
gained the victory; they having previously declared their independence, after which they formed a constitution, heading it with
the declaration that we hold these truths to be self-evident, that
all men are created free and equal, and endowed by their Creator
with certain inalienable rights, among which are life, liberty and
the pursuit of happiness. Now this declaration was just and right,
and was in accordance with the statutes of the King of Light,
and had they carried them out, in their application to others, as
well as to themselves, they would no doubt, have had his special
favor and protection from all harm, and from the powers of both
home and foreign foes.

But it is much to be lamented they did not do unto others, as they wished to be done by, as the King of Light had directed them to do; but instead, they in the face of, and contrary to this broad declaration above named, instituted a form of oppression to the African race, that were among them, that one of their own wisest and best men admitted, a very short period of which to endure, was worse and fraught with more misery than ages of that which their fathers rose in rebellion to oppose. And this unjust and miserable state of things continued long, notwithstanding it was spoken against by many of their wise and best men, but to little or no purpose, as their warning voice was generally disregarded by those who had the rule of government in their hands, who generally were not soldiers in the Army of Light, nor subject to King Alpha; therefore it is not so strange that they should do so unjustly, seeing they were subject to the King of Darkness, instead of the King of Light. But it is much more surprising that any who professed adherence to King Alpha, should so far contradict their profession, as to support so wicked and unjust a thing, yet it was nevertheless done by many who professed to stand high in the Army of Light; and there are great reasons to believe that had those professed servants of Light fully discharged their duty, this great evil might much sooner have been remedied, and with much less cost of blood and treasure. But many of those who should have been the watchmen on the walls, to see the sword coming and warn the people, they miserably and shamefully failed to do so, and consequently did not clear their skirts of the blood of the people, and are therefore accountable to the king, whom they profess to serve, for the neglect of a known duty.

Sad and lamentable were the scenes these things in process of time brought on, of which we propose speaking more minutely hereafter, but for the present we conceive it to be our duty to take a brief review of the past and the present state of the grand division of the Army of Light, occupying the United States, which as we have before said, was first organized by detachments that were transferred from the grand army of occupation of the eastern continent, to the western, which as before said, were detached from the various regiments comprising the grand army in the eastern continent. Now these detachments, it is reasonable to suppose, were composed of true and valiant hearted men, who ably defended the cause of their king, and faithfully performed the arduous duties that were committed to their trust; and the numerous volunteers and recruits that were enlisted for the service by them, were generally well drilled in the arts and tactics of christian warfare, so that when they were by their proper officers, led forth to battle, it was generally to certain victory; and in those days there were many great battles fought, which resulted in victory to the King of Light's army, while the Army of Darkness was often defeated and put to flight. Now the cause of their great success in battle, was their being so very careful to observe, and do the commands of their commander in chief and the subordinate officers, who were generally on hand, and in front when the hottest battles were fought, and therefore very much exposed to the fire of the enemy; and those who had not on the whole armor, were greatly endangered thereby. Now the most of the regiments admitted the possibility and necessity of putting the whole armor on, but strange to say, many of them contended that it could not be got, and put on fully, until the war was nearly over, and they were done fighting; others contended it could not be put on instantly, but gradually, a piece at a time, until the whole was put on.

Now in this, the Methodist regiment differed from the others, for the founder thereof, who was its first colonel, ascertained that it could, by asking for and in faith believing, be obtained instantly, and that there was nothing that the king desired more, than that his soldiers should have on the whole armor; and therefore when they make application to him earnestly for it, they always receive it at his hands. And with the knowledge of this, the Methodist regiment adopted as a part of their creed, that each soldier should believe this, and believing it, that it was their duty to importune the king to admit them into the armor house, in order that they might obtain and put on the whole armor, and that thereby they might be able to withstand in the evil day; having done all, to stand against all the wiles of Abadon and his forces, for every soldier of Light, more or less, before completing the time of their service, experiences an evil day in which all the artillery of Abadon is levelled at them, at which time it is impossible for them to stand firm without having on the whole armor; therefore it is very essential that every soldier of Light, should have and keep it on, for it is unknown to them at what time this evil day may come; and therefore it is one of the king's ancient war orders, by one of his chosen officers, that his soldiers should put it on; therefore their tears were many, and their cries to him great, that he would condescend to heal them, promising that if he would, they would never rebel against him any more. Then does he on his part, when they have become sufficiently humble, undertake their cause, and speedily makes a perfect cure of them, and gives them great joy and comfort; they then willingly become soldiers in the Army of Light, having laid down their weapons of rebellion.

Many of these same, through the instrumentality of Methodist regiments, made very valiant soldiers, and after having fought many severe battles, and gained many great conquests, at length died and were buried in the honors of war, being called home by their king to the celestial country, there to receive a proper reward of merit due. Thus did the Methodist regiment continue many days to operate, and while so doing they had the approval of their king, who often visited them and anointed them greatly by his presence; for it was due to this that they were so successful in their efforts. Now in those days slavery was not admitted among them, they knowing that it was displeasing to the king, neither did prejudice against their fellow-soldiers, merely on account of the color of the coat the king had put on them, exist to the extent it now does among them, for this twin brother to slavery which has not in vindication thereof the same excuse, for they who held them, considered it to be their temporal interest to do so; for this last named interest should not govern the actions of a true soldier of Light, for they undoubtedly will have to be accountable to their sovereign for all their actions and motives.

Now this true that not all the members of the Methodist regiments, nor of the other various regiments composing the army, that professed to be the Army of Light, had this prejudice against their brethern and fellow-soldiers, because their king had given them a coat of a darker hue than that of their own, yet we must with sorrow admit that the majority of those who profess to belong to the true Army of Light, have become so corrupt, and conformed to the world and Abadon's army, that they practice and do this very unjust thing. Now as we have previously remarked, it is not so surprising that the soldiers of Abadon's army, who are under the command of the World, the Flesh, and himself should do so, but that those who profess to belong to the Army of Light, which is commanded by the Comforter, and such great and good officers as Faith, Hope, and Charity, should do so; it is astonishing above measure, insomuch so that it is impossible to reconcile prejudice with all its train, and those who are supporters thereof, as belonging to the true Army of Light, which is certainly at variance with all such, as being contrary to the known will of the King of Light.

Now in regard to the injustice and inconsistency of this prejudice, volumes might be written concerning it and its effects, in the United States. And as it is a very momentous subject and one that deeply interests the soldiers of light, in the United States, I propose to enter into its merits and demerits, in regard to what has been its effects in time past in the United States, and what it now is, and what it is likely to be, and how it is undoubtedly viewed, by the King of Light himself, for in the first place he made of one blood all nations that dwell upon the face of the earth, they all proceeding from the first pair, the color of whose skin it is reasonably believed, was a medium between the darkest and lightest of their descendants of the present day; their different shades of color or complexion and features, and hair, are attributed to various causes, all of which are beyond their control, making it the more unreasonable that one should despise the other for that which is no fault of his, for it is generally admitted by the most wise and intelligent amongst men of all classes, that one of the main causes of the difference of color, and hair, is through the different climates in which they have for successive ages dwelt, for those who have always dwelt in a hot and burning climate, are found to be the most dark, with curly hair, whilst those who have always lived in a temperate climate, are the most light and have generally straight hair.

Now as the climates and their effects are governed by the King of Light himself, therefore, to despise any on account of their color, is offering an insult to the King of Light himself, who has seen fit in his infinite wisdom to beautify all nature by a variety of shades and colors, and it is not by men in the United States, or elsewhere thought a sufficient cause to despise anything else but mankind in all creation for this same cause, and the idea is certainly absurd and ridiculous to any intelligent mind, for one person to think himself superior to another, merely on account of the difference of his features, or the color of their skin, yet is this great absurdity cultivated, supported, and sustained, by men of all classes of the light colored population of the United States. For even in the Army of Light, the place where it should never be found, there are many who hold very high positions therein, and very many of lower standing, who make a line of demarkation between their colored and white fellow soldiers.

And now we proceed first to describe what has been, and are still the effects of this unjust spirit, in the professed Army of Light in the United States, beginning with the Methodist regiment, with which my predecessors were identified, but were caused to leave on the account of this same prejudice and oppression, and organize a regiment of their own, consisting altogether of colored soldiers. Now the cause that forced them to leave was, that they saw that there was a great deviation in the Methodist regiment, from what it had formerly been, and that impartial love they found among them when they first joined them, and that caused them to leave the alien army and come to them, had become so cold, that the Methodist regiment too, like the alien army they had left, could and did make a line of demarkation between them and their fellow-soldiers of a lighter hue merely on that account, insomuch so that they would not drill them at the same time they did the others, and would not suffer them to set on the same seats as others; and though soldiers of their regiment, they sometimes turned them out of the tent to admit others, who were not. And though one of their number had a special commission from the King of Light, as a watchman or a trumpeter, yet was he not permitted to blow the trumpet nor sound an alarm, and it matters not how much those colored watchmen and ambassadors were in favor of the King of Light, or what their qualifications as competent officers were, yet if the king had clothed them with a dark skin, that alone was considered a sufficient reason why they should not serve in the regiments, in the position their office entitled them to, through their appointment by the king; which thing as a matter of course was offensive both to their king, and these his despised servants. For though he himself stooped so low, as to die for these his colored servants as well as his white, and adopt them into his family, owning them as his children, and giving them the right to claim him as their father, and also to prepare for them splendid mansions in the celestial country, such as is not seen by the eyes of man in the terrestrial land; and unto which happy place and pleasant situation he intended to bring his colored soldiers when they have finished their warfare and accomplished the work he has given them to do, as much so as he will his white soldiers, where they shall set down with him in his kingdom, and associate with his prime ministers, and those who hold the most honorable positions in all the celestial country, and have no lack of anything that is good and desirable.

Now all of these things being left on record in the King's documents, which generally are accessible to all, and which makes it so much the more astonishing that the well-informed Methodist regiments, together with the others equally well informed, should make this marked distinction on account of color, when even to have common judgment, they must know that it is so far contrary to the will of their King, as set forth above, and more fully so in his statute book, to which, for further information, we would refer all those in the Methodist regiments, or any others who are ignorant of these things, and want information; for the colored soldiers, who had long been kept intentionally in ignorance and bondage by their white brethren, as they emerged therefrom, very soon discovered that it was not in accordance with the will of their King that they should be dealt with as they had been both by the Army of Darkness and that which represented itself to be the Army of Light, in which the Methodist regiments and others acted so inconsistent with what these colored soldiers found to be the will of their King, therefore they lost confidence in them, and resolved to form a regiment of their own, in which there would be no distinction on account of color. Now the first regiment of this kind that was organized in the United States was the African Union regiment, now called the American Union regiment; it was first organized by a Peter Spencer and others of the despised race, who were soldiers and trumpeters in the Methodist regiment, and who saw and lamented the oppression of their fellow colored soldiers therein, and for that reason came out and formed an independent regiment of their own, but retained the most essential and important rules and regulations which formerly existed in the Methodist regiments, which rules had been first given to its founder by the Comforter, and were therefore good and right, and whilst keeping them, the King was well pleased with this newly formed and despised regiment, and showed them many marked favors by visiting them himself, and also sending the Comforter, who instructed them in the arts of war, so that this regiment in numbers and efficiency became notable, and produced many valiant soldiers, who fought nobly in the defence of the Kingdom of Light, and gained many conquests.

[. . .]

Now these poor despised colored soldiers, many of whom were slaves, some of them to their fellow-soldiers, who professed to be fighting for the same sovereign, one of the petitions which they sent up ran in this wise, and which for many years was sung by them even thus:

> When will Jehovah hear my cry,
> And free the sons of Africa?

And the answer to this that was brought back to them by Mr. Faith and his comrades was thus: That the King in his own time would make a way to free the sons of Africa. Now your humble servant, the author, who is a member and watchman in the Union regiment, is happy to record that he with others has been blessed to live to see the day that this promise made by the King and reported by Mr. Faith a number of years ago, has now been fulfilled to the great satisfaction of the descendants of the African race, and all other true soldiers of light. The manner in which the King has brought this to pass, we intend to take further notice of hereafter, if permitted by our King. Now although this great and mighty work has been accomplished, we have yet to lament the remains of prejudice under which the writer, together with others of his race, have yet to labor and combat with, for it greatly affects both the Church and State. Now the Church is the various regiments composing the grand Army of Light, and the State is the moral or civil law of the land, and is in close affinity with the Church, one defending the other, and as regards the putting down of slavery, the State was in the advance of the professed

Church, for it must be admitted that if the Church had done its duty, slavery could not have existed as long as it did, neither could prejudice be so abundant in the land as it now is, and it is certain that the Congress of the United States has made greater efforts and done more to do away with prejudice and to establish equal rights before the law for all men, irrespective of color or complexion, than what the Church in general has ever yet done, which is a great shame to those who profess to belong to the Army of Light—that the children of this world should supersede them in doing that which is just and right; yet this we can say in the defence of the Methodist regiment of the Army of Light, North, that they for a number of years have not admitted their members to hold slaves, and that they finally dissolved their connection with the Church South on this account, and it was greatly to their credit to do so, for in so doing, they conformed to the regulation under which their regiment was first organized, thus far pleasing the King of Light. Nevertheless, it must be confessed that prejudice to color which years ago became a guest of theirs, in common with other regiments, is still entertained and cherished by them greatly to their hurt. Now soon after the organization of the Union regiment, the African Methodist regiment was organized by a Richard Allen and others, who were its founders, being descendants of Africa, and who disconnected themselves from their white brethren of the Methodist regiment, for the same cause that the African Union regiment had previously done so, calling themselves by the name of the same regiment from which they came, with only African attached, and forming themselves on the same basis, with the same rules and regulations, and differing but little if any from what they had formerly been, with the exception that they were Africans subject to their own independent government.

But being formed after the manner of the aforesaid regiment, therefore they were not so original as the African Union regiment, so that those of their colored brethren who were members of the Methodist regiment, and were so partial to all the rules and regulations thereof, had little or no sacrifice to make in coming out, and becoming members of the African, for it was rather a gain to them, as they thereby obtained equal rights among their brethren, of which they were deprived in the white Methodist regiment;

this will account in a measure for their greater increase than that of the Union regiment, seeing they had to differ so little from what they formerly were, and therefore there were more came to them out of the Methodist regiment, than there did to the Uuion [Union]; and in addition to this, both of these regiments have taken in many recruits, who were formerly in Abadon's army, but now rejoice to fight under the blood-stained banner of King Alpha, so that if these two regiments continue to observe all the commands of their general in chief, they will do much to establish the Kingdom of Light in the United States and elsewhere. But we must here remark that there is scarcely any regiment now in existence, who have not deviated from their first principles, and become greatly adulterated and consequently lost the power they once had; and here the writer who has a partiality and a deep regard for the Methodist regiment, notwithstanding all its present failings, as being the one from which the regiment in which he is a member sprang, is caused with sorrow to pause and remark, that by their leaving some of their first principles, and conforming more to the spirit of this world, and adopting many of the customs of other regiments, who have long since lost the power they once enjoyed, they like them have lost in a large degree the power they once had, which could, and did cause the powers of Darkness to tremble, in which time very many were slain by the sword of the spirit handled by the valiant soldiers of this regiment, and the arrows of the watchmen of the same.

Now they had been told by their former officers who were under the immediate direction of the Comforter, to be exemplary in dress and other outward things, and to love not the world, nor the things of it, and that whosoever did, the love of King Alpha was not in them; yet did the Methodist regiment, that is, many of their members, but not all so far deviate from this wholesome instruction, that they like the world, and other luke-warm regiments, gave themselves up to gay and costly apparel, and grand and costly drill-houses, with bells and high steeples attached thereto, which cost much that had better been given to the poor among them; also in the inside there were splendid decorations and ornaments, and also whereas they had been directed by the order of the king, when they sing, to sing with the spirit and the understanding.

They so far deviated from this that they often employed the enemies of the King of Light, and friends of the King of Darkness, to lead the singing part of their devotion, which they undoubtedly could not do in the spirit, that is to say through the assistance of the Comforter, and therefore it could not be acceptable nor pleasing to King Alpha. Moreover, they at length got to using instrumental music in their devotion, like other regiments who had lost the power, and had nothing left but the form. Now none of these things would have been admitted by the founders of Methodism, who were under the immediate direction of the Comforter, and was careful to observe all that he commanded them, not caring to please the world, which seems to be the reverse of the mind of their ancestors, who in adopting the above named things, appear to have in view the pleasing of the world as their especial object, rather than as a command that they must needs do in order to please the King of Light, for we have no knowledge of any command under the Gospel dispensation being given by him to that effect. Therefore we are sorry to see that the African Methodist regiment, has made great progress in the same direction, and we are still more sorry the colored Union American regiment with which we are identified, are taking steps in the same direction, and have at this date so far advanced as to have choirs introduced into two tents in our encampment, and which are as above said composed of some of the enemies of the King of Light, and friends to the King of Darkness, and consequently cannot be pleasing to King Alpha.

And therefore, as a watchman on the walls of Zion, being appointed by my great and glorious king, I lift my warning voice in protestation against all of these things, especially in any of the Methodist regiments, who were opposed to them in the beginning.

[. . .]

Now the meeting of these two vast armies, will be joyful in the extreme, there never having been such a meeting before since time commenced, and when they have been introduced by their commanding officers, they will congratulate each other on the success they have each had in the wars in which they have been engaged, and the victory they have each achieved, for the celestial army was first engaged in battle against the powers of darkness in the celestial country, and through the King of Light, succeeded in overcoming them, and casting them out of all the celestial country, and the same powers of darkness was that which afterwards fought so severely against the terrestrial Army of Light, and was likewise overcome by them through the power of the great King of Light, therefore will each of these great armies congratulate each other on the victory they have obtained, and vie with each other in giving praise to the King of Light, for the great victory they have each gained through him, and for all the wonderful work which he has done.

Now the celestial army will be able to speak more of the creating power and goodness of the King, and of that song they will sing the loudest and most fully. But the song of redemption, the terrestrial army will be able to sing to perfection, and to talk of it will be their chief delight; and in singing and talking thereof, they will be able to excel the celestial army, as the celestial army was created but not redeemed, therefore they cannot take so active a part in singing and talking thereof, as the terrestrial army; but each will be as completely happy as will be possible for them to be, the celestial escorting the terrestrial up with the loud sound of trumpets and singing of creation, whilst the terrestrial will be as earnestly engaged in singing equally as loud of redemption, and playing on golden harps as upward they go, the whole of both armies keeping time with the music, King Alpha and the Comforter going before on white horses, and when the innumerable host shall arrive in front of the great and glorious city which we have above described, then will be caused a halt, whilst they shall surround it preparatory to their entering into the great city through each of the twelve gates, and when this manœuvre is performed, the King will command with a loud voice, saying, open ye the gates that the righteous nation that keeps the true way may enter in, and the porter will say, lift up the gates and be ye lifted up ye everlasting doors, and the King of glory shall come in, then will the gates be opened wide, and the king shall enter in leading his triumphant hosts through the gates into the city, which on this occasion will be put in the most splendid order, to receive and do honor to the victorious army of the great King of Light, and every bell in the city will ring welcome in, welcome in, and

as they tread the gold paved streets, being led by the king and
conducted by the angelic escort on their way to the throne, as
they pass by the splendid mansion, which the king will have previously prepared for them, as they view them they will behold
such dazzling splendor, as the eyes of mortals had never before
witnessed, perfectly agreeing with the words the King had left on
record, namely, eye has not seen nor ear heard, neither has it entered into the heart of man to conceive, the things that he has
prepared for them that love him and keep his commands; this
will be fully realized by the soldiers of light, when they shall have
arrived inside of the city, and King Alpha will lead them into the
presence of his majestic father, into which when they have arrived, and have been introduced by him to his very great and
Majestic Highness, as those he had redeemed from the earth,
having purchased their pardon by shedding his blood, then will
every knee be bowed, both of the celestial and terrestrial armies,
in adoration to the Father, the Son and the Comforter. . . . Then
will these three agree as always they had done before, and bear
accord in the holy city; for, as we have before said, the Father,
Son and Comforter are three in person, yet are they one Supreme
Being, in perfect unity in all their actions, and they having now
concluded all the necessary ceremonies between them, and agreed
in their future course of proceedings in their kingdom and towards their subjects, they will then turn their face to review the
grand united army that will by their officers be drawn up and
marshaled before the throne on the broad fields of eternal day for
that purpose, and they being arrayed in dazzling splendor, and
clothed with the garments of salvation which the King had previously prepared for them out of his rich bounty, they will appear
to great advantage, and being well drilled as they go through
their various evolutions, the Father will express himself well satisfied with their past and present proceedings, and He will look
approvingly on the Son and smile, and the Son will smile approvingly on the officers and army, and proclaim to them that they
have done well, and that their warfare is now accomplished, and
that henceforth they shall rest from all their labor, and that their
suffering and toiling is all now over, and that they now shall
enter in and possess forever and ever the splendid mansions he
has prepared for them in his Father's house, and inherit all things;

and sickness and sorrow, pain and death by them will be felt and feared no more, for the former things will be done away; for he that sits upon the throne will proclaim to them that he has made all things new, and when the ransomed host shall hear and realise all these great and glorious things, they will be filled with joy unspeakable and full of glory, and will break forth in loud acclamations of praise and thinksgivings [thanksgivings] to him that sets on the throne for ever and ever, and the sound shall be like mighty thundering; when the whole united army with one accord shall sing hallelujah unto Him that loved us and washed us from our sins in his own blood. This theme will inspire the innumerable host, whose names are written in the Book of Life, with love to the King of Light, who has thus brought them to reign with him for ever and ever; they will then be escorted, each individual to the mansion prepared for them, for as many as they be yet will there be enough for all; and from the fact that the very streets of the city are pure gold, an idea may be formed of the grandeur and splendor of the mansions that the servants of light shall inhabit therein, where they will have plenty of time to set down and rest, and talk their sufferings over, and to pay and receive calls from all the inhabitants of the city of the New Jerusalem, and to become intimately acquainted with all the great and good who have preceded them, and all who shall come after them; very pleasant and joyful will be the interviews had between them, while they converse freely on past and present experience, and very interesting will be the experience of many who lived in the different ages, from the most ancient antediluvian down to the most modern times, and those who lived in the days before the flood, when men lived over nine hundred years, will undoubtedly have a long and interesting experience to tell; and all will have much to say concerning the great kindness and goodness of the King towards them, and of the great and wonderful works he has wrought. Neither will their intimacy be confined to those who have fought in the terrestrial army in the defence of the Kingdom of Light alone, but it will also extend to those who fought in the celestial army against the powers of darkness, and in favor of the Kingdom of Light. The soldiers of the celestial army will have very great and wonderful things to relate concerning the first great battle fought, how it was com-

menced, continued and ended, and how it finally terminated in
the complete rout and overthrow of the enemy, and a decisive
victory in favor of the Kingdom of Light, all of which will be due
to the almighty wisdom and power of the great King of Light,
and those shining warriors, from Gabriel and Michael down to
the least of their number, will delight to ascribe all the glory and
praise to the Father, the Son and the Comforter, who sets on the
throne, for the victory they have gained.

So, attentive reader, it is very evident that there will be great
joy in that city, and in addition to all the other great blessings
spoken of, will be this also, that loving friends that have long
been separated shall there meet again with joy, no more to part,
under much more favorable circumstances than when they
parted, and what will augment their happiness will be the knowledge that their joy and happiness shall never end, but shall be
eternal.

(LORENZO DOW BLACKSON, PHILADELPHIA: 1867,
PP. 62–67, 149–66, 231–35)

# Science and Health with Key to the Scriptures

Mary Baker Eddy (1821–1910) wanted nothing more than to be healed physically, and once this was accomplished, she wanted to share with the world the spiritual principles that had brought her relief. She was brought up as a member of a Congregational Church in New Hampshire and reported to have been a sickly child and young adult, struggling with a series of illnesses and accidents that encouraged her to seek remedies from a variety of healing techniques, including special diets, water cure, homeopathy, and hypnosis. After a debilitating fall on the ice in 1866 she lay in bed and read accounts in the Bible of Jesus' healings and was suddenly cured; years later, she recalled this as the moment she discovered "Christian Science," the spiritual principle of healing. After a decade of healing, teaching, and study, Eddy published her findings in 1875 as *Science and Health with Key to the Scriptures,* a volume that explained the principles behind her techniques that she felt were immutable and could be learned by anyone.

*Science and Health* was only the beginning of Eddy's effort to institutionalize her teachings. In 1879 she obtained a charter for the Church of Christ, Scientist, an organization dedicated to reinstating primitive Christianity and its emphasis on healing. A prolific writer and organizer, she opened reading rooms in Boston, founded a newspaper and training college, and established the Christian Science Publishing Society in 1898 as a means to disseminate her ideas. Today services in the First Church of Christ, Scientist, alternate readings of the Bible with passages from *Science and Health,* a book now understood within the organization as the definitive interpretation of biblical teachings.

The selections presented here span a broad range of Eddy's teachings but demonstrate her core reliance on prayer as the focus of Christian practice. Real faith, she insists, lies not in creeds or beliefs but in the demonstration of healing. Illness, she argues, is a human conceptual mistake that springs from our belief that there is a material world apart from the world of spirit. She calls on readers to shift their understanding of God from a personality to an unchanging principle of life, truth, and love. In turn, she faults mistaken human understandings that the material world is real and calls on individuals to recognize that God is available at all times. According to her teachings, Christ is less a savior than a scientific principle that everyone can access, once they recognize that evil is only an illusion. In the final chapter Eddy places her own teachings in a history of divine revelation within a biblical lineage: Christ, "God's idea," was represented first by a man and now, through her, by a woman.

# Science and Health with Key to the Scriptures

## CHAPTER I

### PRAYER

*For verily I say unto you, That whosoever shall say unto this mountain, Be thou removed, and be thou cast into the sea; and shall not doubt in his heart, but shall believe that those things which he saith shall come to pass; he shall have whatsoever he saith. Therefore I say unto you, What things soever ye desire when ye pray, believe that ye receive them, and ye shall have them.*

*Your Father knoweth what things ye have need of, before ye ask Him.*

—CHRIST JESUS.

The prayer that reforms the sinner and heals the sick is an absolute faith that all things are possible to God,—a spiritual understanding of Him, an unselfed love. Regardless of what another may say or think on this subject, I speak from experience. Prayer, watching, and working, combined with self-immolation, are God's gracious means for accomplishing whatever has been successfully done for the Christianization and health of mankind.

Thoughts unspoken are not unknown to the divine Mind. Desire is prayer; and no loss can occur from trusting God with our desires, that they may be moulded and exalted before they take form in words and in deeds.

What are the motives for prayer? Do we pray to make ourselves better or to benefit those who hear us, to enlighten the infinite or to be heard of men? Are we benefited by praying? Yes, the desire which goes forth hungering after righteousness is blessed of our Father, and it does not return unto us void.

God is not moved by the breath of praise to do more than He has already done, nor can the infinite do less than bestow all good, since He is unchanging wisdom and Love. We can do more for ourselves by humble fervent petitions, but the All-loving does not grant them simply on the ground of lip-service, for He already knows all.

Prayer cannot change the Science of being, but it tends to bring us into harmony with it. Goodness attains the demonstration of Truth. A request that God will save us is not all that is required. The mere habit of pleading with the divine Mind, as one pleads with a human being, perpetuates the belief in God as humanly circumscribed,—an error which impedes spiritual growth.

God is Love. Can we ask Him to be more? God is intelligence. Can we inform the infinite Mind of anything He does not already comprehend? Do we expect to change perfection? Shall we plead for more at the open fount, which is pouring forth more than we accept? The unspoken desire does bring us nearer the source of all existence and blessedness.

Asking God to *be* God is a vain repetition. God is "the same yesterday, and to-day, and forever;" and He who is immutably right will do right without being reminded of His province. The wisdom of man is not sufficient to warrant him in advising God.

Who would stand before a blackboard, and pray the principle of mathematics to solve the problem? The rule is already established, and it is our task to work out the solution. Shall we ask the divine Principle of all goodness to do His own work? His work is done, and we have only to avail ourselves of God's rule in order to receive His blessing, which enables us to work out our own salvation.

The Divine Being must be reflected by man,—else man is not the image and likeness of the patient, tender, and true, the One "altogether lovely;" but to understand God is the work of eternity, and demands absolute consecration of thought, energy, and desire.

How empty are our conceptions of Deity! We admit theoretically that God is good, omnipotent, omnipresent, infinite, and then we try to give information to this infinite Mind. We plead for unmerited pardon and for a liberal outpouring of benefactions. Are we really grateful for the good already received? Then we shall avail ourselves of the blessings we have, and thus be fitted to receive more. Gratitude is much more than a verbal expression of thanks. Action expresses more gratitude than speech.

If we are ungrateful for Life, Truth, and Love, and yet return thanks to God for all blessings, we are insincere and incur the sharp censure our Master pronounces on hypocrites. In such a case, the only acceptable prayer is to put the finger on the lips and remember our blessings. While the heart is far from divine Truth and Love, we cannot conceal the ingratitude of barren lives.

What we most need is the prayer of fervent desire for growth in grace, expressed in patience, meekness, love, and good deeds. To keep the commandments of our Master and follow his example, is our proper debt to him and the only worthy evidence of our gratitude for all that he has done. Outward worship is not of itself sufficient to express loyal and heartfelt gratitude, since he has said: "If ye love me, keep my commandments."

The habitual struggle to be always good is unceasing prayer. Its motives are made manifest in the blessings they bring,—blessings which, even if not acknowledged in audible words, attest our worthiness to be partakers of Love.

Simply asking that we may love God will never make us love Him; but the longing to be better and holier, expressed in daily watchfulness and in striving to assimilate more of the divine character, will mould and fashion us anew, until we awake in His likeness. We reach the Science of Christianity through demonstration of the divine nature; but in this wicked world goodness will "be evil spoken of," and patience must bring experience.

Audible prayer can never do the works of spiritual understanding, which regenerates; but silent prayer, watchfulness, and devout obedience enable us to follow Jesus' example. Long prayers, superstition, and creeds clip the strong pinions of love, and clothe religion in human forms. Whatever materializes worship hinders man's spiritual growth and keeps him from demonstrating his power over error.

Sorrow for wrong-doing is but one step towards reform and the very easiest step. The next and great step required by wisdom is the test of our sincerity,—namely, reformation. To this end we are placed under the stress of circumstances. Temptation bids us repeat the offence, and woe comes in return for what is done. So it will ever be, till we learn that there is no discount in the law of justice and that we must pay "the uttermost farthing." The measure ye mete "shall be measured to you again," and it will be full "and running over."

Saints and sinners get their full award, but not always in this world. The followers of Christ drank his cup. Ingratitude and persecution filled it to the brim; but God pours the riches of His love into the understanding and affections, giving us strength according to our day. Sinners flourish "like a green bay tree;" but, looking farther, the Psalmist could see their end,—the destruction of sin through suffering.

Prayer is not to be used as a confessional to cancel sin. Such an error would impede true religion. Sin is forgiven only as it is destroyed by Christ,—Truth and Life. If prayer nourishes the belief that sin is cancelled, and that man is made better merely by praying, prayer is an evil. He grows worse who continues in sin because he fancies himself forgiven.

An apostle says that the Son of God [Christ] came to "destroy the *works* of the devil." We should follow our divine Exemplar, and seek the destruction of all evil works, error and disease included. We cannot escape the penalty due for sin. The Scriptures say, that if we deny Christ, "he also will deny us."

Divine Love corrects and governs man. Men may pardon, but this divine Principle alone reforms the sinner. God is not separate from the wisdom He bestows. The talents He gives we must improve. Calling on Him to forgive our work badly done or left undone, implies the vain supposition that we have nothing to do but to ask pardon, and that afterwards we shall be free to repeat the offence.

To cause suffering as the result of sin, is the means of destroying sin. Every supposed pleasure in sin will furnish more than its equivalent of pain, until belief in material life and sin is destroyed. To reach heaven, the harmony of being, we must understand the divine Principle of being.

"God is Love." More than this we cannot ask, higher we cannot look, farther we cannot go. To suppose that God forgives or punishes sin according as His mercy is sought or unsought, is to misunderstand Love and to make prayer the safety-valve for wrong-doing.

Jesus uncovered and rebuked sin before he cast it out. Of a sick woman he said that Satan had bound her, and to Peter he said, "Thou art an offence unto me." He came teaching and showing men how to destroy sin, sickness, and death. He said of the fruitless tree, "[It] is hewn down."

It is believed by many that a certain magistrate, who lived in the time of Jesus, left this record: "His rebuke is fearful." The strong language of our Master confirms this description.

The only civil sentence which he had for error was, "Get thee behind me, Satan." Still stronger evidence that Jesus' reproof was pointed and pungent is found in his own words,—showing the necessity for such forcible utterance, when he cast out devils and healed the sick and sinning. The relinquishment of error deprives material sense of its false claims.

Audible prayer is impressive; it gives momentary solemnity and elevation to thought. But does it produce any lasting benefit? Looking deeply into these things, we find that "a zeal . . . not according to knowledge" gives occasion for reaction unfavorable to spiritual growth, sober resolve, and wholesome perception of God's requirements. The motives for verbal prayer may embrace too much love of applause to induce or encourage Christian sentiment.

Physical sensation, not Soul, produces material ecstasy and emotion. If spiritual sense always guided men, there would grow out of ecstatic moments a higher experience and a better life with more devout self-abnegation and purity. A self-satisfied ventilation of fervent sentiments never makes a Christian. God is not influenced by man. The "divine ear" is not an auditory nerve. It is the all-hearing and all-knowing Mind, to whom each need of man is always known and by whom it will be supplied.

The danger from prayer is that it may lead us into temptation. By it we may become involuntary hypocrites, uttering desires which are not real and consoling ourselves in the midst of sin with the recollection that we have prayed over it or mean to ask forgiveness at some later day. Hypocrisy is fatal to religion.

A wordy prayer may afford a quiet sense of self-justification, though it makes the sinner a hypocrite. We never need to despair of an honest heart; but there is little hope for those who come only spasmodically face to face with their wickedness and then seek to hide it. Their prayers are indexes which do not correspond with their character. They hold secret fellowship with sin, and such externals are spoken of by Jesus as "like unto whited sepulchres . . . full . . . of all uncleanness."

If a man, though apparently fervent and prayerful, is impure and therefore insincere, what must be the comment upon him? If he reached the loftiness of his prayer, there would be no occasion for comment. If we feel the aspiration, humility, gratitude, and love which our words express,—this God accepts; and it is wise not to try to deceive ourselves or others, for "there is nothing covered that shall not be revealed." Professions and audible prayers are like charity in one respect,—they "cover the multitude of sins." Praying for humility with whatever fervency of expression does not always mean a desire for it. If we turn away from the poor, we are not ready to receive the reward of Him who blesses the poor. We confess to having a very wicked heart and ask that it may be laid bare before us, but do we not already know more of this heart than we are willing to have our neighbor see?

We should examine ourselves and learn what is the affection and purpose of the heart, for in this way only can we learn what we honestly are. If a friend informs us of a fault, do we listen patiently to the rebuke and credit what is said? Do we not rather give thanks that we are "not as other men"? During many years the author has been most grateful for merited rebuke. The wrong lies in unmerited censure,—in the falsehood which does no one any good.

The test of all prayer lies in the answer to these questions: Do we love our neighbor better because of this asking? Do we pursue the old selfishness, satisfied with having prayed for something better, though we give no evidence of the sincerity of our requests by living consistently with our prayer? If selfishness has given place to kindness, we shall regard our neighbor unselfishly, and bless them that curse us; but we shall never meet this great duty simply by asking that it may be done. There is a cross to be taken up before we can enjoy the fruition of our hope and faith.

Dost thou "love the Lord thy God with all thy heart, and with all thy soul, and with all thy mind"? This command includes much, even the surrender of all merely material sensation, affection, and worship. This is the El Dorado of Christianity. It involves the Science of Life, and recognizes only the divine control of Spirit, in which Soul is our master, and material sense and human will have no place.

Are you willing to leave all for Christ, for Truth, and so be counted among sinners? No! Do you really desire to attain this point? No! Then why make long prayers about it and ask to be Christians, since you do not care to tread in the footsteps of our dear Master? If unwilling to follow his example, why pray with the lips that you may be partakers of his nature? Consistent prayer is the desire to do right. Prayer means that we desire to walk and will walk in the light so far as we receive it, even though with bleeding footsteps, and that waiting patiently on the Lord, we will leave our real desires to be rewarded by Him.

The world must grow to the spiritual understanding of prayer. If good enough to profit by Jesus' cup of earthly sorrows, God will sustain us under these sorrows. Until we are thus divinely qualified and are willing to drink his cup, millions of vain repetitions will never pour into prayer the unction of Spirit in demonstration of power and "with signs following." Christian Science reveals a necessity for overcoming the world, the flesh, and evil, and thus destroying all error.

Seeking is not sufficient. It is striving that enables us to enter. Spiritual attainments open the door to a higher understanding of the divine Life.

One of the forms of worship in Thibet is to carry a praying-machine through the streets, and stop at the doors to earn a penny by grinding out a prayer. But the advance guard of progress has paid for the privilege of prayer the price of persecution.

Experience teaches us that we do not always receive the blessings we ask for in prayer. There is some misapprehension of the source and means of all goodness and blessedness, or we should certainly receive that for which we ask. The Scriptures say: "Ye ask, and receive not, because ye ask amiss, that ye may consume it upon your lusts." That which we desire and for which we ask, it is not always best for us to receive. In this case infinite Love will not grant the request. Do you ask wisdom to be merciful and not to punish sin? Then "ye ask amiss." Without punishment, sin would multiply. Jesus' prayer, "Forgive us our debts," specified also the terms of forgiveness. When forgiving the adulterous woman he said, "Go, and sin no more."

A magistrate sometimes remits the penalty, but this may be no moral benefit to the criminal, and at best, it only saves the criminal from one form of punishment. The moral law, which has the right to acquit or condemn, always demands restitution before mortals can "go up higher." Broken law brings penalty in order to compel this progress.

Mere legal pardon (and there is no other, for divine Principle never pardons our sins or mistakes till they are corrected) leaves the offender free to repeat the offence, if indeed, he has not already suffered sufficiently from vice to make him turn from it with loathing. Truth bestows no pardon upon error, but wipes it out in the most effectual manner. Jesus suffered for our sins, not to annul the divine sentence for an individual's sin, but because sin brings inevitable suffering.

Petitions bring to mortals only the results of mortals' own faith. We know that a desire for holiness is requisite in order to gain holiness; but if we desire holiness above all else, we shall sacrifice everything for it. We must be willing to do this, that we may walk securely in the only practical road to holiness. Prayer cannot change the unalterable Truth, nor can prayer alone give us an understanding of Truth; but prayer, coupled with a fervent habitual desire to know and do the will of God, will bring us into all Truth. Such a desire has little need of audible expression. It is best expressed in thought and in life.

"The prayer of faith shall save the sick," says the Scripture. What is this healing prayer? A mere request that God will heal the sick has no power to gain more of the divine presence than is always at hand. The beneficial effect of such prayer for the sick is on the human mind, making it act more powerfully on the body through a blind faith in God. This, however, is one belief casting out another,—a belief in the unknown casting out a belief in sickness. It is neither Science nor Truth which acts through blind belief, nor is it the human understanding of the divine healing Principle as manifested in Jesus, whose humble prayers were deep and conscientious protests of Truth,—of man's likeness to God and of man's unity with Truth and Love.

Prayer to a corporeal God affects the sick like a drug, which has no efficacy of its own but borrows its power from human faith and belief. The drug does nothing, because it has no intelligence. It is a mortal belief, not divine Principle or Love, which causes a drug to be apparently either poisonous or sanative.

The common custom of praying for the recovery of the sick finds help in blind belief, whereas help should come from the enlightened understanding. Changes in belief may go on indefinitely, but they are the merchandise of human thought and not the outgrowth of divine Science.

Does Deity interpose in behalf of one worshipper, and not help another who offers the same measure of prayer? If the sick recover because they pray or are prayed for audibly, only petitioners (*per se* or by proxy) should get well. In divine Science, where prayers are mental, *all* may avail themselves of God as "a very present help in trouble." Love is impartial and universal in its adaptation and bestowals. It is the open fount which cries, "Ho, every one that thirsteth, come ye to the waters."

In public prayer we often go beyond our convictions, beyond the honest standpoint of fervent desire. If we are not secretly yearning and openly striving for the accomplishment of all we ask, our prayers are "vain repetitions," such as the heathen use. If our petitions are sincere, we labor for what we ask; and our Father, who seeth in secret, will reward us openly. Can the mere public expression of our desires increase them? Do we gain the omnipotent ear sooner by words than by thoughts? Even if prayer is sincere, God knows our need before we tell Him or our fellow-beings about it. If we cherish the desire honestly and silently and humbly, God will bless it, and we shall incur less risk of overwhelming our real wishes with a torrent of words.

If we pray to God as a corporeal person, this will prevent us from relinquishing the human doubts and fears which attend such a belief, and so we cannot grasp the wonders wrought by infinite, incorporeal Love, to whom all things are possible. Because of human ignorance of the divine Principle, Love, the Father of all is represented as a corporeal creator; hence men recognize themselves as merely physical, and are ignorant of man as God's image or reflection and of man's eternal incorporeal existence. The world of error is ignorant of the world of Truth,—blind to the reality of man's existence,—for the world of sensation is not cognizant of life in Soul, not in body.

If we are sensibly with the body and regard omnipotence as a corporeal, material person, whose ear we would gain, we are not "absent from the body" and "present with the Lord" in the demonstration of Spirit. We cannot "serve two masters." To be "present with the Lord" is to have, not mere emotional ecstasy or faith, but the actual demonstration and understanding of Life as revealed in Christian Science. To be "with the Lord" is to be in obedience to the law of God, to be absolutely governed by divine Love,—by Spirit, not by matter.

Become conscious for a single moment that Life and intelligence are purely spiritual,—neither in nor of matter,—and the body will then utter no complaints. If suffering from a belief in sickness, you will find yourself suddenly well. Sorrow is turned into joy when the body is controlled by spiritual Life, Truth, and Love. Hence the hope of the promise Jesus bestows: "He that believeth on me, the works that I do shall he do also; . . . because I go unto my Father,"—[because the Ego is absent from the body, and present with Truth and Love.] The Lord's Prayer is the prayer of Soul, not of material sense.

Entirely separate from the belief and dream of material living, is the Life divine, revealing spiritual understanding and the consciousness of man's dominion over the whole earth. This understanding casts out error and heals the sick, and with it you can speak "as one having authority."

"When thou prayest, enter into thy closet, and, when thou hast shut thy door, pray to thy Father which is in secret; and thy Father, which seeth in secret, shall reward thee openly."

So spake Jesus. The closet typifies the sanctuary of Spirit, the door of which shuts out sinful sense but lets in Truth, Life, and Love. Closed to error, it is open to Truth, and *vice versa*. The Father in secret is unseen to the physical senses, but He knows all things and rewards according to motives, not according to speech. To enter into the heart of prayer, the door of the erring senses must be closed. Lips must be mute and materialism silent, that man may have audience with Spirit, the divine Principle, Love, which destroys all error.

In order to pray aright, we must enter into the closet and shut the door. We must close the lips and silence the material senses. In the quiet sanctuary of earnest longings, we must deny sin and plead God's allness. We must resolve to take up the cross, and go forth with honest hearts to work and watch for wisdom, Truth, and Love. We must "pray without ceasing." Such prayer is answered, in so far as we put our desires into practice. The Master's injunction is, that we pray in secret and let our lives attest our sincerity.

Christians rejoice in secret beauty and bounty, hidden from the world, but known to God. Self-forgetfulness, purity, and affection are constant prayers. Practice not profession, understanding not belief, gain the ear and right hand of omnipotence and they assuredly call down infinite blessings. Trustworthiness is the foundation of enlightened faith. Without a fitness for holiness, we cannot receive holiness.

A great sacrifice of material things must precede this advanced spiritual understanding. The highest prayer is not one of faith merely; it is demonstration. Such prayer heals sickness, and must destroy sin and death. It distinguishes between Truth that is sinless and the falsity of sinful sense.

Our Master taught his disciples one brief prayer, which we name after him the Lord's Prayer. Our Master said, "After this manner therefore pray ye," and then he gave that prayer which covers all human needs. There is indeed some doubt among Bible scholars, whether the last line is not an addition to the prayer by a later copyist; but this does not affect the meaning of the prayer itself.

In the phrase, "Deliver us from evil," the original properly reads, "Deliver us from the evil one." This reading strengthens our scientific apprehension of the petition, for Christian Science teaches us that "the evil one," or one evil, is but another name for the first lie and all liars.

Only as we rise above all material sensuousness and sin, can we reach the heaven-born aspiration and spiritual consciousness, which is indicated in the Lord's Prayer and which instantaneously heals the sick.

Here let me give what I understand to be the spiritual sense of the Lord's Prayer:

Our Father which art in heaven,

*Our Father-Mother God, all-harmonious,*

Hallowed be Thy name.

*Adorable One.*

Thy kingdom come.

*Thy kingdom is come; Thou art ever-present.*

Thy will be done in earth, as it is in heaven.

*Enable us to know,—as in heaven, so on earth,—God is omnipotent, supreme.*

Give us this day our daily bread;

*Give us grace for to-day; feed the famished affections;*

And forgive us our debts, as we forgive our debtors.

*And Love is reflected in love;*

And lead us not into temptation, but deliver us from evil;

*And God leadeth us not into temptation, but delivereth us from sin, disease, and death.*

For Thine is the kingdom, and the power, and the glory, forever.

*For God is infinite, all-power, all Life, Truth, Love, over all, and All.*

# CHAPTER XVI

## The Apocalypse

*Blessed is he that readeth, and they that hear the words of this prophecy, and keep those things which are written therein: for the time is at hand.*

—REVELATION.

*Great is the Lord, and greatly to be praised in the city of our God, in the mountain of His holiness.*

—PSALMS.

St. John writes, in the tenth chapter of his book of Revelation:—

And I saw another mighty angel come down from heaven, clothed with a cloud: and a rainbow was upon his head, and his face was as it were the sun, and his feet as pillars of fire: and he had in his hand a little book open: and he set his right foot upon the sea, and his left foot on the earth.

This angel or message which comes from God, clothed with a cloud, prefigures divine Science. To mortal sense Science seems at first obscure, abstract, and dark; but a bright promise crowns its brow. When understood, it is Truth's prism and praise. When you look it fairly in the face, you can heal by its means, and it has for you a light above the sun, for God "is the light thereof." Its feet are pillars of fire, foundations of Truth and Love. It brings the baptism of the Holy Ghost, whose flames of Truth were prophetically described by John the Baptist as consuming error.

This angel had in his hand "a little book," open for all to read and understand. Did this same book contain the revelation of divine Science, the "right foot" or dominant power of which was upon the sea,—upon elementary, latent error, the source of all error's visible forms? The angel's left foot was upon the earth; that is, a secondary power was exercised upon visible error and audible sin. The "still, small voice" of scientific thought reaches over continent and ocean to the globe's remotest bound. The inaudible voice of Truth is, to the human mind, "as when a lion roareth." It is heard in the desert and in dark places of fear. It arouses the "seven thunders" of evil, and stirs their latent forces to utter the full diapason of secret tones. Then is the power of Truth demonstrated,—made manifest in the destruction of error. Then will a voice from harmony cry: "Go and take the little book. . . . Take it, and eat it up; and it shall make thy belly bitter, but it shall be in thy mouth sweet as honey." Mortals, obey the heavenly evangel. Take divine Science. Read this book from beginning to end. Study it, ponder it. It will be indeed sweet at its first taste, when it heals you; but murmur not over Truth, if you find its digestion bitter. When you approach nearer and nearer to this divine Principle, when you eat the divine body of this Principle,—thus partaking of the nature, or primal elements, of Truth and Love,—do not be surprised nor discontented because you must share the hemlock cup and eat the bitter herbs; for the Israelites of old at the Paschal meal thus prefigured this perilous passage out of bondage into the El Dorado of faith and hope.

The twelfth chapter of the Apocalypse, or Revelation of St. John, has a special suggestiveness in connection with the nineteenth century. In the opening of the sixth seal, typical of six thousand years since Adam, the distinctive feature has reference to the present age.

*Revelation* xii. 1. And there appeared a great wonder in heaven; a woman clothed with the sun, and the moon under her feet, and upon her head a crown of twelve stars.

Heaven represents harmony, and divine Science interprets the Principle of heavenly harmony. The great miracle, to human sense, is divine Love, and the grand necessity of existence is to gain the true idea of what constitutes the kingdom of heaven in man. This goal is never reached while we hate our neighbor or entertain a false estimate of anyone whom God has appointed to voice His Word. Again, without a correct sense of its highest visible idea, we can never understand the divine Principle. The botanist must know the genus and species of a plant in order to classify it correctly. As it is with things, so is it with persons.

Abuse of the motives and religion of St. Paul hid from view the apostle's character, which made him equal to his great mission. Persecution of all who have spoken something new and better of God has not only obscured the light of the ages, but has been fatal to the persecutors. Why? Because it has hid from them the true idea which has been presented. To misunderstand Paul, was to be ignorant of the divine idea he taught. Ignorance of the divine idea betrays at once a greater ignorance of the divine Principle of the idea—ignorance of Truth and Love. The understanding of Truth and Love, the Principle which works out the ends of eternal good and destroys both faith in evil and the practice of evil, leads to the discernment of the divine idea.

Agassiz, through his microscope, saw the sun in an egg at a point of so-called embryonic life. Because of his more spiritual vision, St. John saw an "angel standing in the sun." The Revelator beheld the spiritual idea from the mount of vision. Purity was the symbol of Life and Love. The Revelator saw also the spiritual ideal as a woman clothed in light, a bride coming down from heaven, wedded to the Lamb of Love. To John, "the bride" and "the Lamb" represented the correlation of divine Principle and spiritual idea, God and His Christ, bringing harmony to earth.

John saw the human and divine coincidence, shown in the man Jesus, as divinity embracing humanity in Life and its demonstration,—reducing to human perception and understand-

ing the Life which is God. In divine revelation, material and corporeal selfhood disappear, and the spiritual idea is understood.

The woman in the Apocalypse symbolizes generic man, the
spiritual idea of God; she illustrates the coincidence of God and
man as the divine Principle and divine idea. The Revelator symbolizes Spirit by the sun. The spiritual idea is clad with the radi-
ance of spiritual Truth, and matter is put under her feet. The
light portrayed is really neither solar nor lunar, but spiritual Life,
which is "the light of men." In the first chapter of the Fourth
Gospel it is written, "There was a man sent from God . . . to bear
witness of that Light."

John the Baptist prophesied the coming of the immaculate
Jesus, and John saw in those days the spiritual idea as the Messiah, who would baptize with the Holy Ghost,—divine Science.
As Elias presented the idea of the fatherhood of God, which Jesus
afterwards manifested, so the Revelator completed this figure
with woman, typifying the spiritual idea of God's motherhood.
The moon is under her feet. This idea reveals the universe as secondary and tributary to Spirit, from which the universe borrows
its reflected light, substance, life, and intelligence.

The spiritual idea is crowned with twelve stars. The twelve
tribes of Israel with all mortals,—separated by belief from man's
divine origin and the true idea,—will through much tribulation
yield to the activities of the divine Principle of man in the harmony of Science. These are the stars in the crown of rejoicing.
They are the lamps in the spiritual heavens of the age, which
show the workings of the spiritual idea by healing the sick and
the sinning, and by manifesting the light which shines "unto the
perfect day" as the night of materialism wanes.

*Revelation* xii. 2. And she being with child cried, travailing in
birth, and pained to be delivered.

Also the spiritual idea is typified by a woman in travail, waiting to be delivered of her sweet promise, but remembering no
more her sorrow for joy that the birth goes on; for great is the
idea, and the travail portentous.

*Revelation* xii. 3. And there appeared another wonder in
heaven; and behold a great red dragon, having seven heads and
ten horns, and seven crowns upon his heads.

Human sense may well marvel at discord, while, to a diviner

sense, harmony is the real and discord the unreal. We may well be astonished at sin, sickness, and death. We may well be perplexed at human fear; and still more astounded at hatred, which lifts its hydra head, showing its horns in the many inventions of evil. But why should we stand aghast at nothingness? The great red dragon symbolizes a lie,—the belief that substance, life, and intelligence can be material. This dragon stands for the sum total of human error. The ten horns of the dragon typify the belief that matter has power of its own, and that by means of an evil mind in matter the Ten Commandments can be broken.

The Revelator lifts the veil from this embodiment of all evil, and beholds its awful character; but he also sees the nothingness of evil and the allness of God. The Revelator sees that old serpent, whose name is devil or evil, holding untiring watch, that he may bite the heel of truth and seemingly impede the offspring of the spiritual idea, which is prolific in health, holiness, and immortality.

*Revelation* xii. 4. And his tail drew the third part of the stars of heaven, and did cast them to the earth: and the dragon stood before the woman which was ready to be delivered, for to devour her child as soon as it was born.

The serpentine form stands for subtlety, winding its way amidst all evil, but doing this in the name of good. Its sting is spoken of by Paul, when he refers to "spiritual wickedness in high places." It is the animal instinct in mortals, which would impel them to devour each other and cast out devils through Beelzebub.

As of old, evil still charges the spiritual idea with error's own nature and methods. This malicious animal instinct, of which the dragon is the type, incites mortals to kill morally and physically even their fellow-mortals, and worse still, to charge the innocent with the crime. This last infirmity of sin will sink its perpetrator into a night without a star.

The author is convinced that the accusations against Jesus of Nazareth and even his crucifixion were instigated by the criminal instinct here described. The Revelator speaks of Jesus as the Lamb of God and of the dragon as warring against innocence. Since Jesus must have been tempted in all points, he, the immaculate, met and conquered sin in every form. The brutal barbarity of his foes could emanate from no source except the highest degree of human depravity. Jesus "*opened not his mouth.*" Until the majesty of Truth should be demonstrated in divine Science, the spiritual idea was arraigned before the tribunal of so-called mortal mind, which was unloosed in order that the false claim of mind in matter might uncover its own crime of defying immortal Mind.

From Genesis to the Apocalypse, sin, sickness, and death, envy, hatred, and revenge,—all evil,—are typified by a serpent, or animal subtlety. Jesus said, quoting a line from the Psalms, "They hated me without a cause." The serpent is perpetually close upon the heel of harmony. From the beginning to the end, the serpent pursues with hatred the spiritual idea. In Genesis, this allegorical, talking serpent typifies mortal mind, "more subtle than any beast of the field." In the Apocalypse, when nearing its doom, this evil increases and becomes the great red dragon, swollen with sin, inflamed with war against spirituality, and ripe for destruction. It is full of lust and hate, loathing the brightness of divine glory.

*Revelation* xii. 5. And she brought forth a man child, who was to rule all nations with a rod of iron: and her child was caught up unto God, and to His throne.

Led on by the grossest element of mortal mind, Herod decreed the death of every male child in order that the man Jesus, the masculine representative of the spiritual idea, might never hold sway and deprive Herod of his crown. The impersonation of the spiritual idea had a brief history in the earthly life of our Master; but "of his kingdom there shall be no end," for Christ, God's idea, will eventually rule all nations and peoples—imperatively, absolutely, finally—with divine Science. This immaculate idea, represented first by man and, according to the Revelator, last by woman, will baptize with fire; and the fiery baptism will burn up the chaff of error with the fervent heat of Truth and Love, melting and purifying even the gold of human character. After the stars sang together and all was primeval harmony, the material lie made war upon the spiritual idea; but this only impelled the idea to rise to the zenith of demonstration, destroying sin, sickness, and death, and to be caught up unto God,—to be found in its divine Principle.

*Revelation* xii. 6. And the woman fled into the wilderness, where she hath a place prepared of God.

As the children of Israel were guided triumphantly through the Red Sea, the dark ebbing and flowing tides of human fear,—as they were led through the wilderness, walking wearily through the great desert of human hopes, and anticipating the promised joy,—so shall the spiritual idea guide all right desires in their passage from sense to Soul, from a material sense of existence to the spiritual, up to the glory prepared for them who love God. Stately Science pauses not, but moves before them, a pillar of cloud by day and of fire by night, leading to divine heights.

If we remember the beautiful description which Sir Walter Scott puts into the mouth of Rebecca the Jewess in the story of Ivanhoe,—

> When Israel, of the Lord beloved,
>   Out of the land of bondage came,
> Her fathers' God before her moved,
>   An awful guide, in smoke and flame,—

we may also offer the prayer which concludes the same hymn,—

> And oh, when stoops on Judah's path
>   In shade and storm the frequent night,
> Be Thou, longsuffering, slow to wrath,
>   A burning and a shining light!

*Revelation* xii. 7, 8. And there was war in heaven: Michael and his angels fought against the dragon; and the dragon fought, and his angels, and prevailed not; neither was their place found any more in heaven.

The Old Testament assigns to the angels, God's divine messages, different offices. Michael's characteristic is spiritual strength. He leads the hosts of heaven against the power of sin, Satan, and fights the holy wars. Gabriel has the more quiet task of imparting a sense of the ever-presence of ministering Love. These angels deliver us from the depths. Truth and Love come nearer in the hour of woe, when strong faith or spiritual strength wrestles and prevails through the understanding of God. The Gabriel of His presence has no contests. To infinite, ever-present Love, all is Love, and there is no error, no sin, sickness, nor death. Against Love, the dragon warreth not long, for he is killed by the divine Principle. Truth and Love prevail against the dragon because the dragon cannot war with them. Thus endeth the conflict between the flesh and Spirit.

*Revelation* xii. 9. And the great dragon was cast out, that old serpent, called the devil, and Satan, which deceiveth the whole world: he was cast out into the earth, and his angels were cast out with him.

That false claim—that ancient belief, that old serpent whose name is devil (evil), claiming that there is intelligence in matter either to benefit or to injure men—is pure delusion, the red dragon; and it is cast out by Christ, Truth, the spiritual idea, and so proved to be powerless. The words "cast unto the earth" show the dragon to be nothingness, dust to dust; and therefore, in his pretence of being a talker, he must be a lie from the beginning. His angels, or messages, are cast out with their author. The beast and the false prophets are lust and hypocrisy. These wolves in sheep's clothing are detected and killed by innocence, the Lamb of Love.

Divine Science shows how the Lamb slays the wolf. Innocence and Truth overcome guilt and error. Ever since the foundation of the world, ever since error would establish material belief, evil has tried to slay the Lamb; but Science is able to destroy this lie, called evil. The twelfth chapter of the Apocalypse typifies the divine method of warfare in Science, and the glorious results of this warfare. The following chapters depict the fatal effects of trying to meet error with error. The narrative follows the order used in Genesis. In Genesis, first the true method of creation is set forth and then the false. Here, also, the Revelator first exhibits the true warfare and then the false.

*Revelation* xii. 10-12. And I heard a loud voice saying in heaven, Now is come salvation, and strength, and the kingdom of our God, and the power of His Christ: for the accuser of our brethren is cast down, which accused them before our God day and night. And they overcame him by the blood of the Lamb, and by the word of their testimony; and they loved not their lives unto the death. Therefore rejoice, ye heavens, and ye that dwell in them. Woe to the inhabiters of the earth and of the sea! for the devil is come down unto you, having great wrath, because he knoweth that he hath but a short time.

For victory over a single sin, we give thanks and magnify the Lord of Hosts. What shall we say of the mighty conquest over all sin? A louder song, sweeter than has ever before reached high heaven, now rises clearer and nearer to the great heart of Christ; for the accuser is not there, and Love sends forth her primal and everlasting strain. Self-abnegation, by which we lay down all for Truth, or Christ, in our warfare against error, is a rule in Christian Science. This rule clearly interprets God as divine Principle,— as Life, represented by the Father; as Truth, represented by the Son; as Love, represented by the Mother. Every mortal at some period, here or hereafter, must grapple with and overcome the mortal belief in a power opposed to God.

The Scripture, "Thou hast been faithful over a few things, I will make thee ruler over many," is literally fulfilled, when we are conscious of the supremacy of Truth, by which the nothingness of error is seen; and we know that the nothingness of error is in proportion to its wickedness. He that touches the hem of Christ's robe and masters his mortal beliefs, animality, and hate, rejoices in the proof of healing,—in a sweet and certain sense that God is Love. Alas for those who break faith with divine Science and fail to strangle the serpent of sin as well as of sickness! They are dwellers still in the deep darkness of belief. They are in the surging sea of error, not struggling to lift their heads above the drowning wave.

What must the end be? They must eventually expiate their sin through suffering. The sin, which one has made his bosom companion, comes back to him at last with accelerated force, for the devil knoweth his time is short. Here the Scriptures declare that evil is temporal, not eternal. The dragon is at last stung to death by his own malice; but how many periods of torture it may take to remove all sin, must depend upon sin's obduracy.

*Revelation* xii. 13. And when the dragon saw that he was cast unto the earth, he persecuted the woman which brought forth the man child.

The march of mind and of honest investigation will bring the hour when the people will chain, with fetters of some sort, the growing occultism of this period. The present apathy as to the tendency of certain active yet unseen mental agencies will finally be shocked into another extreme mortal mood,—into human indignation; for one extreme follows another.

*Revelation* xii. 15, 16. And the serpent cast out of his mouth water as a flood, after the woman, that he might cause her to be carried away of the flood. And the earth helped the woman, and the earth opened her mouth, and swallowed up the flood which the dragon cast out of his mouth.

Millions of unprejudiced minds—simple seekers for Truth, weary wanderers, athirst in the desert—are waiting and watching for rest and drink. Give them a cup of cold water in Christ's name, and never fear the consequences. What if the old dragon should send forth a new flood to drown the Christ-idea? He can neither drown your voice with its roar, nor again sink the world into the deep waters of chaos and old night. In this age the earth will help the woman; the spiritual idea will be understood. Those ready for the blessing you impart will give thanks. The waters will be pacified, and Christ will command the wave.

When God heals the sick or the sinning, they should know the great benefit which Mind has wrought. They should also know the great delusion of mortal mind, when it makes them sick or sinful. Many are willing to open the eyes of the people to the power of good resident in divine Mind, but they are not so willing to point out the evil in human thought, and expose evil's hidden mental ways of accomplishing iniquity.

Why this backwardness, since exposure is necessary to ensure the avoidance of the evil? Because people like you better when you tell them their virtues than when you tell them their vices. It requires the spirit of our blessed Master to tell a man his faults, and so risk human displeasure for the sake of doing right and benefiting our race. Who is telling mankind of the foe in ambush? Is the informer one who sees the foe? If so, listen and be wise. Escape from evil, and designate those as unfaithful stewards who have seen the danger and yet have given no warning.

At all times and under all circumstances, overcome evil with good. Know thyself, and God will supply the wisdom and the occasion for a victory over evil. Clad in the panoply of Love, human hatred cannot reach you. The cement of a higher humanity will unite all interests in the one divinity.

[. . .]

This heavenly city, lighted by the Sun of Righteousness,—this New Jerusalem, this infinite All, which to us seems hidden in the mist of remoteness,—reached St. John's vision while yet he tabernacled with mortals.

In Revelation xxi. 22, further describing this holy city, the beloved Disciple writes:—

And I saw no temple therein: for the Lord God Almighty and the Lamb are the temple of it.

There was no temple,—that is, no material structure in which to worship God, for He must be worshipped in spirit and in love. The word *temple* also means *body*. The Revelator was familiar with Jesus' use of this word, as when Jesus spoke of his material body as the temple to be temporarily rebuilt (John ii. 21). What further indication need we of the real man's incorporeality than this, that John saw heaven and earth with "no temple [body] therein"? This kingdom of God "is within you,"—is within reach of man's consciousness here, and the spiritual idea reveals it. In divine Science, man possesses this recognition of harmony consciously in proportion to his understanding of God.

The term Lord, as used in our version of the Old Testament, is often synonymous with Jehovah, and expresses the Jewish concept, not yet elevated to deific apprehension through spiritual transfiguration. Yet the word gradually approaches a higher meaning. This human sense of Deity yields to the divine sense, even as the material sense of personality yields to the incorporeal sense of God and man as the infinite Principle and infinite idea,—as one Father with His universal family, held in the gospel of Love. The Lamb's wife presents the unity of male and female as no longer two wedded individuals, but as two individual natures in one; and this compounded spiritual individuality reflects God as Father-Mother, not as a corporeal being. In this divinely united spiritual consciousness, there is no impediment to eternal bliss,—to the perfectibility of God's creation.

This spiritual, holy habitation has no boundary nor limit, but its four cardinal points are: first, the Word of Life, Truth, and Love; second, the Christ, the spiritual idea of God; third, Christianity, which is the outcome of the divine Principle of the Christ-idea in Christian history; fourth, Christian Science, which today and forever interprets this great example and the great Exemplar. This city of our God has no need of sun or satellite, for Love is the light of it, and divine Mind is its own interpreter. All who are saved must walk in this light. Mighty potentates and dynasties will lay down their honors within the heavenly city. Its gates open towards light and glory both within and without, for all is good, and nothing can enter that city, which "defileth, . . . or maketh a lie."

The writer's present feeble sense of Christian Science closes with St. John's Revelation as recorded by the great apostle, for his vision is the acme of this Science as the Bible reveals it.

In the following Psalm one word shows, though faintly, the light which Christian Science throws on the Scriptures by substituting for the corporeal sense, the incorporeal or spiritual sense of Deity:—

## PSALM XXIII

[DIVINE LOVE] is my shepherd; I shall not want.

[LOVE] maketh me to lie down in green pastures: [LOVE] leadeth me beside the still waters.

[LOVE] restoreth my soul [spiritual sense]: [LOVE] leadeth me in the paths of righteousness for His name's sake.

Yea, though I walk through the valley of the shadow of death, I will fear no evil: for [LOVE] is with me; [LOVE'S] rod and [LOVE'S] staff they comfort me.

[LOVE] prepareth a table before me in the presence of mine enemies: [LOVE] anointeth my head with oil; my cup runneth over.

Surely goodness and mercy shall follow me all the days of my life; and I will dwell in the house [the consciousness] of [LOVE] for ever.

(MARY BAKER EDDY, 1875; REV. ED., BOSTON, MA, 1913;
PP. 1–17, 558–71, 576–78)

# OAHSPE:
# A New Bible in the Words of Jehovih and His Angel Embassadors

In 1880 a New York City dentist, John Ballou Newbrough, was gripped by a strong impression that he must write a book. Sitting before a novel device called a typewriter, Newbrough claimed that a bright light enveloped his hands. He later recounted that he had no conscious knowledge of what he was recording and was told by angels not to read it until it was completed. Newbrough wrote "automatically" for more than a year before publishing OAHSPE, his volume of nearly nine hundred pages, with the help of a group of anonymous financial supporters. OAHSPE (which, according to Newbrough's glossary, stands for "Sky, earth [corpor] and spirit") relates twenty-four thousand years of world history through the voice of a father-mother Jehovah the Creator, thousands of gods and goddesses, and a delegation of angel ambassadors. It introduces many new names but also enfolds much familiar biblical and world history, outlining the rise and fall of civilizations and predicting the ultimate defeat of Buddhism, Hinduism, Islam, Christianity, and other world religions and the emergence of a true universal faith. OAHSPE also contains pencil sketches composed by the angels who, according to Newbrough, controlled his hands as he drew.

Within a few years of its publication, the OAHSPE Lodge of Faithists formed and made plans to found a community, Shalam, in New Mexico. Newbrough, a lifelong follower of Spiritualism, a vegetarian, a pacifist, and a social reformer, spearheaded the settlement of several dozen believers along with Andrew Howland, a wealthy Quaker businessman from Massachusetts. Located in the Mesilla Valley along the Rio Grande, the community took into their social experiment orphans and abandoned children in an attempt to live out the ideals related in Newbrough's text. Members ate only two meals a day, children were given names drawn from OAHSPE, and leaders relied on the advice of angels to guide the development of the community. After Newbrough's death in 1891, Howland assumed control of day-to-day operations, but within a decade Shalam was bankrupt and the residents dispersed. Still, Faithists into the late twentieth century remained convinced they saw signs in world events of the fulfillment of the predictions outlined in OAHSPE.

The selections here are drawn from "the book of Es," a portion of the text that describes three central events: the founding of the American Republic; the fall of the major world religions to the strengthening ranks of those espousing liberty of conscience and social harmony; and the dawn of the new order of "kosmon." Warriors on Earth are aided by thousands of angels, and the four false gods fall to the power of Jehovih. The final defeat of the various sects (Christian denominations) marks the beginning of the kosmon era, in which slavery is overthrown and race no longer plays a role in human relationships. By weaving a cosmic story into recent events in American history, OAHSPE offers divine sanction to the nation as the instigator of this culminating era of sacred history, even as it critiques its majority Christian culture.

# OAHSPE:

# A New Bible in the Words of Jehovih and His Angel Embassadors

## BOOK OF ES, DAUGHTER OF JEHOVIH

To His etherean Gods and Goddesses, Jehovih said: Behold, in twelve generations My dawn of kosmon will reach the earth.

2. Go ye down to the earth, and provide mortals and angels unto the work of My cycle.

3. In other times, My Gods and Goddesses said unto man: Thou shalt, and thou shalt not. Behold, in kosmon, ye shall declare the glory of My works and the plans of My heavens unto the nations of the earth. In all My fullness shall ye declare the glories of My creations.

4. But ye shall not say to this man nor to that man: Thou shalt believe, nor that thou shalt not believe.

5. Neither shall ye say to man: Thou shalt do this, and thou shalt not do that.

6. Such were the ancient cycles and the custom of My revelators; but such shall not be the custom of My revelators in this day.

7. But man, having heard and seen, shall judge what he will do; he shall believe, or not believe; and do, or not do, according to his own judgment.

8. Because I hold man responsible, even so should he have liberty to choose.

9. And if he strive to choose Me, by doing righteously, he shall not fail.

10. Though he accept none of the ancient doctrines, nor rites, nor ceremonies, nor Gods, nor Lords, nor Saviors, but strive for Me in doing good unto others, he shall be My chosen, even though he accept not My name.

11. Liberty, first of all, unto all people; then discipline and harmony, and then the improvement of all the talents I created with all.

12. Next to this, to have no leader, nor any one to think for another; nor to abandon one's own judgment contrary to wisdom and truth.

13. But to contend not, nor to be stubborn and positive as to the righteousness of one's own opinion. For I created no two men to see alike the same thing on earth or in heaven.

14. As to which matters, the highest wisdom is to suffer all men to have full liberty to think on all subjects in their own way.

15. In the olden times, they had inquisitors, to watch as to what another did, or said, or intimated; now, behold, in kosmon, exactly the opposite of this shall be the behavior of My chosen.

16. Though man seeth his neighbor do differently from what he himself would, he shall look the other way; or, if he speak to him of the matter, it shall be with respect, even as he would to his own mother or father.

17. And for any shortness of speech, or error, or evil expression, man shall not reprove his neighbor, nor find fault with him, more than he would with his own mother, or father, or sister, or brother. Rather shall he strive, not to see, nor hear the shortness of any man.

18. They shall be taught to see the good that is in others; to speak of the delights of all My living creatures.

19. To reprove with words, to circumspect the doings of one's neighbors, their opinions and behavior, these shall I put away in kosmon.

20. Neither shall one man advise another without becoming bound to him that followeth his advice. This, also, shall man be made to understand in kosmon.

21. In other cycles, I sent My loo'is to raise up certain mortals, through whom I could reveal My commandments unto others. In kosmon, behold, I shall not raise up any great leader-forth; My light shall fall upon thousands and thousands. Of many varieties of talents shall be My chosen in that day.

22. For which reason, when ye have descended to the earth, ye shall appoint loo'is unto millions of mortals, and they shall raise up a numerous offspring unto Me.

23. And it shall be born with them to see and feel, that a new era is at hand; and they shall be born skeptical to the ancient doctrines, Gods, Lords and Saviors.

24. Nevertheless, they shall be the best of men, and wise and charitable and most considerate of the opinions of others.

25. And it shall come to pass, that when the western continent is inhabited across from east to west, all the earth will be circumscribed with men of wisdom and learning.

26. And the year of the circumscribing shall be the beginning of kosmon.

27. And the heavens of the earth shall be opened, and the angels thereof shall descend to the earth, and make themselves known to mortals; even through them which your loo'is shall have born unto the work.

28. And from that time forth, the old order shall decline, to be put away forever; and the new order shall take its place, to triumph over all the earth.

29. Thereafter, shall the virtue of preaching come to an end; but practice, in fulfilling good works and living up to My commandments, shall be all that will avail for the establishing of My kingdom on earth.

30. Go ye forth, My beloved; fulfill the seasons of the earth, that My people may rejoice in their lives, in peace and love, for the glory of My heavens, which I created for them.

[. . .]

## CHAPTER XIII.

### The Republic Established.

Es said: Since three hundred years, the loo'is of God's allotment to the earth, had been providing the generations of men unto the coming work of God.

2. And through these had God, Jehovih's Son, raised up one thousand two hundred men, to be directly under the inspiration of the second resurrection, for establishing an emancipated government for mortals.

3. And these one thousand two hundred men were raised to grades above sixty, and some of them to eighty.

4. Chief of these men raised up by God, to establish the foundation of Jehovih's kingdom with mortals, were the following, all of whom stood above grade eighty, to wit:

5. Paine, Jefferson, Adams, Franklin, Carroll, Hancock and Washington.

6. Into the hands of these seven men did Jehovih, through God, His Son, place the leadership of the mortal hosts; and they were under the guidance of Jehovih's Lord, Yotahiza.

7. And the Lord caused Paine, to proclaim the new doctrines, as against Looeamong and the sacred books, on which the inquisitions had been carried out.

8. These, then, were the doctrines of Paine, inspired by the Lord, Jehovih's Son, to wit:

9. One, the Creator, Who is Almighty, matchless in wisdom, truth, power and unity of purpose; the author of all things, on the earth and on all other worlds, seen and unseen.

10. That the soul of man is immortal and everlasting, and shall ultimately attain to peace and joy in the heavens of the Almighty.

11. That, according to man's good or evil deeds, words, thoughts and actions whilst on earth, even so shall he inherit in heaven, light or darkness, joy or unhappiness.

12. That all the world is my country, and the same right alike to all men.

13. To do good, with all of one's wisdom and strength, is the highest religion.

14. That man hath a natural right, above all kings, priests and sacred writings, to serve his Creator in his own way.

15. That this is an age of reason, in which all men should be inspired, to read and think, and judge with their own judgment and not through any priest or church or Savior.

16. That the doctrine of a Savior is unjust; that no honest man should accept another's dying for him.

17. That the so-called sacred books are not the writings of the Creator; that their multiplicity of defects prove them to have been manufactured by corruptible authors.

18. That, in practice, the said sacred books have been used by

unprincipled priests to promote wars, inquisitions, tyranny and destruction.

19. That man should rise up in his might to embrace his Creator, by the practice of good works, and by promoting brotherly love toward all men; and by charity and independence elicit the protection, the pride and the glory of the Almighty.

20. The doctrines of God, Paine proclaimed publicly; and they were printed, and circulated amongst the inhabitants of Guatama.

21. And it came to pass, that they fell into the hands of such men and women as had been previously prepared by God to receive them. And these people applauded the new doctrines to so great an extent that the colonies repudiated the Divine right (Divan laws) of kings to govern without the consent of the governed.

22. Looeamong, the false Kriste, perceived the design of God, Jehovih's Son, and immediately sent down to the earth, to Guatama, two thousand angel warriors, to overthrow Paine's doctrines, and to precipitate the colonies into war against the home government in western Uropa.

23. So, war in Guatama, on earth, and in the heavens thereof, set in, mortals against mortals and angels against angels.

24. The Lord, Yotahiza, now assigned the army of the inquisition, the seven thousand angels sent of God, to be the protecting hosts to the seven leaders of the Guatama revolt.

25. Besides these angels, who were generals and captains of the hosts, there were of non-commissioned angel officers, two thousand seven hundred and eighty-four, who had also been martyred as to earth-life, by scourging, and by the rack, and by being pulled in quarters, and by being burnt, who were distributed amongst the mortal armies of soldiers. And these angel officers had angel armies and companies, disciplined and quartered in the camps of the mortals with the soldiers.

26. Such, then, were the inspiring hosts, varying in number from six million to twelve million, who remained with the soldiers of the republic during the war, day and night, inspiring them to fortitude, and manipulating them to give them health and strength and endurance.

27. God spake to the angel commander of these hosts, saying: Though thy hosts inspire these mortals to liberty as to earthly

things, yet thou shalt also take advantage of this opportunity to sow the seed of higher spiritual light amongst them. Remember, then, the sermon of the All High: There is but one Great Spirit, Jehovih. And this shall thy hosts forever inspire mortals with.

28. For seven years the war lasted, and during all the while, the earthly commander, Washington, was under the guardianship of the commander of the angel hosts. And there were detailed to guard Washington, day and night, one thousand angels. And though he was shot at, and in many ways sought for to be destroyed, these angels saved him, even catching in their hands the bullets that were fired at him.

29. And in like manner were many other mortal leaders and privates in the war protected and saved from harm by the angels.

30. And yet all this while the angels of Looeamong fought on the other side, endeavoring to pull away the guardian angels, and so make the mortal leaders vulnerable.

31. But these angels were lower in grade and less potent, and, withal, not so enthusiastic, for they had not suffered martyrdom.

32. Jehovih hath said: Rather let a man glory in martyrdom for righteousness' sake; for herein he taketh high resolves against evil; which resolves are a great power to the soul when it entereth heaven.

33. And it came to pass that the republic was established.

34. And God caused the commander of the angels who had accomplished this work, to call his hosts together, that they might hear the voice of Jehovih. And there thus assembled eighteen million three hundred and forty thousand in number, in an extemporized heaven above the Haguan mountains, where the chiefs of Paradise had already prepared an altar to Jehovih for the occasion.

35. Of the higher grades from other plateaux, were here assembled in the sacred circle, seventy million angels, to promote the Voice. Of which matters God had previously sent word to Aroqu, that a chain of light might be made to the upper heavens.

36. Now, when the angels of the inquisition were thus assembled before God, and duly placed by the marshals, God caused the light to be lowered, so that they might rejoice rather than suffer because of its brilliancy.

37. And when God sat on the throne, and the es'enaurs had chanted unto Jehovih glory for having founded the republic of

mortals, a ray of light was seen descending from the upper realms, and it extended down to the throne of God, where now, on all sides, the illumination was in splendor. Presently, just above the throne, a single star of light was formed, and out of this came the Voice of Jehovih, saying:

38. Peace, My beloved. The way is open: liberty to the conscience of mortals is founded on earth. Ye have lifted them above the bondage of Gods.

39. Because ye were cut down before ye had finished your labor on earth, I suffered ye to come back to mortals to complete your own aspirations.

40. Because you united with one another in companies and phalanxes for a good work, instead of working single-handed, ye are now admitted into the second resurrection of My kingdoms.

41. By the light of My throne are ye this day absolved from the bondage of earth and first resurrection.

42. The Voice ceased; but God spake unto his marshals, saying: Provide ye an avalanza sufficient for the ascension of these my beloved angels, and take them to the fields and forests of Attusasabak, in the Ortheon plateau, where I have already provided them ample residences.

43. And, after they are delivered, grade them, and give unto them suitable instructors and companions, that in due time they may become Brides and Bridegrooms to Jehovih, and ascend to the emancipated kingdoms in the etherean worlds.

44. Suffer them now to pass before the throne, that they may receive badges from the Most High! For these will be to them a connection with the exalted kingdoms.

45. The marshals then filed them past the throne, and there fell, from the heavens above, upon them, badges of immortal light, unchangeable.

46. And the builders in Yutis brought them an avalanza, and they went therein, to the sound of the singing of three million voices in Jehovih's praise. And when they were within, God again spake to them, saying:

47. Ye go now far off from the earth. But as ye freed this land unto itself, and now go away, behold, I will call ye back again before another hundred years, to free the people from the doctrines and creeds of the ancients. No God nor Lord nor Savior

shall be enforced in this land! Till then, Jehovih be with you all,
and give you joy and happiness!

48. Thereupon, the officers of the avalanza set it in motion, rising upward. And the musicians, they that remained and they that
ascended, sang and trumpeted until the fire-ship ascended out of
sight.

## CHAPTER XIV.

For three hundred years prior to the above transactions, the four
false Gods had been in war to a limited extent in their heavens,
and for certain earth possessions also.

2. In Chine'ya, the Ka'yuans (Confucians) had made great
progress, to the injury of the false Brahma, Ennochissa. But the
latter had pushed his people into Vind'yu and Par'si'e.

3. On the part of Kabalactes, the false Budha, he had pushed
his people into Chine'ya and Par'si'e also. And in many parts of
Vind'yu, these Budhists had treated the Brahmans with great
slaughter.

4. But neither of the above false Gods was a match for Thoth,
alias God-Gabriel. Under the name and doctrines of Moham-
med, he had made great inroads upon the possessions of the other
two false Gods, both as to the earth and the heavens thereof.

5. And yet, on the other hand, Looeamong, the false Kriste,
had taken advantage of all the other three false Gods. He had
found mortal emissaries in Britain (western Uropa) whom he
had inspired under the name, EAST INDIA COMPANY. To these
he had said: Come, I will lead you where there is great wealth
and most luxurious enjoyment. Behold, ye shall possess the place,
and overcome the heathen of a rich country.

6. So, Looeamong led them, and they took with them missionaries and bibles and swords and cannons and war-ships. And
when they arrived at Vind'yu, Looeamong, through his angel
hosts, said unto them; Tell these heathen, ye are worshippers of
the Lamb of Peace; that ye have come in love and for righteousness' sake. And, behold, they will receive you. And it shall come
to pass, when ye are once within, ye shall fall upon them, and
destroy them by the million, men, women and children. And ye

shall fall upon their aqueducts, which irrigate the lands, and ye shall destroy them also; and, behold, millions of these heathen shall starve every year, because of the famines that shall surely come upon them.

7. Now, all these came to pass; the idolaters of Looeamong did fall upon the Budhists' earthly possessions, and did possess the land of Vind'yu, and, in the name of Kriste and the Holy Ghost, did kill seven million men, women and children.

8. And they also destroyed the aqueducts whereby famines came upon the Vind'yuans, so that, in course of time, thirty million more perished of starvation.

9. Now, although Kabalactes thus lost, in a great measure, his earthly possessions, he still maintained the heavens of Vind'yu, so that Looeamong really gained but few souls, in heaven, after all his destructions.

10. Looeamong had also led his mortal emissaries into Chine'ya, in hope to possess that country also. He had said to them: Go thither, and enforce upon them the opium trade. And it shall come to pass, they will become a drunken and worthless people, and ye shall fall upon them, and overcome them, and possess all their country, wherein there are stored great riches.

11. And the idolaters of the false Kriste did fall upon the Chine'yans and enforce the opium trade, and did also make many of them a drunken and worthless people. And after they were thus drunk, the idolaters of the false Kriste raised the cry: Behold, the drunken heathen! The indulgers in opium!

12. Nevertheless, the Ka'yuans of Chine'ya were a mighty power, and they baffled Looeamong's emissaries in all further encroachments.

13. Now, although Looeamong had been beaten by the wisdom of God, in possessing the colonies of Guatama, nevertheless, Looeamong still hoped to regain the country to himself. And to carry out his designs, he sent two thousand million angel warriors to accomplish the destruction of the Algonquin tribes that inhabited the country.

14. And this also came to pass, the idolaters of Looeamong did fall upon the Algonquins, and caused three million of them to be put to death, men, women and children.

# CHAPTER XV.

## God, Jehovih's Son, Casteth out the Four False Gods.

When the right time came, Jehovih spake to God, saying: My Son, behold, the kosmon era is near, and the light of the arc of su'is entereth the fields of Paradise. Stretch forth thy hand over the nations of the earth and over the heavens thereof, and sweep clean thy kingdoms for My everlasting light.

2. The four false Gods, the perpetuators of the beast, will call out in agony, but thou shalt heed them not in My judgments.

3. Then God sent forth his disciplined hosts, twelve thousand million, to cut off the supplies of the earth. Even as a mortal general cutteth off the supplies of a wicked city to subdue it, so was cut off the accumulated power of the four false Gods, they that had proclaimed themselves the Saviors of mortals and angels.

4. And the angels of God spread around about the whole earth! In armies of millions and tens of millions, well disciplined, they gathered together in the mortal cities, and in the country places, amongst all nations, tribes and peoples.

5. And these angel armies were officered and drilled to work in concert, with lines of light extending to the throne of God.

6. And God spake in Paradise, by means of the lines of light, and his voice went into all the mighty armies of his hosts, the twelve thousand million, saying:

7. Cut off the earth supplies of the four beasts of the earth! They and their countless legions of followers have become profitless in the resurrection of mortals and angels.

8. Their names have become a stench upon the earth. Their mortal followers are grovelers in all manner of uncleanness. Their spirits have become as vagabonds on the earth and in the heavens thereof.

9. My hosts have tried to persuade them, but they will not hear; the light of the upper kingdoms, they will not receive.

10. But I will make them look up. Like beasts that are untamed, they shall cry out for sustenance, but they shall not find it in the places of their old haunts.

11. Then, the hosts of God marched in betwixt the drujas, the worshippers of the four false Gods, and their mortal harvests.

12. And the drujas turned to their respective Gods, the false Brahma, the false Budha and Gabriel of Kalla, and the false Kriste, crying out: Behold, our supplies are cut off! Is not the earth thy kingdom, and the place of thy footstool? Saidst thou not that thou wert the Almighty? How, then, hath another God come between? If thou art, indeed, our Savior, now save us! But if thou hast been all this while deceiving, then shall hell be thy portion!

13. The four false Gods heard the cry of anger and suspicion in their mighty kingdoms; heard the wailings of the sixty thousand million. And they feared, and trembled.

14. Most of all in fear was the false Kriste, for, for sake of aggrandizing his own kingdom, he had had it proclaimed on the earth that: Whosoever believeth in me, shall be saved; but whosoever believeth not in me, shall be in danger of hell-fire!

15. And countless millions of mortals had taken no thought as to self-resurrection, but taken him at his word; and so had lived and died and become his slaves for hundreds of years. Millions of these angels had heavenly banners made, with the promises of this false Lord inscribed thereon, aud with these went in processions in heaven, crying out: Bread or blood! Bread or blood! We come not to bring peace in heaven; we come to bring a sword! We come to set angel against angel! Give unto us, O thou, our God, or hell shall be thy portion!

16. Thus, it came to pass, as had been foretold by God, whereof he had said: Anarchy shall encompass your heavenly kingdoms, and ye shall yet own that ye are false before Jehovih.

17. And the four false Gods, fearing the fires of hell, went about, crying out: I am not the true Brahma! I am not the true Budah! I am not the true God! I am not the true Kriste!

18. For they hoped thereby to save themselves. But, alas, for them. Their thousands of millions fell upon their heavenly cities, palaces and thrones, and robbed them.

19. And, when their fury was started, behold, the vast multitudes rushed for the false Gods, and fell upon them, beat them, suffocated them with foul smells, covered them up with suffocating gases, walled them in with sulphurous fires.

20. And they brought the officers and priests and monks and high officers, and cast them into hells also, millions and millions of high-ruling angels of the false Gods.

21. Thus were these four false Gods hemmed in, even within their own dissolute kingdoms, and every day and every hour grew more terrible. It was the infuriated madness of sixty thousand million deceived angels, broken loose from slavery, turned upon them.

22. Then Jehovih's God, from Paradise, went forth in a ship of fire, brilliant, past the endurance of drujas; went forth with ten million high in the grades; ten million against sixty thousand million. God brought these from the realms of Aroqu and Harivya, well disciplined for the purpose.

23. And on the ship, and on the banners thereof, were inscribed these words: THERE IS BUT ONE GREAT SPIRIT, JEHOVIH. TO ASSIMILATE WITH HIM, IS THE SALVATION OF MORTALS AND ANGELS.

24. He crieth out: Come unto Me; My kingdoms are ample unto all the living. Be ye strong in resurrection, for I am come to deliver.

25. And God gathered in from the highest grades of the disrupted heavenly kingdoms thirteen thousand million homeless angels, who had been worshippers of the four false Gods. And God had them sent to Luana, on the plateau, Hivestos, where he officered them in colonies, with places for education and labor.

26. God said unto them: Ye hoped to ascend to Jehovih's highest kingdom by prayers and confessions to false Gods. Behold, I say unto you, there is no resurrection but by developing the talents Jehovih created unto all men. Go ye to work, therefore, and to places of education, that ye may become fit companions to Jehovih's exalted angels.

[. . .]

## CHAPTER XVIII.

Es said: Such, then, was the fate of the chief false Gods in the lower heavens.

2. But, during the last three or four hundred years, many of the officers of these false Gods had seceded from them, and had set up small heavenly kingdoms of their own. And their mortal followers were called sects.

3. These little heavens were, for the most part, situated on the earth, and usually these small Gods inhabited the churches where mortals came to worship.

4. And the preachers within these churches fell under the inspiration of these itinerant Gods and their gangs of wandering spirits.

5. In Guatama, these inspirations were carried to such an extent, by these drujan Gods, that the mortals of one sect were made hostile, one sect against another.

6. An enmity, therefore, existed betwixt protestants and catholics, and betwixt protestants themselves, and betwixt all of these and the Jews. And, not only on earth, betwixt mortals, did these things take place, but these petty Gods had small kingdoms of their own; as a presbyterian heaven; a methodist heaven; a baptist heaven, and so on. And, when a mortal member died, his spirit fell into his heaven, where he had lived, becoming a servant to these drujas. And, when he cried out: I want to go to Jesus, I want to go to Kriste, he was shown the drujan God, and told: That is he! The which he would believe to be true. For what is bound on earth, is bound in heaven.

7. A drujan God, Piad, established a sect, and named it Mormon, and he located his kingdom on earth with his mortal followers, and he became master over the spirits of his mortal followers in the same way, calling himself, the TRUE KRISTE.

8. Piad taught, that all good Mormons would ultimately attain to rule over some planet and her heavens. But, he never permitted the angels of his kingdom to go out of his reach. He also taught mortals, that the more numerous progeny a man begot, the greater would be his heavenly kingdom, in time to come. For this was Piad's scheme, to make his own heavenly kingdom large and powerful.

9. Another drujan God, Lowgannus, established a kingdom on earth, and named it Shaker Heaven, pretending he was the TRUE KRISTE. And his place became a heavenly bondage unto himself.

10. Another drujan God, Sayawan, established a heavenly kingdom on earth, and called it THE ALL HIGHEST HEAVEN.

11. This Lord called himself THE LORD. He raised up a mortal, Swedenborg, whom he took in spirit, subjectively, into many of the lowest heavens and hells, saying to him:

12. Behold, they that serve not THE LORD! How hard it is with

them! And he further said: This place of darkness is the Brahman heaven; that place of darkness is the Budhist heaven! But this place of light is my heaven, I, THE LORD.

13. Thus did this drujan God establish a Swedenborg heaven, and mortals looked upon him as the true Kriste, and, after death, their souls went thither.

14. So, it came to pass, as had been prophesied of old: Lo, Kriste, here! Lo, Kriste, there!

15. And, as it was with Looeamong's heavenly kingdoms, thus split into hundreds of remnants, even so was it with the heavenly kingdoms of the other false Gods, Brahma, the false, and Budha, the false, so that there were on the earth thousands of petty Gods' heavenly kingdoms of darkness and misery.

16. Now, all of these drujan Gods, whether of Chine'ya, or Vind'yu, or Arabin'ya, or Uropa, or Guatama, rejected Jehovih, but took the name of some one of the four false Gods, and protested that he himself was the real and true God and Savior.

17. And mortal sects, that followed them, did the same thing. The presbyterian professed the true Kriste, but denounced all others as false; the methodist professed the true Kriste, but denounced all others as false; the Mormon professed the true Kriste, but denounced all others; the Roman catholics also professed the true Kriste, but denounced all others as false. Even so was it with all of them, and none of them practiced righteousness and good works, but were warriors and money-getters, for self sake.

18. God had said: Behold, I give a new testimony unto the nations of the earth: In the time I overcame, and cast out the four heads of the beast, the acrimony existing between different sects began, suddenly, to die out, and they spake friendly to one another.

19. And it was so.


# CHAPTER XIX.

## The Dawn of Kosmon.

Es said: Now, whilst the Holy Council were still sitting in Paradise, a light, like a star, came, and stood above the throne of God. And the Voice came out of the light, saying:

2. Behold, the false Gods are cast out, and sent unto their places.

3. Never more shall there be any other false God, or Lord, or Savior, to lead My people away.

4. I am sufficient unto Mine own creations.

5. Let this, therefore, be the beginning of the kosmon era.

6. My people have settled the whole earth around, from east to west; the lands on the western borders of Guatama have become inhabited.

7. Go, then, My God, My Son, open the gates of heaven unto mortals.

8. Let My angels meet them, and talk with them, face to face.

9. Behold, My etherean embassadress, Che'sivi'anathaotes, cometh in a sea of fire!

10. The ship of the etherean Goddess was seen descending from the higher heavens, coming as an open ring, to embrace the whole earth.

11. Again, the Voice spake out of the light, saying:

12. I know no distinctions of men, of races, or sects, or doctrines, or past revelations. All people are My people!

13. Open the gates of heaven; let My angels speak to mortals!

14. Swifter and swifter came the etherean archangels, till all the heavens of Paradise were encircled in the love of the Almighty.

15. Then, God called out the legions who had the matter in charge, where mortals had been born for the work of Jehovih's kingdom. And God said:

16. Open the gates of heaven; let the angels of Jehovih speak with mortals; the time of the Father's kingdom is at hand!

17. Open the gates of heaven! Let the angels come forth in power!

18. And in Hidesville, in Guatama, on the earth, the angels opened the door in Jehovih's name, to be not closed again forever, forever!

# CHAPTER XX.

## Jehovih Overthroweth Slavery in Guatama.

Es said: In the olden times, and in the eastern countries, Jehovih began His revelations. The western continent He left for the finishing thereof.

2. Now, when God looked abroad over Guatama, he saw four million people in bondage, as slaves; and he saw that they must be liberated. And so, God inquired of the chief mathematician in the Holy Council, one Arak, saying: Who, of all the kings of earth, hath had the greatest number of slaves?

3. And Arak said: Xerxes, who dwelleth in Yope'gah, in atmospherea.

4. God said: Send thou a heavenly ship for him, and for a thousand million of his angels. And send also for the Argos'yan, Leonidas, and for a thousand million of his angels. And, when they are brought here, they shall descend to the earth, to these barbarians, and liberate their slaves.

5. Arak saluted, and departed, giving his instructions to the heavenly marshals, who at once sent ships and messengers as directed.

6. God, then, said: I will now recall the ashars, who hold guard over these mortals; and, for a season, they shall dwell in drujan darkness.

7. And this was accomplished, and straightway a war ensued betwixt the owners of the slaves and the neighboring states.

8. Then came the Gods and angels, high in the grades, to witness the play of mortal death, and to determine how best to win to liberty and to Jehovih, the inhabitants of this great land.

9. God had said: It is an easy matter to win in war; but to make mortals see the triumph of righteousness, is not so easy. Therefore, be discreet in appropriating testimony unto Jehovih.

10. And, there rose up two million men in arms, pushing on in war on every side, coursing the rich soil in mortal blood. And yet, neither side had defined its principles, or taken stand for righteousness' sake. But went on in fearful destruction, laying in death tens of thousands, and tens of thousands!

11. Jehovih said: Send thou, thy Par'si'e'an and Argos'yan an-

gels, down to these mortals, and, by inspiration and by dreams and by visions, thy angels shall say to them: Whoso professeth the earth, shall battle in vain; but whoso professeth righteousness in My name, shall win. And millions of angels descended, and tried to persuade them.

12. But mortals would not hear. Even the chief general, on liberty's side, closed his soul against Jehovih. Aye, himself, enforced slavery with his mighty army.

13. And years went on, and all the people began to perceive that, without righteousness, there would be no end to the war.

14. Jehovih said: Only death can reach these people, or make them behold My hand. Yet, thou shalt send thy angel hosts over all the north regions and inspire them to call out for liberty.

15. Then went forth Xerxes and Leonidas, with their two thousand million angels, to overspread the north, to inspire mortals to a more heavenly stand, to make them see justice and liberty.

16. And, for a hundred days, these angels dwelt with mortals; but many mortals were too gross in the earth to comprehend. Then, Xerxes came to New York, and took hence the guardian angels, those of holiness, and he left the city in the hand of drujas. And, at once, the city was plunged in hell [riots, anarchy—ED.], and the people were as a mad people, wild and fearful.

17. Again, Jehovih spake in the Holy Council in heaven, saying: Let My angels go once more, and inspire mortals to rise to the light of My will.

18. Again, the angels overrun the land, inspiring mortals day and night to demand freedom for the slaves. And the Embassadress of Jehovih said to her inspiring hosts of angels: Number ye the mortals, north and south, as to their majority voice for freedom.

19. Now, when the Gods numbered the mortals and graded them, they discovered the majority had turned to freedom's side.

20. Jehovih said to His Embassadress: Take thine own inspiring host, and go down to the earth, to Washington, to the president, and hold this matter up to him, that he may understand Me. For he is not bound in doctrines. For which reason My angels made him president, and for this purpose which I have in hand.

21. And it shall come to pass that the president will hear thee, and he shall resolve in his own mind unto freedom for the slaves.

But he will seek for some external sign, fearing he may have mistaken the angels that minister unto him. But I will provide a way for this end also.

22. And the angels of Jehovih went to the president in a vision, like a dream, and they called unto him. And he answered and said: Who art thou?

23. And the angels said: Such as come in Jehovih's name for freedom's sake. Behold, millions of His angels look down from heaven, and would come to thy armies, if thou wouldst but proclaim freedom to the slaves. Jehovih's hand is in this matter.

24. The president awoke, and was troubled with his dream.

25. The next night, the angels came again, and re-told their words, and added thereunto: The great majority of the country is ripe for this matter. Thou fearest this is but a foolish dream. Behold, we will give thee proof to-morrow.

26. The president awoke more troubled than before, but remembered, the angels said: We will give thee proof to-morrow.

27. Jehovih said: I will make this matter a testimony to this nation, so that no man may gainsay it. And I will show also how My angels work singly and in mighty legions.

28. Now, at that time, there was living in Washington a seeress, through whom spirits spake in her entrancement. And on the day mentioned, the angels spake through her, saying: Go and fetch the president into the presence of this woman.

29. And the president was told what was said. And when the president came before the seeress, the angel of Jehovih entranced her, and said unto him: We said, we would give thee proof to-morrow. Behold, we repeat unto thee, Jehovih is in this matter. Save thou proclaimest the freedom of the slaves thou shalt not succeed. Do thou this, and the enemy's armies shall melt away like snow in the sun.

30. The president's eyes were opened, and he went straight away, and proclaimed freedom to the whole four million slaves.

31. Xerxes said to Leonidas: Thou, great conqueror, thou shalt conquer me. Take thy thousand million angels, and go with the armies of the north, and inspire them on to victory. Give them such strength and courage as they have not before manifested. And, as for myself and my hosts, we will go to the armies of the

south, and we will inspire them to believe they are conquered, and so make them flee before thy soldiers.

32. Thus, these great angel warriors allotted themselves to the war. And, lo and behold, the northern armies ran forth over the enemy's country as if war were but play; and the southern armies vanished, disarming themselves, and returning to their homes.

33. The slaves were free!

34. Jehovih said: Let this be a testimony, that this land is the place of the beginning of the kosmon era. There shall be no caste amongst My people.

35. Behold, I went to the Israelites, and in that day, I said: Keep yourselves as a separate people! For I had work for them; which was to travel westward, and establish Me, the All One. And they came westward, and fulfilled My commandments. Wherefore I have blessed them.

36. And I went to Chine'ya, and I said: Let the followers of Chine keep themselves as an exclusive people; for I have a work for them; which was to establish Me, the All One, and to demonstrate the most numerous people in all the world united as one people, peacefully. And they have accomplished their work. And I blessed them. And I went to Vind'yu also, and established a mighty people with a multiplicity of Gods and languages. For I had a work for them to do, which was to preserve My revelations of some of the divisions in My heavens above; and to prove, in after-time, things which I had revealed to the ancients. They have accomplished their work also, and I have blessed them.

37. But, in this era, I come not to an exclusive people, but to the combination of all peoples commingled together as one people. Hence, I have called this the KOSMON ERA.

38. Henceforth, My chosen shall be of the amalgamated races, who choose Me. And these shall become the best, most perfect of all peoples on the earth.

39. And they shall not consider race or color, but health and nobleness as to the mortal part; and as to spirit, peace, love, wisdom and good works, and one Great Spirit only.

40. Leonidas said to Xerxes: It will be revealed ere long that we have been here with our angel hosts. As a testimony of this, let us allot a number of our angels to remain a season with mortals.

And they shall inspire them to athletic sports peculiar to the Argos'yans and Par'si'e'ans.

41. To this, Xerxes consented, and they asked for six hundred thousand angel volunteers; and they received them, and officered them, and distributed them in such way that their inspiration should develop mortals in health, strength and endurance, by means of athletic games.

42. And it came to pass that the angels of heaven established athletic games amongst this people, far and near. Jehovih said: Even in this shall man behold the Cause of causes which lieth behind all things done on the earth.

43. And man searched as to the Cause of these things, and tried to persuade himself of any cause but the true one!

44. Jehovih said: I will show these people, that the chief causes of great affairs amongst mortals come from the angels of My heavens.

45. I come in kosmon not to free only the corporeal man, but the spiritual man. I raised My hand against a God being founded in their constitution; neither will I have them to fight battles for Me. The past is past; angels and mortals shall be free!

(JOHN BALLOU NEWBROUGH, 1882; REV. ED., BOSTON, MA: 1891)

# The Archko Volume

Late-nineteenth-century Christians, like their first century C.E. predecessors, thrilled to the possibility of finding documents that might shed further light on the life and death of Jesus. So when W. D. Mahan (1824–1906), a minister in the Cumberland Presbyterian Church in Boonville, Missouri, claimed in 1884 to have translated a series of rare documents during a trip to the Vatican Library in Rome and the Mosque of St. Sophia in Constantinople, many Americans took notice. The volume, *The Archeological Writings of the Sanhedrim and Talmuds of the Jews* (later referred to as the *Archko Volume* or *Archko Library*), contained interviews with some of the principal figures in the life of Jesus, Caiaphas's report to the Sanhedrin, and Herod's defense before the Senate for the slaughter of the innocents. Mahan said that all were found in either Rome or Constantinople, and that he had been aided in his translation by two British scholars.

Mahan's work found a ready audience. New editions appeared in St. Louis in 1887, Dalton, Georgia, in 1895, and Philadelphia, in 1896, even as controversy swirled around Mahan and his claims. Although he validated his documents with notarized statements about his European trip, receipts from his research, testimonies about his good character, and a lengthy introduction placing the texts in a larger history of rare documents, observers attacked his assertions from the very start. Some pointed to historical inaccuracies in his work; others noted that none of the participants, including the European archivists and the British academics, had ever been located; still others charged that large sections of some of the documents appeared to have been lifted from *Ben-Hur*, the bestselling novel published in 1880 by the American minister to Turkey, Lew Wallace. Mahan's local presbytery suspended him from ministry for a year after convicting him of falsehood and plagiarism in 1885. But none of this impeded sales of the work or affected its credibility among a wide range of Protestant Americans who continued to believe that it offered new perspectives on the life of Jesus.

The two documents featured here include an interrogation of the shepherds who declared they had witnessed the birth of Jesus, and Gamaliel's interviews of Joseph, Mary, and others about the young man (reported, according to the writer, during Jesus' lifetime). Both paint a portrait that conforms, roughly, to the narrative of Jesus in the canonical Gospels, but also add new information and suggest how best to understand Jesus' future roles as a king of the Jews and the Christ. A few notable features stand out, including the rather rough treatment of Joseph and the nobility of Mary. Mahan himself referred to the book as "one of the strangest and most interesting books ever read," and he believed it would convince readers of the truth of Christianity.

# The Archko Volume

## CHAPTER IV.

*Jonathan's Interview with the Bethlehem Shepherds—*
*Letter of Melker, Priest of the Synagogue At Bethlehem.*
*Sanhedrim, 88 B. By R. Jose. Order No. 2.*

Jonathan, son of Heziel, questions the shepherds and others at Bethlehem in regard to the strange circumstances reported to have occurred there, and reports to this court:

"*Jonathan to the Masters of Israel, Servants of the True God*: In obedience to your order, I met with two men, who said they were shepherds, and were watching their flocks near Bethlehem. They told me that while attending to their sheep, the night being cold and chilly, some of them had made fires to warm themselves, and some of them had laid down and were asleep; that they were awakened by those who were keeping watch with the question, 'What does all this mean? Behold, how light it is!' That when they were aroused it was light as day. But they knew it was not daylight, for it was only the third watch. All at once the air seemed to be filled with human voices, saying, 'Glory! Glory! Glory to the most high God!' and, 'Happy art thou, Bethlehem, for God hath fulfilled His promise to the fathers; for thy chambers is born the King that shall rule in righteousness.' Their shoutings would rise up in the heavens, and then would sink down in mellow strains, and roll along at the foot of the mountains, and die away in the most soft and musical manner they had ever heard; then it would begin again high up in the heavens, in the very vaults of the sky, and descend in sweet and melodious strains, so that they could not refrain from shouting and weeping at the same time. The light would seem to burst forth high up in the heavens, and then descend in softer rays and light up the hills and valleys, making everything more visible than the light of the sun, though it was not so brilliant, but clearer, like the brightest moon. I asked them how they felt—if they were not afraid; they said at first they were; but after awhile it seemed to calm their spirits, and so fill their hearts with love and tranquillity that they felt more like giving thanks than anything else. They said it was around the whole city, and some of the people were almost scared to death. Some said the world was on fire; some said the gods were coming down to destroy them; others said a star had fallen; until Melker the priest came out shouting and clapping his hands, seeming to be frantic with joy. The people all came crowding around him, and he told them that it was the sign that God was coming to fulfil His promise made to their father Abraham. He told us that fourteen hundred years before God had appeared to Abraham, and told him to put all Israel under bonds—sacred bonds of obedience; and if they would be faithful, he would give them a Saviour to redeem them from sin, and that he would give them eternal life, and that they should hunger no more; that the time of their suffering should cease forever; and that the sign of his coming would be that light would shine from on high, and the angels would announce his coming, and their voices should be heard in the city, and the people should rejoice: and a virgin that was pure should travail in pain and bring forth her first born, and he should rule all flesh by sanctifying it and making it obedient. After Melker had addressed the people in a loud voice, he and all the old Jews went into the synagogue and remained there praising God and giving thanks.

"I went to see Melker, who related to me much the same as the shepherds had reported. He told me that he had lived in India, and that his father had been priest at Antioch; that he had studied the sacred scrolls of God all his life, and that he knew that the time had come, from signs given, for God to visit and save the Jews from Roman oppression and from their sins; and as evidence he showed me many quotations on the tripod respecting the matter.

"He said that next day three strangers from a great distance called on him, and they went in search of this young child; and they found him and his mother in the mouth of the cave, where there was a shed projecting out for the sheltering of sheep; that his mother was married to a man named Joseph, and she related to them the history of her child, saying that an angel had visited her, and told her that she should have a son, and she should call him Jesus, for he should redeem his people from their sins; and he should call her blessed forever more.

"Whether this is true or not remains to be proved in the future. There have been so many impostors in the world, so many babes born under pretended miracles, and all have proved to be a failure, that this one may be false, this woman only wishing to hide her shame or court the favor of the Jews.

"I am informed that she will be tried by our law, and, if she can give no better evidence of her virtue than she has given to Melker, she will be stoned according to our law, although, as Melker says, there never has been a case before with such apparent divine manifestations as were seen on this occasion. In the past, in various instances, virgins have pretended to be with child by the Holy Ghost, but at the time of their delivery there was no light from the heavens, and no angels talking among the clouds and declaring that this was the King of the Jews. And, as to the truth of these things, the whole of the people of Bethlehem testify to having seen it, and the Roman guard also came out and asked what it meant, and they showed by their actions that they were very much alarmed. These things, Melker says, are all declared in the Scriptures to be the sign of His coming. Melker is a man of great learning and well versed in the prophecies, and he sends you this letter, referring you to those prophecies:

"'*Melker, Priest of the Synagogue of Bethlehem, to the Higher Sanhedrim of the Jews at Jerusalem:*

"'HOLY MASTERS OF ISRAEL: I, your servant, would call your attention to the words of the prophet in regard to the forerunner, and the rise as well as the conductor of a great and mighty nation, wherein should dwell the true principles of righteousness and the conductor of the outward formation of a national domain of God upon earth. As evidence of the fact, the vision and affliction that has befallen Zacharias of late is enough to satisfy all men of the coming of some great event; and this babe of Elizabeth is the beginning of better times.

"'What has occurred here in the last few days, as Jonathan will inform you, forever settles the question that the day of our redemption is drawing nigh. The sections of these divisions are three: First, the general survey; the original foundation and destiny of man in his single state; the proto-evangel; the full development of mankind; the promises to the fathers of the covenant people; Judah, the leader tribe; section second, the Mosaic law and the Mosaic outlook; the prophecy of Baalam; section third, the anointed one; and the prophets of the past exile: Haggai, Zechariah, and Malachi; Malachi's prophecy of the forerunner of the Lord. Now, noble masters of Israel, if you will refer to the several sections of the divine word, you will not fail to see that all that has been spoken by the prophets in regard to the works of God upon earth has been fulfilled in the last few days in the two events, the birth of the child of Elizabeth and that of Mary of Bethlehem.

"'The unlimited freedom which some men take with these holy writings of God, as to the above prophecy, subjects us to the severest criticism. It is, however, most satisfactory to see and hear that the divine grandeur and authority of the sacred oracles are in no way dependent on the solution of carnal critics, but rest on an inward light shining everywhere out of the bosom of a profound organic unity and an interconnected relation with a consistent and united teleology; overleaping all time, the historical present as well as the past, and all the past brought to light in these two events that have just transpired. Indeed, all past time is blending with the present horizon, and the works of God in ages past are just beginning to develop themselves at this particular time, and the present scenes are bringing us close on to the ways of God upon earth. While we reverence these men of God, we should not misquote their language. Take, for example, the third section of Isaiah, where he prophesies of the captive Israelites, instead of his consolation to the captive. While one of his words refers to the future condition and the reason therefor, the other is sweet in consolation of the Israelites while in this state of captivity, and full of the blessed promises in the future.

"'But let the spirit of prophecy bear us on with the prophet into future time, far beyond the kingdoms of this world into a glorious future, regardless of the Roman, Babylonian, or even the Maccabeean rule or rulers; but never forgetting that the prophet is one who is divinely inspired, and is called, commissioned, and qualified to declare the will as well as the knowledge of God. Yes, he is a seer. His prophecy is of the nature of a vision, involving and enveloping all the faculties of the soul, and placing the prophet in the attitude to God of being outside the body and independent of it. Yea, far better without the body than with it; for the further the soul gets from the body the more active it becomes. This fact is demonstrated in our dreams. The vivid powers of the soul are much more active in dreams than at any other time, the perception is clearer, and the sensitive faculties are much more alive when asleep than when awake. We see this verified in the man dying. His eye is usually brighter, his mind is clearer, his soul is freer and less selfish, as he passes on and nears the eternal state.

"'So is the prophet. He becomes so personal with God that he uses the personalities with seeming presumption; while it is the indwelling power of God's spirit inflating the soul and setting the tongue on fire. So was the moving language of the words to which you have been referred. It seems to me those men of God saw distinctly the gathering light; they saw the travailing of the virgin, they saw the helpless infant in the sheep trough; they heard the mighty chanting of the heavenly host; they saw the ambition of human nature in the Roman soldiery aiming to destroy the child's life; and in that infant they saw human nature in its fallen and helpless condition; and it appears as if they saw the advance of that infant into perfect manhood. As he becomes the theme of the world, his advancing nature will triumph over all; as he does escape the Roman authority this day, so he will finally triumph over all the world, and even death itself shall be destroyed.

"'We, as Jews, place too much confidence in the outward appearance, while the idea we get of the kingdom of heaven is all of a carnal nature, consisting of forms and ceremonies. The prophecies referred to, and many other passages that I might mention, all go to show that the kingdom of God is to begin within us, in the inner life, and rule there, and from the inner nature all outward actions are to flow in conformity with the revealed and written teachings and commands of God. So is the spirit of prophecy. While it uses the natural organs of speech, it at the same time controls all the faculties of life, producing sometimes a real ecstacy, not mechanical or loss of consciousness, though cut off for the time from external relations. He is thus circumscribed to speak, as did Baalam, the words of God with human life. This is to be held by us Jews as of the first and greatest importance, and we are to remember that his prophecy has the same reference to the future that it does to the past, and has respect to the whole empire of man. While it specifies individuals and nations, it often has reference to doctrines and principles; and in this light Israel is the result of prophecy, as a nation with her religious teachings. So is this virgin's babe born to be a ruler of all nations of the earth. The Torah itself goes back to prophecy, as well as every prophet stands on the Torah, and on this rests all prophecy pronouncing condemnation on the disobedient and blessings on the faithful. It was on this principle that the covenant of inheritance was made with Abraham, and, in reality, so made with David. Thus all the promises, political, ethical, judicial, and ritual, rest on the Torah. In short, the whole administration finds its authority in the prophetic vision, as set forth by the commands of God, to regulate human life—commencing in the inner life and working outward, until the outward is like the inward; and thus advancing on from individuals to nations.

"'The Messianic prophecy has no other justification than this. On this rests the church, and on this rests the theocracy. On this rests the glory of the future kingdom of God upon earth.

"'The whole chain of prophecy is already fulfilled in this babe; but the development is only commencing. He will abolish the old cultus forever, but with man it will develop commensurate with time itself. There are many types in the shadow, in the plant, in the animal. Every time the Romans celebrated a triumph on the Tiber it shadowed forth the coming Caesar; so every suffering of David, or lamentation of Job, or glory of Solomon—yea, every wail of human sorrow, every throe of human grief, every dying sigh, every falling bitter tear—was a type, a prophecy of the coming King of the Jews and the Saviour of the world. Israel stands as a common factor at every great epoch of history. The shading of the colors of the prophetic painting does not obliterate the prediction of the literal Israel's more glorious future in the kingdom of God. Her historic calling to mediate salvation to the nations is not ended with this new-comer on the stage of earthly life. The prophecy is eschatological, refining the inner life as well as shaping the outer life in conformity to good laws. Looking also to the end of time and its great importance to us, it has something to teach, and we have something to learn. Along the ages past all the great, good, and happy have first learned their duties, and then performed them: and thus for thousands of years Israel has stood, hope never dying in the Hebrew heart, and has been the only appointed source of preserved knowledge of the true God. And this day she stands as the great factor and centre around which all nations of the earth must come for instruction to guide them, that they may become better and happier.

"'These sacred scrolls which we Jews received from God by the hand of Moses are the only hope of the world. If they were lost to mankind, it would be worse than putting out the sun, moon, and all the stars of night, for this would be a loss of sacred light to the souls of men. When we consider the surroundings, there never has been a time more propitious than the present for the establishing of the true religion, and it seems, by reviewing our history for hundreds of years past, that this is the time for the ushering in of the true kingdom of God. The nations of the earth that have been given to idolatry are growing tired of placing confidence in and depending on gods that do not help them in the hour of danger, and they are now wanting a God that can and will answer their calls.

"'King Herod sent for me the other day, and after I related to him of the God of the Jews and His works, of the many and mighty deeds He had performed for our fathers and for us as a nation, he seemed to think, if there was such a God as we professed, it was far better than to depend on such gods as the Romans had made, of timber, stone, and iron; and even the gods of gold were powerless. He said that if he could know that this babe that was declared by the angels, was such a God as he that saved the Israelites in the Red Sea, and saved Daniel, and those three from the fearful heat of fire, he would have pursued quite a different course toward him. He was under the impression that he had come to drive the Romans from their possessions, and to reign as a monarch instead of Caesar. And I find this to be the general feeling throughout the world, so far as I can hear; that the people want and are ready to receive a God that can demonstrate in his life that he is such a God that the race of men can depend on in time of trouble; and if he can show such power to his friends he will be feared by his enemies, and thus become universally obeyed by all nations of the earth. And this, I fear, is going to be a trouble with our nation; our people are going to look to him as a temporal deliverer, and will aim to circumscribe him to the Jews alone; and when his actions begin to flow out to all the inhabitants of the world in love and charity, as is most certainly shown forth in the ninth section of the holy prophet, then I fear the Jews will reject him; and, in fact, we are warned of that already in the third section of Jeremiah's word. To avoid this Israel must be taught that the prophecy of Isaiah does not stop with the Babylonian captivity and return to the kingdom of heaven, and that Ezekiel's wheels do not whirl politically or spiritually in heaven, but upon earth, and have reference to earthly revolutions or changes, and show the bringing to pass of the great events of which this of Bethlehem is the grandest of all.

"'Neither is the outlook of Daniel to be confined to the shade of the Maccabeean wall of Jewish conquest. Nor are these great questions to be decided by our unsuccessful attempts to find out what the prophet meant or what he might have understood himself to mean; but from the unity, totality, and organic connection of the whole body of prophecy, as referring to the kingdom of this world becoming subject to the kingdom of the Saviour of all men. We, as Jews, are the only people that God has intrusted with the great questions, and, of course, the world will look to and expect us to give interpretation to these questions; and as we are intrusted with these things, God will hold us responsible if we fail to give the true light on this subject. Up to this time I am fearful the Jews as a nation are as much divided, and perhaps as much mistaken, as to the nature of His works, as any other people. I find, by conversing with the Romans, Greeks, and others, that all their knowledge of these things of Jewish expectation of a Redeemer has been obtained from the Jews, either directly or indirectly, and it was through them Herod got the idea of his being a temporal King, and to rule and reign by the might of carnal weapons; whereas, if we consult the spiritual import of the prophets, his office is to blend all nations in one common brotherhood, and establish love in the place of law, and that heart should throb high with love to heart, and under this law a universal peace. Wherever one should meet another they should meet as friends; for what else can the prophet mean, in section nine, where he shows that this King shall destroy all carnal weapons and convert them to a helpful purpose, and thus become the active worker in doing good to all men, and teaching all men to do good to each other?

"'By reading all the scrolls of God we find that the unity and totality of all the prophets go to bear us out in this idea, and all have reference to this Babe of Bethlehem. If we consult them as to the time, taking the revolutions of Ezekiel's wheels, they show plainly that the revolutions of the different governments of the world fix this as the time. Next, consult them in regard to the individuals connected with this great event. These are pointed to as the virgin wife, by Zacharias; next, the place has been pointed out and named; then the light and the appearing of the angels have all been set forth, and also the opposition of the Romans has been declared. Now, I ask the High Court of the living God to look well on these things, and tell us how men that lived in different ages of the world, that lived in different portions of the country—men that never knew each other—men that were not prophesying for a party—men that had no personal interest in the subject as men—men that jeopardized, and some of them lost their lives on account of having uttered these prophecies—how could they all point out the place, the time, and the names of the parties so plain and clear, if it was not revealed to them and ordained by God himself? I understand that the Romans and some of the priests have been saying that Zacharias was a hypocrite, and that Mary was a bad woman. Such might be the case, so far as man is able to judge; but who, I ask, can forge such truth as these prophecies, and make them come true? Or who can cause light to descend from the heavens and the angels come down and make the declaration that this was the Son of God, King of the Jews?

"'Noble Masters of the Sanhedrim, I was not alone. I am not the only witness of these things. The principal people of Bethlehem saw them and heard them as I did. I would say to you, if this is not the Jews' King, then we need not look for any other; for every line of prophecy has been most completely fulfilled in him; and if he does not appear and save his own people I shall despair of ever being released, and I shall believe that we have misinterpreted the meaning of all the prophets. But I feel so sure that this is he I shall wait in expectation and with much anxiety, and I have no fears of any harm befalling him. All the Romans in the world cannot harm him; and although Herod may rage, may destroy all the infants in the world, the same angels that attended his birth will watch over him through life, and the Romans will have to contend with the same God that Pharaoh did, and will meet with similar defeat.'"


## CHAPTER V.

### Gamaliel's Interview with Joseph and Mary and others Concerning Jesus.

The *hagiographa* or holy writings, found in the St. Sophia Mosque at Constantinople, made by Gamaliel, in the Talmuds of the Jews, 27 B. It seems Gamaliel was sent by the Sanhedrim to interrogate Joseph and Mary in regard to this child Jesus. He says:

"I found Joseph and Mary in the city of Mecca, in the land of Ammon or Moab. But I did not find Jesus. When I went to the place where I was told he was, he was somewhere else; and thus I followed him from place to place, until I despaired of finding him at all. Whether he knew that I was in search of him and did it to elude me, I cannot tell, though I think it most likely the former was the reason, for his mother says he is bashful and shuns company.

"Joseph is a wood-workman. He is very tall and ugly. His hair looks as though it might have been dark auburn when young. His eyes are gray and vicious. He is anything but prepossessing in his appearance, and he is as gross and glum as he looks. He is but a poor talker, and it seems that yes and no are the depth of his mind. I am satisfied he is very disagreeable to his family. His children look very much like him, and upon the whole I should call them a third-rate family. I asked him who were his parents. He said his father's name was Jacob, and his grandfather was Matthew. He did not like to talk on the subject. He is very jealous. I told him that we had heard that he had had a vision, and I was sent to ascertain the facts in the case. He said he did not call it a vision; he called it a dream. He said after he and Mary had agreed to marry, it seemed that something told him that Mary was with child; that he did not know whether he was asleep or awake, but it made such an impression on his mind that he concluded to have nothing more to do with her; and while he was working one day under a shed, all at once a man in snowy white stood by his side, and told him not to doubt the virtue of Mary, for she was holy before the Lord; that the child conceived in her was not by man, but by the Holy Ghost, and that the child would be free from human passions. In order to do this he must—that is, his humanity must—be of the extract of *almah* (that is the Hebrew word for virgin), that he might endure all things, and not resist, and fill the demands of prophecy. He said the angel told him that this child should be great and should rule all the kingdoms of this world. He said that this child should set up a new kingdom, wherein should dwell righteousness and peace, and that the kingdoms of this world which should oppose him God would utterly destroy. I asked him, How could a virgin conceive of herself without the germination of the male? He said: "This is the work of God. He has brought to life the womb of Elizabeth, so she had conceived and will bear a son in her old age who will go before and tell the people of the coming of this King." After telling me all these things, he disappeared like the melting down of a light. I then went and told Mary what had occurred, and she told me that the same angel, or one like him, had appeared to her and told the same things. So I married Mary, thinking that if what the angel had told us was true, it would be greatly to our advantage; but I am fearful we are mistaken. Jesus seems to take no interest in us, nor anything else much. I call him lazy and careless. I do not think he will ever amount to much, much less be a king. If he does, he must do a great deal better than he has been doing.' I asked him how long after that interview with the angel before the child was born. He said he did not know, but he thought it was seven or eight months. I asked him where they were at the time. He said in Bethlehem. The Roman commander had given orders for all the Jews to go on a certain day to be enrolled as tax-payers, and he and Mary went to Bethlehem as the nearest place of enrollment; and while there this babe was born. I asked if anything strange occurred there that night. He said that the people were much excited, but he was so tired that he had gone to sleep, and saw nothing. He said toward day there were several priests came in to see them and the babe, and gave them many presents. And the news got circulated that this child was to be King of the Jews, and it created such an excitement that he took the child and his mother and came to Moab for protection, for fear the Romans would kill the child to keep it from being a rival to the Romans.

"I discovered that all Joseph's ideas were of a selfish kind. All he thought of was himself. Mary is altogether a different character, and she is too noble to be the wife of such a man. She seems to be about forty or forty-five years of age, abounds with a cheerful and happy spirit and is full of happy fancies. She is fair to see, rather fleshy, has soft and innocent-looking eyes, and seems to be naturally a good woman. I asked her who her parents were, and she said her father's name was Eli, and her mother's name was Anna; her grandmother's name was Pennel, a widow of the tribe of Asher, of great renown. I asked her if Jesus was the son of Joseph. She said he was not. I asked her to relate the circumstances of the child's history. She said that one day while she was grinding some meal there appeared at the door a stranger in shining raiment, which showed as bright as the light. She was very much alarmed at his presence, and trembled like a leaf; but all her fears were calmed when he spoke to her; for he said: 'Mary, thou art loved by the Lord and He has sent me to tell thee that thou shalt have a child; that this child shall be great and rule all nations of the earth.' She continued: 'I immediately thought of my engagement to Joseph, and supposed that was the way the child was to come; but he astonished me the more when he told me that cousin Elisabeth had conceived and would bear a son, whose name was to be John; and my son should be called Jesus. This caused me to remember that Zacharias had seen a vision and disputed with the angel, and for that he was struck with dumbness, so that he could no longer hold the priest's office. I asked the messenger if Joseph knew anything of the matter. He said that he told Joseph that I was to have a child by command of the Holy Ghost, and that he was to redeem his people from their sins, and was to reign over the whole world; that every man should confess to him and he should rule over all the kings of the earth.'

"I asked her how she knew that he was an angel, and she said he told her so, and then she knew he was an angel from the way he came and went. I asked her to describe how he went away from her, and she said that he seemed to melt away like the extinguishing of a light. I asked her if she knew anything of John the Baptist. She said he lived in the mountains of Judea the last she knew of him. I asked her if he and Jesus were acquainted, or did they visit. She said she did not think they knew each other.

"I asked her if at the time this angel, as she called him, visited her, she was *almah* (that is, virgin). She said she was; that she had never showed to man, nor was known by any man. I asked her if she at that time maintained her *fourchette*; and after making her and Joseph understand what I meant, they both said she had, and Joseph said this was the way he had of testing her virtue. I asked her if she knew when conception took place. She said she did not. I asked her if she was in any pain in bearing, or in delivering this child. She said, 'None of any consequence.' I asked her if he was healthy; to give me a description of his life. She said he was perfectly healthy; that she never heard him complain of any pain or dissatisfaction; his food always agreed with him; that he would eat anything set before him, and if anyone else complained he would often say he thought it good enough, much better than we deserved. She said that Joseph was a little hard to please, but this boy had answered him so often, and his answers were so mild and yet so suitable, that he had almost broken him of finding fault. She said he settled all the disputes of the family; that no odds what was the subject or who it was, one word from him closed all mouths, and what gave him such power was his words were always unpretending and spoken as though they were not intended as a rebuke, but merely as a decision. I asked her if she had ever seen him angry or out of humor. She said she had seen him apparently vexed and grieved at the disputes and follies of others, but had never seen him angry. I asked her if he had any worldly aspirations after money or wealth, or a great name, or did he delight in fine dress, like the most of youth. She said that was one thing that vexed her, he seemed to take no care of his person; he did not care whether he was dressed or not, or whether the family got along well or ill; it was all alike to him. She said she talked to him about it, and he would look at her a little grieved and say, 'Woman (for such he always called me), you do not know who I am.' Indeed, she said he takes so little interest in the things of the world and the great questions of the day, they were beginning to despair of his ever amounting to much—much less be a king, as the angel said he would be; if so, he would have to act very differently from what he was acting at that time. I told her that the Jewish doctors contended that the amorous disposition is peculiar to the male. I asked her if she had ever seen in the private life of Jesus any signs of such disposition. She said she had not. I asked if she saw in him any particular fondness for female society. She said she had not; if anything, rather the contrary; that the young *bethaul* (the word in the Hebrew for young women) were all very fond of him, and were always seeking his society, and yet he seemed to care nothing for them; and if they appeared too fond of him, he treated them almost with scorn. He will often get up and leave them, and wander away and spend his time in meditation and prayer. He is a perfect ascetic in his life. 'When I see how the people like to be with him, and ask him questions, and seem to take such delight with his answers—both men and women—it almost vexes me. They say there is a young woman in Bethany whom he intends to marry; but unless he changes his course very much he will never be qualified to have a family. But I do not believe the report. He never seems to me to care anything about women when he is in my presence.'

"Thus it seems that Joseph and Mary have both lost all confidence in his becoming anything. They seem to think that the Sanhedrim should do something for him to get him out and let him show himself to the people. I tried to console them by telling them that my understanding of the prophecy was that he had to come to the high priesthood first, and there, work in the spiritual dominion of the heart; and when he had brought about a unity of heart and oneness of aim, it would be easy enough to establish his political claim; and all who would not willingly submit to him, it would be an easy matter with the sword of Joshua or Gideon to bring under his control. It seemed to me that his parents' ideas are of a selfish character; that they care nothing about the Jewish government nor the Roman oppression. All they think of is self-exaltation, and to be personally benefited by their son's greatness. But I told them they were mistaken; that the building up of the kingdom of heaven was not to be done by might nor by power, but by the Spirit of the Lord, and it would not do for us to use carnal weapons, nor to expect carnal pleasures to be derived there from; that it was not my understanding of the prophecy that this king was to use such weapons either for himself or for the benefit of a party, but for the good of all men; that his dominion was to be universal, and it was to be of a spiritual character; that he was sent to the lost and not to the found.

"His parents told me of an old man who lived on the road to Bethany who had once been a priest, a man of great learning, and well skilled in the laws and prophets, and that Jesus was often there with him reading the law and prophets together; that his name was Massalian, and that I might find Jesus there. But he was not there. Massalian said he was often at Bethany with a young family, and he thought there was some love affair between him and one of the girls. I asked him if he had seen anything like a courtship between them. He said he had not, but inferred from their intimacy and from the fondness on the woman's part, as well as from the laws of nature, that such would be the case. I asked him to give me an outline of the character of Jesus. He said that he was a young man of the finest thought and feeling he ever saw in his life; that he was the most apt in his answers and solutions of difficult problems of any man of his age he had ever seen; that his answers seem to give more universal satisfaction—so much so that the oldest philosopher would not dispute with him, or in any manner join issue with him, or ask the second time. I asked Massalian who taught him to read and interpret the law and the prophets. He said that his mother said that he had always known how to read the law; that his mind seemed to master it from the beginning; and into the laws of nature and the relation of man to his fellow in his teachings or talks, he gives a deeper insight, inspiring mutual love and strengthening the common trust of society. Another plan he has of setting men right with the laws of nature: he turns nature into a great law book of illustrations, showing that every bush is a flame, every rock a fountain of water, every star a pillar of fire, and every cloud the one that

leads to God. He makes all nature preach the doctrine of trust in
the divine Fatherhood. He speaks of the lilies as pledges of God's
care, and points to the fowls as evidence of his watchfulness over
human affairs. Who can measure the distance between God and
the flower of the field? What connection is there between man
and the lily? By such illustrations he creates a solicitude in man
that seems to awe him into reverence, and he becomes attracted
toward heavenly thought, and feels that he is in the presence of
one that is superior. In this talk he brings one to feel he is very
near the presence of God. He says how much more your Father.
The plane is one, though the intermediate points are immeasur-
ably distant. Thus by beginning with a flower he reasons upward
to the absolute, and then descends and teaches lessons of trust in
a loving Father. The lessons of trust in God reassure the anxious
listener and create an appetite that makes him long for more; and
it often seems, when he has brought his hearers to the highest
point of anxiety, he suddenly breaks off and leaves his company
as though he cared nothing for them. Jesus in his talk brings all
these illustrations to make man feel his nearness to his kindred,
man, teaching also their relation to and dependence upon God;
and although his method is happy, it does not seem to me that it
is the most successful. He teaches that man and the flowers and
birds drink from the same fountain and are fed from the same
table, yet at the same time he seems to do everything to excite
suspicion and prejudice. We that are watching him to see his divine mission commence, he is continually tantalizing our expectations, as well as mocking our natural reason and desires. When
a man separates himself from all other men, both in point of doctrine as well as discipline, he takes a very great risk on his part—
especially when he confines God to one channel, and that one of
his own dictation. A man that assumes these responsible positions must have vast resources from which to draw, or he will
sink in the whirlpool which his own impertinence has created.
Through Jesus, in his teachings or talks (his words sound so
much like the teachings of Hillel or Shammai that I must call it
teaching, though he has no special scholars), we learn that God is
Spirit, and God is Father; and he says these are the only two
things that are essential for man to know. Then he illustrates this

to the parents, and asks them what would they do for their children. He was telling some mothers a circumstance of a mother starving herself to feed her child, and then applied it to God as our Father; and they commenced shouting, they were so happy; and Jesus got up and left the house in seeming disgust.

"Massalian says he is tempted at times to become impatient with Jesus, as he devotes so much time to details. It seems almost a waste of time for a man who came to save the world to be lingering over a special case of disease. He thinks he could hasten Jesus's physical deportment. Why not speak one word and remove every sick patient from his sick-bed at the same hour? What a triumph this would be. I asked him if Jesus had healed anyone. He said not as yet; but if he is to be King of the Jews, he was to heal all nations, and why not do it at once? If he would, there would be nothing more required to establish his kingship. But I said to him, 'Is it not equally so with God's creative power? See what time and labor it takes to bring forth a grain of corn. Why not have caused the earth to bring forth every month instead of every year? Christ was talking in defence of his Father. The people must learn to love and obey the Father before they would reverence the Son. Yes, he said the God that Jesus represented was one that the people might love and venerate; that he was a God of love, and had no bloody designs to execute on even a bad man, provided he ceased his evil ways.'

"It is to be noted that in all Jesus's talk there are manifest references to the future. Many of his statements were like a sealed letter—not to be opened but by time. A grain of mustard was to result in a large tree. All his ideas refer to the future; like the parent helping the child with his burden of to-day, by telling of the blessings of to-morrow; and by making to-day the seed-corn of to-morrow; keeping the action of to-day under moral control by making the morrow the day of judgment. He stated further that Jesus was a young man who was the best judge of human nature he had ever seen; that he thought at times he could tell men their thoughts and expose their bad principles; and while he had all these advantages of life, he seemed not to care for them nor to use them abusively. He seems to like all men—one as well as another—so much so that his own parents have become disgusted with him, and have almost cast him off. But Jesus has such a peculiar temperament that he seems not to care, and is as well satisfied with one as another. He said that Jesus seemed fond of Mary and Martha, who lived at Bethany, and probably I might find him there.

"Massalian is a man of very deep thought and most profound judgment. All his life he has made the Scriptures his study. He, too, is a good judge of human nature, and he is satisfied that Jesus is the Christ. He said that Jesus seemed to understand the prophecy by intuition. I asked him where Jesus was taught to read the prophecy. He said that his mother told him that Jesus could read from the beginning; that no one had ever taught him to read. He said that he, in making quotations from the prophets, was sometimes mistaken or his memory failed him; but Jesus could correct him every time without the scroll; and that sometimes he thought Jesus was certainly mistaken, but never in a single instance was he wrong. I asked him to describe his person to me, so that I might know him if I should meet him. He said: 'If you ever meet him you will know him. While he is nothing but a man, there is something about him that distinguishes him from every other man. He is the picture of his mother, only he has not her smooth, round face. His hair is a little more golden than hers, though it is as much from sunburn as anything else. He is tall, and his shoulders are a little drooped; his visage is thin and of a swarthy complexion, though this is from exposure. His eyes are large and a soft blue, and rather dull and heavy. The lashes are long, and his eyebrows very large. His nose is that of a Jew. In fact, he reminds me of an old-fashioned Jew in every sense of the word. He is not a great talker, unless there is something brought up about heaven and divine things, when his tongue moves glibly and his eyes light up with a peculiar brilliancy; though there is this peculiarity about Jesus, he never argues a question; he never disputes. He will commence and state facts, and they are on such a solid basis that nobody will have the boldness to dispute with him. Though he has such mastership of judgment, he takes no pride in confuting his opponents, but always seems to be sorry for them. I have seen him attacked by the scribes and doctors of the law, and they seemed like little children learning their lessons under a master. His strongest points are in the spiritual power of the law and the intentions of the prophets. The young people tried to get him to take a class of them and teach them; but he utterly refused.' This Jew is convinced that he is the Messiah of the world.

"I went from there to Bethany, but Jesus was not there. They said he and Lazarus were away, they could not tell where. I went and saw Mary and Martha, the sisters of Lazarus, and had a long talk with them. They are very pleasant and nice young maids, and Mary is quite handsome. I teased her about Jesus, but they both denied that Jesus was anything like a lover; he was only a friend; though this is so common for young maids I did not know whether to believe them or not until I told them my real business. And when I told them that this was the same person that was born of the virgin in Bethlehem some twenty-six years before, and that his mother had told me all the facts in the case, they seemed deeply interested. They then told me upon their honor that Jesus never talked or even hinted to either one of them on the subject of marriage. Martha blushed, and said she wished he had. If he was to be a king, she would like to be queen. I asked them if they had ever seen him in the company of young virgins. They said they had not. I asked them if they had heard him talk about young girls, or if he sought their society more than that of men; and they both declared they had not; and they were very much surprised that he did not. I asked them what he talked of when in their company; and they said he was not much in their company; that he and their brother would go upon the house-top and stay there half the night, and sometimes all night, talking and arguing points of interest to them both. Mary said she had often gone near, so she could listen to them, for she loved to hear him talk, he was so mild and unpretending, and then was so intelligent that he was different from any and all other young men she had ever seen. I asked them what was their brother's opinion of him. They said he thought there never was such a man on earth. He thought him to be one of God's prophets. He said when they are out in the mountains, as they are most all the time, Jesus can tell him all about the flowers, trees, and rocks, can tell him everything in the world, and that none of the wild animals are afraid of him. He says often the stag and the wolf will come and stand for Jesus to stroke their mane, and seem almost loath to go away from him. He says that no poisonous serpent will offer to hiss at him. Their brother thinks he is perfectly safe if Jesus is with him. I asked them if he had ever told their brother anything about himself. They said that if he had spoken to their brother he had not told them.

"Now, Masters of Israel, after having investigated this matter; after tracing Jesus from his conception to the present time; after obtaining all the information that is to be had on this important subject, getting it from those who are more likely to tell the truth from the fact they are disinterested persons; and then taking a prophetical as well as a historical view of the subject, I have come to the conclusion that this is the Christ that we are looking for. And as a reason for my conclusion, I will call your attention to the following facts: First to the prophecy of Isaiah, section 7: 'And he said, Hear now, saith the Lord. Oh, house of David, is it a small thing for you? Therefore the Lord himself shall give you a sign; behold, a virgin shall conceive and bear a son, and shall call his name God with men. Butter and honey shall he eat, that he may know to refuse the evil and choose the good; for before the child shall know to refuse the evil and choose the good the land that God abhorrest shall be forsaken of her king.' Section 8: 'Bind the testimony; seal the law among his disciples; the Lord will hide his face from the house of Jacob, and he will look for him.' Here is a literal fulfillment of this word of the Most High God, so clear and plain that none may mistake. Jeremiah, 31st section: 'Turn, oh virgin, to thy people, for the hand of the Lord is upon thee; for the Lord shall create a new thing in the earth; a woman shall compass a man.' Here again are set forth the same things that Isaiah speaks of, and the same things that I have learned from Mary. Micah, section 5: 'Thou, Bethlehem Ephratah, thou art little among the thousands of Judah; out of thee shall come forth unto me him that shall rule my people. He is from everlasting; and I will give them up until the time she travaileth to bring forth my first born, that he may rule all people.' Here we have the city, the virgin, the office, his manner of life, the seeking him by the Sanhedrim. All these things are under our eyes as full and complete as I now write them, who have all this testimony given in this letter. How can we as a people dispute these things? In the 49th section of Genesis, making reference to the history, that is now upon us, the writer says: 'A captive shall not depart from Judah, nor a lawmaker from him, until Shiloh come, and gather his people between his feet, and keep them forever.'"

(REV. W. D. MAHAN, 1887; 2ND ED., PHILADELPHIA, PA: 1905;
PP. 64–96)

# The Great Controversy Between
# Christ and Satan

Ellen Gould White (1827–1915) was a religious reformer, writer, and public speaker who described having thousands of visions in her life. Raised in and around Portland, Maine, the young girl had a conversion experience at a Methodist camp meeting at the age of twelve. But her family was exiled from the local church in the early 1840s for their associations with the Millerites, a popular religious movement of the day based on the predictions of William Miller that the second coming of Christ would occur in 1844. Ellen recorded her first vision that same year, when she reported having witnessed the return of Jesus and the advent of the kingdom of God. She later told of visions involving a bright light that would surround her; she then felt herself to be in the presence of Jesus or angels, who would show her past and future events and places. Married in 1846 to James Springer White, another Millerite, Ellen spent the next seventy years reorganizing the Adventist movement in the face of the failure of the Millerite prophecy, and writing the documents that would serve as its theological and doctrinal basis. One of the most important of these is the four-volume *Spirit of Prophecy* series, the last volume of which outlines a cosmic conflict between good and evil, from the destruction of Jerusalem to the end of time. When it was published in 1888, *The Great Controversy* proved enduringly popular, selling fifty thousand copies within three years.

White wrote prolifically, contributing publications for the growing Seventh-day Adventist movement that fostered organizational unity among many disappointed Millerites as well as educational imperative. Her spiritual gifts were well recognized among Adventists, who had established a church organization by the 1860s. She is still considered a prophet and special messenger of God by the more than fifteen million members of the church, who believe that she was called to draw attention to the Bible and, through her written works, to prepare people for the second coming of Christ. One of the first American evangelists who could claim a transcontinental following, White worked actively to spread the message of Christ's imminent return among believers on the Pacific Coast, African Americans in the South, and audiences beyond the United States. In doing so she became one of the most translated American nonfiction authors of all time.

These selections relate elements of a grand and enduring cosmic battle. Beginning with the biblical proof that Christ had promised to return to Earth, White describes the dispersal of the news that the second advent was imminent—the Advent movement—through recent history and a series of messengers. She details the spread of excitement among William Miller's followers in the United States in the antebellum era as a central event in this divine unfolding. Her account also explains why Miller's prophecies did not come true as predicted and justifies the continuing work of Adventists, even in an era of spiritual disappointment. The document concludes with an admonition to continue to be watchful and to follow sacred commands, including the proper observance of the "true Sabbath" that would become a distinguishing mark of the Seventh-day Adventist Church. Prophecy, White asserted, could not be denied.

# The Great Controversy Between Christ and Satan

## A GREAT RELIGIOUS AWAKENING—20

A great religious awakening under the proclamation of Christ's soon coming, is foretold in the prophecy of the first angel's message of Revelation 14. An angel is seen flying "in the midst of heaven, having the everlasting gospel to preach unto them that dwell on the earth, and to every nation, and kindred, and tongue, and people." "With a loud voice" he proclaims the message, "Fear God, and give glory to Him; for the hour of His judgment is come: and worship Him that made heaven, and earth, and the sea, and the fountains of waters."[1]

The fact that an angel is said to be the herald of this warning, is significant. By the purity, the glory, and the power of the heavenly messenger, divine wisdom has been pleased to represent the exalted character of the work to be accomplished by the message, and the power and glory that were to attend it. And the angel's flight "in the midst of heaven," the "loud voice" with which the warning is uttered, and its promulgation to all "that dwell on the earth,"—"to every nation, and kindred, and tongue, and people,"—give evidence of the rapidity and worldwide extent of the movement.

The message itself sheds light as to the time when this movement is to take place. It is declared to be a part of the "everlasting gospel;" and it announces the opening of the judgment. The message of salvation has been preached in all ages; but this message is a part of the gospel which could be proclaimed only in the last days, for only then would it be true that the hour of judgment *had come*. The prophecies present a succession of events leading

1 Rev. 14:6, 7.

down to the opening of the judgment. This is especially true of the book of Daniel. But that part of his prophecy which related to the last days, Daniel was bidden to close up and seal "to the time of the end." Not till we reach this time could a message concerning the judgment be proclaimed, based on a fulfilment of these prophecies. But at the time of the end, says the prophet, "many shall run to and fro, and knowledge shall be increased."[1]

The apostle Paul warned the church not to look for the coming of Christ in his day. "That day shall not come," he says, "except there come a falling away first, and that man of sin be revealed."[2] Not till after the great apostasy, and the long period of the reign of the "man of sin," can we look for the advent of our Lord. The "man of sin," which is also styled the "mystery of iniquity," the "son of perdition," and "that wicked," represents the papacy, which, as foretold in prophecy, was to maintain its supremacy for 1260 years. This period ended in 1798. The coming of Christ could not take place before that time. Paul covers with his caution the whole of the Christian dispensation down to the year 1798. It is this side of that time that the message of Christ's second coming is to be proclaimed.

No such message has ever been given in past ages. Paul, as we have seen, did not preach it; he pointed his brethren into the then far-distant future for the coming of the Lord. The Reformers did not proclaim it. Martin Luther placed the judgment about three hundred years in the future from his day. But since 1798 the book of Daniel has been unsealed, knowledge of the prophecies has increased, and many have proclaimed the solemn message of the judgment near.

Like the great Reformation of the sixteenth century, the Advent Movement appeared in different countries of Christendom at the same time. In both Europe and America, men of faith and prayer were led to the study of the prophecies, and tracing down the inspired record, they saw convincing evidence that the end of all things was at hand. In different lands there were isolated bodies of Christians who, solely by the study of the Scriptures, arrived at the belief that the Saviour's advent was near.

1 Dan. 12:4.
2 2 Thess. 2:3.

In 1821, three years after Miller had arrived at his exposition of the prophecies pointing to the time of the judgment, Dr. Joseph Wolff, "the missionary to the world," began to proclaim the Lord's soon coming. Wolff was born in Germany, of Hebrew parentage, his father being a Jewish rabbi. While very young, he was convinced of the truth of the Christian religion. Of an active, inquiring mind, he had been an eager listener to the conversations that took place in his father's house, as devout Hebrews daily assembled to recount the hopes and anticipations of their people, the glory of the coming Messiah, and the restoration of Israel. One day hearing Jesus of Nazareth mentioned, the boy inquired who He was. "A Jew of the greatest talent," was the answer; "but as He pretended to be the Messiah, the Jewish tribunal sentenced Him to death." "Why," rejoined the questioner, "is Jerusalem destroyed, and why are we in captivity?" "Alas, alas!" answered his father, "because the Jews murdered the prophets." The thought was at once suggested to the child, "Perhaps Jesus was also a prophet, and the Jews killed Him when He was innocent."[1] So strong was this feeling, that though forbidden to enter a Christian church, he would often linger outside to listen to the preaching.

When only seven years old, he was boasting to an aged Christian neighbor of the future triumph of Israel at the advent of the Messiah, when the old man said kindly, "Dear boy, I will tell you who the real Messiah was: He was Jesus of Nazareth, . . . whom your ancestors have crucified, as they did the prophets of old. Go home and read the fifty-third chapter of Isaiah, and you will be convinced that Jesus Christ is the Son of God."[2] Conviction at once fastened upon him. He went home and read the scripture, wondering to see how perfectly it had been fulfilled in Jesus of Nazareth. Were the words of the Christian true? The boy asked of his father an explanation of the prophecy, but was met with a silence so stern that he never again dared to refer to the subject. This, however, only increased his desire to know more of the Christian religion.

The knowledge he sought was studiously kept from him in his Jewish home; but when only eleven years old, he left his father's

---

1 "Travels and Adventures of the Rev. Joseph Wolff," Vol. I, p. 6 (ed. 1860).
2 "Travels and Adventures of the Rev. Joseph Wolff," Vol. I, p. 7.

house, and went out into the world to gain for himself an education, to choose his religion and his life-work. He found a home for a time with kinsmen, but was soon driven from them as an apostate, and alone and penniless he had to make his own way among strangers. He went from place to place, studying diligently, and maintaining himself by teaching Hebrew. Through the influence of a Catholic instructor, he was led to accept the Romish faith, and formed the purpose of becoming a missionary to his own people. With this object he went, a few years later, to pursue his studies in the College of the Propaganda at Rome. Here his habit of independent thought and candid speech brought upon him the imputation of heresy. He openly attacked the abuses of the church, and urged the necessity of reform. Though at first treated with special favor by the papal dignitaries, he was after a time removed from Rome. Under the surveillance of the church he went from place to place, until it became evident that he could never be brought to submit to the bondage of Romanism. He was declared to be incorrigible, and was left at liberty to go where he pleased. He now made his way to England, and professing the Protestant faith, united with the English Church. After two years' study he set out, in 1821, upon his mission.

While Wolff accepted the great truth of Christ's first advent as "a man of sorrows, and acquainted with grief," he saw that the prophecies bring to view with equal clearness His second advent with power and glory. And while he sought to lead his people to Jesus of Nazareth as the Promised One, and to point them to His first coming in humiliation as a sacrifice for the sins of men, he taught them also of His second coming as a king and deliverer.

[. . .]

Wolff believed the coming of the Lord to be at hand, his interpretation of the prophetic periods placing the great consummation within a very few years of the time pointed out by Miller. To those who urged from the scripture, "Of that day and hour knoweth no man," that men are to know nothing concerning the nearness of the advent, Wolff replied: "Did our Lord say that that day and hour should *never* be known? Did He not give us signs of the times, in order that we may know at least the *approach* of

His coming, as one knows the approach of the summer by the fig-tree putting forth its leaves? Matt. 24:32. Are we never to know that period, whilst He Himself exhorteth us not only to read Daniel the prophet, but to understand it? and in that very Daniel, where it is said that the words were shut up to the time of the end (which was the case in his time), and that 'many shall run to and fro' (a Hebrew expression for observing and thinking upon the time), 'and *knowledge*' (regarding that time) 'shall be increased.' Dan. 12:4. Besides this, our Lord does not intend to say by this, that the *approach* of the time shall not be known, but that the *exact 'day* and *hour* knoweth no man.' Enough, He does say, shall be known by the signs of the times, to induce us to prepare for His coming, as Noah prepared the ark."[1]

Concerning the popular system of interpreting, or misinterpreting, the Scriptures, Wolff wrote: "The greater part of the Christian church have swerved from the plain sense of Scripture, and have turned to the phantomizing system of the Buddhists, who believe that the future happiness of mankind will consist in moving about in the air, and suppose that when they are reading *Jews*, they must understand *Gentiles*; and when they read *Jerusalem*, they must understand the *church*; and if it is said *earth*, it means *sky*; and for the coming of the *Lord* they must understand the progress of the *missionary societies*; and going up to the mountain of the Lord's house, signifies a grand *class-meeting of Methodists*."[2]

During the twenty-four years from 1821 to 1845, Wolff traveled extensively: in Africa, visiting Egypt and Abyssinia; in Asia, traversing Palestine, Syria, Persia, Bokhara, and India. He also visited the United States, on the journey thither preaching on the island of St. Helena. He arrived in New York in August, 1837; and after speaking in that city, he preached in Philadelphia and Baltimore, and finally proceeded to Washington. Here, he says, "on a motion brought forward by the ex-president, John Quincy Adams, in one of the houses of Congress, the House unanimously granted to me the use of the Congress Hall for a lecture, which I delivered on a Saturday, honored with the presence of all the

1 Wolff, "Researches and Missionary Labors," pp. 404, 405.
2 "Journal of the Rev. Joseph Wolff," p. 96.

members of Congress, and also of the bishop of Virginia, and of the clergy and citizens of Washington. The same honor was granted to me by the members of the government of New Jersey and Pennsylvania, in whose presence I delivered lectures on my researches in Asia, and also on the personal reign of Jesus Christ."[1]

Dr. Wolff traveled in the most barbarous countries, without the protection of any European authority, enduring many hardships, and surrounded with countless perils. He was bastinadoed and starved, sold as a slave, and three times condemned to death. He was beset by robbers, and sometimes nearly perished from thirst. Once he was stripped of all that he possessed, and left to travel hundreds of miles on foot through the mountains, the snow beating in his face, and his naked feet benumbed by contact with the frozen ground.

When warned against going unarmed among savage and hostile tribes, he declared himself "provided with arms,"—"prayer, zeal for Christ, and confidence in His help." "I am also," he said, "provided with the love of God and my neighbor in my heart, and the Bible is in my hand."[2] The Bible in Hebrew and English he carried with him wherever he went. Of one of his later journeys he says, "I . . . kept the Bible open in my hand. I felt my power was in the book, and that its might would sustain me."[3]

Thus he persevered in his labors until the message of the judgment had been carried to a large part of the habitable globe. Among Jews, Turks, Parsees, Hindoos, and many other nationalities and races, he distributed the word of God in these various tongues, and everywhere heralded the approaching reign of the Messiah.

In his travels in Bokhara he found the doctrine of the Lord's soon coming held by a remote and isolated people. The Arabs of Yemen, he says, "are in possession of a book called 'Seera,' which gives notice of the second coming of Christ and His reign in glory; and they expect great events to take place in the year 1840."[4]

1 "Journal of the Rev. Joseph Wolff," pp. 398, 399.
2 Adams, W. H. D., "In Perils Oft," p. 192.
3 Idem, p. 201.
4 "Journal of the Rev. Joseph Wolff," p. 377.

"In Yemen . . . I spent six days with the children of Rechab. They drink no wine, plant no vineyard, sow no seed, and live in tents, and remember good old Jonadab, the son of Rechab; and I found in their company children of Israel, of the tribe of Dan, . . . who expect, with the children of Rechab, the speedy arrival of the Messiah in the clouds of heaven."[1]

[. . .]

As early as 1826 the advent message began to be preached in England. The movement here did not take so definite a form as in America; the exact time of the advent was not so generally taught, but the great truth of Christ's soon coming in power and glory was extensively proclaimed. And this not among the dissenters and non-conformists only. Mourant Brock, an English writer, states that about seven hundred ministers of the Church of England were engaged in preaching this "gospel of the kingdom." The message pointing to 1844 as the time of the Lord's coming was also given in Great Britain. Advent publications from the United States were widely circulated. Books and journals were republished in England. And in 1842, Robert Winter, an Englishman by birth, who had received the advent faith in America, returned to his native country to herald the coming of the Lord. Many united with him in the work, and the message of the judgment was proclaimed in various parts of England.

In South America, in the midst of barbarism and priest-craft, Lacunza, a Spaniard and a Jesuit, found his way to the Scriptures, and thus received the truth of Christ's speedy return. Impelled to give the warning, yet desiring to escape the censures of Rome, he published his views under the assumed name of "Rabbi Ben-Israel," representing himself as a converted Jew. Lacunza lived in the eighteenth century, but it was about 1825 that his book, having found its way to London, was translated into the English language. Its publication served to deepen the interest already awakening in England in the subject of the second advent.

In Germany the doctrine had been taught in the eighteenth

1 "Journal of the Rev. Joseph Wolff", p. 389.

century by Bengel, a minister in the Lutheran Church, and a celebrated biblical scholar and critic. Upon completing his education, Bengel had "devoted himself to the study of theology, to which the grave and religious tone of his mind, deepened and strengthened by his early training and discipline, naturally inclined him. Like other young men of thoughtful character, before and since, he had to struggle with doubts and difficulties of a religious nature, and he alludes, with much feeling, to the 'many arrows which pierced his poor heart, and made his youth hard to bear.'"[1] Becoming a member of the consistory of Würtemberg, he advocated the cause of religious liberty. "While maintaining the rights and privileges of the church, he was an advocate for all reasonable freedom being accorded to those who felt themselves bound, on grounds of conscience, to withdraw from her communion."[2] The good effects of this policy are still felt in his native province.

It was while preparing a sermon from Revelation 21 for "Advent Sunday" that the light of Christ's second coming broke in upon Bengel's mind. The prophecies of the Revelation unfolded to his understanding as never before. Overwhelmed with a sense of the stupendous importance and surpassing glory of the scenes presented by the prophet, he was forced to turn for a time from the contemplation of the subject. In the pulpit it again presented itself to him with all its vividness and power. From that time he devoted himself to the study of the prophecies, especially those of the Apocalypse, and soon arrived at the belief that they pointed to the coming of Christ as near. The date which he fixed upon as the time of the second advent was within a very few years of that afterward held by Miller.

Bengel's writings have been spread throughout Christendom. His views of prophecy were quite generally received in his own state of Würtemberg, and to some extent in other parts of Germany. The movement continued after his death, and the advent message was heard in Germany at the same time that it was attracting attention in other lands. At an early date some of the believers went to Russia, and there formed colonies, and the faith

1 Encyclopædia Britannica, art. Bengel (ninth edition).
2 Encyclopædia Britannica, art. Bengel (ninth edition).

of Christ's soon coming is still held by the German churches of that country.

The light shone also in France and Switzerland. At Geneva, where Farel and Calvin had spread the truths of the Reformation, Gaussen preached the message of the second advent. While a student at school, Gaussen had encountered that spirit of rationalism which pervaded all Europe during the latter part of the eighteenth and the opening of the nineteenth century; and when he entered the ministry he was not only ignorant of true faith, but inclined to skepticism. In his youth he had become interested in the study of prophecy. After reading Rollin's "Ancient History," his attention was called to the second chapter of Daniel, and he was struck with the wonderful exactness with which the prophecy had been fulfilled, as seen in the historian's record. Here was a testimony to the inspiration of the Scriptures, which served as an anchor to him amid the perils of later years. He could not rest satisfied with the teachings of rationalism, and in studying the Bible and searching for clearer light he was, after a time, led to a positive faith.

As he pursued his investigation of the prophecies, he arrived at the belief that the coming of the Lord was at hand. Impressed with the solemnity and importance of this great truth, he desired to bring it before the people; but the popular belief that the prophecies of Daniel are mysteries and cannot be understood, was a serious obstacle in his way. He finally determined—as Farel had done before him in evangelizing Geneva—to begin with the children, through whom he hoped to interest the parents.

[. . .]

The effort was successful. As he addressed the children, older persons came to listen. The galleries of his church were filled with attentive hearers. Among them were men of rank and learning, and strangers and foreigners visiting Geneva; and thus the message was carried to other parts.

Encouraged by this success, Gaussen published his lessons, with the hope of promoting the study of the prophetic books in the churches of the French-speaking people. "To publish instruction given to the children," says Gaussen, "is to say to adults, who too often neglect such books under the false pretense that they are obscure. 'How can they be obscure, since your children understand them?'" "I had a great desire," he adds, "to render a knowledge of the prophecies popular in our flocks, if possible." "There is no study, indeed, which it seems to me answers the needs of the time better." "It is by this that we are to prepare for the tribulation near at hand, and watch and wait for Jesus Christ."

Though one of the most distinguished and beloved of preachers in the French language, Gaussen was after a time suspended from the ministry, his principal offense being that instead of the church's catechism, a tame and rationalistic manual, almost destitute of positive faith, he had used the Bible in giving instruction to the youth. He afterward became teacher in a theological school, while on Sunday he continued his work as catechist, addressing the children, and instructing them in the Scriptures. His works on prophecy also excited much interest. From the professor's chair, through the press, and in his favorite occupation as teacher of children, he continued for many years to exert an extensive influence, and was instrumental in calling the attention of many to the study of the prophecies which showed that the coming of the Lord was near.

[. . .]

To William Miller and his co-laborers it was given to preach the warning in America. This country became the center of the great Advent Movement. It was here that the prophecy of the first angel's message had its most direct fulfilment. The writings of Miller and his associates were carried to distant lands. Wherever missionaries had penetrated in all the world, were sent the glad tidings of Christ's speedy return. Far and wide spread the message of the everlasting gospel, "Fear God, and give glory to Him; for the hour of His judgment is come."

The testimony of the prophecies which seemed to point to the coming of Christ in the spring of 1844, took deep hold of the minds of the people. As the message went from State to State, there was everywhere awakened wide-spread interest. Many were convinced that the arguments from the prophetic periods were correct, and sacrificing their pride of opinion, they joyfully received the truth. Some ministers laid aside their sectarian views and feelings, left their salaries and their churches, and united in proclaiming the coming of Jesus. There were comparatively few ministers, however, who would accept this message; therefore it was largely committed to humble laymen. Farmers left their fields, mechanics their tools, traders their merchandise, professional men their positions; and yet the number of workers was small in comparison with the work to be accomplished. The condition of an ungodly church and a world lying in wickedness, burdened the souls of the true watchmen, and they willingly endured toil, privation, and suffering, that they might call men to repentance unto salvation. Though opposed by Satan, the work went steadily forward, and the advent truth was accepted by many thousands.

Everywhere the searching testimony was heard, warning sinners, both worldlings and church-members, to flee from the wrath to come. Like John the Baptist, the forerunner of Christ, the preachers laid the axe at the root of the tree, and urged all to bring forth fruit meet for repentance. Their stirring appeals were in marked contrast to the assurances of peace and safety that were heard from popular pulpits; and wherever the message was given, it moved the people. The simple, direct testimony of the Scriptures, set home by the power of the Holy Spirit, brought a weight of conviction which few were able wholly to resist. Professors of religion were roused from their false security. They saw their backslidings, their worldliness and unbelief, their pride and selfishness. Many sought the Lord with repentance and humiliation. The affections that had so long clung to earthly things they now fixed upon heaven. The Spirit of God rested upon them, and with hearts softened and subdued they joined to sound the cry, "Fear God, and give glory to Him; for the hour of His judgment is come."

Sinners inquired with weeping, "What must I do to be saved?" Those whose lives had been marked with dishonesty were anxious to make restitution. All who found peace in Christ longed to see others share the blessing. The hearts of parents were turned to their children, and the hearts of children to their parents. The barriers of pride and reserve were swept away. Heartfelt confessions were made, and the members of the household labored for the salvation of those who were nearest and dearest. Often was heard the sound of earnest intercession. Everywhere were souls in deep anguish, pleading with God. Many wrestled all night in prayer for the assurance that their own sins were pardoned, or for the conversion of their relatives or neighbors.

All classes flocked to the Adventist meetings. Rich and poor, high and low, were, from various causes, anxious to hear for themselves the doctrine of the second advent. The Lord held the spirit of opposition in check while His servants explained the reasons of their faith. Sometimes the instrument was feeble; but the Spirit of God gave power to His truth. The presence of holy angels was felt in these assemblies, and many were daily added to the believers. As the evidences of Christ's soon coming were repeated, vast crowds listened in breathless silence to the solemn words. Heaven and earth seemed to approach each other. The power of God was felt upon old and young and middle-aged. Men sought their homes with praises upon their lips, and the glad sound rang out upon the still night air. None who attended those meetings can ever forget those scenes of deepest interest.

The proclamation of a definite time for Christ's coming called forth great opposition from many of all classes, from the minister in the pulpit down to the most reckless, Heaven-daring sinner. The words of prophecy were fulfilled: "There shall come in the last days scoffers, walking after their own lusts, and saying, Where is the promise of His coming? for since the fathers fell asleep, all things continue as they were from the beginning of the creation."[1] Many who professed to love the Saviour, declared that they had no opposition to the doctrine of the second advent; they merely objected to the definite time. But God's all-seeing eye read their hearts. They did not wish to hear of Christ's coming to judge the world in righteousness. They had been unfaithful servants, their works would not bear the inspection of the heart-searching God, and they feared to meet their Lord. Like the Jews at the time of Christ's first advent, they were not prepared to welcome Jesus. They not only refused to listen to the plain arguments from the Bible, but ridiculed those who were looking for the Lord. Satan and his angels exulted, and flung the taunt in the

1 2 Peter 3:3, 4.

face of Christ and holy angels, that His professed people had so little love for Him that they did not desire His appearing.

"No man knoweth the day nor the hour," was the argument most often brought forward by rejecters of the advent faith. The scripture is, "Of that day and hour knoweth no man, no, not the angels of heaven, but My Father only."[1]

A clear and harmonious explanation of this text was given by those who were looking for the Lord, and the wrong use made of it by their opponents was clearly shown. The words were spoken by Christ in that memorable conversation with His disciples upon Olivet, after He had, for the last time departed from the temple. The disciples had asked the question, "What shall be the sign of Thy coming, and of the end of the world?" Jesus gave them signs, and said, "When ye shall see all these things, know that it is near, even at the doors."[2] One saying of the Saviour must not be made to destroy another. Though no man knoweth the *day* nor the *hour* of His coming, we are instructed and required to know when it is near. We are further taught that to disregard His warning, and refuse or neglect to know when His advent is near, will be as fatal for us as it was for those who lived in the days of Noah not to know when the flood was coming. And the parable in the same chapter, contrasting the faithful and the unfaithful servant, and giving the doom of him who said in his heart, "My Lord delayeth His coming," shows in what light Christ will regard and reward those whom He finds watching, and teaching His coming, and those denying it. "Watch therefore," He says; "blessed is that servant, whom his Lord when He cometh shall find so doing."[3] "If therefore thou shalt not watch, I will come on thee as a thief, and thou shalt not know what hour I will come upon thee."[4]

Paul speaks of a class to whom the Lord's appearing will come unawares. "The day of the Lord so cometh as a thief in the night. For when they shall say, Peace and safety; then sudden destruction cometh upon them, . . . and they shall not escape." But He

---

1 Matt. 24:36, 3, 33, 42–51.
2 Matt. 24:36, 3, 33, 42–51.
3 Matt. 24:36, 3, 33, 42–51.
4 Rev. 3:3.

adds, to those who have given heed to the Saviour's warning, "Ye, brethren, are not in darkness, that that day should overtake you as a thief. Ye are all the children of light, and the children of the day: we are not of the night, nor of darkness."[1]

Thus it was shown that Scripture gives no warrant for men to remain in ignorance concerning the nearness of Christ's coming. But those who desired only an excuse to reject the truth closed their ears to this explanation; and the words, "No man knoweth the day nor the hour," continued to be echoed by the bold scoffer, and even by the professed minister of Christ. As the people were roused, and began to inquire the way of salvation, religious teachers stepped in between them and the truth, seeking to quiet their fears by falsely interpreting the word of God, Unfaithful watchmen united in the work of the great deceiver, crying, Peace, peace, when God had not spoken peace. Like the Pharisees in Christ's day, many refused to enter the kingdom of heaven themselves, and those who were entering in, they hindered. The blood of these souls will be required at their hand.

The most humble and devoted in the churches were usually the first to receive the message. Those who studied the Bible for themselves could not but see the unscriptural character of the popular views of prophecy; and wherever the people were not controlled by the influence of the clergy, wherever they would search the word of God for themselves, the advent doctrine needed only to be compared with the Scriptures to establish its divine authority.

Many were persecuted by their unbelieving brethren. In order to retain their position in the church, some consented to be silent in regard to their hope; but others felt that loyalty to God forbade them thus to hide the truths which He had committed to their trust. Not a few were cut off from the fellowship of the church for no other reason than expressing their belief in the coming of Christ. Very precious to those who bore this trial of their faith were the words of the prophet, "Your brethren that hated you, that cast you out for My name's sake, said, Let the Lord be glorified: but he shall appear to your joy, and they shall he ashamed."[2]

1 1 Thess. 5:2–5
2 Isa. 66:5.

Angels of God were watching with the deepest interest the result of the warning. When there was a general rejection of the message by the churches, angels turned away in sadness. But there were many who had not yet been tested in regard to the advent truth. Many were misled by husbands, wives, parents, or children, and were made to believe it a sin even to listen to such heresies as were taught by the Adventists. Angels were bidden to keep faithful watch over these souls; for another light was yet to shine upon them from the throne of God.

With unspeakable desire those who had received the message watched for the coming of their Saviour. The time when they expected to meet Him was at hand. They approached this hour with a calm solemnity. They rested in sweet communion with God, an earnest of the peace that was to be theirs in the bright hereafter. None who experienced this hope and trust can forget those precious hours of waiting. For some weeks preceding the time, worldly business was for the most part laid aside. The sincere believers carefully examined every thought and emotion of their hearts as if upon their death-beds and in a few hours to close their eyes upon earthly scenes. There was no making of "ascension robes"; but all felt the need of internal evidence that they were prepared to meet the Saviour; their white robes were purity of soul,—characters cleansed from sin by the atoning blood of Christ. Would that there was still with the professed people of God the same spirit of heart-searching, the same earnest, determined faith. Had they continued thus to humble themselves before the Lord, and press their petitions at the mercy-seat, they would be in possession of a far richer experience than they now have. There is too little prayer, too little real conviction of sin, and the lack of living faith leaves many destitute of the grace so richly provided by our Redeemer.

God designed to prove His people. His hand covered a mistake in the reckoning of the prophetic periods. Adventists did not discover the error, nor was it discovered by the most learned of their opponents. The latter said: "Your reckoning of the prophetic periods is correct. Some great event is about to take place; but it is not what Mr. Miller predicts; it is the conversion of the world, and not the second advent of Christ."

The time of expectation passed, and Christ did not appear for the deliverance of His people. Those who with sincere faith and love had looked for their Saviour, experienced a bitter disappointment. Yet the purposes of God were being accomplished: He was testing the hearts of those who professed to be waiting for His appearing. There were among them many who had been actuated by no higher motive than fear. Their profession of faith had not affected their hearts or their lives. When the expected event failed to take place, these persons declared that they were not disappointed; they had never believed that Christ would come. They were among the first to ridicule the sorrow of the true believers.

But Jesus and all the heavenly host looked with love and sympathy upon the tried and faithful yet disappointed ones. Could the veil separating the visible from the invisible world have been swept back, angels would have been seen drawing near to these steadfast souls, and shielding them from the shafts of Satan.

## THE FINAL WARNING—38

"I saw another angel come down from heaven, having great power; and the earth was lightened with his glory. And he cried mightily with a strong voice, saying, Babylon the great is fallen, is fallen, and is become the habitation of devils, and the hold of every foul spirit, and a cage of every unclean and hateful bird." "And I heard another voice from heaven, saying, Come out of her, My people, that ye be not partakers of her sins, and that ye receive not of her plagues."[1]

This scripture points forward to a time when the announcement of the fall of Babylon, as made by the second angel[2] of Revelation 14, is to be repeated, with the additional mention of the corruptions which have been entering the various organizations that constitute Babylon, since that message was first given, in the summer of 1844. A terrible condition of the religious world is here described. With every rejection of truth, the minds of the people will become darker, their hearts more stubborn, until they are entrenched in an infidel hardihood. In defiance of the warn-

1 Rev. 18:1, 2, 4.
2 Rev. 14:8.

ings which God has given, they will continue to trample upon one of the precepts of the decalogue, until they are led to persecute those who hold it sacred. Christ is set at naught in the contempt placed upon His word and His people. As the teachings of Spiritualism are accepted by the churches, the restraint imposed upon the carnal heart is removed, and the profession of religion will become a cloak to conceal the basest iniquity. A belief in spiritual manifestations opens the door to seducing spirits, and doctrines of devils, and thus the influence of evil angels will be felt in the churches.

Of Babylon, at the time brought to view in this prophecy, it is declared, "Her sins have reached unto heaven, and God hath remembered her iniquities."[1] She has filled up the measure of her guilt, and destruction is about to fall upon her. But God still has a people in Babylon; and before the visitation of His judgments, these faithful ones must be called out, that they "partake not of her sins, and receive not of her plagues." Hence the movement symbolized by the angel coming down from heaven, lightening the earth with his glory, and crying mightily with a strong voice, announcing the sins of Babylon. In connection with his message the call is heard, "Come out of her, My people." These announcements, uniting with the third angel's message, constitute the final warning to be given to the inhabitants of the earth.

Fearful is the issue to which the world is to be brought. The powers of earth, uniting to war against the commandments of God, will decree that all, "both small and great, rich and poor, free and bond,"[2] shall conform to the customs of the church by the observance of the false sabbath. All who refuse compliance will be visited with civil penalties, and it will finally be declared that they are deserving of death. On the other hand, the law of God enjoining the Creator's rest-day demands obedience, and threatens wrath against all who transgress its precepts.

With the issue thus clearly brought before him, whoever shall trample upon God's law to obey a human enactment, receives the mark of the beast; he accepts the sign of allegiance to the power which he chooses to obey instead of God. The warning from

1 Rev. 18:5.
2 Rev. 13:16.

heaven is, "If any man worship the beast and his image, and receive his mark in his forehead, or in his hand, the same shall drink of the wine of the wrath of God, which is poured out without mixture into the cup of His indignation."[1]

But not one is made to suffer the wrath of God until the truth has been brought home to his mind and conscience, and has been rejected. There are many who have never had an opportunity to hear the special truths for this time. The obligation of the fourth commandment has never been set before them in its true light. He who reads every heart, and tries every motive, will leave none who desire a knowledge of the truth, to be deceived as to the issues of the controversy. The decree is not to be urged upon the people blindly. Every one is to have sufficient light to make his decision intelligently.

The Sabbath will be the great test of loyalty; for it is the point of truth especially controverted. When the final test shall be brought to bear upon men, then the line of distinction will be drawn between those who serve God and those who serve Him not. While the observance of the false sabbath in compliance with the law of the state, contrary to the fourth commandment, will be an avowal of allegiance to a power that is in opposition to God, the keeping of the true Sabbath, in obedience to God's law, is an evidence of loyalty to the Creator. While one class, by accepting the sign of submission to earthly powers, receive the mark of the beast, the other, choosing the token of allegiance to divine authority, receive the seal of God.

Heretofore those who presented the truths of the third angel's message have often been regarded as mere alarmists. Their predictions that religious intolerance would gain control in the United States, that church and state would unite to persecute those who keep the commandments of God, have been pronounced groundless and absurd. It has been confidently declared that this land could never become other than what it has been,—the defender of religious freedom. But as the question of enforcing Sunday observance is widely agitated, the event so long doubted and disbelieved is seen to be approaching, and the third message will produce an effect which it could not have had before.

[1] Rev. 14:9, 10.

In every generation God has sent His servants to rebuke sin, both in the world and in the church. But the people desire smooth things spoken to them, and the pure, unvarnished truth is not acceptable. Many reformers, in entering upon their work, determined to exercise great prudence in attacking the sins of the church and the nation. They hoped, by the example of a pure Christian life, to lead the people back to the doctrines of the Bible. But the Spirit of God came upon them as it came upon Elijah, moving him to rebuke the sins of a wicked king and an apostate people; they could not refrain from preaching the plain utterances of the Bible,—doctrines which they had been reluctant to present. They were impelled to zealously declare the truth, and the danger which threatened souls. The words which the Lord gave them they uttered, fearless of consequences, and the people were compelled to hear the warning.

Thus the message of the third angel will be proclaimed. As the time comes for it to be given with greatest power, the Lord will work through humble instruments, leading the minds of those who consecrate themselves to His service. The laborers will be qualified rather by the unction of His Spirit than by the training of literary institutions. Men of faith and prayer will be constrained to go forth with holy zeal, declaring the words which God gives them. The sins of Babylon will be laid open. The fearful results of enforcing the observances of the church by civil authority, the inroads of Spiritualism, the stealthy but rapid progress of the papal power,—all will be unmasked. By these solemn warnings the people will be stirred. Thousands upon thousands will listen who have never heard words like these. In amazement they hear the testimony that Babylon is the church, fallen because of her errors and sins, because of her rejection of the truth sent to her from heaven. As the people go to their former teachers with the eager inquiry, Are these things so? the ministers present fables, prophesy smooth things, to soothe their fears, and quiet the awakened conscience. But since many refuse to be satisfied with the mere authority of men, and demand a plain "Thus saith the Lord," the popular ministry, like the Pharisees of old, filled with anger as their authority is questioned, will denounce the message as of Satan, and stir up the sin-loving multitudes to revile and persecute those who proclaim it.

As the controversy extends into new fields, and the minds of the people are called to God's down-trodden law, Satan is astir. The power attending the message will only madden those who oppose it. The clergy will put forth almost superhuman efforts to shut away the light, lest it should shine upon their flocks. By every means at their command they will endeavor to suppress the discussion of these vital questions. The church appeals to the strong arm of civil power, and in this work, papists and Protestants unite. As the movement for Sunday enforcement becomes more bold and decided, the law will be invoked against commandment-keepers. They will be threatened with fines and imprisonment, and some will be offered positions of influence, and other rewards and advantages, as inducements to renounce their faith. But their steadfast answer is, "Show us from the word of God our error,"—the same plea that was made by Luther under similar circumstances. Those who are arraigned before the courts, make a strong vindication of the truth, and some who hear them are led to take their stand to keep all the commandments of God. Thus light will be brought before thousands who otherwise would know nothing of these truths.

Conscientious obedience to the word of God will be treated as rebellion. Blinded by Satan, the parent will exercise harshness and severity toward the believing child; the master or mistress will oppress the commandment-keeping servant. Affection will be alienated; children will be disinherited, and driven from home. The words of Paul will be literally fulfilled, "All that will live godly in Christ Jesus shall suffer persecution."[1] As the defenders of truth refuse to honor the Sunday-sabbath, some of them will be thrust into prison, some will be exiled, some will be treated as slaves. To human wisdom, all this now seems impossible; but as the restraining Spirit of God shall be withdrawn from men, and they shall be under the control of Satan, who hates the divine precepts, there will be strange developments. The heart can be very cruel when God's fear and love are removed.

As the storm approaches, a large class who have professed faith in the third angel's message, but have not been sanctified through obedience to the truth, abandon their position, and join the ranks

1  2 Tim. 3:12.

of the opposition. By uniting with the world and partaking of its spirit, they have come to view matters in nearly the same light; and when the test is brought, they are prepared to choose the easy, popular side. Men of talent and pleasing address, who once rejoiced in the truth, employ their powers to deceive and mislead souls. They become the most bitter enemies of their former brethren. When Sabbath-keepers are brought before the courts to answer for their faith, these apostates are the most efficient agents of Satan to misrepresent and accuse them, and by false reports and insinuations to stir up the rulers against them.

In this time of persecution the faith of the Lord's servants will be tried. They have faithfully given the warning, looking to God and to His word alone. God's Spirit, moving upon their hearts, has constrained them to speak. Stimulated with holy zeal, and with the divine impulse strong upon them, they entered upon the performance of their duties without coldly calculating the consequences of speaking to the people the word which the Lord had given them. They have not consulted their temporal interests, nor sought to preserve their reputation or their lives. Yet when the storm of opposition and reproach bursts upon them, some, overwhelmed with consternation, will be ready to exclaim, "Had we foreseen the consequences of our words, we would have held our peace." They are hedged in with difficulties. Satan assails them with fierce temptations. The work which they have undertaken seems far beyond their ability to accomplish. They are threatened with destruction. The enthusiasm which animated them is gone; yet they cannot turn back. Then, feeling their utter helplessness, they flee to the Mighty One for strength. They remember that the words which they have spoken were not theirs, but His who bade them give the warning. God put the truth into their hearts, and they could not forbear to proclaim it.

The same trials have been experienced by men of God in ages past. Wycliffe, Huss, Luther, Tyndale, Baxter, Wesley, urged that all doctrines be brought to the test of the Bible, and declared that they would renounce everything which it condemned. Against these men, persecution raged with relentless fury; yet they ceased not to declare the truth. Different periods in the history of the church have each been marked by the development of some special truth, adapted to the necessities of God's people at that time. Every new truth has made its way against hatred and opposition; those who were blessed with its light were tempted and tried. The Lord gives a special truth for the people in an emergency. Who dare refuse to publish it? He commands His servants to present the last invitation of mercy to the world. They cannot remain silent, except at the peril of their souls. Christ's ambassadors have nothing to do with consequences. They must perform their duty, and leave results with God.

As the opposition rises to a fiercer height, the servants of God are again perplexed; for it seems to them that they have brought the crisis. But conscience and the word of God assure them that their course is right; and although the trials continue, they are strengthened to bear them. The contest grows closer and sharper, but their faith and courage rise with the emergency. Their testimony is: "We dare not tamper with God's word, dividing His holy law; calling one portion essential and another non-essential, to gain the favor of the world. The Lord whom we serve is able to deliver us. Christ has conquered the powers of earth; and shall we be afraid of a world already conquered?"

Persecution in its varied forms is the development of a principle which will exist as long as Satan exists and Christianity has vital power. No man can serve God without enlisting against himself the opposition of the hosts of darkness. Evil angels will assail him, alarmed that his influence is taking the prey from their hands. Evil men, rebuked by his example, will unite with them in seeking to separate him from God by alluring temptations. When these do not succeed, then a compelling power is employed to force the conscience.

But so long as Jesus remains man's intercessor in the sanctuary above, the restraining influence of the Holy Spirit is felt by rulers and people. It still controls, to some extent, the laws of the land. Were it not for these laws, the condition of the world would be much worse than it now is. While many of our rulers are active agents of Satan, God also has His agents among the leading men of the nation. The enemy moves upon his servants to propose measures that would greatly impede the work of God; but statesmen who fear the Lord are influenced by holy angels to oppose such propositions with unanswerable arguments. Thus a few men will hold in check a powerful current of evil. The opposition of the enemies of truth will be restrained that the third angel's message may do its work. When the final warning shall be given, it will arrest the attention of these leading men through whom the Lord is now working, and some of them will accept it, and will stand with the people of God through the time of trouble.

The angel who unites in the proclamation of the third angel's message, is to lighten the whole earth with his glory. A work of world-wide extent and unwonted power is here foretold. The Advent Movement of 1840–44 was a glorious manifestation of the power of God; the first angel's message was carried to every missionary station in the world, and in some countries there was the greatest religious interest which has been witnessed in any land since the Reformation of the sixteenth century; but these are to be exceeded by the mighty movement under the last warning of the third angel.

The work will be similar to that of the day of Pentecost. As the "former rain" was given, in the outpouring of the Holy Spirit at the opening of the gospel, to cause the up-springing of the precious seed, so the "latter rain" will be given at its close, for the ripening of the harvest. "Then shall we know, if we follow on to know the Lord: His going forth is prepared as the morning; and He shall come unto us as the rain, as the latter and former rain unto the earth."[1]

"Be glad then, ye children of Zion, and rejoice in the Lord your God: for He hath given you the former rain moderately, and He will cause to come down for you the rain, the former rain, and the latter rain."[2] "In the last days, saith God, I will pour out of My Spirit upon all flesh." "And it shall come to pass, that whosoever shall call on the name of the Lord shall be saved."[3]

The great work of the gospel is not to close with less manifestation of the power of God than marked its opening. The prophecies which were fulfilled in the outpouring of the former rain at the opening of the gospel, are again to be fulfilled in the latter rain at its close. Here are "the times of refreshing" to which the apostle Peter looked forward when he said, "Repent ye therefore,

---

1 Hosea 6:3.
2 Joel 2:23.
3 Acts 2:17, 21.

and be converted, that your sins may be blotted out when the times of refreshing shall come from the presence of the Lord; and He shall send Jesus."[1]

Servants of God, with their faces lighted up and shining with holy consecration, will hasten from place to place to proclaim the message from heaven. By thousands of voices, all over the earth, the warning will be given. Miracles will be wrought, the sick will be healed, and signs and wonders will follow the believers. Satan also works with lying wonders, even bringing down fire from heaven in the sight of men.[2] Thus the inhabitants of the earth will be brought to take their stand.

The message will be carried not so much by argument as by the deep conviction of the Spirit of God. The arguments have been presented. The seed has been sown, and now it will spring up and bear fruit. The publications distributed by missionary workers have exerted their influence, yet many whose minds were impressed have been prevented from fully comprehending the truth or from yielding obedience. Now the rays of light penetrate everywhere, the truth is seen in its clearness, and the honest children of God sever the bands which have held them. Family connections, church relations, are powerless to stay them now. Truth is more precious than all besides. Notwithstanding the agencies combined against the truth, a large number take their stand upon the Lord's side.

(ELLEN G. WHITE, 1888; REV. ED., MOUNTAIN VIEW, CA: 1911;
PP. 355–66, 368–74, 603–12)

1 Acts 3:19, 20.
2 Rev. 13:13.

# The Unknown Life of Jesus Christ

One of the great mysteries surrounding the life of Jesus is the "missing period" of his life from the ages of approximately thirteen to thirty. The canonical Gospels say nothing about his whereabouts during this time, a fact that left plenty of room for speculation as nineteenth-century Christians increasingly sought scientific certainty about his life. *The Unknown Life of Jesus Christ* both fed and fueled this interest. Its origins, as with many of these texts, are contested. Nicolas Notovitch (1858–?) was a Russian war correspondent, and he claimed to have heard rumors about a great prophet named Issa (the Tibetan form of the name Jesus) during his travels in India and Kashmir in 1887. By coincidence, he also had a riding accident during his visit and spent several months being nursed to health in the monastery of Hemis. It was there, in one of the spiritual centers of Tibetan Buddhism, where he was shown a book called the *Life of Saint Issa*. Convinced that this Issa was, in fact, Jesus Christ, Notovitch had a translator help him record the book as it was read aloud to him. The resulting volume was published in French in 1894, but almost immediately it created a sensation throughout the West. Within a year, eight editions appeared in French, four in English, and one each in German, Spanish, and Italian.

*The Unknown Life of Christ* related the story of Jesus' travels through India and Tibet prior to his ministry in Palestine. There he studied Buddhist and Hindu texts, then traveled to Persia to study Zoroastrianism. Finally he returned to his home, where he was ultimately killed by the Roman authorities and later resurrected. Just as striking as the new accounting for his whereabouts is the implication that his message was informed by his encounters with Eastern religious traditions. That claim drew the attention of scholars, including the most renowned Indologist of the day, Max Müller, who swiftly rejected Notovitch's claims of the ancient origins of the document. Investigators who returned to Hemis were never able to locate anyone who remembered meeting the Russian traveler.

Despite those denunciations, Notovitch's story did not die. Since its publication, many New Age and Spiritualist authors have incorporated some of his basic claims—that Jesus traveled to India and was influenced by Buddhist and Hindu teachings—into their belief systems. The Ahmadiyya movement, an offshoot of orthodox Islam founded in the late nineteenth century, teaches that Jesus did not die on the cross but instead fled to Kashmir, where he became a great teacher. Levi Dowling repeated some of the same ideas in the *Aquarian Gospel*. More recently, Elizabeth Clare Prophet, leader of the American-based Summit Lighthouse and the Church Universal and Triumphant, published a book titled *The Lost Years of Jesus* that drew heavily from Notovitch's work. In all of these instances, religious groups have tied Jesus' travels in the East with their own spiritual blending of Eastern and Western ideas.

# The Unknown Life of Jesus Christ

## THE LIFE OF SAINT ISSA.
## THE BEST OF THE SONS OF MEN.

### I.

—1—

The earth trembled and the heavens wept because of the great crime just committed in the land of Israel.

—2—

For they have just finished torturing and executing there the great, just Issa in whom dwelt the soul of the universe,

—3—

Who incarnated himself in a simple mortal in order to do good to men and to exterminate evil thoughts

—4—

And in order to bring back man degraded by sins to a life of peace, love and good, and to recall him to the only and indivisible Creator, whose mercy is infinite and boundless.

—5—

This is what the merchants, who came from Israel, relate on the subject.

### II.

—1—

The people of Israel lived on a very fertile land, yielding two harvests a year, and possessed large flocks; they excited by their sins the wrath of God,

—2—

Who inflicted on them a terrible punishment, taking away their land, their flocks and their possessions. Israel was reduced to slavery by the powerful and rich Pharaohs who then reigned in Egypt.

—3—

The latter had made slaves of the Israelites and treated them worse than beasts, overloading them with heavy and difficult work and putting them in irons and covering their bodies with wounds and scars, denying them sufficient food and shelter.

—4—

This was in order to keep them in a state of continual fear and deprive them of all resemblance to human beings;

—5—

And in this great calamity the people of Israel, remembering their heavenly Protector, prayed and implored His grace and pity.

—6—

An illustrious Pharaoh reigned in Egypt at this time who rendered himself famous by his numerous victories and riches which he had accumulated and the large palaces which his slaves had erected with their own hands.

—7—

This Pharaoh had two sons, the younger of whom was called Mossa; the wise men of Israel taught him different sciences.

—8—

And they loved Mossa in Egypt for his kindness and for the compassion which he showed to all those who suffered.

—9—

Seeing that the Israelites would not, in spite of the intolerable sufferings which they endured, abandon their God to worship those which the hand of man had made and which were the gods of the Egyptians,

—10—

Mossa believed in their invisible God who did not allow their weakened forces to fail,

—11—

And the Israelite teachers excited the ardor of Mossa and implored him to intercede with Pharaoh his father, in favor of his co-religionists.

—12—

The Prince Mossa applied to his father imploring him to ameliorate the fate of the unfortunate people, but Pharaoh was enraged against him and only increased the torments of his slaves.

—13—

Shortly afterwards, a great misfortune visited Egypt; the plague cut down the young and the old, the sick and the well, Pharaoh believed that his own gods were angry with him;

—14—

But Prince Mossa told his father that it was the God of the slaves who was interceding in favor of the unfortunates and was punishing the Egyptians;

—15—

Pharaoh then ordered Mossa to take all the slaves of the Jewish race and lead them out of the city, and to found at a great distance from the capital another city and there to live with them.

—16—

Mossa told the Hebrew slaves that he had freed them in the name of his God, the God of Israel; he departed with them from the city and from the land of Egypt.

—17—

He led them into the land which they had formerly lost by their many sins; he gave them laws and advised them always to pray to the invisible Creator whose kindness is infinite.

—18—

After the death of the Prince Mossa the Israelites observed his laws rigorously; God too recompensed them for the evils to which they had been subjected in Egypt.

—19—

Their kingdom became the most powerful in all the world, their kings became illustrious on account of their treasures and peace reigned long among the people of Israel.

## III.

—1—

The fame of the riches of Israel was spread throughout the earth and the neighboring nations envied them.

—2—

But God led the victorious armies of the Hebrews and the heathen dared not attack them.

—3—

Unfortunately, man does not always obey his own better self, so the fidelity of the Israelities to their God did not long endure.

—4—

They soon forgot all the favors which He had heaped upon them, and rarely invoked His name, but begged protection of the magicians and sorcerers;

—5—

The kings and captains submitted their own laws for those that Moses had left to them; the temples of God and the customs of worship were abandoned, and the people gave themselves up to pleasures and lost their original purity.

—6—

Several centuries had elapsed since their departure from Egypt, when God again thought of inflicting punishment on them.

—7—

Strangers began to invade the country of Israel, devastating the land, ruining the villages and forcing the inhabitants into captivity.

—8—

Heathens at one time came from beyond the seas from the country of Romulus; they subdued the Hebrews and appointed commanders of the army who goverened them under the orders of Cæsar.

—9—

They destroyed the temples, compelling the people to sacrifice victims to the heathen gods instead of worshiping the invisible God.

—10—

Warriors were made of the nobles, the women were torn from their husbands; the lower class of the people, reduced to slavery, were sent by thousands across the sea.

—11—

As to the children they were killed by the sword, and throughout the whole country of Israel nothing but weeping and groaning was heard.

—12—

In their sore distress the people remembered again their great God; they implored His mercy and prayed Him to forgive them. Our Father in His inexhaustible kindness listened to their appeal.

# IV.

## —1—

The time had now come when the merciful Judge had chosen to incarnate Himself in a human being.

## —2—

And the Eternal Spirit who remained in a condition of complete inaction and of supreme beatitude, aroused and detached Himself for an indefinite time from the Eternal Being,

## —3—

In order to show, by assuming the human form, the means of identifying one's self with divinity and attaining eternal felicity;

## —4—

And to show by His example how we may attain moral purity and separate the soul from its material envelope so that it may reach the perfection necessary to pass into the Kingdom of Heaven, which is unchangeable and where eternal happiness reigns.

## —5—

Soon after, a wonderful child was born in the land of Israel; God Himself spoke by the mouth of this child of the insignificance of body, and the grandeur of soul.

## —6—

The parents of this child were poor people, belonging by birth to a family distinguished for their piety, who had forgotten their ancient grandeur on earth, in celebrating the name of the Creator and thanking Him for the misfortunes with which He was pleased to try them.

## —7—

To reward this family for remaining firm in the path of truth, God blessed their first-born child and elected him to go forth and uplift those that had fallen in evil and to cure those that were suffering.

## —8—

The divine child, to whom they gave the name of Issa, began to speak, while yet a child, of the one indivisible God, exhorting the erring souls to repent and to purify themselves from those sins, of which they were guilty.

## —9—

People came from all parts to listen to him and they marvelled at the words of wisdom which issued from his childish mouth; all the Israelites affirmed that in this child dwelt the Eternal Spirit.

—10—

When Issa reached the age of thirteen years, the time when an Israelite should take a wife,

—11—

The house where his parents earned a livelihood by means of modest labor, began to be a place of meeting for the rich and noble people who desired to have the young Issa for a son-in-law, who was already well-known by his edifying discourses in the name of All-Powerful;

—12—

It was then that Issa disappeared secretly from his father's house, left Jerusalem, and with a caravan of merchants, went toward Sindh,

—13—

With the purpose of perfecting himself in the divine knowledge and of studying the laws of the great Buddhas.

## V.

—1—

In the course of his fourteenth year, the young Issa, blessed of God, crossed the Sindh and established himself among the Aryas, in the cherished country of God.

—2—

The fame of this wonderful youth spread throughout Northern Sindh; when he crossed the country of the five rivers and Rajputana, the worshippers of the Jaina God implored him to dwell with them.

—3—

But he left them and went to Jagannath, in the country of Orissa, where lie the mortal remains of Vyasa-Krishna. Here the white priests of Brahma received him joyfully.

—4—

They taught him to read and understand the Vedas, to cure with the aid of prayers, to teach and explain the holy scriptures to the people, to drive away the evil spirit from the body of man, and to restore to him the human form.

—5—

He spent six years in Jagannath, Rajagriha, Benares and other holy cities. Every one loved Issa, for he lived in peace with the Vaishyas and Shudras, to whom he taught the holy scripture.

—6—

But the Brahmins and Kshatriyas said to him that the great Para-Brahma had forbidden them to approach those whom he had created from his belly and from his feet;

—7—

That the Vaishyas were authorized to hear the reading of the Vedas only on the festival days,

—8—

That the Shudras were not only forbidden to attend the reading of the Vedas, but even to look at them; for their condition was to serve forever as slaves to the Brahmins, the Kshatriyas and even the Vaishyas;

—9—

"Death alone can free them from their servitude," Para-Brahma has said: "Leave them, therefore, and come and worship with us the gods that will be angry with you if you disobey them."

—10—

But Issa did not heed their words, and went among the Shudras to preach against the Brahmins and the Kshatriyas.

—11—

He strongly denounced the doctrine that gives to men the power of robbing their fellow-men of their human rights; in truth, he said: "God the Father has established no difference between his children, who are all equally dear to him."

—12—

Issa denied the divine origin of the Vedas and the Puranas, for he taught his followers that one law had been given to man to guide him in his actions:

—13—

"Fear thy God, bend thy knee only before Him, and bring to Him alone thy offerings which come from thy labors."

—14—

Issa denied the Trimurti and the incarnation of Para-Brahma in Vishnu, Shiva and other gods; for he said:

—15—

"The Eternal Judge, the Eternal Spirit composes the one individual soul of the universe, which alone creates, contains and vivifies the whole."

—16—

"It is He alone who has willed and created, who exists from eternity, whose existence will have no end; there is none equal to Him either in heaven or on earth."

—17—

"The great Creator has shared His power with no one, still less with inanimate objects, as they have taught you, for He alone possesses all power."

—18—

"He willed and the world appeared; by one divine thought He united the waters and separated from them the dry part of the globe. He is the cause of the mysterious life of man, into whom He has breathed a part of His own."

—19—

"He has subordinated to man the land, the water, the beasts and all that He has created, and which He Himself preserves in an unchangeable order by fixing the proper duration of each."

—20—

"The anger of God will soon fall on man, for he has forgotten his Creator; he has filled His temples with abominations, and he adores numerous creatures which God has subordinated to him."

—21—

"For, in order to please stones and metals, he sacrifices human beings, in whom dwells a part of the spirit of God."

—22—

"For he humiliates those who toil by the sweat of their brow to gain the favor of the idle, who sit at sumptuously furnished tables."

—23—

"Those who deprive their brothers of the divine gift shall be deprived of it themselves, and the Brahmins and the Kshatriyas will become Shudras of the Shudras, with whom the Eternal will dwell forever."

—24—

"Because on the day of the last Judgment, the Shudras and the Vaishyas shall be pardoned on account of their ignorance; on the other hand, God will pour His wrath upon those who have arrogated His rights."

—25—

"The Vaishyas and the Shudras greatly admired these words of Issa, and begged him to teach them how to pray, so that they might secure their happiness."

—26—

He said to them: "Do not worship idols, for they do not hear you; do not listen to the Vedas, in which the truth is perverted; do not believe yourselves superior to others everywhere; do not humiliate your neighbor."

—27—

"Help the poor, sustain the feeble; do no evil to anyone; do not covet what others possess and you do not."

## VI.

—1—

The white priests and the warriors having learnt of the discourse which Issa had addressed to the Shudras, determined upon his death, and with this intention sent their servants to search for the young prophet.

—2—

But Issa, warned of the danger by the Shudras, left Jagannath by night, reached the mountains, and established himself in the country of the Gautamides, where the great Buddha Shakya-Muni was born, amidst the people who worshiped the one and only sublime Brahma.

—3—

Having learned perfectly the Pali language, the just Issa devoted himself to the study of the sacred rolls of the Sutras.

—4—

Six years afterwards, Issa, whom the Buddha had chosen to spread the holy doctrine, was able to explain perfectly the sacred rolls.

—5—

Then he left Nepal and the Himalaya mountains, descended into the valley of Rajputana and journeyed toward the west, preaching to various peoples the possibility of man's attaining the supreme perfection,

—6—

And the good which each one should do to his neighbor, which is the surest means of being quickly absorbed into the Eternal Spirit; "he who had recovered his primitive purity," Issa said, "would die having obtained pardon for his sins, and the right to contemplate the majestic figure of God."

—7—

In traversing the heathen territories the divine Issa taught that the worship of visible gods was contrary to natural law.

—8—

"For man," he said, "has not been favored with the power to see the image of God and to construct a host of divinities resembling the Eternal One."

—9—

"Besides, it is incompatible with the human conscience to esteem the grandeur of divine purity less than animals or works executed by the hand of man in stone or metal."

—10—

"The Eternal Legislator is one infinite; there are no other gods but Him, He has not shared the world with anyone, nor has He informed anyone of His intentions."

—11—

"Just as a father would act toward his children, so shall God judge men after their death according to His merciful laws; never will He humiliate His child by making his soul migrate into the body of a beast as in purgatory."

—12—

"The celestial law," said the Creator through the mouth of Issa, "scorns the immolation of human beings to a statue or to an animal, for I have dedicated to the use of man all animals and all that the world contains."

—13—

"All has been given to man who is thus directly and intimately bound to me his Father; he who has taken away my child will be severely judged and chastised by the divine law."

—14—

"To the Eternal Judge man is nil, just as an animal is to a man."

—15—

"Therefore I say unto you, leave your idols, do not perform ceremonies that separate you from your Father, and link and bind you to priests against whom Heaven is turned."

—16—

"For it is they who have led you astray from the true God and whose superstitions and cruelty are leading you to the perversion of spirit and to the loss of all moral sense."

## VII.

—1—

The words of Issa were spread abroad among the heathen in the countries through which he traveled and the people abandoned their idols.

—2—

Seeing this the priests demanded from him who glorified the name of the true God, proofs of the reproaches that he had heaped upon them and the demonstration of the powerlessness of their idols, in the presence of the people.

—3—

And Issa replied to them: "If your idols and animals are powerful and really possess a supernatural power, let them annihilate me on the spot."

—4—

"Perform a miracle," the priests answered him, "and let thy God confound ours if they inspire him with disgust."

—5—

But Issa answered: "The miracles of our God began with the creation of the universe, they take place now every day, every moment, and whosoever does not see them is deprived of one of the most beautiful gifts of life."

—6—

"And it is not upon pieces of inanimate stone or metal or wood that the anger of God will fall, but it will fall upon men, who must for their own safety destroy all the idols which they have made":

—7—

"Just as a stone and grain of sand which are as nothing before men, wait with resignation the time when he will utilize and make of them something useful and beautiful,"

—8—

"Just so man must wait for the great favor which God will accord him in honoring him with a decision."

—9—

"But alas for you, opponents of men! if it is not the favor but the wrath of Divinity that you await; woe unto you if you wait for Him to show His power by miracles!"

—10—

"For it is not the idols which He shall destroy in His wrath, but those who have erected them; their hearts shall be a prey to an eternal fire and their lacerated bodies will be given to satisfy the appetite of wild beasts."

—11—

"God will expel the contaminated animals from His flocks but He will take back to Himself those who were misled by having misunderstood the celestial spark which dwelt in them."

—12—

Seeing the powerlessness of their priests these people believed in the teachings of Issa and adopted his faith and in fear of the anger of the Divinity broke their idols in pieces; seeing this the priests fled to escape the popular vengeance.

—13—

And Issa taught the heathen not to try to see the Eternal Spirit with their own eyes, but rather to feel it with their heart and by a soul truly pure render themselves worthy of His favors.

—14—

He said to them: "Not only must you desist from making human sacrifices, but in general from sacrificing any animal to which life has been given, for all that has been created is for the benefit of man."

—15—

"Steal not the property of another, for this would be taking away from your neighbor the things which he has acquired by the sweat of his brow."

—16—

"Deceive not any one, thus you shall not be deceived yourselves; try to justify yourselves before the last judgment, for then it will be too late."

—17—

"Do not give yourselves up to debauchery, for that is violating the laws of God."

—18—

"Supreme happiness shall be attained not only by purifying yourselves, but also by guiding others in the way which will achieve for them the primitive perfection."

# VIII.

—1—

The neighboring countries were filled with the renown of the teachings of Issa, and when he entered Persia the priests became alarmed and forbade the people to listen to him.

—2—

But when they saw all the villages greeting him with joy and piously listening to his sermons, they caused him to be arrested and brought before the high priest where he was submitted to the following questions.

—3—

"Of what new God dost thou teach? Dost thou not know, unfortunate one that thou art, that the holy Zoroaster is the only just man admitted to the honor of receiving communications from the Supreme Being?"

—4—

"He has ordered the angels to record in writing the words of God for the use of his people—the laws that were given to Zoroaster in paradise."

—5—

"Who then art thou that darest to blaspheme our God and sow doubt in the hearts of believers?"

—6—

And Issa said unto them: "I do not speak of a new God, but of

our Heavenly Father who existed before the beginning and who
will exist after the eternal end."

—7—

"It is of Him that I have taught the people, who like an innocent child cannot yet understand God by the only force of their
intelligence and penetrate His divine and spiritual sublimity."

—8—

"But as a new-born child recognizes in the dark its mother's
breast, just so your people who have been led in error by your erroneous doctrine and religious ceremonies have recognized in-
stinctively their Father in the God, of whom I am the prophet."

—9—

"The Eternal Being says to your people through the medium of
my mouth: 'You should not worship the sun for it is only a part
of the world which I have created for man.'"

—10—

"'The sun rises in order to warm you during your labors; it sets
so as to give you rest which I have fixed.'"

—11—

"'It is only to me and to me alone that you owe all that you
possess, all that surrounds you, either above or below.'"

—12—

"But," began the priests, "how could a people live according to
the laws of justice, if they had no teachers?"

—13—

Issa answered: "As long as the people had no priests, they were
governed by natural laws and preserved the candour of their souls."

—14—

"Their souls were in God and when they wanted to communicate with the Father they did not have recourse to the mediation
of an idol, an animal or a fire as you practise here."

—15—

"You pretend that one must worship the sun, the spirit of good
and of evil; well, I say to you that your doctrine is detestible. The
sun does not act spontaneously, but by the will of the invisible
God who has created it,"

—16—

"And who has willed that this star should light the day and
should warm the labor and the crops of man."

—17—

"The eternal spirit is the soul of all that it animates. You commit a great sin in dividing Him into the spirit of evil and that of good, for there is no God except that of good,"

—18—

"Who like unto the father of a family does only good to his children, whose faults he forgives if they repent of them."

—19—

"And the evil spirit dwells upon the earth in the heart of those men who turn the children of God from the right path."

—20—

"Therefore I say unto you: Fear the judgement day for God will inflict a terrible punishment upon those who have forced His children to deviate from the true light and who have filled them with superstition and prejudice,"

—21—

"Upon those who have blinded the seeing, carried contagion to the strong, and taught the worship of those things which God has given to man for his own good and to aid him in his labors."

—22—

"Your doctrine is therefore the fruit of your error, for in desiring to approach the God of truth you have created for yourselves false gods."

—23—

After having listened to him the priests resolved to do no evil to him, but during the night while all in the city slept, they led him outside the walls and there left him to his fate upon the highway in the hope that he would soon become the prey of wild beasts.

—24—

But protected by our God, Saint Issa continued his way unharmed.

# IX.

—1—

Issa, whom the Creator had chosen to bring back the true God to men plunged in sin, was twenty-nine years old when he arrived in the land of Israel.

—2—

Since the departure of Issa the heathen had caused the Israelites to endure still more atrocious sufferings, and they were now a prey to the greatest dispair.

—3—

Many among them had already abandoned the laws of their God and those of Moses, hoping to soften their fierce conquerors.

—4—

In the presence of this situation Issa exhorted his countrymen not to dispair because the day of redemption of sins was near, and he strengthened their belief in the God of their fathers.

—5—

"Children, do not give yourselves up to dispair," said the Heavenly Father by the mouth of Issa, "for I have heard your voice and your cries have reached even unto me."

—6—

"Do not weep, O my beloved, for your cries have touched the heart of your Heavenly Father, and He has forgiven you as He forgave your ancestors."

—7—

"Do not forsake your family to plunge yourselves into iniquity, lose not the nobility of your feelings, and worship not idols which will remain deaf to your voice."

—8—

"Fill my temple with your hope and your patience and do not abjure the religion of your fathers, for I alone have guided them and heaped favors on them."

—9—

"You shall raise those who have fallen, you shall give food to those that are hungry, and you shall help the sick that you may be pure and just at the day of judgment which I am preparing for you."

—10—

The Israelites came in throngs to hear the words of Issa, and asked him where they should praise their Heavenly Father, since the enemy had rased their temples to the ground and lain profane hands on their sacred vessels.

—11—

Issa answered them that God had no reference to temples built by the hand of man, but that He meant the hearts of men which are the true temples of God.

—12—

"Enter into your temple, into your heart, enlighten it with good thoughts, with patience and with firm confidence which you should place in your Father."

—13—

"And your sacred vessels, these are your heads and eyes; see and do that which is pleasing to God, for in doing good to your neighbor you perform a ceremony which beautifies the temple where He lives who has given you life."

—14—

"For God has created you in His own image innocent, with the soul pure, the heart filled with kindness, and not intended for the conception of evil schemes, but made to be the sanctuary of love and justice."

—15—

"Do not therefore defile your heart, I say unto you, for the Eternal Being dwells there always."

—16—

"If you wish to accomplish works of piety or love, do them with an open heart and let not your action be governed by hope of gain or mercenary thoughts."

—17—

"For these actions will not bring you salvation and you will then fall into a state of moral degredation where lying, theft and assassination pass as generous deeds."

## X.

—1—

Holy Issa went from one city to another, confirming with the word of God the courage of the Israelites who were ready to seccumb under the weight of despair, and thousands of men followed to hear his teachings.

—2—

But the rulers of the cities feared him and informed the principal Governor who dwelt at Jerusalem that a man called Issa had arrived in the country, that by his sermons he was rousing the people against the authorities, that the multitude listened to him eagerly and neglected the works of the state, stating that in a short time it would be rid of its ruling intruders.

—3—

Then Pilate, the governor of Jerusalem, ordered them to seize the person of the preacher Issa, bring him into the city and lead him before the judges; but so as to not excite discontent among the people, Pilate ordered the priests and the wise men, aged Hebrews, to judge him in the temple.

—4—

Meanwhile, Issa continuing his preaching came to Jerusalem; having learned of his arrival, all the inhabitants who knew him already by reputation went to meet and greet him.

—5—

They saluted him respectfully and opened the doors of their temple to him in order to hear from his lips what he had said in the other towns of Israel.

—6—

And Issa said unto them: "The human race is perishing because of its lack of faith, for the darkness and the tempest have confused the flock of mankind and they have lost their shepherd."

—7—

"But the tempest will not last forever, the darkness will not hide the light forever, the heavens will soon become serene, the heavenly brightness will soon spread over the whole earth and the wandering flocks will gather themselves around their shepherd."

—8—

"Do not try to seek for the direct roads in darkness for fear of falling in a ditch, but gather together your lost forces, aid each other, place all your confidence in your God and wait till the first light appears."

—9—

"He who aids his neighbor aids himself and whoever protects his own family protects his people and his country."

—10—

"For be sure that the day is near when you will be delivered from darkness; you shall gather yourselves together in one family and your enemy who ignores the favor of the great God shall tremble in fear."

—11—

The priests and the elders who listened to him, full of wonder at his words, asked him if it was true that he had tried to arouse the people against the authorities of the country as had been reported to Governor Pilate.

—12—

"Can one rise against misled men to whom darkness has hidden the way and the door?" answered Issa. "I have only warned the unfortunate as I do here in this temple so that they may not advance further on dark roads, for an abyss is open at their feet."

—13—

"Earthly power is not of long duration and it is subject to many changes. It would be of no use for a man to revolt against it, for one power always succeeds another and it will thus be until the extinction of humanity."

—14—

"On the contrary do you not see that the powerful and the rich sow among the sons of Israel a spirit of rebellion against the eternal power of Heaven?"

—15—

And then the elders said: "Who art thou and from what country art thou come even unto us? Heretofore we have not heard thee spoken of, and we are even ignorant of thy name."

—16—

"I am an Israelite," answered Issa, "and on the day of my birth I saw the walls of Jerusalem, and heard the wailings of my brothers reduced to slavery and the lamentations of my sisters carried away among the heathen."

—17—

"And my soul was painfully grieved when I saw that my brothers had forgotten the true God; while yet a child I left my father's house to go and settle among other nations."

—18—

"But hearing that my brothers suffered still greater torturers I returned to the country where my parents dwelt, to recall my brothers to the faith of their ancestors, which teaches us patience upon earth so that we may obtain perfect and sublime happiness above."

—19—

And the learned elders asked him this question: "They claim that thou deniest the laws of Mossa and that thou teachest the people to abandon the temple of God?"

—20—

And Issa answered: "We do not demolish what has been given by our heavenly Father and what has been destroyed by sinners, but I have advised them to purify their heart of every stain, for *there* is the true temple of God."

—21—

"As for the laws of Mossa I have tried to re-establish them in the heart of men, but I tell you that you do not understand their true meaning, for it is not vengeance, but pardon that they teach; only the sense of these laws has been perverted."

## XI.

—1—

Having heard Issa, the priests and the learned elders decided among themselves not to judge him for he did no evil to anyone, and presenting themselves before Pilate, the Governor of Jerusalem, chosen by the heathen King of the country of Romulus, they addressed him thus:

—2—

"We have seen the man whom thou accusest of exciting our people to revolt, we have heard his teachings and we know that he is our fellow-countryman."

—3—

"But the rulers of the towns have sent thee false reports, for he is a just man who teaches the people the word of God. After having questioned him we let him go in peace."

—4—

The Governor became violently enraged and sent his servants in disguise to spy after Issa and to report to the authorities every word that he addressed to the people.

—5—

The holy Issa continued, however, to visit the neighboring towns and preach the true ways of the Creator, exhorting the Hebrews to patience and promising them a speedy deliverance.

—6—

During all this time many people followed him wherever he went; many did not quit him, but they served him as servants.

—7—

And Issa said: "Do not believe in miracles performed by the hand of man, for He who commands nature is alone able to perform supernatural things, while man is powerless to soften the rage of winds and to distribute rain."

—8—

"There is one miracle, however, that it is possible for man to perform; it is, when full of sincere belief, he decides to uproot from his heart all bad thoughts, and to attain this end, he goes no more into the paths of evil."

—9—

"And all the things which are done without God are but great errors, seductions and enchantments, which show only how far the soul of him who practices this art is full of shamelessness, falsehood and impurity,"

—10—

"Put no faith in oracles, for God alone knows the future; he who has recourse to sorcerers, defiles the temple which is in his heart and shows distrust for his Creator."

—11—

"Faith in sorcerers and their oracles destroys the innate simplicity in man and his child-like purity; an infernal power takes possession of him and forces him to commit all sorts of crimes and worship idols;"

—12—

"While the Lord, our God, who has no equal, is one, all-powerful, all-knowing and present everywhere; it is He who alone possesses all wisdom and all light."

—13—

"It is to Him that you must pray for being comforted in your griefs, aided in your works, cured in your sickness; whoever will have recourse to Him will not suffer refusal."

—14—

"The secret of nature is in the hands of God, for the world, before it appeared, existed in the depths of the Divine thought; it has become material and visible by the will of the Most High."

—15—

"When you would seek Him, become children, for you know neither the past, nor the present nor the future and God is master of time."

## XII.

—1—

"Just man!" said the disguised servants of the Governor of Jerusalem, "tell us whether we should execute the will of our Cæsar or await our near deliverance."

—2—

And Issa having recognized in the questioners the people bribed to follow him, said to them: "I have not said that you would be delivered from Cæsar; it is the soul which is plunged into error that will have deliverance."

—3—

"There can be no family without a head and there can be no order among a people without a Cæsar whom they must obey blindly, for he alone shall answer for his acts before the supreme tribunal."

—4—

"Does Cæsar possess a divine right," the spies again asked, "and is he the best of mortals?"

—5—

"There is none best among men, but truly there are some that are sick whom chosen men charged with this mission should care for, by using the means which the sacred law of our Heavenly Father confers upon them."

—6—

"Clemency and justice are the highest gifts granted to Cæsar, his name will be illustrious if he holds to them."

—7—

"But he who acts otherwise, who transgresses the limits of his power over those under his rule, endangering their life, offends the great Judge and wrongs His dignity in the opinion of men."

—8—

Meanwhile an old woman who had approached the crowd to hear Issa better was pushed aside by one of the disguised men who placed himself before her.

—9—

Issa then said: "It is not good for a son to push aside his mother so that he may occupy the front place which should be hers. Whoever does not respect his mother, the most sacred being after God, is unworthy of the name of son."

—10—

"Listen to these words: Respect woman for she is the mother of the universe and the truth of divine creation lies within her."

—11—

"She is the foundation of all that is good and beautiful, as also the germ of life and death. Upon her depends the whole life of man for she is his moral and natural support in his labors."

—12—

"She gives birth to you amid suffering; by the sweat of her brow she attends your growth and until her death you cause her the greatest anxiety. Bless her and adore her, for she is your only friend and support upon earth."

—13—

"Respect and defend her; in acting thus you will win her love and her heart, and you will please God, and many of your sins will be forgiven."

—14—

"Therefore, love your wives and respect them, for they will be mothers to-morrow, and later elders of a whole nation."

—15—

"Be submissive to your wife; her love ennobles a man, softens his hardened heart, tames the beast and makes a lamb of it."

—16—

"Wife and mother are inestimable treasures bestowed of God; they are the most beautiful ornaments of the universe, and of them will be born all who shall inhabit the world."

—17—

"Just as the God of armies formerly separated the light from earkness and the land from waters, so woman possesses the divine talent to separate the good from evil intentions in man."

—18—

"Therefore I say unto you, after God your best thoughts should belong unto women and to your wives; she is the divine temple where you will obtain easily perfect happiness."

—19—

"Draw from this temple your moral force; there you will forget your troubles and your failures; there you will recover your wasted forces which are necessary in helping your neighbors."

—20—

"Do not expose her to humiliations, for thereby you humiliate yourself and lose the sentiment of love, without which nothing exists here below."

—21—

"Protect your wife that she may protect you and all your family; all that you will do for your mother, your wife, for a widow or another woman in distress, you shall have done for your God."

## XIII.

—1—

Holy Issa thus taught the people of Israel for three years in every town and village, on the highways and on the plains, and all that he predicted was realized.

—2—

During all this time the disguised servants of the Governor Pilate observed him closely without hearing anything resembling the reports formerly made against Issa by the rulers of the towns.

—3—

But the Governor Pilate, fearing the great popularity of the Saint Issa, whom his opponents believed to be inciting the people to have himself chosen for king, ordered one of his spies to accuse him.

—4—

Then he ordered the soldiers to proceed to arrest him, and they imprisoned him in a dungeon, where they caused him to endure various torments, hoping thereby to force him to accuse himself, which would permit them to put him to death.

—5—

The Saint, desiring only the perfect happiness of his brothers, endured these torments in the name of his Creator.

—6—

The servants of Pilate continued torturing him, reducing him to a state of extreme weakness; but God was with him and did not suffer him to die.

—7—

Learning of the sufferings and tortures which their Saint endured, the principal priests and wise elders requested the Governor to set Issa free on the occasion of a great feast which was near at hand.

—8—

But the Governor refused them decidedly. They asked him then to have Issa appear before the tribunal of the elders in order that he might be condemned or acquitted before the feast; Pilate consented to this.

—9—

The next day the Governor called together the principal captains, priests, wise elders and legislators for the purpose of having them judge Issa.

—10—

They brought the Saint from his prison, and seated him before the Governor between two robbers, who were then on trial, and to show the people that he was not the only one to be condemned.

—11—

And Pilate, addressing Issa, said: "O man! is it true that thou dost incite the people against the authorities with the intention of becoming the king of Israel thyself?"

—12—

"One does not become king by his own will," answered Issa, "and they have spoken falsely to you in asserting that I was inciting the people. I have never spoken but of the King of Heaven, and it is He whom I taught the people to worship."

—13—

"For the sons of Israel have lost their original purity, and if they do not have recourse to the true God they will be sacrificed and their temple will fall in ruin."

—14—

"Temporal power maintains order in a country; I have therefore taught them not to forget it; I said to them: 'Live according to your position and fortune, so as not to disturb public order;' and I exhorted them also to remember that disorder reigned in their heart and in their soul."

—15—

"Thus the King of Heaven has punished them and suppressed their national kings. Nevertheless I said to them: 'If you resign yourselves to your fate, the Kingdom of Heaven will be reserved to you as a reward.'"

—16—

At this moment the witnesses were introduced, one of whom testified, saying: "Thou hast taught the people that the temporal power was nothing before that of the king who would soon free the Israelites from the heathen yoke."

—17—

"Blessed be thou," said Issa, "for having told the truth; the King of Heaven is greater and more powerful than terrestial law, and His Kingdom surpasses all kingdoms here below."

—18—

"And the time is not far distant when conformably to the Divine will, the people of Israel shall purify themselves of their sins, for it is said that a precusor shall come and announce the deliverance of the people and unite them in one family."

—19—

And the Governor addressing the judges, said: "Do you hear this? The Israelite Issa acknowledges the crime of which he is accused. Judge him then according to your laws and pronounce upon him capital punishment."

—20—

"We cannot condemn him;" answered the priests and the elders, "thou hast thyself heard that he alluded to the King of Heaven, and that he has preached nothing which constitutes insubordination against our laws."

—21—

The Governor then summoned the witness who at the instigation of his master, Pilate, had betrayed Issa; this man came and addressing Issa, said: "Didst thou not make thyself pass as king of Israel when thou didst say that He who reigns in Heaven had sent thee to prepare His people?"

—22—

And Issa having blessed him, said: "Thou shalt be forgiven, for what thou sayest cometh not from thee." Then addressing the

Govenor he said: "Why humiliate thy dignity and teach thy inferiors to live in falsehood, since even without this thou hast the power to condemn an innocent person?"

—23—

At these words the Governor became violently enraged and ordered Issa to be condemned to death and the two robbers to be acquitted,

—24—

The judges having consulted together, said to Pilate: "We will not take upon ourselves the great sin of condemning an innocent man, and of acquitting robbers, which is contrary to our laws."

—25—

"Do, therefore, as thou pleaseth." Having said this the priests and the wise men went out and washed their hands in a sacred vessel, saying: "We are innocent of the death of this just man."

## XIV.

—1—

By order of the Governor the soldiers seized Issa and the two robbers and led them to a place of punishment and there nailed them upon crosses which they erected.

—2—

All day long the bodies of Issa and the two robbers remained suspended dripping with blood, under the guard of the soldiers; the people stood round about them, the relatives of the tortured praying and weeping.

—3—

At sunset the suffering of Issa ended. He lost his consciousness and the soul of this just man freed itself from his body to be absorbed in the Divinity.

—4—

Thus ended the terrestial life of the reflection of the Eternal Spirit in the form of a man who endured so much suffering, saving hardened sinners.

—5—

Pilate, however, through his own actions feared the throng, and returned the body of the Saint to his relatives, who interred it near the place of execution; the people came to pray at his tomb filling the air with weeping and wailings.

—6—

Three days afterwards fearing a general uprising, the Governor sent soldiers to raise secretly the body of Issa and bury it in some other place.

—7—

The next day the throng found the tomb open and empty; so that the rumor was spread that the Supreme Judge had sent His angels to carry away the mortal remains of the Saint in whom had dwelt on earth a part of the Divine Spirit.

—8—

When the rumor reached Pilate he was very angry and forbade them under penalty of slavery and death ever to utter the name of Issa, or to pray to the Lord for him.

—9—

But the people continued to weep and to glorify their Master aloud; so that many of them were led into captivity and subjected to torture and put to death.

—10—

Then many of the disciples of the Holy Issa left the country of Israel and went among the heathen, preaching that they must abandon their errors and think of the safety of their souls and the perfect happiness awaiting human beings in the immaterial world of light and wisdom wherein reposes in all His purity and perfect majesty, the great Creator.

—11—

The heathen, their kings and their warriors, listened to these preachers, abandoned their absurd beliefs, left their priests and their idols to celebrate the praises of the very wise Creator of the Universe, the King of Kings, whose heart is filled with infinite mercy.

(NICOLAS NOTOVITCH, 1890; TRANS. VIRCHAND R. GANDHI, CHICAGO, IL: 1907)

# Autobiography by Jesus of Nazareth

This text, published in 1870 by American spiritualist Olive G. Pettis, presents a testimony about the life of Jesus. Claiming to be a scribe for the "holy Hebrew family" of Mary, Joseph, and their four children (including Jesus), Pettis explained in a preface to the volume that the words had appeared to her as gifts from departed spirits, printed in "bright electric letters" that she felt compelled to write down. The goal of these spirits, apparently, was to "finish up what had been begun ages on ages ago," to help humanity understand the truth of Jesus' teachings that had been imperfectly passed down through the ages.

Followers of Spiritualism like Olive G. Pettis insisted that departed spirits could communicate with the living, and many writings published by believers in nineteenth-century America suggested that living humans were conduits into the thoughts of those in the spirit world. Her book was only one among many channeled "spirit writings" produced in this era; like the *Autobiography,* quite a few of them reinterpreted elements of the Christian tradition in ways that fit the more liberal religious convictions of the Spiritualists. In Pettis's gospel account, Jesus' powers come from the aid of his "controller," a spirit named Leiah who had in his own lifetime been a "king of ancient Arabia." Many of Jesus' miracles were aided, the text explains, by the electrical current that Spiritualists believed surrounded human bodies and which could be manipulated by skilled human beings, although the story indicates that his family and most observers understood these scientific principles as the work of God.

The following selections from Pettis's text recount the beginning of Jesus' earthly ministry, the harassment experienced by his family that forced him to flee his home as a young man, and the end of his life. This telling explains that after the crucifixion Jesus was cremated on a funeral pyre, after which his spirit left the earth. He now tells his story through living scribes. Although the events echo the canonical Gospels, the *Autobiography* affirms that scientific principles and laws of nature—aided by angels and spirits—were the foundation of Jesus' power, rather than the workings of a divine God. It presents a fascinating example of the use of modern scientific principles to explain what an earlier generation of Christians would have accepted as miracles.

# Autobiography by Jesus of Nazareth

## CHAPTER VII.

### Jesus Carried to the Synagogue at Antioch.

Eight days passed away ere Leiah returned. I was kneeling in prayer when he entered our house. He breathed upon me and controlled me; in an instant bore me away down the mountain side; my feet did not touch the ground in many places, and I felt like a feather blown by the wind. I could see all I passed, but I had no power to stop. All day we sped along; night came, and we halted not. There was a great feast at Antioch, and we arrived there the third day and the third hour, even as they had begun to assemble. Leiah relinquished his grasp, and I sat down by the wayside, faint and exhausted. I fell back, and a beggar came to me and said, "Boy, are you dying?" I answered, "Give me bread, give me water." He brought me water, but bread he had none. I drank freely, then I lay there for hours. There came a poor, despised female; man had cursed her, God never. I breathed deep, and my controller exclaimed, "Give this boy bread, or he dies." She took from her bundle a piece of bread; she handed it toward me, but I had no power to reach for it, and then she knelt beside me and said, "Poor boy, he is dying." Here I breathed deep again, and said, "Crumble it into the water, he cannot eat it dry." Then she started back, and looked at me again, and said, "Holy God, this the holy child Jesus, that healed me when I was sick, gave me light when I was in darkness; let me die for him even here." I answered, "Your dying would do me no good; but live to take care of this poor holy until I can begin a work for humanity, that God may be glorified through his own children." The bread and water gave me strength, and I ate all I desired; then I arose to my feet, it being high noon, and I was controlled on that instant. Leiah bore me into the synagogue, beggarly clad as I was, through the multitude, upon the very altar. He held me there one hour and a little more. Then the Jews cried out against the beggar, declaring the Devil had control, because he was all over light. Then the shout arose, "Drag him out, drag him out." One of the laymen approached me, and laid his hand upon me, then he fell back entranced. After a few moments he sprang to his feet, shouting, "Holy, Almighty God is here, because the synagogue is filled with angels. Light is everywhere; catch its rays, O ye children of darkness! shout, O ye children of Antioch, God is here!" Then the congregation shouted louder than before, "The Devil is here filling us with light." The people began to flee; he stood there still like a ray of light, while I had fallen to the floor. He shouted to them to stop, saying, "If you bring in your battle-axe, God will curse you forever." They heeded him not, but brought in their magistrate and his followers. They sought to aim a blow at him that was declaring God, but they could not reach him. They became so electrified that they dropped the battle-axe and fled, filled with fear. As soon as they had gone I arose to my feet, and in an instant I was folded to the bosom of my guardian angel, and how she bore me away from there I never knew. . . . All that day and night I was borne on until the sun stood high in the ether; then I was accosted by a herdsman. He said, "Are you the boy Jesus that is making such a great commotion all about the lowlands." I answered, "God begets commotion in order that his holy electric air can purify." He said, "Have you any electricity that I can feel the shock."—"God holds his own electricity," I answered, "and uses it at his own will and pleasure."—"Boy," he said, "I am freezing now; are you binding me with electricity?" I saw Leiah fold him in his arms, and I knew he would control him. He breathed deep, his face became livid, and his eyes glazed, then he spoke to me, and said, "The hour has come, my boy, for us to begin our work in earnest. There is to be a wedding in Cana, I must bear you there in order that God can turn their water into wine, that they can behold his works. Help me, my angel boy, and I will bear you back to your mother in eight days." I said, "Let me go home to my mother, then I will die for you if it be needed."— "Then it will be too late for God to be glorified," he said. "There," he said, "I will bear you to friends that will give you food and rest ere you go back towards the mountain." Leiah then breathed out of that body, and left him in a natural sleep, in order that I could get away, because he was determined to get the price for my head, which was one hundred pieces of silver, if I was dead or alive. I was caught up again, and borne onward, not knowing whither. Four days and four nights passed away, and I was in Cana. I stopped at a humble home and said, "Can I have a cup of cold water and a place to lie down; I am exhausted, and must sleep."— "Come in little boy, I have seen you before. Have you a brother that had his leg cut off?" I answered, "I have, and his name is Jesse."—"Is your name Jesus?" she said, covering her face with her hands. "It is," I said; "my father's name is Joseph, and my mother's name is Mary."—"My father and mother belong to the Hebrews, and I thought you looked like them." The mother came forward with a cup of water; I drank it, and then she said, "I know your mother; we were children together, and she was my own dear cousin, I am Hester. The ways of God were wonderful how your family escaped death; it is the hand of God that held them, else they would have been cut off ere this." Then she said, "Come in, boy, lie down and rest, you look so pale; but tell me how came you here alone?"—"God bade me come, and he will bear me back again if it be his will," I said. Then I fell asleep. When I awoke, I found myself in the midst of a large assembly, holding in my hand a glass of pure, cold water, shouting, "Holy, Almighty God, change this water into wine, that they can behold thy glory." At that moment I saw a hand held over that glass, and a crimson stream run therein. "Here," I said, "is your wine, drink and be merry; bring me more pure water, that you can have a plenty and to spare." They brought four gourds and one bucketful. The same hand was held over them, and they became wine. "Here," I said, "drink, but do not become drunken; but let God be glorified through the works done here." I was controlled, declaring that the same body before them must be hung upon the cross, in order that God's children might know who to worship in truth.

[. . .]

I had been wandering about my home all day, but as night closed in I was controlled by Leiah. He told Mary that he must bear me away on a long journey, and it would be months before he could bring me back again. She asked, "Where are you going?" He answered, "I am going to a king that is about to be dethroned by the Amalekites. If timely warning is given he will be saved, and his people. Trust him to me; I will bring him back by the middle of the fourth month." The influence left me; I went away by myself and asked God to assist me. God's child came and sat down beside me. She laid her hand in mine; she said, "Dear boy, your journey is a fearful one. God will direct you; my father will care for you, while I must remain with Mary and the children; but I will come to you and comfort you whenever I can." Mary prepared my garments, and at early dawn I set out barefooted, and alone as for human aid, not knowing whither I was going, but trusting to him that walked beside me, an angel bright. I had learned to love him as my father, and his daughter as my sister. Down we went from crag to crag, a way that I never went before. Deep cuts in the mountain made me stop; then I would glide down as easy as if it was a smooth surface. Night came on, and we were still upon the mountains. I sat down by a green bush, and there I fell asleep. I arose at early dawn, still descending the mountains; noon came, and I began to find the habitation of man. I entered a herdsman's home and asked for a piece of bread. I got for an answer, "Bread we have not; but you can have a piece of meat and a cup of milk." I said, "Give me the milk; but meat I cannot eat."—"Drink all the milk you want, for by and by I shall have more." She was the daughter of an aged herdsman, and they dwelt there alone. As I handed the cup back I said, "You have many in family." Her answer was, "My father and myself." I said, "I see a female here old enough for your mother, four beautiful damsels, and a young man; he says you are his sister." Then the father came in. She told him all. He looked kindly at me, and said, "Angel boy, your doom is sealed. I saw a band of confessors not more than an hour ago, and they were inquiring after such a boy as you, and they said you had fled them." The damsel said, "Let us hide him until they have left the country, lest they cut him off." I remained there the rest of that day and that night, but started again at early dawn. Night came again, and I was still among the herdsmen. I asked for a cup of milk, a piece of bread, and a place to lie down to sleep. I drank the milk, but the bread I laid in my bosom for my breakfast. I arose before any of them were astir. Day after day I journeyed onward until I reached Armenia; there I inquired for the king, and was told he was not able to be seen. The gatekeeper said, "Boy, come in. It may be business of importance; at any rate, this little boy can't do any harm." I was directed into the servants' apartment. They asked if I was hungry. I answered, "I have come a long way to see the king; do let me see him ere it is too late." One said, "Is it business that concerns the kingdom?" I answered, "The Amalekites are preparing to cut him off and destroy the people and take the kingdom. Do let me see him now, else it be too late"—"Come, little boy," said one of the kind-hearted females, "eat now while we send word to the king, that he may prepare for your coming to his chamber; for he has been ill for days." I answered, "Drink I cannot, eat I dare not, until I have delivered my message to the king." The king called for an audience, and I hastened to meet him. He looked at me as I entered there, and said, "You are a frail little thing, but you are covered all over with light." Then I saw Leiah. He reached out his hand to me. I laid my palm in his. He breathed upon me, and I had a fearful vision. I saw a mighty army all around, with battle-axes, javelins, and spears. I saw they had chariots, whose wheels would turn in any direction; burnished steel-like blades cut in pieces whatever they came in contact with. Then I shouted "O king, they are already crossing your border country, and if you do not prepare to defend yourself you will surely be cut to pieces." Then the king shouted, "Bring in my council, even now." He was obeyed; and the chamber was filled with brave-looking men. There I stood before them, and was controlled. What was said I know not; but this I do know, when the influence left me I fell down like one dead. I could hear and see all, but move I could not. In their excitement they had forgotten me, stepping around and over me. . . . The king . . . reached out his hand, and said, "Here, boy, take this; eat and drink all you want before you go: this will buy you more. What you do not need, bear it home to your father; say to him, 'It is sent to you for letting your frail little boy come to me in my hour of need.'"—"God sent me," I said, "else I could not have found the way."—"Farewell, frail little boy; how I wish you were mine!"—"Good-by," I said; then left King Lear, but not forever.

## Joseph's Contest with a Confessor,
## When Going to the Lowlands

I had been at home one year and a half, and had become stronger than I had ever been before in my life. I was now in my twenty-fourth year, and my communion with the Angel World was daily and hourly. I had still continued to go forth daily from my home, although the chilly winds pierced me; yet God's children were ever beside me, and gave me comfort. The time did come when I was borne again into the midst of confusion, and there declared God would cleanse earth of anointed priests and confessors. Here I must breathe a few words fresh from the light that is around me; even while I am tracing lines for coming ages, the inspiration that was breathed upon me high in the mountains of Helam is daily being made manifest through God's changes during the past eighteen hundred and fifty years. I am made to feel when eighteen hundred and fifty years have rolled away, that all of your creeds and isms will not be known but by name, and that name will be "chains that bound us." Holy, Eternal God! assist me in finishing up my earth mission, when earth's children are ready to say, "Thou art my Father, God, and the humble Nazarene is my brother; and God is father of us all, one as the other, and we are all a part of the mighty whole." Then I am free from earth's chains, light will dispel darkness; then humanity will learn that I am but the humble man, and they are all my brothers and sisters. Here I must exclaim, "Who are my brothers and my sisters?" They that are willing to free me from my earthly chains, and let me go free. Here I am, a poor crushed spirit, because man holds me as an idol, and God is robbed of his glory. Hasten the day, holy Creator, God, that I can lay down the cross that humanity has nailed me upon, and holds me as a hostage for their evil deeds; but I cannot forgive sins, any more than God could be nailed to the cross and breathe out his life there. Humanity, O humanity! God must hold you accountable hereafter for all the human sacrifices that are to be laid on the altar of wicked ambition and priestly devices of those that dare hold human souls chained and bound longer! I will declare myself what I am, but a man, and if you receive my declaration as truth, you will be blessed by it; but if you seek to hold me longer chained to earth, as an idol, God will cut you off in the midst of your hypocrisy and deceit, and you will be accountable for the misery you caused. O ye men in priestly robes, the hand of God is upon you! Live but to undo what you have done in damning God's children; in teaching what you did not believe, and extracting from them their last penny they needed for bread. I have come with a scourge in order to drive you from the temple of the living God, which is the hearts of his children. Free oh, free me from the chains that you are seeking to draw around me tighter and tighter! You are seeking to bind me to the cross; and if you do not free me from those chains, facts will be revealed that will curse you forever. Hypocrisy and deceit have possession of your souls, and a hell of guilty conscience awaits you. Go back, go back among the priestly robed, damned! When I walked the earth, I was compelled to flee into the mountains like a felon that despoiled his neighbor of his inheritance. There I was compelled to endure the severest hardships among the clefts of the rocks in order that I should not chill to death. It was not weeks or months, but years, that I dragged out such a life; except when God's children in spirit breathed upon me, and bore me down into the lowlands and the border country, denouncing their idolatrous worship and the Jewish ritual, declaring God ever present among his children. "Blessed are they that hunger after righteousness, for they shall be filled." "Blessed are they that seek God daily; he will surely be found of them." "Blessed are the pure in heart; they shall behold their Creator as he is." "Blessed are they that love the light; their garments shall be covered all over with God's dewdrops of light." "Blessed are they that remember the poor in their needs; God will surely feed them with the bread of eternal life." "All that seek God will seek to bless humanity; and they will have their reward in this life, and a crown of light in the bright home beyond." "Happy are they that love God's wonders, and scan them over and over, filled with holy adoration for him that created all things." I must now go back in my history, and detail simple facts of my earth life, in order that my chains may be broken; and let all idols be buried. They are earthly devices; and all that bow to idols are damned already, and the light of the living God is not within them.

# CHAPTER XVI.

## An Experience in a Holier Sphere of Life.

I was borne along through the crowd by the strong arm of Bartholomew, even back to the fisherman's hut on the bank of the stream. That day Peter had caught his net full of fishes, and he had exchanged a part for barley meal; and that night we supped on bread and fish. Here the brothers came in, even as we were breaking the bread, and John exclaimed, "God feeds us with barley bread still, that we may go on with our work for coming ages; but none can ever know how dearly the knowledge will be bought by those that lay down all they have, even their lives, that the veil of mystification may be torn away, and God's wonders be laid bare by the light within the human soul." I said, "Come, brother, come and eat; then we will ask for light from eternal distance to guide us on our way."

That night we slept; but ere morning dawned I heard deep groans come welling up from the heart of Stephen. I spoke to him and said, "Stephen, are you dreaming?" He said, "I have had a fearful dream. I saw my four beautiful sisters dragged away by confessors. I called on God to assist me, and no answer came, until God's child answered, 'Brother, you have had a fearful dream, but you must leave them in their Creator's hands. You must work for coming ages, that the inhabitants of earth can discern good from evil; then they will learn that man has sought to bind, but God would have them free.'" I said, "Sleep, brother, sleep; God has a work for us on the morrow; here will be many gather on the bank of the stream, and we will bless them there." Then I fell asleep and did not awake until the sun arose. That day was fair until midday; many had gathered together; I went out and greeted them in early morn; then I ate and gave God the glory. I then went out in their midst, and said, "Friends, beloved God is in our midst; let us give him the glory forever." Now I was entranced by the holy Jephthah. I saw him approach me; he folded me to his bosom and I forgot all earthly things; he breathed deep from God's wondrous creation, and I floated away into a holy, heavenly condition, and found rest. I breathed from the inner life of all things, and that breath filled me with holy resignation to the will of my Creator, God. There I saw the aged patriarchs; there I saw the holy angels filled with holy adoration to their Creator, God; there I saw the holy angelic band singing praises to the great first cause, and as I approached them they made me feel I was one of them. There I saw the holy Sabilla; he reached out his hand to me, bade me welcome, then he said, "Brother, your earth work is nearly finished, and you will be one of us." I shouted, "Holy Creator, God, leave me as I am among thy children, freed from earth." Here I got answer from one still beyond us, "I will bring thee back when thine earth mission is finished in this holy condition, until humanity's demand for another human sacrifice cannot be appeased; then you must go back again to finish up by being nailed to the cross. I will breathe upon you in your hour of agony, and I will fold you in my bosom, and you shall be blessed." Then I held my breath. I knew I must go back to earth and suffer death in that earthly body. While I was made to feel the death agonies come over me, I heard an angel voice say, "Come, brother, the day is far spent, and you must come back to your earthly body, and Sabilla must leave it even now, Amen." I answered, "God's will, not mine, be done." Then I found myself trying to breathe into that body again as it lay there on the cold ground. John raised the body up and held it close in his warm bosom, warm with earth magnetism, and warm with holy love for the poor bruised body. He called his brother. Then Bartholomew came forward and held the palm of his hands on the hollow of my feet. God's child laid her hands upon my brow, and asked God to assist them, and then I began to breath into that body again.

## CHAPTER XXV.

### The Last Day Ere Jesus Entered Jerusalem.

Morning did dawn. I was calm, knowing full well I had nearly reached my journey's end. Hunger held control. I had not tasted one morsel of food now for two days. I knew the rest had nothing, therefore I asked not for bread. My good brother Bartholomew writhed in agony; it was fearful to see so strong a man starving for bread. John came and said, "Holy brother, the day is wearing away. Had we better enter the city?" I answered, "God's command is upon me. Let us hasten there, even now. They are preparing the cross, and I will hasten even there to find rest."

Then I rose to my feet, and a holy calm came over me. I said, "Who will lead me?" John answered, "I will lead the brother to where the ass is tied that the good brother Bartholomew has brought from his father's barn."—"Bring me my mother," I said, "that I may fold her in my bosom for the last time on earth." Mary was brought to me, and I folded her to my bosom. At first bitter tears of anguish flowed from my inmost being. My mother folded her arms around me, and naught but deep groans came welling up from her inmost soul. I held her there until my heart ceased to beat, and I fell to the earth, and Mary fell beside me. Here Mary made an expression like this: "Holy God, give me back my boy, and I will endure all things for thee and thine. Oh, give him back to me; it is all I will ask of thee, thou God of immensity." Peter came and said, "Dear brother, the ass is waiting; we are all ready to go. Come, let us not delay." I answered, "Lead, oh, lead me, that I may find rest." I then arose to my feet, and said, "I am ready." Then the ass was led forward. They assisted me upon his back. As we rode forward, I began to feel that I grew stronger by the warmth of the animal. After we began our journey for the last time, ere we reached the great gate, the poor, famished creatures cried out, "Hail, Jesus of Nazareth!" And soon the beggars shouted, "Hail, King of the Jews!" I said, "They will enrage the priesthood; bid them be silent." But they shouted still, "Hail, Jesus of Nazareth, King of the Jews! He will surely give us bread; for the inhabitants of Jerusalem will not deny him." I felt my life nearly go out of me ere I could make my followers hold their peace. Then I said, "Let us ask God to direct us, and we will hold our peace." As I rode on, Mary and Martha kept beside me. I would ofttimes speak to them and encourage them as much as I could. As we drew near the city I saw the gates were swung back, and the inhabitants were all within doors. I remarked to Mark, "They have left the gates open for the poor famishing creatures, but their homes are closed." I made my way to the great square, and the poor dying creatures followed, and sat down on the ground. Filled with hope, I said, "Let us go in front of Pontius Pilate's house; perhaps he may come to me there."

Here many had begun to fill the streets; and ere I could reach the court, the king's eldest daughter came forward, and spread a costly garment in front of the ass. I said to her, "Take up that garment, go and feed the poor starving Hebrews, and God will bless you." Here she took up the garment; then she reached her hand to me, and said, "Dear brother, how glad I am to see you, that I can tell you to hide, because Caiaphas is going to have you crucified." I answered, "If you would save me, go to the king, your father, and ask him what I have done to deserve death." She answered, "He cannot save you, because Caiaphas has already sealed your death in the council chamber." I said, "Go to your father; say to him, if he will release me from death I will live but as his servant hereafter." She answered, "I will go and beg with my life at the king's feet." Here Caiaphas caught her by the arm, and said, "Come, beauty, this is no place for you. If you remain here you will become contaminated with heresy." She said, "Release Jesus from death, Caiaphas, and I will bless you." That was the last I heard her speak; but, as he hurried her away, she gave me one look so full of fear and despair, I could not forget it, even when I hung upon the cross.

I then called for the chamberlain of the king's house, but no answer was given me. John said, "Let us go to the inhabitants and ask for bread." Ere I could answer, the chief magistrate came forward. He reached his hand to me, and said, "Come; you are the felon I have been looking for." I laid my hand in his, and answered, "I am a subject of the law; and if I have violated the law, I alone am accountable. But feed, oh, feed the poor starving Hebrews, and I will enter the council chamber to receive my sentence." "Get off," said the magistrate; "I have no time to waste on beggars."—"I cannot stand upon my feet," I said. "If you will assist me I will make no resistance." He then assisted me down from the ass; but my feet gave way beneath that emaciated body; but he raised me up, putting one arm around my waist, and bore me along, until we reached the great entrance leading into the council chamber. My mother led me by the hand; but when we reached the entrance, the magistrate said, "You cannot enter here; this is no place for females." I looked at my mother. She burst into tears, and said, "Leave me with my boy but one moment, and I will bless you forever." The magistrate said to a confessor, "Take her away among the Hebrews, and don't let me hear anything more from her." He then bore me up a long flight of wooden steps leading to the great hall. Here I beheld the hall filled with priests and confessors; and in their centre here sat Pontius Pilate, on a seat a little elevated above the others and there, a little below, sat Josephus and four other Jews from the synagogue, with their accusations against me; and beside them sat Caiaphas and his accomplices. I was set away by myself, all but the magistrate; he sat beside me.

Josephus arose to his feet and unrolled a piece of parchment, and began like this: "Jesus of Nazareth is condemned to die upon the cross because of his deceiving the people, causing them to believe he had a power at his command by which he could heal the sick, cast out devils, raise the dead, and cause the deaf to hear, the blind to see, and the lame to walk. He also stole corn on the Jewish sabbath, to feed the beggars that followed him from place to place. He ate with publicans and sinners; he lived with drunkards and harlots. He also denounced the Jewish creed, and declared heathen, idolatrous worshippers were damned by the priests and confessors; and he bowed not to the idols, nor acknowledged the traditions of the Jews; and, after all of his unholy acts, he has declared himself the king of the Jews: and the council have decided that he deserves death, and he is to be hung upon the cross, and there hang until he is dead." He then sat down, and Caiaphas arose, and said, "Heresy is destroying the control of the priesthood, and the confessors, in many instances, are compelled to labor for bread." He also brought accusation against me for telling him to his face he was a brute and a debauchee; also for casting insinuations against him among the king's children.

He then sat down, and Pontius Pilate said, "Among all of your accusations, I find nothing worthy of putting him to death. Leave him with me for a time; let me question him alone." Then they all went out. Then the king commenced like this: "Have you been causing a disturbance in the Jewish synagogue?" I answered, "Not of my will have I caused disturbance; but I was borne in their midst in a deep sleep. What I said I know not; but when I awoke I was lying in a humble hut of a faithful Hebrew family. But I must acknowledge I was folded in the bosom of an angel, even as I was in your presence at the feast." Then he answered, "The accusations brought against you arise from the heathen confessors' hate and jealousy against you; but, my friend, I fear you must die. If I attempt to hold you, I know full well I shall be beheaded, and my family will be destroyed, and my people will be held by Caiaphas; and he will control but to destroy." I answered, "I would die, O king, for you and your children; but Caiaphas is damning your daughters, and they are poor crushed flowers that cannot bloom earthly, but they will bloom beyond God's ether blue. There they will bless you, my dear friend, as they cannot bless you earthly." When I ceased to speak I looked at him, and big tears rolled down his cheeks. I said, "I am dying, king, even now; I am starving for bread, and the poor Hebrews are dying with utter starvation. Feed, oh, feed them, even while I am hanging on the cross. Let me feel they are not suffering the pangs of starvation." Here he gave a deep groan from his inmost life, and said, "I am helpless. I am a slave to Caiaphas and his accomplices."—"Let them come in," I said, "else I cannot live until they nail me to the cross. If I do not, God will be robbed of his glory and humanity of her sacrifice."

Here the king gave the signal. They all came in. As the court had ever allowed the felon to speak in his own defence, and as I looked around and saw they were all seated, I attempted to rise to my feet, but I fell back. Then I said to the magistrate, "If you will assist me to my feet and hold me there, I will have this matter brought to a close." He assented, and raised me up. Then Josephus said, "What have you to say in your defence?" I answered, "Humanity is my judge, and I bow to her decree." I then breathed deep, and I knew a power was resting upon me; yet I could hear all that was said, and could comprehend its meaning. I saw a band of bright angels gathering around me and the magistrate, as we stood away by ourselves. Then I began like this: "Who among you have aught to say against the law being held unbroken, as there is nothing brought against this man worthy of death? Who among you can say, in every crime you have sought to bring against him, that ye are not thrice guilty,—nay, a hundred times more guilty? But him you would slay." Here I breathed deep again, and I saw Jephthah beside me. He then brought his ideas before me, and I gave them utterance, loud and clear. The first expression was like this: "Who among you live in the holy ordinance of the law of the living God, and hold yourselves in a condition to make humanity better by your lives, and cause the holy influence from God's angel children to find a resting-place in the human mind, that they may learn they belong to God, and seek to do his will? Held by the will of Almighty God, this body is, in order that humanity may know that God has held him from death until he can be lain on the altar of the heathen bigots, and prepare the way for coming ages to ask for light from beyond, that they may be lighted through the dark passage; that they may not fall in darkness, and remain in darkness until they can draw light from eternal distance, which is eternal and forever unchangeable, because it is the first great cause." Then Leiah drew near. I felt his influence folding me in his embrace, and then he shouted, "Who among you are ready to acknowledge you are damned already by your own hellish desires? But you are not content to damn yourselves; you would damn all of the human family, and drag them down to hell with you. And you, Caiaphas, are a brute and a drunken debauchee, and the fiends of darkness await your coming. Lay down your hate and your damning ambition ere it is too late. Let the good king feel you are ready to make amends, as far as you can, for damning his daughters and diseasing his concubines, which are dying by your brutish, filthy body; and you are diseased even now, and by it you will die, and all you have destroyed will rise up in judgment against you. And you, Josephus, would destroy this poor frail body for giving warning to your people to prepare to defend themselves against this brute by your side, who instigated the plot of destroying all the Hebrews in the land, that they could control in Antioch as well as in Jerusalem. Answer me, Josephus," Leiah shouted, "how many Jews did they behead, and how many females did they damn in one night? And here you are, in league one with the other, against the humble child of Joseph and Mary; and you would crucify him because he sought to save the Jews from utter destruction." Then the king arose to his feet, and said, "Do with him as you will, but I find no fault in him. But lead me to my chamber; I am filled with sorrow." Here I answered, "The king was my friend; he is my friend, and God will bless him when he reaches a condition where disease cannot fall upon him from that brute Caiaphas." Here Caiaphas' hate knew no bounds, but he was compelled to hold his peace until I was done. Then I addressed Josephus, and said, "Your synagogue will be taken from you before two years, and your men will be slaughtered, and your females will be dragged about by these heathen priests and confessors until they are all blasted by their filthy, diseased bodies. They will fall to rise no more on earth; but God will surely take his own. But if you are a man, defend the weak from these fiends of darkness, which are even now planning your utter destruction. Hell cannot hold them, but in God's own time he will hold control, and these miserable wretches will be lost in oblivion, and neither root nor branch will remain to declare they ever have been."

Here the influence left me, and I dropped down beside the magistrate. Then again I said, "Raise me to my feet." There I stood, trembling all over from my head to my feet, not with fear, but with utter exhaustion. I then bowed my head, and said, "Now I am ready to die for God and humanity." Then they cried out from all parts of the hall, "Crucify, crucify him, that the heretics can see their God cannot save him!" Here the magistrate held me up, and we made our way toward the stairway. Here I became filled with electricity, and I walked down those stairs as if I had been a strong man. The confessors had stationed themselves on each side of the entrance, and one raised his hand to strike me; but ere I reached him, his hand fell by his side powerless. I saw him in the after part of the day, and his arm hung by his side, a blasted thing. But as I stepped upon the floor of the entrance, my angel friend laid her hand in mine; and, as we walked out of the hall together, she said, "God is with us, and hell cannot destroy my brother. His body will writhe in agony upon the cross, but his spirit will gain its freedom during that agony." I said, "My dear friend, do not leave me again until I breathe out of my body." But I got no answer; but she bowed her head, and a bitter sigh escaped her. That was the first time I had ever heard a sigh from spirit, and I hoped it would be the last. I then asked a bystander where my mother was. He answered, "Her cries rent our hearts, and the priests commanded her to be borne away among the heretics."—"My God!" I said, "can I never behold her again?" At that moment I heard a scream. I burst from the magistrate. Dart-ing forward, feeble as I was, I gained the spot, and knelt beside my poor dear mother. I said, "But look upon me once more, and then I am ready to die." Her head was resting in Martha's lap. I bent down, and imprinted a kiss upon her forehead. She raised one hand; I held it against my beating heart. At that moment a confessor caught me by my hair, and drew me back upon the ground, as he said, "Fool of a heretic thou art, to think you are going to evade the law!" Then he dragged me into the main street, and bound me, hands and feet. Here I saw four confessors bearing along a cross, and they laid it down near by me. Then they unbound my feet, in order to nail me upon that cross, in the midst of the inhabitants of Jerusalem. They cried out against it; and I heard one Hebrew say, "He cannot be nailed to the cross here; he has not taken life, and if you will destroy him, carry him out of the city." The inhabitants saw they were determined to destroy me, and they advised them to bear me out of the city to the Mount of Olives, where they had hanged and burned and stoned to death their felons for a long time. Then they said, "Get up; your feet are not tied, and you must walk out of the city." In an instant an electric flash went over me, and I sprang to my feet, and shouted, "Holy, Creator, God! fill all earth with thy light, until all of thy creations shall exclaim, 'Thou art my Light, thou art my Life, thou art my Father, God!' and these fiends in priestly garb cannot damn thy children, because the light around them will cause darkness to flee, and the sweet breath of the angels will bless the earth flowers."

Here the confessor that held the cord that bound me shouted, "He ought to be nailed to the cross here, that the heretics may look upon their deceiver, and then swear allegiance to the priesthood!" As I stood there I was felled to the ground by the handle of a battle-axe in the hands of a priest. Then a confessor kicked me as I lay there, and said, "Damned heretic, you will soon find out the priesthood are not to be insulted by a felon like you." John drew near, and a confessor struck at him; then John felled him to the ground, jumped upon him with both feet, and exclaimed, "Hell's damned, thou art chained and bound forever!" Here the authorities stepped forward and demanded peace. John stepped back into the crowd, and they lost sight of him. Then the magistrate commanded them to bear away the cross to where it was to be set, and he would see the heretic was brought in due time. Four confessors came forward, raised the cross, and bore it away. . . . The magistrate said, "get up, it is half-past ten, and the hour for crucifixion was to be at ten." Then I arose to my feet and my holy controller breathed upon me. Again I caught up the cross, sped up the hill, and held it until Caiaphas commanded me to lay it down. Then Leiah exclaimed, "He that assists in crucifying this child of Joseph and Mary will surely be crucified in spirit forever." I then sat down, while the sweat was pouring from my forehead, and ere I could get a deep breath Caiaphas came forward and put a spade in my hand, and said, "Dig the hole where the cross is to be set." I answered, "I am too weak to dig that hard earth." My head was aching fearfully, and my back was in agony. Then I made an attempt to get up and my strength was mighty again. Then I said, "Give me the spade, and I will dig as long as need be." The earth was hard alluvial soil, and I could hardly make an impression upon it until the incrustation gave away, then I could raise my spade full of dirt, and I soon was bade "get out of there; that will do." That harsh expression caused me to feel bitterness in my heart, and how I was held from dashing upon Caiaphas with that spade and striking him down. I know not, but my hand was staid, and I dropped to the earth unable to rise again until I asked God to assist me to my knees. There I raised my hands in prayer for the last time in my earthly body. "Father, God, forgive, oh, forgive them, they know not what they do. Light, my God, to guide me through the dark valley of death. Hold and lead me until I can reach that home Thou hast prepared for thy children, and holy God, care for my mother and bring her to the bosom of her family ere another year shall pass away." I had but spoken the last word when I was thrown back, and four confessors caught me and laid me on the cross. Then an high priest stepped forward with nails in one hand and a hammer in the other. Five nails he drove in each hand, and four in each foot. Then my groans could not be suppressed. I heard a bitter shriek, then I opened my eyes. There was my mother, fallen upon that body as it lay upon the cross. Her shrieks rent the air, her breath left her, and she fell like one dead. Then I said, "Holy God, hold her in Thy bosom until I am borne away." But her breath came again and she knelt beside me. I was caused to feel her cup was full and would soon run over. Then she smoothed back my hair and laid one arm beneath my head for the last time on earth. There she covered my forehead with kisses, and bathed my bosom with tears. When nearly a half-hour had passed away then they came forward, and said, "Let us raise him up." Now they did raise me up. There I hung and writhed in agony until my mother fell at the foot of the cross, and I knew, by the one deep, bitter groan of despair that forced itself up from her inmost life, that her heart was broken, and I did know that she had drank the bitter cup to the dregs. Then for a moment I lost myself, but soon again I came back to consciousness; then the furies were at work. My followers were being cut to pieces with battle-axes; heads were strewn upon the ground. As Mary fell at the foot of the cross, her head rested against my feet, and I saw a priest drag her away by the hair and give her into the hands of two confessors, and they dragged her out of sight toward the dark side of the hill. Three hours had passed away, and I began to feel the pain less and less in my hands and feet. My head was nearly bursting, and my heart was beating fearfully, when I caught a glimpse of Bartholomew. I said, "Can you get me some water?" He answered, "I will get some for you or die in the attempt." In a short time I saw him approaching; he had a gourd in one hand and a cup in the other. Then I saw the glimmer of a battle-axe and I saw his head roll on the ground. Judas caught up the gourd and cup and hastened toward me. As he was about raising the cup to my lips, I saw a heathen priest strike down his arm with a battle-axe, and he then struck off his head. I said to the brute, "God will dash you to atoms, even as you dashed that cup from me." I was now folded in the embrace of my controller at least two hours. What he said, I know not, but I have been told since that he denounced them fearfully, and the first thing I did know some one had dealt a fearful blow across the chest, a little above the heart. Then my agony was inexpressible. All the blood in my body seemed to rush to my head and then to my feet. I must have continued in that state for at least two hours. I heard a voice, I knew it was John, say, "His death is a fearful one, and God will curse all that have assisted in this dreadful deed." I called and said, "John, John, come here. Dear brother John, do care for my mother." He answered, "I will care for Mary." I looked around and I saw my followers all lying dead around me. I learned afterwards that four hundred and eighteen were beheaded that day. As my agony began to subside, and night was closing in, Caiaphas commanded them all to begone, even then, or the city gates should be closed on them, and they should not go in unless they would go then. My head had dropped upon my bosom. Although I could breathe no longer, yet I could hear, and I did hear Caiaphas say, "We will drive the inhabitants within the gates, then we will return and care for the body." They did return; and I heard them digging, and then one said, "We will splinter up the cross, and that will be sufficient with this brush."

I knew when they came to take me down, but breathe I could not; but I did know my heart beat. They took the spade and chopped my hands from the cross; then, as I pitched forward, they struck off my feet also. Then they left me on the ground until they had dug up the cross and split it in many pieces. I heard the fagots crackling, and I knew a funeral pile was prepared for me. They then came and took me by my head and feet, and bore me a few paces; then they laid me upon the blazing heap. As the flames curled up around my head and face it caused the blood to circulate again, and in the midst of the flames my breath came back, and I exclaimed, "My God, my God! how much longer must I suffer in this body?" There my agony was fearful. It did seem that the heat would never penetrate the vitals and free my spirit from its mortal agony. But it did free itself; then I could understand why they were burning that body. They were aware that the acts that had been performed by an unseen power could not be crushed out of the minds of the inhabitants, even of that day, and they conceived of the idea of holding the body from the knowledge of all. They, the priesthood, could easily make the idolatrous worshippers believe the idols had come and taken me to themselves, and they could still hold them in darkness, subservient to their will. Here I also observed that after the body was nearly consumed they were very careful to heap on the dirt and tread it down, to make it appear like the rest of the earth, that had been worn by the many feet that were constantly walking about while I hung upon the cross; and they knew if the cross was left it would be carried away in pieces by the Hebrews, if none else.

Here I am held by the Almighty power of the Creator, God. I

have come back in order to finish up that which was begun ages on
ages ago; and they that are willing to behold me as I am, nothing
but a man, will surely be blessed by these historical facts, bereft of
fiction. I have drawn these facts from their true source. Humble
life of a humble family that were driven about the country because a price was so often set upon my head. And in order to shield
me from the battle-axe they would flee to the mountain. Here I
will now leave my history in the hands of God's children that ask
for light; and may the light of inspiration give them the true design
of this work.

Even while I hung upon the cross, a mighty rumbling was
heard in the bowels of the earth, and about four in the after part
of the day Mount Sinai did belch forth her thunders, and the
smoke was so dense that the top of the mountain could not be
discerned. Even if fire and smoke were thrown from the bosom of
earth, it was not because I was hanging upon the cross. It would
have belched forth even the same if I had not been crucified at all.
The natural causes were there, controlled by a mightier power
than could have been brought about by the death of one man or
a thousand. But through the designing priesthood it has been
held before the poor, deluded, benighted, deceived, confiding,
that dare not ask light for themselves, lest they should be called
to an account by their deceivers, that do teach what they do not
believe; but they withhold their knowledge, because they dare
not infringe on their isms and creeds, lest they would be set aside,
and then, from their necessities, eat the bread earned by the sweat
of their brows, and become honest men. Who among them all is
ready to go to his toil-worn brother, that has bent beneath his
burden, and say, "Brother, I will use the spade for you to-day; go
ye and rest"? When find I a priest or a dispenser of creeds, no
matter what the name may be, that is willing to go to his brother's destitute family, that once fed and clothed him, and say, "I
have bread, come, eat with me; I have a home, come and I will
comfort you"? And, above all, are you, any of you, ready to say,
"I have the light, and infallible knowledge, that God's angel children come to me, and would bless me, so far as I blend my ideas
with theirs, and they bring me tidings of a brighter home beyond"? Dare any of you say, "My loved ones are there, awaiting
my coming, and I long to breathe in their presence"? Live, oh,

live for the good of humanity, that when thou hast ceased to be earthly, that thy last breath may say, "Angels beloved, I am coming to thee; my labor is done for humanity. I am going home." And to you, O mothers, that God has entrusted with gifts divine, live in a way that you can feed those tender minds with the bread of life, which is life eternal. Do not crush the tender bud that your father, God, has laid in your bosom, the bosom of its love. Let God unfold its tender leaves; then the child will be prepared to say, "Thy will be done;" and behold, through wondrous formations, their God is there. Then the Soul of souls will answer, "I am here, I am there, I am everywhere, throughout all time, throughout all space; I am the father of the human race." Then come, my own beloved children, and gaze upon me, as I am in all things I have created. Heaven divides not its own. Then let heaven begin within each human breast. Then if you seek, you will be sure to find for every bruise a healing balm that will not leave you as long as time rolls on. And now I will bow to thee, my father and my God, although I bow to kiss the rod, if it be for thy glory and the good of humanity.


## My Humble Prayer to my Creator, God, for Assisting me in Finishing up my Earth History.

Holy, almighty, infinite as thou art; humble as I am, I am but of thee a part. Held by thy almighty hand, humbly I bow at thy command. Here I am, but a speck in thine immensity, made to feel that I can bless thy children by giving them truth, bereft of fiction, that has been held among the holy records of the past, free from spot or blemish.

Although earth's dark, benighted children have sought to destroy all traces of the Hebrew family, yet thou hast held them in thy own bosom, until changes could be made for them to come back to earth and declare God's mercies still; and I could not rob humanity of her inheritance,—that is, God's wonders wrought through his children. Ages ago, Mount Sinai did belch forth her thunder, not because of thy anger, but through the wondrous working of thy elements, held by thy almighty hand, the law that changes not, even from the beginning, and endureth forever. Oh, give me light from thy inner light, that I may understand how best to live out the measure of time, in order that thy glory may fill all minds, that thy children may exclaim, The glory of our Father, God, fills us full to overflowing! and we can say, Thou art ever present, and we behold thy wonders through thy mighty works. Assist thy angel children to lead and guide all of thy children still in earthly forms to flee the cruel devices of man, that has sought to chain and bind them to creeds and dogmas that fill the land, which are but devices of heathen bigots, and none other. And may they all understand that it is because I am in their churches, as an idol, thy command has been put upon me to go back to the poor benighted souls that are in darkness, and give them freedom by declaring myself, as I am, a friend and a brother. Assist, oh, assist, them, thou source of life divine, to read and be blessed. If they could but know what I have suffered in order to give them facts in relation to thee, my God, they would all answer, "Let us search the law; let us be guided by the law,—and then we shall not need another human sacrifice,—that we may inquire of the law how it is we are held accountable for every act of our lives." When all learn life is God; light is God; love is God; knowledge is God; and all of the angels bright are but a part of thee, thou Almighty Creator, and creative, are but component parts of immensity, held by the law, and nothing else; and let thy children ask of thee, thou Father, God, the inner life of all things; then an answer sure will come, "As they live, so they will receive from thy own bounteous gifts, free from hypocrisy and deceit, fresh from eternal distance." They will receive it; then the glory will be thine, Creator, God, all thine own, light, eternal light divine. Lead and guide thy children on to a higher, holier clime, and let nothing come between thee and thy highest created, that has come forth from the inner life of all things; and may they learn they are of thee, and they will surely go back again into the bosom of immensity, from whence they came. And may they learn, through the knowledge of the law, that they have existed co-equal with the Almighty whole, and not one jot or tittle of mind or matter can be lost or created anew. All things are held by the law of attraction; and the attraction is thee, my God, that begets all things, but through blending of essences, extracted from other formations. Through thus blending, all things become new; yet nothing is taken from, nothing is added to, the great

Almighty whole. Then held as all things are, sustained as all things are, let us breathe but one word; let that be God. Then let all understand that nothing can be created but by the law; then you will answer: "He is my friend and my brother. He is but a man. Then I should be free. Then, Holy God, thy kingdom will be established on earth, as it is in the brighter worlds beyond. Then anointed priests will lose their power to chain human souls, and man will not know that his blood has been held, as the bond people's were, in the wicked chains of heathen bigots' devices. O my God, let thy light enter every human mind, and darkness will fade away. Then thou wilt be acknowledged as the one God, and the one God only; and thine own inner life blending with all created things that has been begotten by thee, the First Great Cause, Eternal Light. Holy Creator, God, bless her that has laid down all she has earthly, that I may declare myself as I am, but a humble beggar, still begging of thee humanity to make condition to receive the bread of life, which is thy knowledge. Then they will be robed in their wedding garments, crowned all over with the dewdrops bright, fresh from thy fountain of love, which has ever flowed since creations were. Plant flowers earthly, my God, that they may bloom in a holier condition than earth ever knew. May I bow low before thee, my Creator, and ask humanity if they are willing to receive my blessing, and relieve me from earth, that I may go back to that bright land of light, and say to my angel loved ones there, that "My earth labor is finished, and I have come back home, and we will give God the glory for all his mercies, forever and forever."

Here, reader, I must bid you farewell, hoping to meet you beyond God's ether blue. There, dear brother and dear sister, I will await your coming. There my home has been for ages on ages, and I long to go back again. O humanity! thy demands must be appeased. Oh, do not call me! I cannot come again, but to die. But if humanity demands another human sacrifice I will die for them, if it be God's will. And now, reader, I must bid you a long farewell! I am your friend and brother, Jesus of Nazareth, and none other; the first-born of Joseph and Mary. Farewell!

(OLIVE G. PETTIS, 1870; REPRINT ED., BOSTON, 1894; PP. 23–29,
46–47, 63–64, 97–106)

# The Woman's Bible

The nineteenth-century feminist and reformer Elizabeth Cady Stanton (1815–1902) had long planned a thorough revision of the Bible that would restore the rightful place of women in both the text and in the Christian church. For many decades a critic of the second-class treatment of women in Protestant congregations, Stanton nonetheless believed that the Bible contained true principles that simply needed to be extracted from the oppressive interpretations of generations of male religious leaders. She gathered a committee of nearly two dozen women from the United States and Europe, most of them women's rights activists interested in biblical interpretation but not trained scholars themselves, to write commentaries on biblical passages in order to prove that women should not be subservient to men.

Appearing in two volumes in 1895 and 1898, *The Woman's Bible* came right on the heels of one of the major biblical revision projects of the day, the Revised Version (published 1881–1894). Stanton was not satisfied with the treatment of women in that text, or with the fact that no female scholars played major roles in the revision committee. In response, *The Woman's Bible* was biting and pointed in its criticism of traditional teachings about women's place in the church and society. While the text was a bestseller, it was roundly condemned by clergy from the pulpits as "the work of Satan." It also received mixed responses from women's rights advocates, who questioned whether an overhaul of the Christian tradition was the best use of the activists' time. Nonetheless, it has continued to inspire subsequent Christian feminists who see it as a milestone for the study of gender and scriptural interpretation.

The passages selected here include the book of Genesis, with extensive commentary on the creation of man and woman; several of the Gospels, in which contributors discuss the women surrounding Jesus; and the Epistle to the Corinthians, in which authors comment on Paul's discussion of marriage. All of these issues were of the utmost importance to nineteenth-century Protestant women reformers as they tried to reconcile Christian teachings with their belief in gender equality.

# THE WOMAN'S BIBLE.

## THE BOOK OF GENESIS.

### CHAPTER I.

*Genesis i: 26, 27, 28*

26 ¶ And God said, Let us make man in our image, after our likeness: and let them have dominion over the fish of the sea, and over the fowl of the air, and over the cattle, and over all the earth, and over every creeping thing that creepeth upon the earth.

27 So God created man in his *own* image, in the image of God created he him; male and female created he them.

28 And God blessed them, and God said unto them, Be fruitful, and multiply, and replenish the earth, and subdue it; and have dominion over the fish of the sea, and over the fowl of the air, and over every living thing that moveth upon the earth.

Here is the sacred historian's first account of the advent of woman; a simultaneous creation of both sexes, in the image of God. It is evident from the language that there was consultation in the Godhead, and that the masculine and feminine elements were equally represented. Scott in his commentaries says, "this consultation of the Gods is the origin of the doctrine of the trinity." But instead of three male personages, as generally represented, a Heavenly Father, Mother, and Son would seem more rational.

The first step in the elevation of woman to her true position, as an equal factor in human progress, is the cultivation of the religious sentiment in regard to her dignity and equality, the recognition by the rising generation of an ideal Heavenly Mother, to whom their prayers should be addressed, as well as to a Father.

If language has any meaning, we have in these texts a plain declaration of the existence of the feminine element in the Godhead, equal in power and glory with the masculine. The Heavenly Mother and Father! "God created man in his *own image, male and female.*" Thus Scripture, as well as science and philosophy, declares the eternity and equality of sex—the philosophical fact, without which there could have been no perpetuation of creation, no growth or development in the animal, vegetable, or mineral kingdoms, no awakening nor progressing in the world of thought. The masculine and feminine elements, exactly equal and balancing each other, are as essential to the maintenance of the equilibrium of the universe as positive and negative electricity, the centripetal and centrifugal forces, the laws of attraction which bind together all we know of this planet whereon we dwell and of the system in which we revolve.

In the great work of creation the crowning glory was realized, when man and woman were evolved on the sixth day, the masculine and feminine forces in the image of God, that must have existed eternally, in all forms of matter and mind. All the persons in the Godhead are represented in the Elohim the divine plurality taking counsel in regard to this last and highest form of life. Who were the members of this high council, and were they a duality or a trinity? Verse 27 declares the image of God male and female. How then is it possible to make woman an afterthought? We find in verses 5-16 the pronoun "he" used. Should it not in harmony with verse 26 be "they," a dual pronoun? We may attribute this to the same cause as the use of "his" in verse 11 instead of "it." The fruit tree yielding fruit after "his" kind instead of after "its" kind. The paucity of a language may give rise to many misunderstandings.

The above texts plainly show the simultaneous creation of man and woman, and their equal importance in the development of the race. All those theories based on the assumption that man was prior in the creation, have no foundation in Scripture.

As to woman's subjection, on which both the canon and the civil law delight to dwell, it is important to note that equal dominion is given to woman over every living thing, but not one word is said giving man dominion over woman.

Here is the first title deed to this green earth giving alike to the sons and daughters of God. No lesson of woman's subjection can be fairly drawn from the first chapter of the Old Testament.

E.C.S.

The most important thing for a woman to note, in reading Genesis, is that that portion which is now divided into "the first three chapters" (there was no such division until about five centuries ago), contains two entirely separate, and very contradictory, stories of creation, written by two different, but equally anonymous, authors. No Christian theologian of to-day, with any pretensions to scholarship, claims that Genesis was written by Moses. As was long ago pointed out, the Bible itself declares that all the books the Jews originally possessed were burned in the destruction of Jerusalem, about 588 B. C., at the time the people were taken to Babylonia as slaves to the Assyrians, (see II Esdras, ch. xiv, v. 21, Apocrypha). Not until about 247 B. C. (some theologians say 226 and others 169 B. C.) is there any record of a collection of literature in the re-built Jerusalem, and, then, the anonymous writer of II Maccabees briefly mentions that some Nehemiah "gathered together the acts of the kings and the prophets and those of David" when "founding a library" for use in Jerusalem. But the earliest mention anywhere in the Bible of a book that might have corresponded to Genesis is made by an apocryphal writer, who says that *Ezra* wrote "all that hath been done in the world since the beginning," after the Jews returned from Babylon, under his leadership, about 450 B. C. (see II Esdras, ch. xiv, v. 22, of the Apocrypha).

When it is remembered that the Jewish books were written on rolls of leather, without much attention to vowel points and with no division into verses or chapters, by uncritical copyists, who altered passages greatly, and did not always even pretend to understand what they were copying, then the reader of Genesis begins to put herself in position to understand how it can be contradictory. Great as were the liberties which the Jews took with Genesis, those of the English translators, however, greatly surpassed them.

The first chapter of Genesis, for instance, in Hebrew, tells us, in verses one and two, "As to origin, created the gods (Elohim) these skies (or air or clouds) and this earth . . . And a wind moved upon the face of the waters." Here we have the opening of a poly-theistic fable of creation, but, so strongly convinced were the English translators that the ancient Hebrews must have been originally monotheistic that they rendered the above, as follows: "In the beginning God created the heaven and the earth. . . . And the spirit of God (!) moved upon the face of the waters."

It is now generally conceded that some one (nobody pretends to know who) at some time (nobody pretends to know exactly when), copied two creation myths on the same leather roll, one immediately following the other. About one hundred years ago, it was discovered by Dr. Astruc, of France, that from Genesis ch. i, v. 1 to Genesis ch. ii, v. 4, is given one complete account of creation, by an author who always used the term "the gods" (*Elohim*), in speaking of the fashioning of the universe, mentioning it altogether thirty-four times, while, in Genesis ch. ii, v. 4, to the end of chapter iii, we have a totally different narrative, by an author of unmistakably different style, who uses the term "Iahveh of the gods" twenty times, but "Elohim" only three times. The first author, evidently, attributes creation to a council of gods, acting in concert, and seems never to have heard of Iahveh. The second attributes creation to Iahveh, a tribal god of ancient Israel, but represents Iahveh as one of two or more gods, conferring with them (in Genesis ch. xiii, v. 22) as to the danger of man's acquiring immortality.

[. . .]

Now as it is manifest that both of these stories cannot be true; intelligent women, who feel bound to give the preference to either, may decide according to their own judgment of which is more worthy of an intelligent woman's acceptance. Paul's rule is a good one in this dilemma, "Prove all things: hold fast to that which is good." My own opinion is that the second story was manipulated by some Jew, in an endeavor to give "heavenly authority" for requiring a woman to obey the man she married. In a work which I am now completing, I give some facts concerning ancient Israelitish history, which will be of peculiar interest to those who wish to understand the origin of woman's subjection.

E. B. D.

# Chapter II.

*Genesis ii: 21-25.*

21  And the Lord God caused a deep sleep to fall upon Adam, and he slept; and he took one of his ribs, and closed up the flesh thereof.

22  And the rib which the Lord God had taken from man, made he a woman, and brought her unto the man.

23  And Adam said, This *is* now bone of my bone, and flesh of my flesh: she shall be called Woman, because she was taken out of man.

24  Therefore shall a man leave his father and his mother, and shall cleave unto his wife; and they shall be one flesh.

25  And they were both naked, the man and his wife, and were not ashamed.

As the account of the creation in the first chapter is in harmony with science, common sense, and the experience of mankind in natural laws, the inquiry naturally arises, why should there be two contradictory accounts in the same book, of the same event? It is fair to infer that the second version, which is found in some form in the different religions of all nations, is a mere allegory, symbolizing some mysterious conception of a highly imaginative editor.

The first account dignifies woman as an important factor in the creation, equal in power and glory with man. The second makes her a mere afterthought. The world in good running order without her. The only reason for her advent being the solitude of man.

There is something sublime in bringing order out of chaos; light out of darkness; giving each planet its place in the solar system; oceans and lands their limits; wholly inconsistent with a petty surgical operation, to find material for the mother of the race. It is on this allegory that all the enemies of women rest their battering rams, to prove her inferiority. Accepting the view that man was prior in the creation, some Scriptural writers say that as the woman was of the man, therefore, her position should be one of subjection. Grant it, then as the historical fact is reversed in our day, and the man is now of the woman, shall his place be one of subjection?

The equal position declared in the first account must prove more satisfactory to both sexes; created alike in the image of God— The Heavenly Mother and Father.

Thus, the Old Testament, "in the beginning," proclaims the simultaneous creation of man and woman, the eternity and equality of sex; and the New Testament echoes back through the centuries the individual sovereignty of woman growing out of this natural fact. Paul, in speaking of equality as the very soul and essence of Christianity, said, "There is neither Jew nor Greek, there is neither bond nor free, there is neither male nor female; for ye are all one in Christ Jesus." With this recognition of the feminine element in the Godhead in the Old Testament, and this declaration of the equality of the sexes in the New, we may well wonder at the contemptible status woman occupies in the Christian Church of to-day.

All the commentators and publicists writing on woman's position, go through an immense amount of fine-spun metaphysical speculations, to prove her subordination in harmony with the Creator's original design.

It is evident that some wily writer, seeing the perfect equality of man and woman in the first chapter, felt it important for the dignity and dominion of man to effect woman's subordination in some way. To do this a spirit of evil must be introduced, which at once proved itself stronger than the spirit of good, and man's supremacy was based on the downfall of all that had just been pronounced very good. This spirit of evil evidently existed before the supposed fall of man, hence woman was not the origin of sin as so often asserted.

                                                                      E. C. S.

In v. 23 Adam proclaims the eternal oneness of the happy pair, "This is now bone of my bone and flesh of my flesh;" no hint of her subordination. How could men, admitting these words to be divine revelation, ever have preached the subjection of woman!

Next comes the naming of the mother of the race. "She shall be called Woman," in the ancient form of the word Womb-man. She was man and more than man because of her maternity.

The assertion of the supremacy of the woman in the marriage relation is contained in v. 24: "Therefore shall a man leave his father and his mother and cleave unto his wife." Nothing is said of the headship of man, but he is commanded to make her the head of the household, the home, a rule followed for centuries under the Matriarchate.                                    L. D. B.

———

Note the significant fact that we always hear of the "fall of man," not the fall of woman, showing that the consensus of human thought has been more unerring than masculine interpretation. Reading this narrative carefully, it is amazing that any set of men ever claimed that the dogma of the inferiority of woman is here set forth. The conduct of Eve from the beginning to the end is so superior to that of Adam. The command not to eat of the fruit of the tree of Knowledge was given to the man alone before woman was formed. Genesis ii, 17. Therefore the injunction was not brought to Eve with the impressive solemnity of a Divine Voice, but whispered to her by her husband and equal. It was a serpent supernaturally endowed, a seraphim as Scott and other commentators have claimed, who talked with Eve, and whose words might reasonably seem superior to the second-hand story of her companion—nor does the woman yield at once. She quotes the command not to eat of the fruit to which the serpent replies "Dying ye shall not die," v. 4, literal translation. In other words telling her that if the mortal body does perish, the immortal part shall live forever, and offering as the reward of her act the attainment of Knowledge.

Then the woman fearless of death if she can gain wisdom takes of the fruit; and all this time Adam standing beside her interposes no word of objection. "Her husband with her" are the words of v. 6. Had he been the representative of the divinely appointed head in married life, he assuredly would have taken upon himself the burden of the discussion with the serpent, but no, he is silent in this crisis of their fate. Having had the command from God himself he interposes no word of warning or remonstrance, but takes the fruit from the hand of his wife without a protest. It takes six verses to describe the "fall" of woman, the fall of man is contemptuously dismissed in a line and a half.

The subsequent conduct of Adam was to the last degree dastardly. When the awful time of reckoning comes, and the Jehovah

God appears to demand why his command has been disobeyed, Adam endeavors to shield himself behind the gentle being he has declared to be so dear. "The woman thou gavest to be with me, she gave me and I did eat," he whines—trying to shield himself at his wife's expense! Again we are amazed that upon such a story men have built up a theory of their superiority!

Then follows what has been called the curse. Is it not rather a prediction? First is the future fate of the serpent described, the enmity of the whole human race—"it shall lie in wait for thee as to the head" (v. 15, literal translation). Next the subjection of the woman is foretold, thy husband "shall rule over thee," v. 16. Lastly the long struggle of man with the forces of nature is portrayed. "In the sweat of thy face thou shalt eat food until thy turning back to the earth" (v. 19, literal translation). With the evolution of humanity an ever increasing number of men have ceased to toil for their bread with their hands, and with the introduction of improved machinery, and the uplifting of the race there will come a time when there shall be no severities of labor, and when women shall be freed from all oppressions.

"And Adam called his wife's name Life for she was the mother of all living" (v. 20, literal translation).

It is a pity that all versions of the Bible do not give this word instead of the Hebrew Eve. She was Life, the eternal mother, the first representative of the more valuable and important half of the human race.                                                              L. D. B.

———

## Myths of Creation.

Nothing would be more interesting in connection with the "Woman's Bible" than a comparative study of the accounts of the creation held by people of different races and faiths. Our Norse ancestors, whose myths were of a very exalted nature, recorded in their Bible, the Edda, that one day the sons of Bor (a frost giant), Odin, Hoener, and Loder, found two trees on the sea beach, and from them created the first human pair, man and woman. Odin gave them life and spirit, Hoener endowed them with reason and motion, and Loder gave them the senses and physical characteristics. The man they called Ask, and the woman Embla. Prof. Anderson finds in the brothers the threefold Trinity of the Bible. It is easy to fancy that there is some philological connection between the names of the first pair in the Bible and in the Edda. Perhaps the formation of the first pair out of trees had a deep connection with the tree of life, Ygdrasil, which extended, according to Norse mythology throughout the universe, furnishing bodies for mankind from its branches. It had three great roots, one extending to the nebulous world, and this was constantly gnawed by the serpent Nidhug. There was nothing in the Norse mythology that taught the degradation of woman, and the lay of Sigdrifa, in the Edda, is one of the noblest conceptions of the character of woman in all literature.

North American Indian mythology has the human race born of the earth, but the writer cannot learn that women held an inferior place. Among the Quiches the mothers and fathers of old slept in the waters, covered with green, under a limpid twilight, from which the earth and they were called out by a mighty wind. The Algonkins believed the human family were the children of Michabo, the spirit of the dawn, and their supreme deity. In their language the words earth, mother and father were from the same root. Many tribes claim descent from a raven, symbolizing the clouds; others from a dog, which is the symbol of the water goddess.

Dr. and Madame Le Plongeon relate that in their discoveries among the buried remains of the Mayas in Yucatan, everything marks a very high state of civilization. In one of the exhumed temples they found pictures on the walls, which seem to be a combination of the stones of the Garden of Eden and Cain and Abel. The Serpent was always the royal emblem, because the shape of Yucatan is that of a serpent ready to spring. It was the custom among the Mayas for the oldest son of the king to be a priest, and the second son to marry the oldest daughter. The pictures represent that the oldest son in this particular case was dissatisfied with this arrangement, and wanted to marry the sister himself. To tempt her he sends a basket of apples by a messenger. He stands watching the way in which the present is received, and the serpent in the picture (indicating the royal family), makes it curiously suggestive of the temptation of Eve. The sister, however, rejects the present, and this so enrages the elder brother that he kills the younger, who accordingly is deified by the Mayas. The image of Chacmohl was discovered by the Le Plongeons, and is now in the possession of the Mexican Government. Perhaps these brothers were twins, as the commentator says Cain and Abel were, and that gave rise to the jealousy.

Nothing can surpass in grandeur the account in the first chapter of Genesis of the creation of the race, and it satisfies the highest aspirations and the deepest longings of the human soul. No matter of what material formed, or through how many ages the formative period ran, or is to run, the image of God is the birthright of man, male and female. Whatever the second chapter may mean, it cannot set aside the first. It probably has a deep spiritual significance which mankind will appreciate when cavilling about the letter ceases. To the writer's mind its meaning is best expressed in the words of Goethe: "The eternal womanly leads us on."

C. B. C.

# THE BOOK OF MATTHEW.

## Chapter I.

*Matthew i.*

16  And Jacob begat Joseph the husband of Mary, of whom was born Jesus, who is called Christ.

17  So all the generations from Abraham to David are fourteen generations; and from David until the carrying away into Babylon are fourteen generations; and from the carrying away into Babylon unto Christ are fourteen generations.

Saint Matthew is supposed to be distinguished from the other Apostles by the frequency of his references to the Old Testament. He records more particulars of Jesus than the others do, far more of his birth, his sayings and his miracles.

There has been much difference of opinion among writers of both sacred and profane history as to the paternity of Jesus, and whether he was a real or an ideal character. If, as the Scriptures claim, he descended from heaven, begotten by the Holy Ghost, the incarnation of God himself, then there was nothing remarkable in his career, nor miraculous in the seeming wonders which he performed, being the soul and the centre of all the forces of the Universe of matter and of mind. If he was an ideal character, like the gifted hero of some novel or tragedy, his great deeds and his wise sayings the result of the imagination of some skilful artist, then we may admire the sketch as a beautiful picture. But if Jesus was a man who was born, lived and died as do other men, a worthy example for imitation, he is deserving of our love and reverence, and by showing us the possibilities of human nature he is a constant inspiration, our hope and salvation; for the path, however rough, in which one man has walked, others may follow. As a God with infinite power he could have been no example to us; but with human limitations we may emulate his virtues and walk in his footsteps.

Some writers think that his mother was a wise, great and beautiful Jewish maiden, and his father a learned rabbi, who devoted much time and thought to his son's education. At a period when learning was confined to the few, it was a matter of surprise that as a mere boy he could read and write, and discuss the vital questions of the hour with doctors in the sacred temples. His great physical beauty, the wisdom of his replies to the puzzling questions of the Pharisees and the Sadducees, his sympathy with the poor and the needy, his ambition for all that is best in human development, and his indifference to worldly aggrandizement, altogether made him a marked man in his day and generation. For these reasons he was hated, reviled, persecuted, like the long line of martyrs who followed his teachings. He commands far more love and reverence as a true man with only human possibilities, than as a God, superior to all human frailties and temptations.

What were years of persecution, the solitude on the mountain, the agonies on the cross, with the power of a God to sustain him? But unaided and alone to triumph over all human weakness, trials and temptation, was victory not only for Jesus but for every human being made in his image.

*Matthew ii.*

1   Now when Jesus was born in Bethlehem of Judea in the days of Herod the king, behold, there came wise men from the east to Jerusalem,

2   Saying, Where is he that is born King of the Jews? for we have seen his star in the east, and are come to worship him.

3   When Herod the king had heard these things, he was troubled, and all Jerusalem with him.

4   And when he had gathered all the chief priests together, he demanded of them where Christ should be born.

5   And they said unto him, In Bethlehem of Judea:

8   And he sent them to Bethlehem, and said, Go and search diligently for the young child; and when ye have found him, bring me word.

9   And they departed; and lo, the star, which they saw in the east, went before them, till it came and stood over where the young child was.

11   And when they were come into the house, they saw the young child with Mary his mother, and fell down, and worshiped him: and when they had opened their treasures, they presented unto him gifts; gold, and frankincense, and myrrh.

12   And being warned of God in a dream that they should not return to Herod, they departed into their own country another way.

13   And the angel of the Lord appeareth to Joseph in a dream, saying, Arise, and take the young child and his mother, and flee into Egypt; for Herod will seek to destroy him.

14   And he arose, and departed into Egypt;

19   But when Herod was dead, behold, an angel of the Lord appeareth in a dream to Joseph

20   Saying, Arise, and take the young child and his mother, and go into the land of Israel.

These sages were supposed to be men of great learning belonging to a sect called Magians, who came from Arabia. There was a general feeling that the king of the Jews was yet to be born, and that they were soon to see the long expected and promised Messiah. Herod was greatly troubled by the tidings that a child had been born under remarkable circumstances. The star spoken of was supposed to be a luminous meteor the wise men had seen in their own country before they set out on their journey for Bethlehem, and which now guided them to the house where the young child was. Notwithstanding the common surroundings, the wise men recognizing something more than human in the child, fell down and worshiped him and presented unto him the most precious gifts which their country yielded. Some have supposed that the frankincense and the myrrh were intended as an acknowledgment of his deity, as the gold was of his royalty.

To defeat the subtle malice of Herod, who was determined to take the child's life, Joseph was warned in a dream to flee into Egypt with the child and his mother. The wise men did not return to Herod as commanded, but went at once to their own country.

*Matthew ix.*

18   Behold, there came a certain ruler, saying, My daughter is even now dead; but come and lay thy hand upon her, and she shall live.

19   And Jesus arose and followed him.

20   And behold, a woman, which was diseased twelve years, came behind him, and touched the hem of his garment:

21   For she said within herself, If I may but touch his garment, I shall be whole.

22   But Jesus turned him about, and when he saw her, he said, Daughter, be of good comfort: thy faith hath made thee whole. And the woman was made whole from that hour.

23   And when Jesus came into the ruler's house, * * *

24   He said, Give place: for the maid is not dead, but sleepeth. And they laughed him to scorn.

25   But when the people were put forth, he went in, and took her by the hand, and the maid arose.

*Matthew xiv.*

3   For Herod had laid hold on John, and put him in prison for Herodias' sake, his brother Philip's wife.

4   For John said unto him, It is not lawful for thee to have her.

5   And when he would have put him to death, he feared the multitude, because they counted him as a prophet.

6   But when Herod's birthday was kept, the daughter of Herodias danced before them, and pleased Herod.

7   Whereupon he promised to give her whatsoever she would ask.

8 And she, being before instructed of her mother, said, Give me here John Baptist's head in a charger.

9 And the king was sorry: nevertheless for the oath's sake he commanded it to be given her.

10 And he sent, and beheaded John in the prison.

11 And his head was brought in a charger, and given to the damsel: and she brought it to her mother.

12 And his disciples came, and took up the body, and buried it, and went and told Jesus.

Josephus says that Herodias was niece both to her former husband, Philip, and to Herod, with whom she at this time lived. Herod had divorced his own wife in order to take her; and her husband Philip was still living, as well as the daughter Salome, whom he had by her. No connection could be more contrary to the law of God than this. John, therefore, being a prophet and no courtier, plainly reproved Herod, and declared that it was not lawful for him to retain Herodias. This greatly offended Herod and Herodias, and they cast John into prison. Herodias waited her opportunity to wreak her malice on him, counting John's reproof an insult to her character as well as an interference with her ambition.

At length when Herod celebrated his birthday, entertaining his nobles with great magnificence, the daughter of Herodias danced before them all, with such exquisite grace as to delight the company, whereupon Herod promised her whatever she desired, though equal in value to half his kingdom. Salome consulted her mother, who urged her to demand the head of John the Baptist. By the influence of Herodias, Herod, contrary to his own conscience, was induced to put John to death, for he feared him as a righteous man.

It must have been a great trial to the daughter, who might have asked so many beautiful gifts and rare indulgences, to yield all to her wicked mother's revenge. But these deeds were speedily avenged. It is said that Salome had her head cut off by the ice breaking as she passed over it. Herod was shortly after engaged in a disastrous war on account of Herodias, and was expelled from his territories; and both died in exile, hated by everybody and hating one another.                                    E. C. S.

In regard to the charge against Herodias, which is current among theological scandal-mongers, there is not a moderately intelligent jury of Christendom (if composed half of men and half of women) which, after examining all the available evidence, would not render a verdict in her favor of "Not Guilty." The statement that she "paid the price of her own daughter's debasement and disgrace for the head of John the Baptist," is an assertion born wholly of the ecclesiastical, distorted imagination. Not even a hint, much less an iota of proof, to warrant such an assertion, is found anywhere in history—sacred or profane. While some anonymous writer of the early Christian centuries did put in circulation the charge that John the Baptist was put to death at the instigation of Herodias (without implicating her daughter's character, however), Josephus, on the contrary, explicitly declares that his death was wholly a political matter, with which the names of Herodias and her daughter are not even connected by rumor. Says Josephus: "When others came in crowds about him (John the Baptist), for they were greatly moved by hearing his words, Herod, who feared lest the great influence John had over the people might put it into his power and inclination to raise a rebellion (for they seemed ready to do anything he should advise), thought it best, by putting him to death, to prevent any mischief he might cause. . . . Accordingly he was sent a prisoner, *out of Herod's suspicious temper*, to Macherus, the castle I before mentioned, and was there put to death."

Now, the jury must remember that Josephus was born in Jerusalem about 38 A. D., that he was an educated man and in a position to know the facts in this case, owing both to his prominent position among the Jews and to his study of contemporaneous history. But that, on the other hand, the anonymous writers who bring Herodias' name into the transaction, are not traceable further back than the fourth century of our era, and that even they do not bring any charge against her character as a mother.        E. B. D.

*Matthew xv.*

21   Then Jesus departed into the coasts of Tyre and Sidon.

22   And, behold, a woman of Canaan cried unto him, saying, Have mercy on me, O Lord, thou son of David; my daughter is grievously vexed with a devil.

23    But he answered her not a word. And his disciples besought him to send her away.

24    But he answered and said, I am not sent but unto the lost sheep of the house of Israel.

25    Then came she and worshiped him, saying, Lord, help me.

26    But he said, It is not meet to take the children's food, and to cast it to dogs.

27    And she said. Truth, Lord: yet the dogs eat of the crumbs which fall from their master's table.

28    Then Jesus answered and said unto her, O woman, great is thy faith: be it unto thee even as thou wilt. And her daughter was made whole from that very hour.

Peter had a house in Capernaum; and his wife's mother lived with them; and Jesus lodged with them when in that city. It is hoped that his presence brought out the best traits of the mother-in-law, so as to make her agreeable to Peter. As soon as Jesus rebuked the fever, she was able without delay to rise and to wait on Jesus and his disciples. These displays of the power of Christ in performing miracles, according to the text, are varied, in almost every conceivable way of beneficence; but he wrought no miracles of vengeance, even the destruction of the swine was doubtless intended in mercy and conducive to much good—so say the commentators. He not only healed the sick and cast out devils, but he made the blind to see and the dumb to speak.

The woman of Canaan proved herself quite equal in argument with Jesus; and though by her persistency she tired the patience of the disciples, she made her points with Jesus with remarkable clearness. His patience with women was a sore trial to the disciples, who were always disposed to nip their appeals in the bud. It was very ungracious in Jesus to speak of the Jews as dogs, saying, "It is not meet to take the children's food, and to cast it to dogs." Her reply, "Yet the dogs eat of the crumbs which fall from the master's table," was bright and appropriate. Jesus appreciated her tact and her perseverance, and granted her request; and her daughter, the text says, was healed.

We might doubt the truth of all these miracles did we not see so many wonderful things in our own day which we would have pronounced impossible years ago. The fact of human power developing in so many remarkable ways proves that Jesus's gift of performing miracles is attainable by those who, like him, live pure lives, and whose blood flows in the higher arches of the brain. If one man, at any period of the world's history, performed miracles, others equally gifted may do the same.

*Matthew xx.*

20   Then came to him the mother of Zebedee's children with her sons, worshiping him, and desiring a certain thing of him.

21   And he said unto her, What wilt thou? She saith unto him, Grant that these my two sons may sit, the one on thy right hand, and the other on the left, in thy kingdom.

Zebedee, the father of James and of John, was dead; and he was not so constant a follower of Christ as his wife; so she is mentioned as the mother of Zebedee's children, which saying has passed into a conundrum, "Who was the mother of Zebedee's children?" Scott in his commentaries gives her name as Salome. Whatever her name, she had great ambition for her sons, and asked that they might have the chief places of honor and authority in his kingdom. Her son James was the first of the Apostles who suffered martyrdom. John survived all the rest and is not supposed to have died a violent death.

A mother's ambition to lift her sons over her own head in education and position, planning extraordinary responsibilities for ordinary men, has proved a misfortune in many cases. Many a young man who would be a success as a carpenter would be a failure as the governor of a State. Mothers are quite apt to overestimate the genius of their children and push them into niches which they cannot fill.

*Matthew xxii.*

23   The same day came to him the Sadducees, which say that there is no resurrection and asked him,

24   Saying, Master, Moses said, If a man die, having no children, his brother shall marry his wife, and raise up seed unto his brother.

25   Now there were with us seven brethren: and the first,

when he had married a wife, deceased, and, having no issue, left his wife unto his brother:

26  Likewise the second also, and the third, unto the seventh.

27  And last of all the woman died also.

28  Therefore in the resurrection, whose wife shall she be of the seven? for they all had her.

29  Jesus answered and said unto them, Ye do err, not knowing the Scriptures, nor the power of God.

30  For in the resurrection they neither marry, nor are given in marriage, but are as the angels of God in heaven.

Jesus reminded the Sadducees that marriage was intended only for the present world, to replenish the earth and to repair the ravages which death continually makes among its inhabitants; but as in the future state there was to be no death, so no marriage. There the body even would be made spiritual; and all the employments and the pleasures pure and angelic. The marriage relation seems to have been a tangled problem in all ages. Scientists tell us that both the masculine and feminine elements were united in one person in the beginning, and will probably be reunited again for eternity.

E.C.S.

## Chapter II.

*Matthew xxv.*

1  Then shall the kingdom of heaven be likened unto ten virgins, which took their lamps, and went forth to meet the bridegroom.

2  And five of them were wise, and five were foolish

3  They that were foolish took their lamps, and took no oil with them:

4  But the wise took oil in their vessels with their lamps.

5  While the bridegroom tarried, they all slumbered and slept.

6  And at midnight there was a cry made, Behold, the bridegroom cometh; go ye out to meet him.

7  Then all those virgins arose, and trimmed their lamps.

8  And the foolish said unto the wise, Give us of your oil; for our lamps are gone out.

9   But the wise answered, saying, Not so, lest there be not enough for us and you: but go ye rather to them that sell, and buy for yourselves.

10   And while they went to buy, the bridegroom came; and they that were ready went in with him to the marriage: and the door was shut.

11   Afterward came also the other virgins, saying, Lord, Lord, open to us.

12   But he answered and said, Verily I say unto you, I know you not.

In this chapter we have the duty of self-development impressively and repeatedly urged in the form of parables, addressed alike to man and to woman. The sin of neglecting and of burying one's talents, capacities and powers, and the penalties which such a course involve, are here strikingly portrayed.

This parable is found among the Jewish records substantially the same as in our own Scriptures. Their weddings were generally celebrated at night; yet they usually began at the rising of the evening star; but in this case there was a more than ordinary delay. Adam Clarke in his commentaries explains this parable as referring chiefly to spiritual gifts and the religious life. He makes the Lord of Hosts the bridegroom, the judgment day the wedding feast, the foolish virgins the sinners whose hearts were cold and dead, devoid of all spiritual graces, and unfit to enter the kingdom of heaven. The wise virgins were the saints who were ready for translation, or for the bridal procession. They followed to the wedding feast; and when the chosen had entered *the door was shut.*

This strikes us as a strained interpretation of a very simple parable, which, considered in connection with the other parables, seems to apply much more closely to this life than to that which is to come, to the intellectual and the moral nature, and to the whole round of human duties. It fairly describes the two classes which help to make up society in general. The one who, like the foolish virgins, have never learned the first important duty of cultivating their own individual powers, using the talents given to them, and keeping their own lamps trimmed and burning. The idea of being a helpmeet to somebody else has been so sedulously drilled into most women that an individual life, aim, purpose and ambition are never taken into consideration. They oftimes do so much in other directions that they neglect the most vital duties to themselves.

We may find in this simple parable a lesson for the cultivation of courage and of self-reliance. These virgins are summoned to the discharge of an important duty at midnight, alone, in darkness, and in solitude. No chivalrous gentleman is there to run for oil and to trim their lamps. They must depend on themselves, unsupported, and pay the penalty of their own improvidence and unwisdom. Perhaps in that bridal procession might have been seen fathers, brothers, friends, for whose service and amusement the foolish virgins had wasted many precious hours, when they should have been trimming their own lamps and keeping oil in their vessels.

And now, with music, banners, lanterns, torches, guns and rockets fired at intervals, come the bride and the groom, with their attendants and friends numbering thousands, brilliant in jewels, gold and silver, magnificently mounted on richly caparisoned horses—for nothing can be more brilliant than were those nuptial solemnities of Eastern nations. As this spectacle, grand beyond description, sweeps by, imagine the foolish virgins pushed aside, in the shadow of some tall edifice, with dark, empty lamps in their hands, unnoticed and unknown. And while the castle walls resound with music and merriment, and the lights from every window stream out far into the darkness, no kind friends gather round them to sympathize in their humiliation, nor to cheer their loneliness. It matters little that women may be ignorant, dependent, unprepared for trial and for temptation. Alone they must meet the terrible emergencies of life, to be sustained and protected amid danger and death by their own courage, skill and self-reliance, or perish.

Woman's devotion to the comfort, the education, the success of men in general, and to their plans and projects, is in a great measure due to her self-abnegation and self-sacrifice having been so long and so sweetly lauded by poets, philosophers and priests as the acme of human goodness and glory.

Now, to my mind, there is nothing commendable in the action of young women who go about begging funds to educate young men for the ministry, while they and the majority of their sex are too poor to educate themselves, and if able, are still denied admittance into some of the leading institutions of learning throughout our land. It is not commendable for women to get up fairs and donation parties for churches in which the gifted of their sex may neither pray, preach, share in the offices and honors, nor have a voice in the business affairs, creeds and discipline, and from whose altars come forth Biblical interpretations in favor of woman's subjection.

It is not commendable for the women of this Republic to expend much enthusiasm on political parties as now organized, nor in national celebrations, for they have as yet no lot or part in the great experiment of self-government.

In their ignorance, women sacrifice themselves to educate the men of their households, and to make of themselves ladders by which their husbands, brothers and sons climb up into the kingdom of knowledge, while they themselves are shut out from all intellectual companionship, even with those they love best; such are indeed like the foolish virgins. They have not kept their own lamps trimmed and burning; they have no oil in their vessels, no resources in themselves; they bring no light to their households nor to the circle in which they move; and when the bridegroom cometh, when the philosopher, the scientist, the saint, the scholar, the great and the learned, all come together to celebrate the marriage feast of science and religion, the foolish virgins, though present, are practically shut out; for what know they of the grand themes which inspire each tongue and kindle every thought? Even the brothers and the sons whom they have educated, now rise to heights which they cannot reach, span distances which they cannot comprehend.

The solitude of ignorance, oh, who can measure its misery!

The wise virgins are they who keep their lamps trimmed, who burn oil in their vessels for their own use, who have improved every advantage for their education, secured a healthy, happy, complete development, and entered all the profitable avenues of labor, for self-support, so that when the opportunities and the responsibilities of life come, they may be fitted fully to enjoy the one and ably to discharge the other.

These are the women who to-day are close upon the heels of

man in the whole realm of thought, in art, in science, in literature and in government. With telescopic vision they explore the starry firmament, and bring back the history of the planetary world. With chart and compass they pilot ships across the mighty deep, and with skilful fingers send electric messages around the world. In galleries of art, the grandeur of nature and the greatness of humanity are immortalized by them on canvas, and by their inspired touch, dull blocks of marble are transformed into angels of light. In music they speak again the language of Mendelssohn, of Beethoven, of Chopin, of Schumann, and are worthy interpreters of their great souls. The poetry and the novels of the century are theirs; they, too, have touched the keynote of reform in religion, in politics and in social life. They fill the editors' and the professors' chairs, plead at the bar of justice, walk the wards of the hospital, and speak from the pulpit and the platform.

Such is the widespread preparation for the marriage feast of science and religion; such is the type of womanhood which the bridegroom of an enlightened public sentiment welcomes to-day; and such is the triumph of the wise virgins over the folly, the ignorance and the degradation of the past as in grand procession they enter the temple of knowledge, and *the door is no longer shut.*

## THE BOOK OF MARK.

*Mark iii.*

31 There came then his brethren and his mother, and, standing without, sent unto him,

32 And the multitude sat about him, and said unto him, Behold, thy mother and thy brethren seek for thee.

33 And he answered them, saying, Who is my mother, or my brethren?

34 And he looked round about and said. Behold my mother and my brethren!

35 For whosoever shall do the will of God, the same is my brother, and my sister, and mother.

Many of the same texts found in the Book of Matthew are repeated by the other Evangelists. It appears from the text that the earnestness of Jesus in teaching the people, made some of his friends, who did not believe in his mission, anxious. Even his mother feared to have him teach doctrines in opposition to the public sentiment of his day. His words of seeming disrespect to her, simply meant to imply that he had an important work to do, that his duties to humanity were more to him than the ties of natural affection.

Many of the ancient writers criticise Mary severely, for trying to exercise control over Jesus, assuming rightful authority over him. Theophylact taxes her with vainglory; Tertullian accuses her of ambition; St. Chrysostom of impiety and of disbelief; Whitby says it is plain that this is a protest against the idolatrous worship of Mary. She was generally admitted to be a woman of good character and worthy of all praise; but whatever she was, it ill becomes those who believe that she was the mother of God to criticise her as they would an ordinary mortal.

*Mark x.*

2  And the Pharisees came to him, and asked him, Is it lawful for a man to put away his wife? tempting him.

3  And he answered and said unto them, What did Moses command you?

4  And they said, Moses suffered to write a bill of divorcement, and to put her away.

5  And Jesus answered and said unto them, For the hardness of your heart he wrote you this precept.

6  But from the beginning of the creation God made them male and female.

7  For this cause shall a man leave his father and mother, and cleave to his wife;

8  And they twain shall be one flesh:

9  What therefore God hath joined together, let not man put asunder.

The question of marriage was a constant theme for discussion in the days of Moses and of Jesus, as in our own times. The Pharisees are still asking questions, not that they care for an answer on the highest plane of morality, but to entrap some one as opposed to the authorities of their times. Life with Jesus was too short and his mission too stern to parley with pettifoggers; so he gives to them a clear cut, unmistakable definition as to what marriage is: "Whoever puts away his wife save for the cause of unchastity, which violates the marriage covenant, commits adultery." Hence, under the Christian dispensation we must judge husband and wife by the same code of morals.

If this rule of the perfect equality of the sexes were observed in all social relations the marriage problem might be easily solved. But with one code of morals for man and another for woman, we are involved in all manner of complications. In England, for example, a woman may marry her husband's brother; but a man may not marry his wife's sister. They have had "a deceased wife's sister's bill" before Parliament for generations. Ever and anon they take it up, look at it with their opera glasses, air their grandfather's old platitudes over it, give a sickly smile at some well-worn witticism, or drop a tear at a pathetic whine from some bishop, then lay the bill reverently back in its sacred pigeon-hole for a period of rest.

The discussion in the United States is now in the form of a homogeneous divorce law in all the States of the Union, but this is not in woman's interest. What Canada was to the Southern slaves under the old régime, a State with liberal divorce laws is to fugitive wives. If a dozen learned judges should get together, as is proposed, to revise the divorce laws, they would make them more stringent in liberal States instead of more lax in conservative States. When such a commission is decided upon, one-half of the members should be women, as they have an equal interest in the marriage and divorce laws; and common justice demands that they should have an equal voice in their reconstruction. I do not think a homogeneous law desirable; though I should like to see New York and South Carolina liberalized, I should not like to see South Dakota and Indiana more conservative.

*Mark xii.*

41   And Jesus sat over against the treasury, and beheld how the people cast money into the treasury; and many that were rich cast in much.

42   And there came a certain poor widow, and she thew in two mites, which make a farthing.

43  And he called unto him his disciples, and saith unto them, Verily I say unto you, That this poor widow hath cast more in than all they which have cast into the treasury:

44  For all *they* did cast in of their abundance; but she of her want did cast in all that she had, *even* all her living.

The widow's gift no doubt might have represented more generosity than all beside, for the large donations of the rich were only a part of their superfluities, and bore a small proportion to the abundance which they still had, but she gave in reality of her necessities. The small contribution was of no special use in the treasury of the Church, but as an act of self-sacrifice it was of more real value in estimating character. Jesus with his intuition saw the motives of the giver, as well as the act.

This woman, belonging to an impoverished class, was trained to self-abnegation; but when women learn the higher duty of self-development, they will not so readily expend all their forces in serving others. Paul says that a husband who does not provide for his own household is worse than an infidel. So a woman, who spends all her time in churches, with priests, in charities, neglects to cultivate her own natural gifts, to make the most of herself as an individual in the scale of being, a responsible soul whose place no other can fill, is worse than an infidel. "Self-development is a higher duty than self-sacrifice," should be woman's motto henceforward.

E. C. S.

# THE BOOK OF JOHN.

Is it not astonishing that so little is in the New Testament concerning the mother of Christ? My own opinion is that she was an excellent woman, and the wife of Joseph, and that Joseph was the actual father of Christ. I think there can be no reasonable doubt that such was the opinion of the authors of the original Gospels. Upon any other hypothesis it is impossible to account for their having given the genealogy of Joseph to prove that Christ was of the blood of David. The idea that he was the Son of God, or in any way miraculously produced, was an afterthought, and is hardly entitled now to serious consideration. The Gospels were written so long after the death of Christ that very little was known of him, and substantially nothing of his parents. How is it that not one word is said about the death of Mary, not one word about the death of Joseph? How did it happen that Christ did not visit his mother after his resurrection? The first time he speaks to his mother is when he was twelve years old. His mother having told him that she and his father had been seeking him, he replied: "How is it that ye sought me? Wist ye not that I must be about my father's business?" The second time was at the marriage feast in Cana, when he said to her: "Woman, what have I to do with thee?" And the third time was at the cross, when "Jesus, seeing his mother standing by the disciple whom he loved, said to her: 'Woman, behold thy son;' and to the disciple: 'Behold thy mother.'" And this is all.

The best thing about the Catholic Church is the deification of Mary; and yet this is denounced by Protestantism as idolatry. There is something in the human heart that prompts man to tell his faults more freely to the mother than to the father. The cruelty of Jehovah is softened by the mercy of Mary.

Is it not strange that none of the disciples of Christ said anything about their parents—that we know absolutely nothing of them? Is there any evidence that they showed any particular respect even for the mother of Christ? Mary Magdalene is, in many respects, the tenderest and most loving character in the New Testament. According to the account, her love for Christ knew no abatement, no change—true even in the hopeless shadow of the cross. Neither did it die with his death. She waited at the sepulchre; she hastened in the early morning to his tomb; and yet the only comfort Christ gave to this true and loving soul lies in these strangely cold and heartless words: "Touch me not."          ANON.

# EPISTLES TO THE CORINTHIANS.

*I Corinthians vii.*

2   Let every man have his own wife, and let every woman have her own husband.

3   Let the husband render unto the wife due benevolence: and likewise also the wife unto the husband.

10   And unto the married I command, yet not I, but the Lord, Let not the wife depart from her husband:

11   But if she depart, let her remain unmarried, or be reconciled to her husband, and let not the husband put away his wife.

12   But to the rest speak I, not the Lord: If any brother hath a wife that believeth not: and she be pleased to dwell with him, let him not put her away.

13   And the woman which hath a husband that believeth not, and if he be pleased to dwell with her, let her not leave him.

14   For the unbelieving husband is sanctified by the wife, and the unbelieving wife is sanctified by the husband: else were your children unclean: but now are they holy.

16   For what knowest thou, O wife, whether thou shalt save thy husband? or how knowest thou, O man, whether thou shalt save thy wife?

The people appear to have been specially anxious to know what the Christian idea was in regard to the question of marriage. The Pythagoreans taught that marriage is unfavorable to high intellectual development. On the other hand, the Pharisees taught that it is sinful for a man to live unmarried beyond his twentieth year. The Apostles allowed that in many cases it might be wise for a man to live unmarried, as he could be more useful to others, provided that he were able to live with that entire chastity which the single life required.

The Apostle says that Christians should not marry unbelievers, but if either should change his or her opinions after, he would not advise separation, as they might sanctify each other. Scott thinks that the children are no more holy with one unbelieving parent, than when both are unbelieving; and he has not much faith in their sanctifying each other, except in a real change of faith. A union with an unbeliever would occasion grief and trouble, yet that ought patiently to be endured, for God might make use of the unbelieving wife or husband as an instrument in converting the other by affectionate and conscientious behavior; as this might not be the case, there is no reason to oppose the dissolution of the marriage.

There are no restrictions in the Scriptures on divorced persons marrying again, though many improvised by human laws are spoken of as in the Bible.                                   E. C. S.

In this chapter Paul laments that all men are not bachelors like himself; and in the second verse of that chapter he gives the only reason for which he was willing that men and women should marry. He advised all the unmarried and all widows to remain as he was. Paul sums up the whole matter, however, by telling those who have wives or husbands to stay with them—as necessary evils only to be tolerated; but sincerely regrets that anybody was ever married, and finally says that, "they that have wives should be as though they had none;" because, in his opinion, "he that is unmarried careth for the things that belong to the Lord, how he may please the Lord; but he that is married careth for the things that are of the world, how he please his wife."

"There is this difference, also," he tells us, "between a wife and a virgin. The unmarried woman careth for the things of the Lord, that she may be holy both in body and spirit; but she that is married careth for the things of the world, how she may please her husband." Of course, it is contended that these things have tended to the elevation of woman. The idea that it is better to love the Lord than to love your wife or husband is infinitely absurd. Nobody ever did love the Lord—nobody can—until he becomes acquainted with him.

Saint Paul also tells us that "man is the image and glory of God; but woman is the glory of man." And, for the purpose of sustaining this position, he says: "For the man is not of the woman, but the woman of the man; neither was the man created for the woman, but the woman for the man." Of course we can all see that man could have gotten along well enough without woman. And yet this is called "inspired!" and this Apostle Paul is supposed to have known more than all the people now upon the earth. No wonder Paul at last was constrained to say: "We are fools for Christ's sake."                               ANON.

*I Corinthians xi.*

   3   But I would have you know, that the head of every man is Christ; and the head of the woman is the man; and the head of Christ is God.

4  Every man praying or prophesying, having his head covered, dishonoureth his head.

5  But every woman that prayeth or prophesieth with her head uncovered dishonoureth her head.

7  For a man indeed ought not to cover his head, forasmuch as he is the image and glory of God: but the woman is the glory of the man.

8  For the man is not of the woman; but the woman of the man.

9  Neither was the man created for the woman; but the woman for the man.

10  For this cause ought the woman to have power on her head because of the angels.

11  Nevertheless neither is the man without the woman, neither the woman without the man, in the Lord.

13  Judge in yourselves: is it comely that a woman pray unto God uncovered?

14  Doth not even nature itself teach you, that, if a man have long hair, it is a shame unto him?

15  But if a woman have long hair, it is a glory to her: for her hair is given her for a covering.

According to the custom of those days a veil on the head was a token of respect to superiors; hence for a woman to lay aside her veil was to affect authority over the man. The shaving of the head was a disgraceful punishment inflicted on women of bad repute; it not only deprived them of a great beauty, but also of the badge of virtue and honor.

Though these directions appear to be very frivolous, even for those times, they are much more so for our stage of civilization. Yet the same customs prevail in our day and are enforced by the Church, as of vital consequence; their non-observance so irreligious that it would exclude a woman from the church. It is not a mere social fashion that allows men to sit in church with their heads uncovered and women with theirs covered, but a requirement of canon law of vital significance, showing the superiority, the authority, the headship of man, and the humility and the subservience of woman. The aristocracy in social life requires the same badge of respect of all female servants. In Europe they uniformly wear caps, and in many families in America, though under protest after learning its significance.

It is certainly high time that educated women in a Republic should rebel against a custom based on the supposition of their heaven-ordained subjection. Jesus is always represented as having long, curling hair, and so is the Trinity. Imagine a painting of these Gods all with clipped hair. Flowing robes and beautiful hair add greatly to the beauty and dignity of their pictures.     E. C. S.

The injunctions of St. Paul have had such a decided influence in fixing the legal status of women, that it is worth our while to consider their source. In dealing with this question we must never forget that the majority of the writings of the New Testament were not really written or published by those whose names they bear. Ancient writers considered it quite permissible for a man to put out letters under the name of another, and thus to bring his own ideas before the world under the protection of an honored sponsor. It is not usually claimed that St. Paul was the originator of the great religious movement called Christianity; but there is a strong belief that he was Divinely inspired. His inward persuasions, and especially his visions, appeared as a gift or endowment which had the force of inspiration; therefore, his mandates concerning women have a strong hold upon the popular mind; and when opponents to the equality of the sexes are put to bay, they glibly quote his injunctions.

We congratulate ourselves that we may shift some of these Biblical arguments that have such a sinister effect from their firm foundation. He who claims to give a message must satisfy us that he has himself received such a message. The origin of the command that women should cover their heads is found in an old Jewish or Hebrew legend which appears in literature for the first time in Genesis vi. There we are told that the sons of God, that is, the angels, took to wives the daughters of men, and begat the giants and the heroes who were instrumental in bringing about the flood. The Rabbins held that the way in which the angels got possession of women was by laying hold of their hair; they accordingly warned women to cover their heads in public so that the angels might not get possession of them.

Paul merely repeats this warning, which he must often have

heard at the feet of Gamaliel, who was at that time prince or president of the Sanhedrim, telling women to have a power (that is, protection) on their heads because of the angels: "For this cause ought the woman to have power on her head because of the angels." Thus the command had its origin in an absurd old myth. This legend will be found fully treated in a German pamphlet, "Die Paulinische Angolologie und Daemonologie." Otto Everling, Gottingen, 1883.

If the command to keep silence in the churches has no higher origin than that to keep covered in public, should so much weight be given it, or should it be so often quoted as having Divine sanction? L. S.

*I Corinthians xiv.*

34 Let your women keep silence in the churches: for it is not permitted unto them to speak; but they are commanded to be under obedience, as also saith the law.

35 And if they will learn anything, let them ask their husbands at home; for it is a shame for woman to speak in the church.

The church at Corinth was peculiarly given to diversion and to disputation; and women were apt to join in and to ask many troublesome questions; hence they were advised to consult their husbands at home. The Apostle took it for granted that all men were wise enough to give to women the necessary information on all subjects. Others, again, advise wives never to discuss knotty points with their husbands; for if they should chance to differ from each other, that fact might give rise to much domestic infelicity. There is such a wide difference of opinion on this point among wise men, that perhaps it would be as safe to leave women to be guided by their own unassisted common sense. E. C. S.

(ELIZABETH CADY STANTON, NEW YORK: 1895, 1898; PP. 14–18, 20–22, 26–27, 31–33, 116–126, 129–131, 143–144, 155–159)

# The Aquarian Gospel of
# Jesus the Christ

Born in Bellville, Ohio, Levi H. Dowling (1844–1911) spent the early years of his life as a Church of Christ minister and traveling Sunday school evangelist. By the 1880s he was experimenting with the healing art of homeopathy and becoming involved with circles of Spiritualists, Theosophists, and New Thought advocates that he met in his Midwestern travels. Yet his break from mainstream Protestantism did not come until 1903, when he and his wife, Eva, moved to Los Angeles and he took on the the mantle of a messenger who would reveal to twentieth-century audiences the real mission of Jesus Christ for a new spiritual era, what he called the "age of Aquarius." In 1907, Dowling published the *Aquarian Gospel,* a volume he described as a transcription from the grand Cosmic recording library or "Akashic Record," a Sanskrit term for "sky" made popular by Theosophists of the day.

Presented as an account of Jesus' formative years, the *Aquarian Gospel* presents Jesus as a human being who became a spiritual adept through education in religious traditions around the world. Dowling's work, as with many Theosophists and New Thought adherents of the time, affirmed that the "true religion" was composed of many truths from many traditions, and that the world was now entering a particularly fruitful cosmic era in which human beings would be able to better comprehend Jesus' teachings. Dowling played a special role as the messenger or translator of this new dispensation. Elements of Dowling's ideas remained popular among his followers in the Aquarian Commonwealth, an organization that combined Theosophy, New Thought, Spiritualism, and Christian teachings. Although he died suddenly in 1911, his notions of a Cosmic Christ lived on in the later movements of Edgar Cayce, Guy Ballard, and Elizabeth Clare Prophet. The *Aquarian Gospel* also had distinct influences on the early Unification Church of Reverend Sun Myung-Moon.

These excerpts spring from Dowling's belief that Jesus traveled to India and describe his studies of Hinduism and Buddhism. Most notable, perhaps, is that both traditions are rendered as philosophical precepts, or intellectual principles, rather than as spiritual practices. Jesus also seems to be teaching as much as he is learning, a feature that may reflect the author's desire to represent the adept's spiritual development over time; alternately, it may suggest that the otherwise ecumenical Dowling thought Christian teachings superior in some respects to other religious paths. In either case, the hostile reaction of local peoples to Jesus indicates that the world was not yet ready to receive his message. Dowling's conviction, though, was that Aquarian adherents would have reached a spiritual stage that would make them naturally receptive to these teachings.

# The Aquarian Gospel of Jesus the Christ

## SECTION VI.

### Vau.

*Life and Works of Jesus in India.*

### Chapter 21.

*Ravanna sees Jesus in the temple and is captivated. Hillel tells him about the boy. Ravanna finds Jesus in Nazareth and gives a feast in his honor. Ravanna becomes patron of Jesus, and takes him to India to study the Brahmic religion.*

A royal prince of India, Ravanna of Orissa in the south, was at the Jewish feast.

2   Ravanna was a man of wealth; and he was just, and with a band of Brahmic priests sought wisdom in the West.

3   When Jesus stood among the Jewish priests and read and spoke, Ravanna heard and was amazed.

4   And when he asked who Jesus was, from whence he came and what he was, chief Hillel said,

5   We call this child the Day Star from on high, for he has come to bring to men a light, the light of life; to lighten up the way of men and to redeem his people, Israel.

6   And Hillel told Ravanna all about the child; about the prophecies concerning him; about the wonders of the night when he was born; about the visit of the magian priests;

7   About the way in which he was protected from the wrath of evil men; about his flight to Egypt-land, and how he then was serving with his father as a carpenter in Nazareth.

8   Ravanna was entranced, and asked to know the way to Nazareth, that he might go and honor such a one as son of God.

9   And with his gorgeous train he journeyed on the way and came to Nazareth of Galilee.

10   He found the object of his search engaged in building dwellings for the sons of men.

11   And when he first saw Jesus he was climbing up a twelve-step ladder, and he carried in his hands a compass, square and ax.

12   Ravanna said, All hail, most favored son of heaven!

13   And at the inn Ravanna made a feast for all the people of the town; and Jesus and his parents were the honored guests.

14   For certain days Ravanna was a guest in Joseph's home on Marmion Way; he sought to learn the secret of the wisdom of the son; but it was all too great for him.

15   And then he asked that he might be the patron of the child; might take him to the East where he could learn the wisdom of the Brahms.

16   And Jesus longed to go that he might learn: and after many days his parents gave consent.

17   Then, with proud heart, Ravanna with his train, began the journey toward the rising sun; and after many days they crossed the Sind, and reached the province of Orissa, and the palace of the prince.

18   The Brahmic priests were glad to welcome home the prince; with favor they received the Jewish boy.

19   And Jesus was accepted as a pupil in the temple Jagannath; and here he learned the Vedas and the Manic laws.

20   The Brahmic masters wondered at the clear conceptions of the child, and often were amazed when he explained to them the meaning of the laws.

## Chapter 22.

*The friendship of Jesus and Lamaas. Jesus explains to Lamaas the meaning of truth, man, power, understanding, wisdom, salvation and faith.*

Among the priests of Jagannath was one who loved the Jewish boy. Lamaas Bramas was the name by which the priest was known.

2   One day as Jesus and Lamaas walked alone in plaza Jagannath, Lamaas said, My Jewish master, what is truth?

3   And Jesus said, Truth is the only thing that changes not.

4   In all the world there are two things; the one is truth; the other falsehood is; and truth is that which is, and falsehood that which seems to be.

5   Now truth is aught, and has no cause, and yet it is the cause of everything.

6   Falsehood is naught, and yet it is the manifest of aught.

7   Whatever has been made will be unmade; that which begins must end.

8   All things that can be seen by human eyes are manifests of aught, are naught, and so must pass away.

9   The things we see are but reflexes just appearing, while the ethers vibrate so and so, and when conditions change they disappear.

10   The Holy Breath is truth; is that which was, and is, and evermore shall be; it cannot change nor pass away.

11   Lamaas said, You answer well; now, what is man?

12   And Jesus said, Man is the truth and falsehood strangely mixed.

13   Man is the Breath made flesh; so truth and falsehood are conjoined in him; and then they strive, and naught goes down and man as truth abides.

14   Again Lamaas asked, What do you say of power?

15   And Jesus said, It is a manifest; is the result of force; it is but naught; it is illusion, nothing more. Force changes not, but power changes as the ethers change.

16   Force is the will of God and is omnipotent, and power is that will in manifest, directed by the Breath.

17   There is a power in the winds, a power in the waves, a power in the lightning's stroke, a power in the human arm, a power in the eye.

18   The ethers cause these powers to be, and thought of Elohim, of angel, man, or other thinking thing, directs the force; when it has done its work the power is no more.

19   Again Lamaas asked, Of understanding what have you to say?

20   And Jesus said, It is the rock on which man builds him-

self; it is the gnosis of the aught and of the naught, of falsehood and of truth.

21 It is the knowledge of the lower self; the sensing of the powers of man himself.

22 Again Lamaas asked, Of wisdom what have you to say?

23 And Jesus said, It is the consciousness that man is aught; that God and man are one;

24 That naught is naught; that power is but illusion; that heaven and earth and hell are not above, around, below, but in; which in the light of aught becomes the naught, and God is all.

25 Lamaas asked, Pray, what is faith?

26 And Jesus said, Faith is the surety of the omnipotence of God and man; the certainty that man will reach deific life.

27 Salvation is a ladder reaching from the heart of man to heart of God.

28 It has three steps; Belief is first, and this is what man thinks, perhaps, is truth.

29 And faith is next, and this is what man knows is truth.

30 Fruition is the last, and this is man himself, the truth.

31 Belief is lost in faith; and in fruition faith is lost; and man is saved when he has reached deific life; when he and God are one.

## Chapter 23.

*Jesus and Lamaas among the sudras and visyas. In Benares. Jesus becomes a pupil of Udraka. The lessons of Udraka.*

Now, Jesus with his friend Lamaas went through all the regions of Orissa, and the valley of the Ganges, seeking wisdom from the sudras and the visyas and the masters.

2 Benares of the Ganges was a city rich in culture and in learning; here the two rabbonis tarried many days.

3 And Jesus sought to learn the Hindu art of healing, and became the pupil of Udraka, greatest of the Hindu healers.

4 Udraka taught the uses of the waters, plants and earths; of heat and cold; sunshine and shade; of light and dark.

5 He said, The laws of nature are the laws of health, and he who lives according to these laws is never sick.

6 Transgression of these laws is sin, and he who sins is sick.

7   He who obeys the laws, maintains an equilibrium in all his parts, and thus insures true harmony; and harmony is health, while discord is disease.

8   That which produces harmony in all the parts of man is medicine, insuring health.

9   The body is a harpsichord, and when its strings are too relaxed, or are too tense, the instrument is out of tune, the man is sick.

10   Now, everything in nature has been made to meet the wants of man; so everything is found in medical arcanes.

11   And when the harpsichord of man is out of tune the vast expanse of nature may be searched for remedy; there is a cure for every ailment of the flesh.

12   Of course the will of man is remedy supreme; and by the vigorous exercise of will, man may make tense a chord that is relaxed, or may relax one that is too tense, and thus may heal himself.

13   When man has reached the place where he has faith in God, in nature and himself, he knows the Word of power; his word is balm for every wound, is cure for all the ills of life.

14   The healer is the man who can inspire faith. The tongue may speak to human ears, but souls are reached by souls that speak to souls.

15   He is the forceful man whose soul is large, and who can enter into souls, inspiring hope in those who have no hope, and faith in those who have no faith in God, in nature, nor in man.

16   There is no universal balm for those who tread the common walks of life.

17   A thousand things produce in harmony and make men sick; a thousand things may tune the harpsichord, and make men well.

18   That which is medicine for one is poison for another one; so one is healed by what would kill another one.

19   An herb may heal the one; a drink of water may restore another one; a mountain breeze may bring to life one seeming past all help;

20   A coal of fire, or bit of earth, may cure another one; and one may wash in certain streams, or pools, and be made whole.

21   The virtue from the hand or breath may heal a thousand

more; but love is queen. Thought, reinforced by love, is God's great sovereign balm.

22   But many of the broken chords in life, and discords that so vex the soul, are caused by evil spirits of the air that men see not; that lead men on through ignorance to break the laws of nature and of God.

23   These powers act like demons, and they speak; they rend the man; they drive him to despair.

24   But he who is a healer, true, is master of the soul, and can, by force of will, control these evil ones.

25   Some spirits of the air are master spirits and are strong, too strong for human power alone; but man has helpers in the higher realms that may be importuned, and they will help to drive the demons out.

26   Of what this great physician said, this is the sum. And Jesus bowed his head in recognition of the wisdom of this master soul, and went his way.

## Chapter 24.

*The Brahmic doctrine of castes. Jesus repudiates it and teaches human equality. The priests are offended and drive him from the temple. He abides with the sudras and teaches them.*

Four years the Jewish boy abode in temple Jagannath.

2   One day he sat among the priests and said to them, Pray, tell me all about your views of castes; why do you say that all men are not equal in the sight of God?

3   A master of their laws stood forth and said, The Holy One whom we call Brahm, made men to suit himself, and men should not complain.

4   In the beginning days of human life Brahm spoke, and four men stood before his face.

5   Now, from the mouth of Parabrahm the first man came; and he was white, was like the Brahm himself; a brahman he was called.

6   And he was high and lifted up; above all want he stood; he had no need of toil.

7   And he was called the priest of Brahm, the holy one to act for Brahm in all affairs of earth.

8   The second man was red, and from the hand of Parabrahm he came; and he was called shatriya.

9   And he was made to be the king, the ruler and the warrior, whose highest ordained duty was, protection of the priest.

10   And from the inner parts of Parabrahm the third man came; and he was called a visya.

11   He was a yellow man, and his it was to till the soil, and keep the flocks and herds.

12   And from the feet of Parabrahm the fourth man came; and he was black; and he was called the sudras, one of low estate.

13   The sudras is the servant of the race of men; he has no rights that others need respect; he may not hear the Vedas read, and it means death to him to look into the face of priest, or king, and naught but death can free him from his state of servitude.

14   And Jesus said, Then Parabrahm is not a God of justice and of right; for with his own strong hand he has exalted one and brought another low.

15   And Jesus said no more to them, but looking up to heaven he said,

16   My Father-God, who was, and is, and ever more shall be; who holds within thy hands the scales of justice and of right;

17   Who in the boundlessness of love has made all men to equal be. The white, the black, the yellow and the red can look up in thy face and say, Our Father-God.

18   Thou Father of the human race, I praise thy name.

19   And all the priests were angered by the words which Jesus spoke; they rushed upon him, seized him, and would have done him harm.

20   But then Lamaas raised his hand and said, You priests of Brahm, beware! you know not what you do; wait till you know the God this youth adores.

21   I have beheld this boy at prayer when light above the light of sun surrounded him, Beware! his God may be more powerful than Brahm.

22   If Jesus speaks the truth, if he is right, you cannot force him to desist; if he is wrong and you are right, his words will come to naught, for right is might, and in the end it will prevail.

23    And then the priests refrained from doing Jesus harm; but one spoke out and said,

24    Within this holy place has not this reckless youth done violence to Parabrahm? The law is plain; it says, He who reviles the name of Brahm shall die.

25    Lamaas plead for Jesus' life; and then the priests just seized a scourge of cords and drove him from the place.

26    And Jesus went his way and found a shelter with the black and yellow men, the servants and the tillers of the soil.

27    To them he first made known the gospel of equality; he told them of the Brotherhood of Man, the Fatherhood of God.

28    The common people heard him with delight, and learned to pray, Our Father-God who art in heaven.

## Chapter 25.

*Jesus teaches the sudras and farmers. Relates a parable of a nobleman and his unjust sons. Makes known the possibilities of all men.*

When Jesus saw the sudras and the farmers in such multitudes draw near to hear his words, he spoke a parable to them; he said:

2    A nobleman possessed a great estate; he had four sons, and he would have them all grow strong by standing forth and making use of all the talents they possessed.

3    And so he gave to each a share of his great wealth, and bade them go their way.

4    The eldest son was full of self; he was ambitious, shrewd and quick of thought.

5    He said within himself, I am the oldest son, and these, my brothers, must be servants at my feet,

6    And then he called his brothers forth; and one he made a puppet king; gave him a sword and charged him to defend the whole estate.

7    To one he gave the use of lands and flowing wells, and flocks and herds, and bade him till the soil, and tend the flocks and herds and bring to him the choicest of his gains.

8    And to the other one he said, You are the youngest son; the

broad estate has been assigned; you have no part nor lot in anything that is.

9    And then he took a chain and bound his brother to a naked rock upon a desert plain, and said to him,

10    You have been born a slave; you have no rights, and you must be contented with your lot, for there is no release for you until you die and go from hence.

11    Now, after certain years the day of reckoning came; the nobleman called up his sons to render their accounts.

12    And when he knew that one, his eldest son, had seized the whole estate and made his brothers slaves,

13    He seized him, tore his priestly robes away and put him in a prison cell, where he was forced to stay until he had atoned for all the wrongs that he had done.

14    And then, as though they were but toys, he threw in air the throne and armor of the puppet king; he broke his sword, and put him in a prison cell.

15    And then he called his farmer son and asked him why he had not rescued from his galling chains his brother on the desert sands.

16    And when the son made answer not, the father took unto himself the flocks and herds, the fields and flowing wells,

17    And sent his farmer son to live out on the desert sands, until he had atoned for all the wrongs that he had done.

18    And then the father went and found his youngest son in cruel chains; with his own hands he broke the chains and bade his son to go in peace.

19    Now, when the sons had all paid up their debts they came again and stood before the bar of right.

20    They all had learned their lessons, learned them well; and then the father once again divided the estate.

21    He gave to each an equal share, and bade them recognize the law of equity and right, and live in peace.

22    And one, a sudras, spoke and said, May we who are but slaves, who are cut down like beasts to satisfy the whims of priests— may we have hope that one will come to break our chains and set us free?

23    And Jesus said, The Holy One has said, that all his children shall be free; and every soul is child of God.

24  The sudras shall be free as priest; the farmer shall walk hand in hand with king; for all the world will own the brotherhood of man.

25  O men, arise! be conscious of your powers, for he who wills need not remain a slave.

26  Just live as you would have your brother live; unfold each day as does the flower; for earth is yours, and heaven is yours, and God will bring you to your own.

27  And all the people cried, Show us the way that like the flower we may unfold and come unto our own.

## Chapter 26.

*Jesus at Katak. The car of Jagannath. Jesus reveals to the people the emptiness of Brahmic rites, and how to see God in man. Teaches them the divine law of sacrifice.*

In all the cities of Orissa Jesus taught. At Katak, by the river side, he taught, and thousands of the people followed him.

2  One day a car of Jagannath was hauled along by scores of frenzied men, and Jesus said,

3  Behold, a form without a spirit passes by; a body with no soul; a temple with no altar fires.

4  This car of Krishna is an empty thing, for Krishna is not there.

5  This car is but an idol of a people drunk on wine of carnal things.

6  God lives not in the noise of tongues; there is no way to him from any idol shrine.

7  God's meeting place with man is in the heart, and in a still small voice he speaks; and he who hears is still.

8  And all the people said, Teach us to know the Holy One who speaks within the heart, God of the still small voice.

9  And Jesus said, The Holy Breath cannot be seen with mortal eyes; nor can men see the Spirits of the Holy One;

10  But in their image man was made, and he who looks into the face of man, looks at the image of the God who speaks within.

11  And when man honors man he honors God, and what man does for man, he does for God.

12   And you must bear in mind that when man harms in thought, or word or deed another man, he does a wrong to God.

13   If you would serve the God who speaks within the heart, just serve your near of kin, and those that are no kin, the stranger at your gates, the foe who seeks to do you harm;

14   Assist the poor, and help the weak; do harm to none, and covet not what is not yours;

15   Then, with your tongue the Holy One will speak; and he will smile behind your tears, will light your countenance with joy, and fill your hearts with peace.

16   And then the people asked, To whom shall we bring gifts? Where shall we offer sacrifice?

17   And Jesus said, Our Father-God asks not for needless waste of plant, of grain, of dove, of lamb.

18   That which you burn on any shrine you throw away. No blessings can attend the one who takes the food from hungry mouths to be destroyed by fire.

19   When you would offer sacrifice unto our God, just take your gift of grain, or meat and lay it on the table of the poor.

20   From it an incense will arise to heaven, which will return to you with blessedness.

21   Tear down your idols; they can hear you not; turn all your sacrificial altars into fuel for the flames.

22   Make human hearts your altars, and burn your sacrifices with the fire of love.

23   And all the people were entranced, and would have worshipped Jesus as a God; but Jesus said,

24   I am your brother man just come to show the way to God; you shall not worship man; praise God, the Holy One.

## Chapter 27.

*Jesus attends a feast in Behar. Preaches a revolutionary sermon on human equality. Relates the parable of the broken blades.*

The fame of Jesus as a teacher spread through all the land, and people came from near and far to hear his words of truth.

2　At Behar, on the sacred river of the Brahms, he taught for many days.

3　And Ach, a wealthy man of Behar, made a feast in honor of his guest, and he invited every one to come.

4　And many came; among them thieves, extortioners, and courtesans. And Jesus sat with them and taught; but they who followed him were much aggrieved because he sat with thieves and courtesans.

5　And they upbraided him; they said, Rabboni, master of the wise, this day will be an evil day for you.

6　The news will spread that you consort with courtesans and thieves, and men will shun you as they shun an asp.

7　And Jesus answered them and said, A master never screens himself for sake of reputation or of fame.

8　These are but worthless baubles of the day; they rise and sink, like empty bottles on a stream; they are illusions and will pass away;

9　They are the indices to what the thoughtless think; they are the noise that people make; and shallow men judge merit by the noise.

10　God and all master men judge men by what they are and not by what they seem to be; not by their reputation and their fame.

11　These courtesans and thieves are children of my Father-God; their souls are just as precious in his sight as yours, or of the Brahmic priests.

12　And they are working out the same life sums that you, who pride yourselves on your respectability and moral worth, are working out.

13　And some of them have solved much harder sums than you have solved, you men who look at them with scorn.

14　Yes, they are sinners, and confess their guilt, while you are guilty, but are shrewd enough to have a polished coat to cover up your guilt.

15　Suppose you men who scorn these courtesans, these drunkards and these thieves, who know that you are pure in heart and life, that you are better far than they, stand forth that men may know just who you are.

16   The sin lies in the wish, in the desire, not in the act.

17   You covet other people's wealth; you look at charming forms, and deep within your hearts you lust for them.

18   Deceit you practice every day, and wish for gold, for honor and for fame, just for your selfish selves.

19   The man who covets is a thief, and she who lusts is courtesan. You who are none of these speak out.

20   Nobody spoke; the accusers held their peace.

21   And Jesus said, The proof this day is all against those who have accused.

22   The pure in heart do not accuse. The vile in heart who want to cover up their guilt with holy smoke of piety are ever loathing drunkard, thief and courtesan.

23   This loathing and this scorn is mockery, for if the tinseled coat of reputation could be torn away, the loud professor would be found to revel in his lust, deceit, and many forms of secret sin.

24   The man who spends his time in pulling other people's weeds can have no time to pull his own, and all the choicest flowers of life will soon be choked and die, and nothing will remain but darnel, thistles, burs.

25   And Jesus spoke a parable: he said, Behold, a farmer had great fields of ripened grain, and when he looked he saw that blades of many stalks of wheat were bent and broken down.

26   And when he sent his reapers forth he said, We will not save the stalks of wheat that have the broken blades.

27   Go forth and cut and burn the stalks with broken blades.

28   And after many days he went to measure up his grain, but not a kernel could he find.

29   And then he called the harvesters and said to them, Where is my grain?

30   They answered him and said, We did according to your word; we gathered up and burned the stalks with broken blades, and not a stalk was left to carry to the barn.

31   And Jesus said, If God saves only those who have no broken blades, who have been perfect in his sight, who will be saved?

32   And the accusers hung their heads in shame; and Jesus went his way.

# Chapter 28.

*Udraka gives a feast in Jesus' honor. Jesus speaks on the unity of God and the brotherhood of life. Criticises the priesthood. Becomes the guest of a farmer.*

Benares is the sacred city of the Brahms, and in Benares Jesus taught; Udraka was his host.

2    Udraka made a feast in honor of his guest, and many high born Hindu priests and scribes were there.

3    And Jesus said to them, With much delight I speak to you concerning life—the brotherhood of life.

4    The universal God is one, yet he is more than one; all things are God; all things are one.

5    By the sweet breaths of God all life is bound in one; so if you touch a fiber of a living thing you send a thrill from center to the outer bounds of life.

6    And when you crush beneath your foot the meanest worm, you shake the throne of God, and cause the sword of right to tremble in its sheath.

7    The bird sings out its song for men, and men vibrate in unison to help it sing.

8    The ant constructs her home, the bee its sheltering comb, the spider weaves her web, and flowers breathe to them a spirit in their sweet perfumes that gives them strength to toil.

9    Now, men and birds and beasts and creeping things are deities, made flesh; and how dare men kill anything?

10    'Tis cruelty that makes the world awry. When men have learned that when they harm a living thing they harm themselves, they surely will not kill, nor cause a thing that God has made to suffer pain.

11    A lawyer said, I pray you, Jesus, tell who is this God you speak about; where are his priests, his temples and his shrines?

12    And Jesus said, The God I speak about is every where; he cannot be compassed with walls, nor hedged about with bounds of any kind.

13    All people worship God, the One; but all the people see him not alike.

14    This universal God is wisdom, will and love.

15   All men see not the Triune God. One sees him as the God of might; another as the God of thought; another as the God of love.

16   A man's ideal is his God, and so, as man unfolds, his God unfolds. Man's God today, tomorrow is not God.

17   The nations of the earth see God from different points of view, and so he does not seem the same to every one.

18   Man names the part of God he sees, and this to him is all of God; and every nation sees a part of God, and every nation has a name for God.

19   You Brahmans call him Parabrahm; in Egypt he is Thoth; and Zeus is his name in Greece; Jehovah is his Hebrew name; but everywhere he is the causeless Cause, the rootless Root from which all things have grown.

20   When men become afraid of God, and take him for a foe, they dress up other men in fancy garbs and call them priests,

21   And charge them to restrain the wrath of God by prayers; and when they fail to win his favor by their prayers, to buy him off with sacrifice of animal, or bird,

22   When man sees God as one with him, as Father-God, he needs no middle man, no priest to intercede;

23   He goes straight up to him and says, My Father-God! and then he lays his hand in God's own hand, and all is well.

24   And this is God. You are, each one, a priest, just for yourself; and sacrifice of blood God does not want.

25   Just give your life in sacrificial service to the all of life, and God is pleased.

26   When Jesus had thus said he stood aside; the people were amazed, but strove among themselves.

27   Some said, He is inspired by Holy Brahm; and others said, He is insane; and others said, He is obsessed; he speaks as devils speak.

28   But Jesus tarried not. Among the guests was one, a tiller of the soil, a generous soul, a seeker after truth, who loved the words that Jesus spoke; and Jesus went with him, and in his home abode.

## Chapter 29.

*Ajainin, a priest from Lahore, comes to Benares to see Jesus, and abides in the temple. Jesus refuses an invitation to visit*

*the temple. Ajainin visits him at night in the farmer's home, and accepts his philosophy.*

Among Benares' temple priests was one, a guest, Ajainin, from Lahore.

2   By merchantmen Ajainin heard about the Jewish boy, about his words of wisdom, and he girt himself and journeyed from Lahore that he might see the boy, and hear him speak.

3   The Brahmic priests did not accept the truth that Jesus brought, and they were angered much by what he said at the Udraka feast.

4   But they had never seen the boy, and they desired much to hear him speak, and they invited him to be a temple guest.

5   But Jesus said to them, The light is most abundant, and it shines for all; if you would see the light come to the light.

6   If you would hear the message that the Holy One has given me to give to men, come unto me.

7   Now, when the priests were told what Jesus said they were enraged.

8   Ajainin did not share their wrath, and he sent forth another messenger with costly gifts to Jesus at the farmer's home; he sent this message with the gifts:

9   I pray you, master, listen to my words; The Brahmic law forbids that any priest shall go into the home of any one of low estate; but you can come to us;

10   And I am sure these priests will gladly hear you speak. I pray that you will come and dine with us this day.

11   And Jesus said, The Holy One regards all men alike; the dwelling of my host is good enough for any council of the sons of men.

12   If pride of caste keeps you away, you are not worthy of the light. My Father-God does not regard the laws of man.

13   Your presents I return; you cannot buy the knowledge of the Lord with gold, or precious gifts.

14   These words of Jesus angered more and more the priests, and they began to plot and plan how they might drive him from the land.

15   Ajainin did not join with them in plot and plan; he left the temple in the night, and sought the home where Jesus dwelt.

16    And Jesus said, There is no night where shines the sun; I have no secret messages to give; in light all secrets are revealed.

17    Ajainin said, I came from far-away Lahore, that I might learn about this ancient wisdom, and this kingdom of the Holy One of which you speak.

18    Where is the kingdom? where the king? Who are the subjects? what its laws?

19    And Jesus said, This kingdom is not far away, but man with mortal eyes can see it not; it is within the heart.

20    You need not seek the king in earth, or sea, or sky; he is not there, and yet is everywhere. He is the Christ of God; is universal love.

21    The gate of this dominion is not high, and he who enters it must fall down on his knees. It is not wide, and none can carry carnal bundles through.

22    The lower self must be transmuted into spirit-self; the body must be washed in living streams of purity.

23    Ajainin asked, Can I become a subject of this king?

24    And Jesus said, You are yourself a king, and you may enter through the gate and be a subject of the King of kings.

25    But you must lay aside your priestly robes; must cease to serve the Holy One for gold; must give your life, and all you have, in willing service to the sons of men.

26    And Jesus said no more; Ajainin went his way; and while he could not comprehend the truth that Jesus spoke, he saw what he had never seen before.

27    The realm of faith he never had explored; but in his heart the seeds of faith and universal brotherhood had found good soil.

28    And as he journeyed to his home he seemed to sleep, to pass through darkest night, and when he woke the Sun of Righteousness had arisen; he had found the king.

29    Now, in Benares Jesus tarried many days and taught.

[. . .]

# Chapter 31.

*Brahmic priests are enraged because of Jesus' teaching and resolve to drive him from India. Lamaas pleads for him. Priests*

*employ a murderer to kill him. Lamaas warns him and he
flees to Nepel.*

The words and works of Jesus caused unrest through all the land.

2   The common people were his friends, believed in him, and
followed him in throngs.

3   The priests and rulers were afraid of him; his very name
sent terror to their hearts.

4   He preached the brotherhood of life, the righteousness of
equal rights, and taught the uselessness of priests, and sacrificial
rites.

5   He shook the very sand on which the Brahmic system stood;
he made the Brahmic idols seem so small, and sacrifice so fraught
with sin, that shrines and wheels of prayer were all forgot.

6   The priests declared that if this Hebrew boy should tarry
longer in the land a revolution would occur; the common people
would arise and kill the priests, and tear the temples down.

7   And so they sent a call abroad, and priests from every province came. Benares was on fire with Brahmic zeal.

8   Lamaas from the temple Jagannath, who knew the inner
life of Jesus well, was in their midst, and heard the rantings of the
priests,

9   And he stood forth and said, My brother priests, take heed,
be careful what you do; this is a record-making day.

10   The world is looking on; the very life of Brahmic thought
is now on trial.

11   If we are reason-blind; if prejudice be king today; if we
resort to beastly force, and dye our hands in blood that may, in
sight of Brahm, be innocent and pure,

12   His vengeance may fall down on us; the very rock on
which we stand may burst beneath our feet; and our beloved
priesthood, and our laws and shrines will go into decay.

13   But they would let him speak no more. The wrathful
priests rushed up and beat him, spit upon him, called him traitor,
threw him, bleeding, to the street.

14   And then confusion reigned; the priests became a mob;
the sight of human blood led on to fiendish acts, and called for more.

15   The rulers, fearing war, sought Jesus, and they found him
calmly teaching in the market-place.

16   They urged him to depart, that he might save his life; but he refused to go.

17   And then the priests sought cause for his arrest; but he had done no crime.

18   And then false charges were preferred; but when the soldiers went to bring him to the judgment hall they were afraid, because the people stood in his defense.

19   The priests were baffled, and they resolved to take his life by stealth.

20   They found a man who was a murderer by trade, and sent him out by night to slay the object of their wrath.

21   Lamaas heard about their plotting and their plans, and sent a messenger to warn his friend; and Jesus hastened to depart.

22   By night he left Benares, and with haste he journeyed to the north; and everywhere, the farmers, merchants and the sudras helped him on his way.

23   And after many days he reached the mighty Himalayas, and in the city Kapivastu he abode.

24   The priests of Buddha opened wide their temple doors for him.


## Chapter 32.

*Jesus and Barata. Together they read the sacred books. Jesus takes exception to the Buddhist doctrine of evolution and reveals the true origin of man. Meets Vidyapati, who becomes his co-laborer.*


Among the Buddhist priests was one who saw a lofty wisdom in the words that Jesus spoke. It was Barata Arabo.

2   Together Jesus and Barata read the Jewish Psalms and Prophets; read the Vedas, the Avesta and the wisdom of Guatama.

3   And as they read and talked about the possibilities of man, Barata said,

4   Man is the marvel of the universe. He is a part of everything, for he has been a living thing on every plane of life.

5   Time was when man was not; and then he was a bit of formless substance in the molds of time; and then a protoplast.

6   By universal law all things tend upward to a state of perfectness. The protoplast evolved, becoming worm, then reptile, bird and beast, and then at last it reached the form of man.

7   Now, man himself is mind, and mind is here to gain perfection by experience; and mind is often manifest in fleshy form, and in the form best suited to its growth. So mind may manifest as worm, or bird, or beast, or man.

8   The time will come when everything of life will be evolved unto the state of perfect man.

9   And after man is man in perfectness, he will evolve to higher forms of life.

10   And Jesus said, Barata Arabo, who taught you this, that mind, which is the man, may manifest in flesh of beast, or bird, or creeping thing?

11   Barata said, From times which man remembers not our priests have told us so, and so we know.

12   And Jesus said, Enlightened Arabo, are you a master mind and do not know that man knows naught by being told?

13   Man may believe what others say; but thus he never knows. If man would know, he must himself be what he knows.

14   Do you remember, Arabo, when you was ape, or bird, or worm?

15   Now, if you have no better proving of your plea than that the priests have told you so, you do not know; you simply guess.

16   Regard not, then, what any man has said; let us forget the flesh, and go with mind into the land of fleshless things; mind never does forget.

17   And backward through the ages master minds can trace themselves; and thus they know.

18   Time never was when man was not.

19   That which begins will have an end. If man was not, the time will come when he will not exist.

20   From God's own Record Book we read: The Triune God breathed forth, and seven Spirits stood before his face. (The Hebrews call these seven Spirits, Elohim.)

21   And these are they who, in their boundless power, created everything that is, or was.

22   These Spirits of the Triune God moved on the face of boundless space and seven ethers were, and every ether had its form of life.

23   These forms of life were but the thoughts of God, clothed in the substance of their ether planes.

24   (Men call these ether planes the planes of protoplast, of earth, of plant, of beast, of man, of angel and of cherubim.)

25   These planes with all their teeming thoughts of God, are never seen by eyes of man in flesh; they are composed of substance far too fine for fleshly eyes to see, and still they constitute the soul of things;

26   And with the eyes of soul all creatures see these ether planes, and all the forms of life.

27   Because all forms of life on every plane are thoughts of God, all creatures think, and every creature is possessed of will, and, in its measure, has the power to choose,

28   And in their native planes all creatures are supplied with nourishment from the ethers of their planes.

29   And so it was with every living thing until the will became a sluggish will, and then the ethers of the protoplast, the earth, the plant, the beast, the man, began to vibrate very slow.

30   The ethers all became more dense, and all the creatures of these planes were clothed with coarser garbs, the garbs of flesh, which men can see; and thus this coarser manifest, which men call physical, appeared.

31   And this is what is called the fall of man; but man fell not alone for protoplast, and earth, and plant and beast were all included in the fall.

32   The angels and the cherubim fell not; their wills were ever strong, and so they held the ethers of their planes in harmony with God.

33   Now, when the ethers reached the rate of atmosphere, and all the creatures of these planes must get their food from atmosphere, the conflict came; and then that which the finite man has called, survival of the best, became a law,

34   The stronger ate the bodies of the weaker manifests; and here is where the carnal law of evolution had its rise.

35   And now man, in his utter shamelessness, strikes down

and eats the beasts, the beast consumes the plant, the plant thrives on the earth, the earth absorbs the protoplast.

36 In yonder kingdom of the soul this carnal evolution is not known, and the great work of master minds is to restore the heritage of man, to bring him back to his estate that he has lost, when he again will live upon the ethers of his native plane.

37 The thoughts of God change not; the manifests of life on every plane unfold into perfection of their kind; and as the thoughts of God can never die, there is no death to any being of the seven ethers of the seven Spirits of the Triune God.

38 And so an earth is never plant; a beast, or bird, or creeping thing is never man, and man is not, and cannot be, a beast, or bird, or creeping thing.

39 The time will come when all these seven manifests will be absorbed, and man, and beast, and plant, and earth and protoplast will be redeemed.

40 Barata was amazed; the wisdom of the Jewish sage was revelation unto him.

41 Now, Vidyapati, wisest of the Indian sages, chief of temple Kapavistu, heard Barata speak to Jesus of the origin of man, and heard the answer of the Hebrew prophet, and he said,

42 You priests of Kapavistu, hear me speak: We stand today upon a crest of time. Six times ago a master soul was born who gave a glory light to man, and now a master sage stands here in temple Kapavistu.

43 This Hebrew prophet is the rising star of wisdom, deified. He brings to us a knowledge of the secret things of God; and all the world will hear his words, will heed his words, and glorify his name.

44 You priests of temple Kapavistu, stay! be still and listen when he speaks; he is the Living Oracle of God.

45 And all the priests gave thanks, and praised the Buddha of enlightenment.

## Chapter 33.

*Jesus teaches the common people at a spring. Tells them how to attain unto happiness. Relates the parable of the rocky field and the hidden treasure.*

In silent meditation Jesus sat beside a flowing spring. It was a holy day, and many people of the servant caste were near the place.

2   And Jesus saw the hard drawn lines of toil on every brow, in every hand. There was no look of joy in any face. Not one of all the group could think of anything but toil.

3   And Jesus spoke to one and said, Why are you all so sad? Have you no happiness in life?

4   The man replied, We scarcely know the meaning of that word. We toil to live, and hope for nothing else but toil, and bless the day when we can cease our toil and lay us down to rest in Buddha's city of the dead.

5   And Jesus' heart was stirred with pity and with love for these poor toilers, and he said,

6   Toil should not make a person sad; men should be happiest when they toil. When hope and love are back of toil, then all of life is filled with joy and peace, and this is heaven. Do you not know that such a heaven is for you?

7   The man replied, Of heaven we have heard; but then it is so far away, and we must live so many lives before we reach that place!

8   And Jesus said, My brother, man, your thoughts are wrong; your heaven is not far away; and it is not a place of metes and bounds, is not a country to be reached; it is a state of mind.

9   God never made a heaven for man; he never made a hell; we are creators and we make our own.

10   Now, cease to seek for heaven in the sky; just open up the windows of your hearts, and, like a flood of light, a heaven will come and bring a boundless joy; then toil will be no cruel task.

11   The people were amazed, and gathered close to hear this strange young master speak,

12   Imploring him to tell them more about the Father-God; about the heaven that men can make on earth; about the boundless joy.

13   And Jesus spoke a parable; he said, A certain man possessed a field; the soil was hard and poor.

14   By constant toil he scarcely could provide enough of food to keep his family from want.

15 One day a miner who could see beneath the soil, in passing on his way, saw this poor man and his unfruitful field.

16 He called the weary toiler and he said, My brother, know you not that just below the surface of your barren field rich treasures lie concealed?

17 You plow and sow and reap in scanty way, and day by day you tread upon a mine of gold and precious stones.

18 This wealth lies not upon the surface of the ground; but if you will but dig away the rocky soil, and delve down deep into the earth, you need no longer till the soil for naught.

19 The man believed. The miner surely knows; he said, and I will find the treasures hidden in my field.

20 And then he dug away the rocky soil, and deep down in the earth he found a mine of gold.

21 And Jesus said, The sons of men are toiling hard on desert plains, and burning sands and rocky soils; are doing what their fathers did, not dreaming they can do aught else.

22 Behold, a master comes, and tells them of a hidden wealth; that underneath the rocky soil of carnal things are treasures that no man can count;

23 That in the heart the richest gems abound; that he who wills may open up the door and find them all.

24 And then the people said, Make known to us the way that we may find the wealth that lies within the heart.

25 And Jesus opened up the way; the toilers saw another side of life, and toil became a joy.

## Chapter 34.

*The Jubilee in Kapavistu. Jesus teaches in the plaza and the people are astonished. He relates the parable of the unkept vineyard and the vine dresser. The priests are angered by his words.*

It was a gala day in sacred Kapavistu; a throng of Buddhist worshippers had met to celebrate a Jubilee.

2 And priests and masters from all parts of India were there; they taught; but they embellished little truth with many words.

3    And Jesus went into an ancient plaza and he taught; he spoke of Father-Mother-God; he told about the brotherhood of life.

4    The priests and all the people were astounded at his words and said, Is this not Buddha come again in flesh? No other one could speak with such simplicity and power.

5    And Jesus spoke a parable; he said, There was a vineyard all unkept; the vines were high, the growth of leaves and branches great.

6    The leaves were broad and shut the sunlight from the vines; the grapes were sour, and few, and small.

7    The pruner came; with his sharp knife he cut off every branch, and not a leaf remained; just root and stalk, and nothing more.

8    The busy neighbors came with one accord and were amazed, and said to him who pruned, You foolish man! the vineyard is despoiled.

9    Such desolation! There is no beauty left, and when the harvest time shall come the gatherers will find no fruit.

10    The pruner said, Content yourselves with what you think, and come again at harvest time and see.

11    And when the harvest time came on the busy neighbors came again; they were surprised.

12    The naked stalks had put forth branch and leaf, and heavy clusters of delicious grapes weighed every branch to earth.

13    The gatherers rejoiced as, day by day, they carried the rich fruitage to the press.

14    Behold, the vineyard of the Lord! the earth is spread with human vines.

15    The gorgeous forms and rites of men are branches, and their words are leaves; and these have grown so great that sunlight can no longer reach the heart; there is no fruit.

16    Behold, the pruner comes, and with a two-edged knife he cuts away the branches and the leaves of words,

17    And naught is left but unclothed stalks of human life.

18    The priests and they of pompous show, rebuke the pruner, and would stay him in his work.

19    They see no beauty in the stalks of human life; no promises of fruit.

20    The harvest time will come and they who scorned the pruner

will look on again and be amazed, for they will see the human stalks that seemed so lifeless, bending low with precious fruit.

21   And they will hear the harvesters rejoice, because the harvest is so great.

22   The priests were not well pleased with Jesus' words; but they rebuked him not; they feared the multitude.

## Chapter 35.

*Jesus and Vidyapati consider the needs of the incoming age of the world.*

The Indian sage and Jesus often met and talked about the needs of nations and of men; about the sacred doctrines, forms and rites best suited to the coming age.

2   One day they sat together in a mountain pass, and Jesus said, The coming age will surely not require priests, and shrines, and sacrifice of life.

3   There is no power in sacrifice of beast, or bird, to help a man to holy life.

4   And Vidyapati said, All forms and rites are symbols of the things that men must do within the temple of the soul.

5   The Holy One requires man to give his life in willing sacrifice for men, and all the so-called offerings on altars and on shrines that have been made since time began, were made to teach man how to give himself to save his brother man; for man can never save himself except he lose his life in saving other men.

6   The perfect age will not require forms and rites and carnal sacrifice. The coming age is not the perfect age, and men will call for object lessons and symbolic rites.

7   And in the great religion you shall introduce to men, some simple rites of washings and remembrances will be required; but cruel sacrifice of animals, and birds the gods require not.

8   And Jesus said, Our God must loathe the tinseled show of priests and priestly things.

9   When men array themselves in showy garbs to indicate that they are servants of the gods, and strut about like gaudy birds to be admired by men, because of piety or any other thing, the Holy One must surely turn away in sheer disgust.

10    All people are alike the servants of our Father-God, are kings and priests.

11    Will not the coming age demand complete destruction of the priestly caste, as well as every other caste and inequality among the sons of men?

12    And Vidyapati said, The coming age is not the age of spirit life and men will pride themselves in wearing priestly robes, and chanting pious chants to advertise themselves as saints.

13    The simple rites that you will introduce will be extolled by those who follow you, until the sacred service of the age will far outshine in gorgeousness the priestly service of the Brahmic age.

14    This is a problem men must solve.

15    The perfect age will come when every man will be a priest and men will not array themselves in special garb to advertise their piety.

(LEVI DOWLING, 1907; REPRINT ED., LOS ANGELES: 1911; PP. 47–65)